Praise for *Anatomy of Writing for Publicati*
Second Edition

"Cynthia Saver and her colleagues have removed all legitimacy to those who say they cannot write. This very thorough and detailed book walks both the novice and expert through every phase and stage of the writing process. Each chapter 'drills down' into the specifics of writing dynamics and the authoring process in a way that is both revealing and relevant. The tips and gems sprinkled throughout each chapter of this text elucidate the essentials of good writing and empower potential authors with the writing tools essential to publication."

–Tim Porter-O'Grady, DM, EdD, ScD(h), APRN, FAAN
Senior Partner, Tim Porter-O'Grady Associates, Inc.
Clinical Professor, Leadership Scholar, College of Nursing, The Ohio State University
Professor of Practice, College of Nursing and Health Innovation, Arizona State University
Adjunct Professor, School of Nursing, Emory University

"Saver has brought together a dream team of authors in a book that helps novice and experienced nurse authors. This new book is a treasure for helping nurses tell important stories to shape the future of practice. There is a lot of mystery in writing for publication, but Saver and her colleagues have written an inspirational book that captures logical and important steps providing guidance to all who use this reference. This is an important and attractive book for everyone's library. Here at last is an accessible guide for all."

–Jeanette Ives Erickson, DNP, RN, FAAN
Chief Nurse and Senior Vice President for Patient Care Services, Massachusetts General Hospital
Professor, William F. Connell School of Nursing, Boston College
Editorial Board of *Nursing Research* and *The International Journal of Nursing Knowledge*

"Anatomy of Writing is a 'must-have' book for both novice and experienced authors. For others to learn about and use the meaningful and impactful work that we do, we must disseminate it. Each chapter in this book contains golden nuggets of great advice, practical tips for success, and inspirational quotes to make it through those 'character-building' writing times."

–Bernadette Mazurek Melnyk, PhD, RN, CPNP/PMHNP, FNAP, FAAN
Associate Vice President for Health Promotion and University Chief Wellness Officer
Dean and Professor, College of Nursing
Professor of Pediatrics & Psychiatry, College of Medicine
The Ohio State University
Editor, *Worldviews on Evidence-Based Nursing*

"Saver and her coauthors have hit it out of the writing and publishing ballpark! Each chapter elegantly unfolds as the authors expertly present a treasure trove of positive, easy-to-read ideas to help authors and presenters (from beginner to expert) take their writing to the next level and beyond. The inspirational quotes and 'confidence boosters' make me want to grab my keyboard and start clacking away! This is a must-read for anyone seeking practical tips and tools to improve his or her writing acumen and confidence."

–Cynthia Clark, PhD, RN, ANEF, FAAN
Professor, Boise State University, School of Nursing
Author, *Creating and Sustaining Civility in Nursing Education*

"In this comprehensive second edition, Cynthia Saver and her contributors have provided readers with the guidance, tools, and skills they need for publishing success. Anatomy of Writing for Publication for Nurses, *Second Edition*, is a must-have for all aspiring nurse authors."

–Peter I. Buerhaus, PhD, RN, FAAN
Valere Potter Distinguished Professor of Nursing
Director, Center for Interdisciplinary Health Workforce Studies
Institute for Medicine and Public Health, Vanderbilt University Medical Center

"A true 'editor/writing mentor in a box (or a book),' this resource for nurse authors will be of use not only to aspiring academics and nurse leaders, but also to nurses in all roles at every career stage and experience level, whether they are expected to publish, want to share their expertise with others in print, or want to assist others in getting published. Clearly written, upbeat, and action oriented, the chapters provide extensive advice and anticipate reader questions regarding a variety of publishing venues and formats."

–Sean P. Clarke, PhD, RN, FAAN
Professor and Susan E. French Chair in Nursing Research and Innovative Practice
Director, McGill Nursing Collaborative for Education and Innovation in Patient and Family Centered Care,
Ingram School of Nursing, Faculty of Medicine, McGill University
Editor-in-Chief, *CJNR (Canadian Journal of Nursing Research)*

"Saver has compiled the quintessential writing guide for nurses, whether novice or experienced writer, as well as anyone in healthcare and beyond. From getting published in commercial and peer-reviewed journals to writing evidence-based project reports or creating and promoting a blog, Anatomy of Writing for Publication for Nurses covers it all and then some. I refer to it and recommend it often. A must-have for every professional nurse's personal library."

–Donna Cardillo, MA, RN
Author, Columnist, and President, DonnaCardillo.com
Expert blogger at DoctorOz.com
"Dear Donna" columnist at Nurse.com

"This must-needed book serves as a call to action for the entire nursing profession. The authors not only develop a compelling argument for our members to get out the word on our practice through publication, but most importantly, how to face the often daunting task of writing in a clear, understandable, practical manner."

–Margaret Fitzgerald, DNP, FNP-BC, NP-C, FAANP, CSP, FAAN, DCC
President, Fitzgerald Health Education Associates, Inc.

"Many years ago, I read a stack of books and articles as I tried to prepare and position myself to be a writer. This practical book is fun to read and has everything a person needs for writing articles and books. As a seasoned writer, I was delighted by how much I learned. I especially enjoyed the Q&As."

–Kathleen D. Pagana, PhD, RN
Professor Emeritus, Lycoming College
Author, including *The Nurse's Etiquette Advantage*, *The Nurse's Communication Advantage*,
and *Mosby's Diagnostic & Laboratory Test Reference, 11th edition*

"Building upon the valuable information in the first edition, the book is completely updated and enhanced. The book now includes several new chapters on peer review, writing quality- or evidence-based reports, turning academic papers or presentations into publishable articles, and has specific guidance on many other types of writing that nurses may complete during their career. These are wonderful additions to an already outstanding book."

–Marilyn W. Edmunds, PhD, NP
Editor in Chief, *The Journal for Nurse Practitioners*

"Saver and colleagues have done it again, providing an excellent tool for personal development that will help students to experienced professionals. They have addressed practically all forms of writing with numerous case examples, pointers, and confidence-boosting tips. Anatomy of Writing for Publication for Nurses is a practical, comprehensive guide that will inspire nurses to share stories with other nurses and the public. This book demystifies the process for everyday types of writing, such as peer reviews and practice exemplars, as well as scholarly work. It is bound to help boost your success for seeing your name in print."

–Pamela F. Cipriano, PhD, RN, NEA-BC, FAAN
Senior Director, Galloway Consulting
Research Associate Professor, University of Virginia School of Nursing

"Writing is not a core competency for most nursing professionals, but it is an essential part of disseminating the emerging evidence for practice and influencing the advancement of our profession's policy goals. This great book provides clear and strategic means for improving the professional's ability to succinctly and convincingly advance the knowledge of the profession through clear scholarly writing. Kudos to Cynthia Saver for providing this impressive and very much-needed tool!"

–Geraldine Polly Bednash, PhD, RN, FAAN
CEO/Executive Director
American Association of Colleges of Nursing

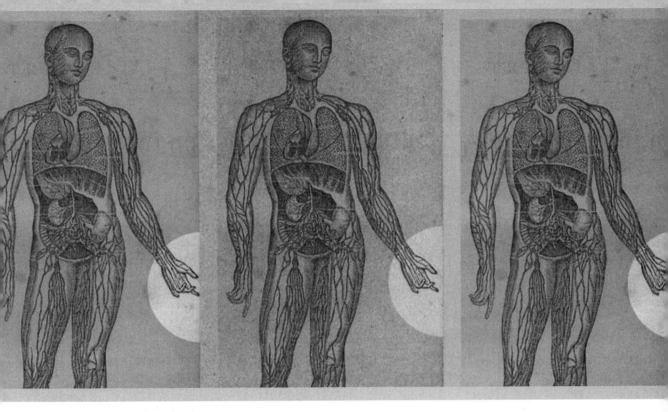

Anatomy of
WRITING
FOR PUBLICATION
FOR NURSES

Second Edition

CYNTHIA SAVER, MS, RN

Sigma Theta Tau International
Honor Society of Nursing®

The Honor Society of Nursing, Sigma Theta Tau International (STTI) is a nonprofit organization whose mission is to support the learning, knowledge, and professional development of nurses committed to making a difference in health worldwide. Founded in 1922, STTI has 130,000 members in 86 countries. Members include practicing nurses, instructors, researchers, policymakers, entrepreneurs and others. STTI's 493 chapters are located at 673 institutions of higher education throughout Australia, Botswana, Brazil, Canada, Colombia, Ghana, Hong Kong, Japan, Kenya, Malawi, Mexico, the Netherlands, Pakistan, Portugal, Singapore, South Africa, South Korea, Swaziland, Sweden, Taiwan, Tanzania, United Kingdom, United States, and Wales. More information about STTI can be found online at www.nursingsociety.org.

Sigma Theta Tau International
550 West North Street
Indianapolis, IN, USA 46202

To order additional books, buy in bulk, or order for corporate use, contact Nursing Knowledge International at 888.NKI.4YOU (888.654.4968/US and Canada) or +1.317.634.8171 (outside US and Canada).

To request a review copy for course adoption, email solutions@nursingknowledge.org or call 888.NKI.4YOU (888.654.4968/US and Canada) or +1.317.634.8171 (outside US and Canada).

To request author information, or for speaker or other media requests, contact Marketing, Honor Society of Nursing, Sigma Theta Tau International at 888.634.7575 (US and Canada) or +1.317.634.8171 (outside US and Canada).

ISBN: 9781938835421
EPUB ISBN: 9781938835438
PDF ISBN: 9781938835445
MOBI ISBN: 9781938835452

Library of Congress Cataloging-in-Publication Data

Saver, Cynthia, 1955- author.
 Anatomy of writing for publication for nurses / Cynthia Saver. -- Second edition.
   p. ; cm.
 ISBN 978-1-938835-42-1 (book : alk. paper) -- ISBN 978-1-938835-43-8 (EPUB) -- ISBN 978-1-938835-44-5 (PDF) -- ISBN 978-1-938835-45-2 (MOBI)
 I. Sigma Theta Tau International, issuing body. II. Title.
 [DNLM: 1. Writing--Nurses' Instruction. 2. Publishing--Nurses' Instruction. WZ 345]
 RT24
 610.73--dc23
                    2014003903

Second Printing, 2015

Publisher: Renee Wilmeth
Acquisitions Editor: Emily Hatch
Editorial Coordinator: Paula Jeffers
Cover Designer: Katy Bodenmiller
Interior Design/Page Layout: Kim Scott

Principal Book Editor: Carla Hall
Development and Project Editor: Jennifer Lynn
Copy Editor: Charlotte Kughen
Proofreader: Barbara Bennett
Indexer: Joy Dean Lee

Dedication

*To all my writing mentors over the years, my family (especially my mother,
who introduced me to the pleasure of reading and writing), and Jackie and David*

Acknowledgments

Thank you to my incredible team of contributors. I am honored to be in such stellar company. The contributors bring a wonderful wealth of knowledge and a desire to help other nurses publish.

Thanks to Joan Borgatti for first linking anatomy to writing, and to Judith Mitiguy and Patricia Dwyer Schull, for their insightful comments and unfailing support.

Special thanks to the talented staff at Sigma Theta Tau International, who always make their authors look great; to Jennifer Lynn, for her expert editing; Charlotte Kughen, for copyediting, an important part of polishing any manuscript; Barbara Bennett, for proofreading; and Katy Bodenmiller, for designing an outstanding cover.

About the Author

Author and speaker Cynthia Saver, MS, RN, president of CLS Development, Inc., an editorial services firm

Cynthia Saver, an award-winning author, has nearly four decades of experience in nursing, including nearly 30 years of publishing experience as a writer, editor, and senior vice president of editorial.

Saver has written for many nursing publications, including *Nursing Management, Nursing Spectrum, American Nurse Today, AORN Journal, NurseWeek, Nurse.com, OR Manager, American Journal of Nursing, The Nurse Practitioner*, and *Journal of Nursing Regulation*, to name a few. Her writing experience includes a 10-part writing for publication series for the *AORN Journal*, research reports, case studies, interviews, clinical articles, and continuing education programs. She has written materials for nurses, physicians, pharmacists, social workers, physical therapists, occupational therapists, dentists, and other healthcare professionals. Saver has worked with the top publishers as an author, editor, and managing editor. Her writing for publication program for nurses produces excellent reviews—and published articles by participants. She received her master's degree in nursing from The Ohio State University.

About the Contributors

Mary Alexander, MA, RN, CRNI®, CAE, FAAN, chief executive officer, Infusion Nurses Society (INS)

Mary Alexander was named chief executive officer of the Infusion Nurses Society (INS) and the Infusion Nurses Certification Corporation (INCC) in 1997. She is responsible for ensuring consistent delivery of professional services to the 7,000 members of INS and 3,400 certificants of INCC. As editor of the *Journal of Infusion Nursing*, Alexander writes bimonthly columns for the *Journal* and has editorial responsibilities for the INS bimonthly membership newsletter, *INS Newsline*. She is editor of the *Core Curriculum for Infusion Nursing* (4th ed.), and editor-in-chief of the INS textbook *Infusion Nursing: An Evidence-Based Approach*. Alexander's areas of expertise include infusion therapy with an emphasis on patient safety, practitioner competency, and standards development. Her clinical experience spans a variety of practice settings, including home care, alternative sites, and acute care settings.

Nancy J. Brent, JD, MS, RN, nurse attorney in private law practice

After practicing and teaching psychiatric nursing for more than 15 years, Nancy J. Brent graduated from Loyola University of Chicago School of Law in 1981. Her private practice is concentrated in professional licensure defense for nurses and other healthcare providers, consultation to nurses and school of nursing faculty, and educational programs in law and nursing practice to nurses and other healthcare groups. She has also published extensively in the area of law and nursing practice. Brent is also the author of Brent's Law, a regular online column at www.nurse.com.

Christopher Burton, DPhil, RN, senior research fellow, Bangor University, Wales

Christopher Burton is codirector of Implement@Bangor, a program of researchers and practitioners who have an interest in untangling the challenges of implementation and improvement within health services. Burton has a special interest in implementation and improvement in stroke and other complex clinical conditions. He currently holds a fellowship from the UK Health Foundation, and is investigating how implementation activities that have strong patient and public involvement create value for professionals and health organizations.

Nan Callender-Price, MA, RN, executive director of continuing nursing education, Gannett Education

Nan Callender-Price, who has worked with Gannett Education for the past 18 years, has helped dozens of nurse authors develop continuing education programs. She holds a BA in English literature from University of California, Berkeley; a BSN from University of California, San Francisco; and an MA in Education from San Francisco State University. She practiced in women and children's health at Kaiser Permanente, San Francisco.

Susan Gennaro, PhD, RN, FAAN, dean and professor, Connell School of Nursing, Boston College

Susan Gennaro is an internationally renowned perinatal clinician and scholar whose research has helped improve healthcare for childbearing women and their families around the world. She is also the editor of the *Journal of Nursing Scholarship*, which is read in more than 100 countries and whose mission is to improve the health of the world's people. Gennaro has been active in supporting that mission by leading an understanding of how best to promote global dissemination of nursing scholarship.

Julie A. Goldsmith, PhD, assistant director of the Institute of American Thought at Indiana University-Purdue University Indianapolis

Julie A. Goldsmith served as editor of the Sigma Theta Tau International (STTI) quarterly, *Reflections,* from 1991 to 2000; and the creator and writer of its television program, *Nursing Approach,* on CNBC-TV's American Medical Television from 1998 to 2000. Following her work for STTI, she received a fellowship from the National Institutes of Health to study bio-medical communications in an interdisciplinary program at the Northwestern University School of Medicine, Kellogg School of Management, and Medill School of Journalism. A recipient of the American Academy of Nursing's Media Award and many other journalism awards, Goldsmith holds a master's degree in journalism from Northwestern University and a doctor of philosophy degree in media and information studies from Michigan State University. A media historian and communications researcher, she has presented her studies on the *Chicago Tribune's art of color images* at the Library of Congress, now seen as a web cast. For the National Endowment for the Humanities, Goldsmith has most recently served as a senior program officer in Washington, DC, counseling cultural and academic institutions on federal grants for intellectual projects. Her book, *Woodward and Bernstein: The People's Right to Know*, is due out in 2014 by Routledge.

Pamela J. Haylock, PhD, RN, FAAN, oncology and cancer survivorship consultant

Pamela J. (PJ) Haylock has held staff, management, teaching, and consultation roles in oncology care, and most recently served as chief executive officer of the Association for Vascular Access. She was a core development team member of the National Coalition for Cancer Survivorship's award-winning *Cancer Survival Toolbox*, audio instructional programs for survivors and family caregivers, and was co-coordinator of the *Life Beyond Cancer* retreats for women survivors. Haylock is coauthor of *Women's Cancers: How to Prevent Them, How to Treat Them, How to Beat Them* (with Kerry A. McGinn); *Cancer Doesn't Have to Hurt* (with Carol P. Curtiss); and author and editor of *Men's Cancers: How to Prevent Them, How to Treat Them, How to Beat Them.* In 2002, Haylock received the Distinguished Alumni Award for Service from the University of Iowa College of Nursing; and in June 2008, received a Distinguished Alumni Award for Service from the University of Iowa.

Shaké Ketefian, EdD, RN, FAAN, professor emerita, University of Michigan, School of Nursing

Shaké Ketefian has had a rich academic, scholarly, and administrative career. Throughout her career, she has worked extensively with U.S. and international students and has consulted with many institutions worldwide, providing curricular consultation, conducting faculty workshops, and teaching. Ketefian's research and scholarly expertise and publications have focused on research utilization, ethical issues in healthcare, measurement of ethical practice, research ethics, global issues in healthcare and knowledge development, and graduate and doctoral education in the United States and worldwide. She has been editor, associate editor, editorial board member, and reviewer for many international and domestic scholarly journals. Ketefian has provided extensive service to the professional community internationally and has been recognized through many awards and honors. She is a cofounder and founding president of the International Network for Doctoral Education in Nursing. Ketefian is retired from the University of Michigan School of Nursing, is professor emerita, and is currently serving as interim director and professor at Western Michigan University Bronson School of Nursing.

Tina M. Marrelli, MSN, MA, RN, FAAN, president, Marrelli and Associates, Inc., and editor-in-chief, *Home Healthcare Nurse*

Tina M. Marrelli is a nurse and the author of 12 books, including the *Handbook of Home Health Standards* (5th edition) and *Home Health Aide: Guidelines for Care*. Marrelli has been editor of peer-reviewed publications, including *Home Care Provider; Home Care Nurse News;* and, for the past 8 years, *Home Healthcare Nurse*. Marrelli worked in policy and operations at the HCFA (now CMS) central office in Maryland for 4 years on home care and hospice issues. She brings 25 years of experience as a manager in systems-based healthcare, particularly home care and hospice. Marrelli and Associates, Inc. (www.marrelli.com), an international firm, provides a range of consulting services and products (written deliverables, new business lines, training/education, operations, and so on) to client organizations, including universities, hospitals, home health agencies, hospices, payers, associations/organizations, publishers, manufacturers, and others related to varying aspects of healthcare.

Cheryl L. Mee, MSN, MBA, RN, CMSRN, manager, faculty engagement, education, Elsevier

Cheryl L. Mee presents to nursing faculty on topics such as test item writing and writing for publication and consults with faculty on analyzing testing data and improving student outcomes. Previously, she was the vice president of US Nursing and Health Professions Journals at Elsevier Publishing, managing 54 journals. Mee was the editor-in-chief of *Nursing* for 7 years and has been in publishing for 18 years. She has received national writing awards for her editorials and helped the journal achieve key publication awards. Her background includes work as a critical care, operating room, and hospice nurse; critical care clinical specialist, and nurse manager. She received her MSN and an MBA from Lasalle University. Mee is active in many nursing organizations. In 2003, she received the Pennsylvania State Nurses Association highest award (the Distinguished Nurse Award); and in 2007, received the association's Volunteer of the Year award.

Judith S. Mitiguy, MS, RN, editorial coach/consultant, Boston Children's Hospital; former executive vice president, nursing communications & initiatives, Gannett Healthcare Group, publisher of *Nurse.com*

Judith S. Mitiguy has worked full time in healthcare publishing as a writer and editor since 1989. She was the editor of *BayState Nurse News* for about 7 years before joining *Nurse.com* (formerly *Nursing Spectrum* and *NurseWeek*). She graduated with a master's degree from Boston University (BU) College of Communication, specializing in print journalism. Before that, she practiced pediatric and maternal-child health nursing and holds a master's degree in that specialty from BU. Mitiguy has presented workshops on writing for publication for nurses since the mid-1980s and has coached many nurses through the publication process from idea generation to manuscript acceptance by clinical and research journals of nursing. She has also written more than 100 articles, including magazine features and clinical and professional journal articles. Mitiguy has received several writing awards: two from the American Medical Writers Association; two from The Honor Society of Nursing, Sigma Theta Tau International; and one from the Association of Critical-Care Nurses. She also received the Staff Nurse Council Recognition Award from Boston Children's Hospital.

Cindy L. Munro, PhD, RN, ANP-BC, FAAN, FAANP, professor and associate dean, research and innovation, University of South Florida College of Nursing, Tampa

Cindy L. Munro has served as coeditor of the *American Journal of Critical Care* for 5 years. Munro, who is an experienced peer reviewer, has published more than 100 articles and presented at many national and international conferences. Munro received a diploma from York Hospital School of Nursing, a BSN from Millersville University of Pennsylvania, and a MS in nursing from University of Delaware. She earned her PhD in nursing and microbiology and immunology at Virginia Commonwealth University. Her NIH-funded research on oral care in critically ill adults has had an important effect on clinical practice. Munro was the American Association of Critical-Care Nurses 2014 Distinguished Research lecturer.

Sandra M. Nettina, MSN, ANP-BC, nurse practitioner, Columbia Medical Practice, Columbia, MD; adjunct clinical instructor, The Johns Hopkins University, School of Nursing, Baltimore; editor, *The Lippincott Manual of Nursing Practice*, Wolters Kluwer Health, Philadelphia

Sandi Nettina attended the Sisters of Charity Hospital School of Nursing in Buffalo, NY; completed a bachelors degree at Marymount College of Virginia; and received her MSN from the University of Pennsylvania, Philadelphia. As an adult nurse practitioner, Nettina's multidimensional career includes part-time clinical practice; clinical mentoring for nurse practitioner students from Johns Hopkins University; writing, editing, and reviewing for several publishing companies; leadership in her state nurse practitioner association; and volunteering for several health-related organizations.

Leslie H. Nicoll, PhD, MBA, RN, principal and owner, Maine Desk, LLC; editor-in-chief, *CIN: Computers, Informatics, Nursing*

Leslie H. Nicoll has more than 36 years of experience in nursing and healthcare and has worked in clinical practice, research, and academia. She founded her own business, Maine Desk, LLC, in 2001. Nicoll has been the editor-in-chief of *CIN: Computers, Informatics, Nursing* since 1995 and served as editor-in-chief of *The Journal of Hospice and Palliative Nursing* for 8 years (2001–2009). She is the author of more than 120 published professional articles, book chapters, and books, including *The Nurse's Guide to the Internet*. She was the founding editor of *Perspectives on Nursing Theory*, the first edition of which was published in 1986. She is the second author of *Contemporary Medical Surgical Nursing* (2nd ed., 2011) and coauthor of *The Editor's Handbook: An Online Resource and CE Course* (2010). Recently, Nicoll published *Manuscript Success: A Guide to Successful Publishing in the Professional Literature* (2012). In the non-nursing literature, she is the author of three *For Dummies* books, the most recent of which, *Kindle Paperwhite For Dummies*, was published in 2013. Nicoll thoroughly enjoys helping nurses and other healthcare professionals achieve their publication goals. She has done this through one-on-one support in her business as well as leading writing workshops for the National League for Nursing, a consortium of universities in Switzerland and various colleges and schools of nursing in the United States. Nicoll is active in INANE: The International Academy of Nursing Editors.

Susanne J. Pavlovich-Danis, MSN, RN, ARNP-C, CDE, CRRN, professor, University of Phoenix, South Florida Campus, Plantation, Florida; director of online content, TeamHealth Institute, Sunrise, Florida

Susanne J. Pavlovich-Danis maintains a private adult primary care practice in Plantation, Florida, and is a certified diabetic educator and a certified rehabilitation nurse (CRRN). She is also an approved continuing nursing education provider for Florida, an Alzheimer's education provider recognized by the Florida Department of Elder Affairs, and has been published in the nursing literature more than 500 times since 1996.

Demetrius J. Porche, DNS, PhD, APRN, FNP, FAANP, FAAN, dean and associate dean, Louisiana State University Health Sciences Center, New Orleans

Demetrius J. Porche is currently chief editor of the *American Journal of Men's Health* and serves on the editorial board of the *Journal for Nurse Practitioners*. He was the associate editor of the *Journal of the Association of Nurses in AIDS* for 10 years. Porche is the president of the Louisiana State Board of Nursing. He is a Virginia Henderson Fellow of Sigma Theta Tau International and a Fellow in Society of Luther Christman Fellows for Contributions to Nursing by Men. He is also a Fellow in the American Academy of Nursing and American Academy of Nurse Practitioners. Porche is the author of *Health Policy: Application for Nurses and Other Health Care Professionals* (2012), and he has published many articles in peer-reviewed journals.

Jo Rycroft-Malone, PhD, MSc, BSc(Hons), RN, professor of implementation & health services research and university director of research for Bangor University, Wales

Jo Rycroft-Malone is a codirector of Implement@Bangor, a program of researchers and practitioners who have an interest in untangling the challenges of implementation and improvement within health services. Rycroft-Malone is a nurse and health services researcher who studies the processes and outcomes of evidence-informed service delivery in different health service contexts across the globe. She was the inaugural editor of *Worldviews on Evidence-Based Nursing*.

Patricia Dwyer Schull, MSN, RN, president, MedVantage Publishing, LLC

Patricia Dwyer Schull has more than 20 years' experience in medical and nursing publishing. She is the editor and author of popular nursing journals, books, websites, and other publications. She has held executive management positions with the top medical publishers in the world. Before entering the publishing industry, she practiced as a registered nurse and held various nursing positions in direct patient care, hospital management, and staff education. She has a master of science degree in nursing and a bachelor of science degree.

Rose O. Sherman, EdD, RN, NEA-BC, CNL, FAAN, director of the Nursing Leadership Institute, Florida Atlantic University

Rose Sherman is a professor at Florida Atlantic University (FAU). Before joining the FAU faculty, she had a 25-year nursing leadership career with the Department of Veterans Affairs. She graduated with a BSN in nursing from the University of Florida. Her master's degree in nursing is from the Catholic University of America, and her doctorate is in nursing leadership from Teachers College, Columbia University. Sherman has extensive experience with both podium and poster presentations at professional conferences. She has also served as an abstract reviewer for numerous professional conferences at the state and national level. Sherman has written more than 50 articles that have been published in nursing journals and books. She completed a 3-year Robert Wood Johnson Executive Nurse Fellowship.

Lorraine Steefel, DNP, RN, CTN-A, president of LTS Writing/Mentoring & Editorial Services for RNs and Students

Lorraine Steefel, who is known for mentoring nurses, nursing faculty, and doctor of nursing practice (DNP) students to write for scholarly and popular publications, lectures and publishes on this topic. She has presented to nursing faculty and provided writing webinars for nurse scholar members of the National Coalition of Ethnic Minority Nurses Associations. Steefel has been widely published in peer-reviewed journals, nursing magazines, and on websites. She is the author of the book *What Nurses Know about Chronic Fatigue Syndrome*, and her short story "Lowe's Legacy" appeared in *Ordinary Miracles in Nursing*. Steefel is a certified transcultural nurse and the founding diversity editor and current editorial board member of the *Journal of Nursing Practice Applications and Reviews of Research* (*JNPARR*), the official journal of the Philippine Nurses Association of America, and an editorial board member of *Creative Nursing: A Journal of Values, Issues, Experience, and Collaboration*. She is adjunct professor at Kean University School of Nursing, Union, New Jersey, and nurse educator/clinical coordinator, Rutgers University Behavioral Health Care/University Correctional Health Care.

Renee Wilmeth, publisher, The Honor Society of Nursing, Sigma Theta Tau International

With more than 23 years of experience in publishing and content creation, Renee Wilmeth oversees Sigma Theta Tau International's publishing operations, including scholarly journals—*Journal of Nursing Scholarship* and *Worldviews for Evidence-Based Nursing*—both copublished with Wiley; *Reflections on Nursing Leadership*, the online daily society magazine, and publication of 14 professional and scholarly books each year. Wilmeth has served in senior-level acquisitions positions for publishers large and small, including Penguin Group (USA), Pearson Education, Macmillan USA, and Webster's New World.

Table of Contents

Part I   A Primer on Writing and Publishing

Foreword

Memorializations of Florence Nightingale's actions on behalf of British soldiers in the Crimea—in poetry, paintings, and even postage stamps—have made her a global icon for caring and compassion and a role model for nurses and nursing students caring for individuals, families, and communities. But Nightingale should as well be a model for writers in nursing, for she was a prolific author—her collected works fill 16 volumes! In her books, monographs and reports, pamphlets, and letters, Nightingale wrote for students, scientists, politicians, and the community to inform, explore, and persuade about all manner of health topics. Her writing style was clear and engaging, her tables and figures were original and informative, and her arguments were well crafted and analytical as she advocated for patients, pioneered nursing education, and advanced reform of health systems.

The worlds of health and nursing have changed dramatically since the time of Nightingale, but the imperative to use the written word has not. Exchange of scientific, technical, and professional information among nurses, other scientists and healthcare professionals and policymakers, and the individuals, families, and communities they serve is more critical than ever. Our digital, globalized age boasts new tools to support creation of written works, novel means for dissemination of written works, and ever-accelerating speeds for information exchange.

In today's writing environment, Cynthia Saver's *Anatomy of Writing for Publication for Nurses,* Second Edition, is an invaluable resource. Nurses and nursing students at all levels, as well as nursing faculty and nurse scientists, will find it to be a critical contemporary guide to professional and scientific writing tailored for nursing. The two parts of the book address writing and publishing basics and approaches to writing many essential types of papers and other documents, including text for the Web. The second edition adds to the contents of the acclaimed first edition, particularly by inclusion of chapters about quality reports and shorter contributions such as letters to the editor and opinion pieces that will be especially useful to practicing nurses who are increasingly called upon to write. The culture of the somewhat shadowy world of publishing is cogently described. Advice about how to effectively communicate with editors is useful and supported by a glossary explaining the terminology and jargon of the publishing world.

Sadly, beginning and experienced writers alike often engage in a war on words. The writing task is an attack on a blank monitor screen. Skirmishes involve the struggle to choose words and compose compelling sentences. Advances are marked only as page numbers and word counts increase. The war is not won unless grades of "A" are assigned or coveted messages beginning with "Congratulations!" are received. It's no wonder battle fatigue sets in and would-be authors retreat from the keyboard in favor of other pursuits.

Engagement with *Anatomy of Writing for Publication for Nurses* is sure to move any reader from a writing-as-war to a writing-as-pleasure frame of mind. Cynthia Saver's conviction that writing is an essential nursing responsibility and her confidence that effective writing can be learned permeates the book. Her enthusiasm for writing is contagious; all of the chapter contributors "caught" it. The tone throughout is inviting, encouraging, and informative. Readers will catch the enthusiasm, too, as they learn how to nurture their ideas and bring them to full bloom in papers and other documents that are mechanisms for sharing their thoughts with others.

Ostensibly, based on my position titles, I have been a teacher of nursing for more than a quarter of a century. During that time, I *have* taught much about nursing. Because my scientific training is in a quantitative field (psychometrics), I've been disciplined to think in numbers and naturally convey this approach to my students. But over the years, I think I have taught composition more than any other subject. As a teacher guiding students, I've seen how quality composition is as essential to effective communication in the nursing notes that students write in fundamentals as it is in the most complex scientific dissertation.

Careers in nursing develop and mature in many directions across the landscape of health services—nurses are direct care providers, educators, administrators, scientists, and lobbyists. Writing is a central activity in all these positions. This is great! As we take on new professional challenges, each step in our careers means an opportunity to renew ourselves as writers, exploring novel forms as we communicate with new readerships—patients, professional and scientific colleagues, and policymakers. Like Nightingale, writing can become the means by which we share our knowledge and passion to improve health as a resource for life.

Susan J. Henly, PhD, RN
Editor, *Nursing Research*
Professor, University of Minnesota

Introduction

"I admire anybody who has the guts to write anything at all."

—*E.B. White*

Writing well is not the result of luck or innate talent. Writing is a skill you can learn—just as you learned nursing skills, such as venipuncture and suctioning.

However, nurses often find it challenging to write. After all, quoting Margaret McClure in *Words of Wisdom from Pivotal Nurse Leaders* (Houser & Player, 2008), "One of nursing's biggest handicaps is that we are in a field where your basic practice requires that you never write in complete sentences."

Anatomy of Writing for Publication for Nurses, Second Edition, is designed to help you bridge the gap between incomplete sentences and a published manuscript. The book's contributors include the best and the brightest from publishing today. Most of the contributors have experience as editors of nursing journals, where their role is to decide which articles to accept for publication. These decision-makers share with you important insights as to how they make their decisions, which will enhance the likelihood your manuscript is accepted for publication.

The many years of writing experience that the contributors bring to this book comprise a comprehensive resource that this book takes advantage of. These authors' long history of success in having their work published enables them to give you important tips that set you on track to seeing your work in print.

Since the first edition of this book, the Web has become a widely used venue for publication. As you read, keep in mind that the information applies regardless of whether the final destination is in print or online. Good writing is the same no matter what the medium, although you'll find a few tips specific to writing for the Web in Chapter 6.

How to Use This Book

This book is divided into two parts that include updated information from the first edition as well as four new chapters.

Part I, "A Primer on Writing and Publishing," describes the basics of publishing, from generating a great idea and writing the article to revising your manuscript and marketing your work. This section is packed with information on how to bolster your chances for having your manuscript accepted for publication. Topics include how to query a journal; writing and submitting the manuscript; legal and ethical issues; and effective use of tables, figures, graphs, illustrations, and photos. If English is your second language, don't miss the chapter for global authors. Part I of this edition also includes a new chapter on peer review. Peer review is a great way to improve your own writing skills. Even if you don't plan to be a peer reviewer, understanding the reviewer's perspective will help you anticipate what comments reviewers might have about your manuscript.

In addition, Part I includes expanded information on topics such as open access, an important issue in today's publishing field; impact factors; determining authorship; and the publishing team. You'll also find new tools, such as a timeline, to help you organize your writing project, and tips for having a successful experience writing as part of a team.

Part II, "Tips for Writing Different Types of Articles," is where you can apply what you learned in Part I. Each chapter takes you through writing a particular type of paper or article, including clinical articles, scholarly journals, abstracts, books, reports, personal narratives, continuing education, and writing for consumers.

Part II includes three new chapters. The first is on writing the quality or evidence-based project report, something that nurses are increasingly being asked to do. The second explains how to turn a presentation or school assignment, such as your capstone project, into a published article. The third new chapter discusses other forms of writing, such as letters to the editor, book reviews, editorials, and newsletters. The expanded material includes information on writing a systematic review and working with contributors when writing a book.

New appendixes include a list of publishing terminology (like nursing, the publishing industry has its own jargon) and the SQUIRE (Standards for Quality Improvement Reporting Excellence) Guidelines. Be sure to also review Appendix F, "What Editors and Writers Want." It's designed to promote the valuable partnership between the two.

Writing Can Be Fun

The contributors and I have forgone the traditional textbook style of writing for something that (we hope) is livelier and more approachable. This doesn't mean that we don't take writing seriously. We do. Writing is a core nursing responsibility, right up there with being a patient advocate.

Our goal is to show you that although it takes some work to write effectively, it is within every nurse's reach to do so—and you can even have some fun while doing it.

Special Elements in This Book

In each chapter of *Anatomy of Writing for Publication for Nurses*, you'll find these features:

- **Opening quotes:** Quotes at the start of each chapter provide pithy words of wisdom related to the craft of writing.

- **Q&A sidebars:** Here you will find answers to some of the common questions related to the chapter's topic.

- **Confidence Booster:** Lack of confidence can hold nurses back from sharing their wealth of knowledge. These special sections are designed to inspire you and to encourage you to break down that barrier.

- **Write Now!:** These exercises at the end of each chapter help you apply what you have learned.

A Call to Action

Remember: The best way to become a better writer is to write! Like any other skill, practice is a key component to success. I hope this book inspires you to take on writing as a lifetime practice.

I also hope you use *Anatomy of Writing for Publication for Nurses* as a guide to getting your work published. We have an obligation to share our knowledge with other nurses, other healthcare professionals, and the public.

References

Houser, B. P., & Player, K. N. (2008). *Words of Wisdom from Pivotal Nurse Leaders*. Indianapolis: Sigma Theta Tau International.

"When asked, 'How do you write?,'
I invariably answer, 'One word at a time.'"

–Stephen King

Anatomy of Writing

Cynthia Saver

1

Writing is a skill. Like other nursing skills—such as starting an IV, suctioning a patient, or analyzing an ECG strip—writing can be learned. That doesn't mean you will necessarily become the next David McCullough or J. K. Rowling, or be able to emulate your favorite nurse author, but you can become confident enough in your writing to achieve a variety of goals, from publishing your first journal article to contributing to your staff newsletter.

Of course, nurses have different levels of expertise for different skills. For example, nurses learn how to insert an IV in nursing school, and for many of us, this becomes a daily part of our routine. However, you likely know of at least one nurse who is particularly adept at IV insertion. When you have a difficult "stick," you can rely on his or her advanced expertise, right?

Writing can be the same way. Some might be much better at it than others, but every nurse can learn the basic skill. Learning how to write is your first step in becoming a published author. You also need to learn the ropes about how publishing works. This chapter gives you an overview of the writing, editing, and publishing process. Subsequent chapters give you many more details, but by the end of this chapter, you should understand the big picture of writing for publication.

WHAT YOU'LL LEARN IN THIS CHAPTER

- Writing something, whether it's an article for a journal or a script for a multimedia program, can be compared with anatomy: If you passed your anatomy course in nursing school, you can write for publication.

- Like nursing, publishing has a specific process that you can follow.

- Collaboration is just as important with your publishing team as it is with a healthcare team.

Why Write?

Many articles have been written about why nurses should write. Although the most basic reason is to disseminate information, others find that writing can help them with job advancement, academic work, and sharing what works in practice. For example, a single nurse speaking in front of an audience about the latest treatment for sepsis might reach, at best, a few hundred nurses. But after your work is in print or online as a journal article, a chapter in a book, a magazine article, or even a newsletter write-up, your contribution is much more widely available, particularly if your published piece is indexed in one of the large databases that researchers and clinicians search for information.

Writing gives you the opportunity to (Adapted from Saver, 2006a):

- Share information (for example, an inspirational experience with a patient)

- Improve patient care (for example, a program for reducing pressure ulcers that improved outcomes)

- Promote yourself (for example, tenure track for faculty, clinical ladder, getting your name known so you can speak at national meetings, and so on)

- Enhance your knowledge (for example, a review article on patient handoff techniques that helps you explore a topic in-depth)

- Advance the profession (for example, publishing in other disciplines' journals or online, coauthorship with people outside nursing, an innovative way of defining nursing outcomes, and so on)

Now that you understand the importance of writing, you're ready to learn more about how to write.

Anatomy of Writing

Like many skills that fall outside our comfort zone, writing can be intimidating. Coaches, mentors, and editors have heard it all:

- "I want to write, but I'm a terrible writer!"

- "I don't know where to start!"

- "I could never finish an article, a paper, or a book!"

Not true! If you passed anatomy and physiology in nursing school, you can write for publication. In fact, grounding writing in an anatomy analogy makes it easier to understand (see Figure 1.1).

As you read this section, keep in mind that these basic principles are the same whether you're writing for online or in print or whether you're writing anything from a blog post to a book.

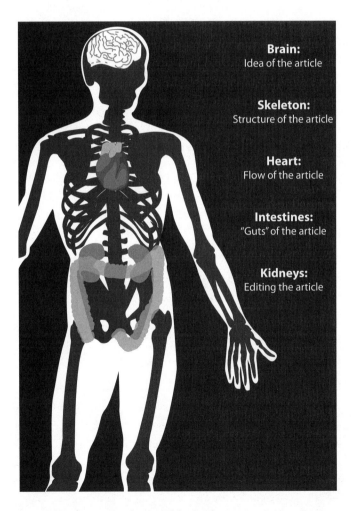

Figure 1.1 Think about writing in terms of parts of the body.

Brain

The brain is the idea for the article. In this discussion, an "article" can be anything from a blog post to a book chapter. Ideas are all around you. Perhaps the most challenging part for you is to take a broad idea (say, reducing readmissions) and narrow it down (how to reduce readmissions in newly diagnosed patients with diabetes).

Heart

The heart pumps the blood through the body, maintaining a constant flow. Like the heart, your article must have a flow to it so that the reader can easily move from point to point. Remember that you never want to make the reader work to understand your message.

Flow is how your article moves from one point to the next: how your article is organized and also how you lead your reader to your conclusion through a flow of information, such as how to manage the patient receiving negative pressure wound therapy. Or, how you move your reader through your idea, opinion, column, or even heart-wrenching story. Here are examples of types of flow:

- **Disease process** provides an overview of a disease. You likely remember this from nursing school: incidence, pathophysiology, assessment, diagnosis, treatment, and nursing care.

- **How-to articles** are well suited to quality improvement projects or clinical tips. For example, the author of one article described how she and her colleagues were able to improve documentation of restraints, and reduce their use, in a neuro ICU (Whitbeck, 2013).

- **Chronology articles** present information in a chronological order. A good example of this is preoperative, intraoperative, and postoperative care.

- **Case studies** are just what they sound like—clear descriptions of a patient's presentation, assessment, diagnosis, treatment, nursing care, and outcomes. A unique patient might present you the opportunity to write about an unusual experience, or you can use a case study as an example within a larger article.

You can use one or more of these techniques in your article. For example, if you are writing an article on the latest surgical technique for a general nursing journal such as *Nursing* or *American Nurse Today*, you might start with a case study to draw the reader in, and then move to a chronological approach: preoperative, intraoperative, and postoperative care.

Skeleton

The skeleton, along with ligaments, muscle, and tendons, holds your body together. Your skeleton is the basic structure that applies to nearly every article—a beginning, a middle, and an end. Your English teacher would call this an *outline*. And just like you learned your skeletal anatomy, your outline will start out with the basics, becoming more complicated as you flesh out (no pun intended) your work. The beginning, middle, and end are critical to communicating your points to your audience.

The Basics of IMRAD

The *IMRAD* format is an example of an article structure. It's typically used to present quantitative research, such as a research study comparing two ways of measuring blood pressure in pediatric patients (Oermann & Hays, 2010).

- **Introduction:** *Why did you do what you did?* This section includes what is known and not known about the topic, the purpose of the study, and the research question(s).
- **Methods:** *What did you do?* You should include the study protocol and procedures, subjects, methods of measurement or observation, and data analysis.
- **Results**: *What did you find?* This includes your findings with statistical details. Stick to the facts, with no discussion, and organize it from the most to the least important results.
- **Discussion:** *What do the results mean?* Include the answer to the research question(s), the supporting evidence, and the implications of the results. In essence, state the results within the context of your study and within the broader body of knowledge. It's here that you address what's important for the reader to take away from the study, the study limitations, and what additional research you are recommending.

The *beginning* sets the tone of the article and lets your reader know what is coming. Editors in newspapers and magazines would call it a *lede*, and it's that opening line, image, or paragraph that sets a compelling scene. This is your chance to grab readers and draw them into your topic or story. Consider the first lines from a few notable books, which you will probably recognize:

"I am the invisible man." *Invisible Man* by Ralph Ellison (1995)

"124 was spiteful." *Beloved* by Toni Morrison (2006)

Each of these opening lines draws in the reader, giving the promise of interesting things to come. You might think that you can't get the same impact from the lede in a nonfiction article, but consider this first line from *Early Birds Have Different Brains Than Night Owls*, by Breanna Draxler (2013):

> If the early bird gets the worm, what does the night owl get? According to a recent study, "sleep disturbances, vulnerability to depression and higher consumption of nicotine and alcohol."

Depending on the tone of your target publication and your audience, you can be creative with your beginning. Look at this example from an article on family presence during resuscitation, published in *American Nurse Today* (Twibell et al., 2009):

> "Hold CPR." "No pulse." "Resume CPR. Give epi 1 milligram now."
>
> Erin, an RN, taps a key on the computer in the resuscitation room and glances at the information: Devon, 22-year-old male, motor vehicle trauma, massive blood loss, shocked three times in transport, mother and brother on the way.

If the publication you are writing for is more scholarly in tone, you can still have strong beginnings, such as the start of this article on older patients' experiences of heart failure by Falk, Ekman, Anderson, Fu, and Granger (2013), which was published in the *Journal of Nursing Scholarship*:

> Almost half of all patients with heart failure (HF) are older than 75 years (Roger et al., 2012) and the condition has been labeled the quintessential disorder of cardiovascular aging…

Keep in mind that you might have "buried" the lede after the first few paragraphs. Often authors need a "warm up" period before they get to the crux of the article. You might find you can delete these early paragraphs. Early on in your manuscript, include what the article will be about and why it's important for the reader to know the information.

The *middle* is the meat of the article. Stick to the topic at hand. Depending on what you're writing about, use one or more of the flow techniques listed earlier in this chapter. You can use paragraphs and subheads to keep yourself organized, breaking text into smaller pieces as necessary. The publication style will dictate some of your middle structure. Some magazines want small sections with many small, related sections—*sidebars or marginalia*—broken out. A book chapter might call for longer sections, more in-depth discussion of your topic, and fewer subheadings.

Q: *How can I decide what structure will fit my article best?*

A: Read what other authors who successfully write for the same publication are doing. After all, a blog post will have a different structure than a journal article or even an article for a newsletter or nursing magazine.

The *end* of the article is the last opportunity you have to make your point with the reader. Depending on the style of article, it might be a simple conclusion or summary of your research, or you could ask your readers to take a stand. Either way, it is just as important as the beginning when it comes to structure.

Examples of endings include:

- A call to action (Nurses can use this tool to quickly screen patients in the emergency department for psychiatric disorders)

- A summary of key points (Plan ahead, keep your cool, and remember to take a step-by-step approach to assessment)

- Suggestions for areas of future research (Future studies should address…)

Ask yourself: What is the most important idea or message that I want the reader to take away from this article?

Intestines

Intestines are the guts of the article, the important part that makes it function, including all the data and information (the *nutrients*) that you need to include. Involve your reader whenever possible.

A basic rule is to *show, not tell*. Here are some ways in which you can *show* the reader:

- **Use examples.** Examples are the most powerful way to engage your reader, yet they are often forgotten. In the earlier example of the article from *American Nurse Today* about family member presence during resuscitation, the authors provided a table of example statements that nurses could use to talk to physicians who are resistant to family members' presence (Twibell et al., 2009).

- **Add anecdotes and case studies when appropriate.** People like reading about people and their experiences. You can use "stories" such as anecdotes and case studies, but be sure not to identify the patient.

- **Add visual elements.** Use photographs, tables, and illustrations. Be sure that your visuals are easy to understand. Visuals are a great way to reduce word count and engage the reader's eye. Some topics, such as wounds and dermatological conditions, particularly lend themselves to photographs. Just remember to not repeat in the text what you are showing.

- **Create sidebars.** These short pieces of key or supplemental information are usually presented in a shaded box. For example, "The Basics of IMRAD" section earlier in this chapter is a sidebar. Another example is a list of key signs and symptoms of pulmonary edema. Sidebars help make your article more succinct because you do not need to repeat what's in the sidebar in the text.

- **Write to the audience.** A common piece of advice is to write how you talk, but that is not necessarily true. Instead, write to the *audience*—the readers of the publication. Adapt your approach to fit the reader the same way that you would teach how to suction differently whether your "audience" was a patient, a patient's family, or a new nurse. For example, your article for the journal *Worldviews on Evidence-Based Nursing* should have a different tone than your article for *Nursing*.

Kidneys

The human body can't live without functioning kidneys, and your article can't live and thrive without editing. Editing comes after you have given yourself permission to write freely, without spending time agonizing over every word, and then revised your work. Just as the kidneys filter out toxins and unnecessary electrolytes, editing is the chance for you to trim the fat from an article. Be on the lookout for unnecessary words and redundant sentences, thoughts, and ideas. Cutting your own work can be painful, but it's necessary. You might want to use an editing checklist like the one in Appendix A.

Q: *What are ways to self-edit my work?*

A: Two items that you should always check for are *qualifiers* and *obvious statements*.

Qualifiers such as "I believe…" or "We think…" make you sound unsure of yourself. As the author, your work implies that it is what you think or believe. You can also quickly eliminate obvious statements, such as "The nursing shortage is a problem in today's society." If you make a statement that you think most people would know, such as "Heart disease is the leading cause of death in the US," back it up with a few interesting statistics.

After you complete your first draft, share it with a few colleagues or readers whom you trust. No matter what their response, take their advice as it is intended—as constructive criticism. For the most part, even a comment that you feel is negative or unsupportive might be just what your writing needs. Most reviewers will truly want your writing to be the best it can be. And you'd rather hear any criticism now, before your writing is published.

Here are some ways to make an outside review more useful:

- **Ask at least one expert on the topic to review your article.** Say that you are writing an article on post-intensive care syndrome with the goal of teaching progressive care unit nurses about this issue. One of your reviewers should be an expert in this area.

- **Ask someone who is not an expert but who represents your target audience for the article.** Now you turn to a progressive care nurse who is not an expert on post-intensive care syndrome. This is a great way to identify unclear areas. Remember that at this stage, you are too close to the article to be objective.

- **Select reviewers who will be honest and objective.** Your friend might be your best support, but perhaps not the best person to give you truly objective feedback.

- **Ask a good writer or editor to read your article.** For your article on post-intensive care syndrome, perhaps you contact a friend (in this case, friends are fine because you are asking only about grammar and style) who has many articles published, or even your neighbor, who teaches English at the local community college. This type of review is a great way to identify awkward sentences and major grammar errors. This step is not essential, because journals have editing experts, but will make your copy "cleaner" and clearer, perhaps boosting your chance of acceptance.

- **Consider each person's input and then decide whether to follow his or her advice.** You do not have to follow everyone's suggestion lest your article turns out to appear to be written by a committee, but think about the reasons behind the suggestions—and then make thoughtful decisions.

- **Remember to always thank your reviewers.** And, if your article is published, send them copies.

Q: *How do I find people to review my article before I submit it for publication?*

A: Network, network, network. Ask your friends for ideas. For your expert reviewer, consider contacting the author of several articles on the topic. Usually, these writers are passionate about their topic and willing to help "get the word out" to others, and will not charge you for this service.

Q: *What should I do if I feel like I need to improve my basic writing skills?*

A: Even professionals need an occasional tune-up when it comes to the basics of writing. One place to start is with grammar and style. As a starting place, try the classic *The Elements of Style*, by Strunk and White.

Breaking Down Barriers

At this stage, you might be thinking that you understand the writing process, but you doubt your ability to produce the finished product. It can be hard to just sit down and write. Consider ways to break down barriers to writing. Two common barriers are lack of confidence and lack of time.

Lack of Confidence

Lack of confidence commonly comes from two sources: self-doubt that you have something worthwhile to share, and discomfort with writing.

For too long, nurses have been passive in acknowledging their expertise. When nurses are praised for their expertise, they frequently say things like, "I was just doing my job" or

"It was no big deal." However, what we do *is* a big deal, and we have a responsibility to share it with others. Believe in your expertise.

Writing something—an article, a paper, a blog, or even a book chapter—can be daunting, especially when it's not something you learned in nursing school. Think back to when you learned a new skill, such as inserting a nasogastric tube. The first time, it was tiring and probably a bit stressful: You had to consciously think about each step because you wanted to do it correctly. Each time thereafter, though, the procedure became easier and easier for you until you felt comfortable with it, and it came naturally.

The way to be more comfortable with writing is to just do it: to just write. Practice helps, which is why we include writing exercises in this book. And amazingly, the more you write, the easier it becomes. For many nurses, writing actually becomes enjoyable.

Confidence Booster

We tell our patients to use positive self-talk to help them make lifestyle changes, and you can do the same to build your confidence with writing for publication. Tell yourself, "I can write!" When potholes mar the road (for example, you just had two staff nurses resign, leaving you short staffed), think of them as temporary setbacks and plan how you'll get back on track.

Also, be sure to reward yourself for small accomplishments. You wrote two paragraphs today? Enjoy the latest fiction bestseller. Finished formatting your reference list? Take a walk to take in a nice day. Of course, you'll need to match your rewards to what is meaningful for you.

Lack of Time

We're all busy these days, rushing to work, driving children to activities ranging from soccer to dance class, volunteering in the community, working out, and more. Here are a few ways to carve out time in your schedule to write (Saver, 2006a).

Think before you write. Don't waste time sitting in front of a blank computer screen waiting for inspiration. Mull over your topic while you are taking a shower or riding the subway to work. Watch for gifts of time: for example, when you are waiting in line at the grocery store or stuck in traffic waiting to pay a toll. Think about the key points that you want to make and how you want to structure the article. You might map out an entire article on compassion fatigue during a pleasant bike ride.

Q: *I always have great ideas, but when I don't write them down, I forget them! What are some techniques for capturing these thoughts?*

A: Have you ever seen writers toting a tiny, black book, scribbling observations as they go? Become one! Whether you choose a pretty blank book as your own or you carry a small notebook in your pocket, keep paper and pen handy so you can write down those fresh ideas. (Don't forget to keep a pen and pad of paper by the side of your bed!) Better yet, take advantage of applications such as Evernote, which lets you dictate a note, or Penultimate, which lets you handwrite a note. These programs allow you to sync your notes across platforms such as your smartphone, tablet, and computer so you can easily retrieve them.

Negotiate. Talk to friends, family members, and significant others. Explain what you are trying to accomplish and ask for their help. We delegate at work, but too often fail to do so at home. After all, how clean does your house really need to be? Talk to your supervisor at work. Some organizations offer time to work on articles as part of staff retention efforts.

Manage the project. Treat your article as you would any other project you expect to accomplish, from developing a new policy and procedure to painting the house. Make a timeline of interim steps. Schedule writing time on your calendar just as you would do any meeting. Just don't expect to be able to devote hours at a time to your writing efforts. That just sets you up for failure. Instead, try 60-, 30-, or even 15-minute blocks of time.

Developing a Writing Timeline

If you don't create a timeline for your writing project, it's likely you will never have a final product. The detail for your timeline depends on how much direction you need. You might want to simply enter major milestones, such as choose topic, send query, research, write, revise, and submit. Or, you might want more detail, such as what is included here:

- Research possible ideas.
- Narrow and choose your topic. (See Chapter 2 for how to accomplish this step.)
- Research possible publications.

- Decide on your target publication and read the author guidelines. (See Chapter 3 for how to accomplish this step.)
- Write a query letter to the appropriate person. (See Chapter 3 for how to accomplish this step.)

If your query is accepted…

- Conduct a literature search.
- Review the results of the search.
- Create a general outline. (See Chapter 2 for how to accomplish this step.)
- Divide the outline into sections you will write, for example: introduction, literature review, methods, results, and discussion. List each section. Or, simply divide your time into a number of segments, such as five to ten, and be more open about what you will work on during those segments. For instance:
  - Writing time #1
  - Writing time # 2, etc.
- Plan to put the manuscript away for 1 to 2 weeks before you revise.
- Revise the manuscript, focusing on organization.
- Revise again, focusing on clarity.
- Revise again, focusing on accuracy.
- Ask at least two people to review.
- Revise based on comments from the reviewers.
- Set the article aside for about three days.
- Read again for clarity and revise as needed.
- Proofread.
- Submit manuscript.

Assign each task a corresponding deadline and treat those dates with the same respect you would other important work or personal projects.

Find a space. You can save time by dedicating one area of your home or office for your writing. That way, all your materials can stay in one place, ready to go. Take steps to avoid interruptions. If you have a door, close it. If you are in a cubicle, hang a "Do not disturb! Genius at work!" sign on the cubicle wall. If someone does interrupt, don't give into temptation to respond. Instead, say when you can get back to him. On the other hand, keep in mind that you can write anywhere you have a laptop or a paper and pen. Some writers work on planes, trains, and even boats. Writing is a mindset, not a location.

Divide and conquer. Consider working with a coauthor to save time—and, if you're a first-time author, to tap into another's expertise. Having an experienced coauthor, coach, or mentor for your first article makes sense and fits with nurses' values. After all, you wouldn't, for example, conduct your first internal ear examination without having someone who could verify you were doing it correctly.

Collaborative or Team Writing

Partnering with others to write a manuscript can be efficient and enhance the quality. Given today's emphasis on collaboration in all areas of heathcare, from quality improvement and evidence-based practice projects to research studies, it's likely that at some point you'll be writing with others.

In addition to writing with other nurses, interdisciplinary teams are becoming more common, so you may be writing with other healthcare professionals such as physicians, social workers, physical therapists, and respiratory therapists. Each person brings his or her different perspective to the topic, which can strengthen the effectiveness of an article. Be sure the team commits to respecting each other's viewpoint.

Use this checklist to ensure your experience on a writing team is a positive one and not a time waster:

☐ Define each person's responsibilities for the manuscript, based on their strengths (L. Nicoll, personal communication, October 6, 2013). For example, who is the most detail oriented team member? He or she would be the perfect person to take responsibility for verifying and finalizing the reference list. Who is best at analyzing data?

☐ Decide on the lead author, who will shoulder the bulk of the work. The lead author will help ensure the manuscript reads like it was written by one person instead of several and keep the process moving. Team members should speak up if during the project it seems that someone other than the lead author is doing most of the work. Sometimes a change is needed, but waiting until the end of the project to raise the issue can cause distress within the team.

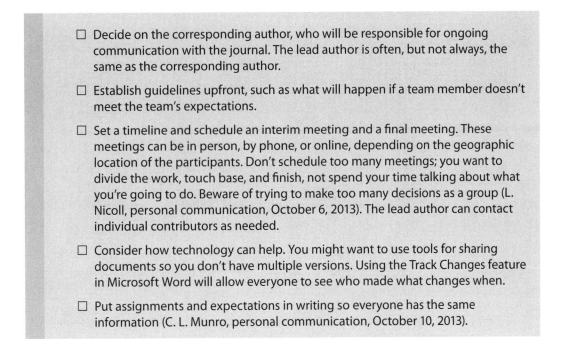

- ☐ Decide on the corresponding author, who will be responsible for ongoing communication with the journal. The lead author is often, but not always, the same as the corresponding author.

- ☐ Establish guidelines upfront, such as what will happen if a team member doesn't meet the team's expectations.

- ☐ Set a timeline and schedule an interim meeting and a final meeting. These meetings can be in person, by phone, or online, depending on the geographic location of the participants. Don't schedule too many meetings; you want to divide the work, touch base, and finish, not spend your time talking about what you're going to do. Beware of trying to make too many decisions as a group (L. Nicoll, personal communication, October 6, 2013). The lead author can contact individual contributors as needed.

- ☐ Consider how technology can help. You might want to use tools for sharing documents so you don't have multiple versions. Using the Track Changes feature in Microsoft Word will allow everyone to see who made what changes when.

- ☐ Put assignments and expectations in writing so everyone has the same information (C. L. Munro, personal communication, October 10, 2013).

Be flexible. Don't feel that you have to start at the beginning, which is often the hardest part of the article to write. Instead of taking time fretting over that, just start writing. For example, say that you are writing an article about your study on how your online education program increased knowledge of hypertension among Asian women. Instead of starting with the introduction, you might decide to start with the methods section.

Give yourself a break. Writing isn't easy (or everyone would do it, right?). Do not expect perfection; editors and peer reviewers can help you polish your manuscript. Be forgiving if your writing session doesn't go as planned. Although some deadlines must be met, there will be other times when the words just don't come. Understanding that this can happen and planning accordingly will keep you from getting discouraged.

Publishing Process

Just like the nursing process, the publishing process has defined steps: submission, peer review, revision, editing and layout, author review and approval, and printed article (Saver, 2006b). Upcoming chapters will provide more details, but here is an overview.

Submission

The days of mailing in an article are gone. Editors and publishers now ask authors to email their manuscripts or upload them via the publisher's manuscript management website. If you're blogging, you can even create your article directly in a special web-based editing interface, inserting photos, illustrations, and hyperlinks as you go.

When making a formal submission for a journal, magazine, website, or book publisher, be sure to follow the publication or publisher's guidelines for submitting your manuscript. Make sure that your article or chapter has all the required elements, including abstract and cover letter with complete contact information. Many journals will have additional guidelines if the article is being submitted for peer review. Carefully review your publisher's guidelines, too, for submitting illustrations or figures with your written work.

To give yourself the best possible chance for a publisher to not reject your work, save time and energy by avoiding these common submission errors. (Don't worry—every author has made one or more of these mistakes many times!)

- **Manuscript does not meet or greatly exceeds suggested word count.** Don't send a textbook instead of a journal article, and don't send a memo instead of an article. Publishers use established word counts to ensure a consistency of coverage within their publication. Plus, they know how much they need to fill the pages, or in the case of an online publication, to be sure an article isn't too long or short for the topic. You don't have to hit the requested number of words exactly, but be fairly close. For example, if 3,500 words are requested, it's acceptable to submit about 3,800, but don't submit 5,000. A good guideline is to be within 5% to 10%.

- **Manuscript is not an appropriate fit for the publication.** The content may be good, but the topic isn't appropriate for the publication's audience, so the article is rejected.

- **Manuscript is too "rough" in its current state; in other words, it feels unfinished or incomplete.** The manuscript will take significant time to edit, so it might be rejected or sent back to the author for edits before it can be reviewed.

- **Manuscript uses fancy fonts and formatting styles.** This can make your submission difficult for the editor to read or accurately gauge its length. Stick to using basic fonts, such as Times New Roman or Arial, and consult the publication's guidelines for specific requirements.

- **Author didn't follow directions for electronic submission.** Electronic submission can be frustrating for authors unfamiliar with it, but for better or worse, it is a trend for the future. The good news is that these systems allow you to track the progress of your manuscript. And, you'll feel more comfortable with this type of submission the more you do it.

- **Manuscript isn't formatted according to the guidelines.** It's a small problem but a frustrating one, nonetheless. Check page sizes, margins, spacing, numbering, and other requirements.

- **Cover letter doesn't include title of manuscript and complete contact information.** Make sure to include the name, address, phone number, and email address for each author.

- **Cover letter doesn't indicate the corresponding author.** When submitting to a journal, be aware that the editors want to work with just one author so that the process is streamlined. This does not have to be the lead author.

- **Submission is incomplete.** Editors cannot begin work on a project until all elements— including photos, illustrations, tables, charts, and parts of the article or book—are submitted.

- **Author hasn't obtained necessary permissions for photos, illustrations, or text.** Most publishers request that you submit letters of permission with your submission, say for a previously published figure.

> **Q:** *Is it ever acceptable to submit a manuscript for publication if I don't have all permissions in place?*
>
> **A:** If you will have to pay for a permission, it's usually acceptable to note the situation, indicating that you will obtain permission should the article be accepted for publication.

- **Artwork files are not prepared according to specifications.** Publishers will include specific requirements in their guidelines for preparing images, including dots per inch (dpi) resolution, file sizes, and file formats.

- **References are incomplete or incorrectly formatted.** Make sure to use the reference style that your publisher requires—and complete each reference. Your publisher might use the American Psychological Association (APA) style instead of Vancouver or

American Medical Association style, where references are cited in the text by number with a complete citation at the end. If your references are incomplete, your editor will likely return your manuscript to you.

- **Submission is late.** Just like you plan your schedule, editors plan a schedule, too, and they count on submissions arriving on time.

After you submit your work, the editor will review the manuscript and decide whether it should be sent for peer review. With most journals, your manuscript is not accepted for publication at this stage. It is just moving to the next step.

Peer Review

Nurses can't be experts in all areas of practice, and it's the same with editors. Editors use peer reviewers to tap into experts who can give them feedback on your submission. Reviewer feedback often includes a recommendation as to whether the work should be rejected, be published, or is acceptable for publication if certain revisions are made.

The peer-review process is common in scholarly or academic research journals: that is, journals with a focus on research and evidence-based practice. Faculty members usually must publish in peer-reviewed journals as part of meeting tenure requirements. Although peer review is common for journals, many publishers will also use a similar process to assess the quality of your work for other outlets such as books and websites.

The editor reviews the peer-reviewer comments, and authors see them as well. If it seems unfair that comments from outside reviewers hold so much weight, keep in mind that it's generally agreed that peer review improves the quality of the final product.

 How long does peer review take?

 Peer review typically takes 4 to 8 weeks, but this timeframe varies considerably by publication. Peer reviewers, who receive nothing or a small honorarium for their work, must fit the task around their already-busy schedules.

Revision

If the peer reviews are favorable, you will be asked to revise your manuscript. You'll base your revisions on comments from the peer reviewers and the publication's editorial staff. It can be stressful to see comments on the manuscript you put so much work into. Remember that it's highly unusual for any manuscript to be accepted without any revision. Editors say that too many times, authors become discouraged at this point and give up. Don't. If you complete the revisions satisfactorily, you have a fairly good chance of being published.

Editing and Layout

After your manuscript has been accepted, publishing staff start to edit it and prepare it for layout, whether in print, online, or both. No matter what you have written and where it will be published, your work will be edited. Here are the most common types of editing.

- **"Substantive" or "developmental."** With this type of editing, the editor focuses on the big picture of your work, from the flow and organization to the tone and style of the text. The editor plays the role of an orthopedic surgeon faced with a complicated fracture, examining the article from all angles, deciding what works to deliver the content so the reader can grasp it, and what might need repair. The editor also makes sure that the style of your article fits the style of the journal or magazine—and in the case of a book, matches the outline of the work the publisher expected to receive.

- **Line editing.** Some editors refer to the subset of substantive editing that focuses on paragraphs and sentences as line editing.

- **Copy editing.** Ever wonder about those miraculous editors who seem to catch every small grammar, spelling, and punctuation mistake? They are *copy editors*, and the process is similar to checking for bleeding before closing a surgical incision. The copy editor eases a weight from your shoulders. Unless you work in communications on a daily basis, no one can keep up on the latest rules of English.

After your manuscript has been edited, it will be returned to you for your author review.

Author Review and Approval

When your edited article is returned to you for review, you will see questions—often called *queries*—included for you to answer. Typical queries include requests for more complete reference information and clarification of the meaning of particular sentences.

At this stage, reorganization of your article or addition of substantial material is not a good idea. Instead, focus on clinical accuracy, such as drug dosages and correct figure labels.

Sometimes an editorial change can inadvertently change the meaning of a sentence, so review all edits carefully. Remember that you are responsible for the final accuracy of the article.

The time you have to review the manuscript varies considerably, depending on the type of publication. For a blog, you might have only an hour. For a journal, you might have 2 to 10 days. For a book or a chapter in a book, you might have 2 to 4 weeks. In some cases, you will review a Word document of the article; other times, you will review the article in its laid-out version as a PDF document or on a website that is not yet "live."

You might also be asked to sign a form attesting that you have reviewed the article either with no changes or the minor changes noted on the form.

Q: *What if I have a change to my article after I've sent in my final submission?*

A: Contact your editor immediately. Depending on the type of publication and stage your paper is in the process, you might have to hold on to your correction for an errata, addendum, or reprint correction. In this digital age, the good news is that corrections can be quickly made to articles online. But it's best to avoid the situation by making sure your final changes are truly your final changes.

Publication

The best part of writing an article is seeing it in print or online! It can take anywhere from 2 months to 2 years or longer for your article to be printed; time for online publication is usually less because websites don't have the same restrictions on number of pages per issue that journals and other print outlets do.

Timing of Print Publications

Several factors go into the decision of when to print an article. One is the importance of the article to the reader. Some journals assign each article a priority number for publication; those with the highest priority are more likely to be printed first. Other factors include how often the journal is published and the number of articles that a journal receives and accepts. Finally, unique innovation or cutting-edge research typically goes to the head of the publishing line and may be published on the journal's website before appearing in print.

After your handiwork is published, be sure to add your accomplishment to your professional portfolio, resume, and curriculum vitae.

Q: *What I was taught as "good writing" in high school now seems unacceptable to many editors. What's going on?*

A: English is a living, evolving language, and styles are different for different audiences. For example, many nurses were taught in high school that starting a sentence with a conjunction (and, or, or but) is an error. It is now acceptable to do so in more informal publications. Scholarly journals typically won't accept informal usages, though. The trick is to tailor your writing to the style required by the publication you're targeting.

All About the Publishing Team

Publishing is a team sport. As with a multidisciplinary healthcare team, each person on the team has a specific role.

- **Authors:** Supply the clinical or research expertise.

- **Peer reviewers:** Provide knowledge expertise that helps authors strengthen their manuscript.

- **Editors:** Supply the editorial expertise so that the article is editorially correct and is presented most effectively to readers. Editors understand what their readers prefer as far as topics and style of article.

Editors plan the content of the publication; in most cases the planning is done months in advance. Editors are professionals who are bound to follow codes of editorial conduct such as those from the Committee on Publication Ethics (2011), the International Committee of Medical Journal Editors (2013), and the Council of Science Editors (2012). Within an editorial department, different editors have different responsibilities, but common roles include:

Editor-in-chief: Has primary responsibility for the overall content of the publication and strategic planning for the mission of the publication. In some cases the editor is full time; in other situations, the editor might be part-time and also hold another job, such as faculty member or dean at a college of nursing.

Managing editor: Oversees the general editorial operations of the publication, ensuring that articles undergo peer review, are edited, designed, and laid out.

Acquisitions editor: Consults with content experts who have expertise in specific areas that have relevance to the mission of the publication and asks them to submit a manuscript for potential publication. The manuscript generally must still undergo peer review before it's accepted for publication.

Developmental editor: Assists the author to ensure that the manuscript meets the expectations of the publication and guides the author in focusing the manuscript to ensure quality of the content. The role may also be called the *clinical editor*, when the person has expertise in the clinical area of the publication, for example, a nurse clinical editor for a nursing publication.

Content editor: Focuses on ensuring that the writing style of the manuscript is consistent with the publication guidelines. This editor may revise the organization of content and change the way it is written to ensure the content is understandable to the reader and follows the style guidelines of the publication. While changing the wording in some cases, this editor is careful not to change the meaning of the content.

Project editor: Responsible for tracking the manuscript through the editorial process, ensuring that it is sent for peer review and ensuring that authors receive the feedback. This editor also works with other editors or copyeditors as well as the art and production departments to ensure that the manuscript is complete and that all the content needed for final publication is included.

Copyeditor: Performs copyediting and proofreading services for your manuscript.

- **Art director, designer, or graphics person:** Creates the visual elements, such as illustrations, graphs, and tables. The editorial staff and the art director work closely together to ensure that your information is presented clearly.

- **Production assistant:** Lays out the publication on the page for printing or web design.

Sometimes members of the publishing team forget and use jargon when communicating with authors. If you don't know what "crop marks," "folio," "marginalia," or other terms mean, refer to Appendix D.

Collaboration within the publishing team is just as important as it is for a healthcare team. Respect each person's expertise and know that all of you have the same goal: an outstanding published product.

Q: *How can I best work with my editor?*

A: Understand that like you, editors are busy people with multiple deadlines. You will endear yourself to the editor, who, after all, can help make your article shine, by following the author guidelines (the most common complaint of editors is that authors don't do this), responding promptly to emails and phone calls, and meeting your deadlines. The good news is that most editors welcome the opportunity to nurture their relationship with you. That means they welcome your questions. If you're struggling with your revisions, for example, it is perfectly fine to make an appointment with your editor to discuss the situation.

Anatomy of Writing Lessons

You now have a solid overview of what it takes to write for publication, all based on something you already know—anatomy and physiology. You also know how to break down barriers to writing and how the publishing process works.

In upcoming chapters, you will learn much more about writing, submitting, and revising your work for publication. As you read, remember—if you passed anatomy and physiology, you can write!

Write Now!

1. List three benefits that you feel will come from writing an article. It might be personal satisfaction, a desire to learn more about a topic, or something else. The point is that it should be personal to you.

2. Now, write a few sentences about how you will carve out time to write in your schedule. Create action steps: for example, when you will set your first writing date in your calendar.

References

Committee on Publication Ethics. (2011). Code of conduct and best practice guidelines for journal editors. Retrieved from http://publicationethics.org/files/Code_of_conduct_for_journal_editors.pdf

Council of Science Editors. (2012). CSE's white paper on promoting integrity in scientific journal publications, 2012 update. Retrieved from http://www.councilscienceeditors.org/i4a/pages/index.cfm?pageid=3331

Draxler, B. (2013). Early birds have different brains than night owls. *Discover*. Retrieved from http://blogs.discovermagazine.com/d-brief/?p=3614#.UkxpBSigWWU

Ellison, R. (1995). *Invisible man*. New York, NY: Vintage Classic.

Falk, H., Ekman, I., Anderson R., Fu, M., & Ganger, B. (2013). Older patients' experiences of heart failure—An integrative literature review. *Journal of Nursing Scholarship, 45*(3), 247–255.

International Committee of Medical Journal Editors. (2013). Retrieved from http://www.icmje.org

Morrison, T. (2006). *Beloved*. New York, NY: Everyman's Library.

Oermann, M. H., & Hays, J. (2010). *Writing for publication in nursing* (2nd ed.). New York, NY: Springer Publishing Company.

Saver, C. (2006a). Reap the benefits of writing for publication. *AORN Journal, 83*(3), 603–606.

Saver, C. (2006b). Demystifying the publishing process. *AORN Journal, 84*(3), 373-376.

Strunk, W., Jr., & White, E.B. (1999). *The elements of style* (4th ed.). Boston, MA: Longman/Pearson Education.

Twibell, R., Siela, D., Riwitis, C., Wheatley, J., Riegle, T., Johnson, D., … Cable, S. (2009). Family presence during resuscitation: Who decides? *American Nurse Today, 4*(8), 8–10.

Whitbeck, A. (2013). What Works: Improving documentation of restraints in the neuro ICU. *American Nurse Today, 8*(6). Retrieved from http://www.americannursetoday.com/article.aspx?id=10386&fid=10320

> *"You can't wait for inspiration.*
> *You have to go after it with a club."*
>
> *–Jack London*

Finding, Refining, and Defining a Topic

2

Patricia Dwyer Schull and Cynthia Saver

Every good article starts with a good idea. Finding the right topic, and then refining and defining it, makes writing easier. The right topic serves as the nervous system for your article; just as your brain, spinal column, and nerves keep you balanced, the right topic keeps you steady on your writing course and guides the entire creation of your article. This chapter describes a three-step process for developing a topic. The process consists of finding your topic, refining your topic, and defining your topic.

Finding a Topic

Perhaps the most frequent question first-time authors ask is simply what to write about. If you plan to publish a study you just completed or you want to write about a recent important clinical experience, you have an easy answer right in front of you. But what if you've been asked to contribute to a nursing magazine, or you want to start a blog? For many nurses, picking a topic requires thought and effort. The good news is that ideas are all around you: in your life, your practice, the literature you read—even your local news.

Think about how you would handle an emergency situation during your everyday practice. It's automatic, right? First, you assess the situation. The same applies to writing: Assess your motivation for writing an article and possible topics. When you write down

WHAT YOU'LL LEARN IN THIS CHAPTER

- Using a variety of questions will help you determine your interest areas so that you can start to think about a topic you want to write on.

- To further explore and narrow your topic, create a mind map.

- You can use the author guidelines to develop some specifications for your article before you send a query to the editor.

your thoughts and ideas in an organized and systematic fashion, it pushes you to more fully and coherently express them. Just as in nursing, practice makes perfect. The more times you work through the exercise of defining your idea, the easier it will become.

Use the questions shown in Figure 2.1 (these questions are described in detail in the following sections) to conduct your assessment. Write your responses to each question in the space provided.

Why Should I Write an Article?

As a practitioner or expert in your field, writing and sharing your ideas with professional colleagues can be a good way to increase your professional recognition, career opportunities, and advancement. You will also gain personal satisfaction and improve your confidence. We need to share our knowledge with our colleagues so we can learn from each other, building the best evidence to improve patient care and further validating the nursing profession and what nurses do day to day.

Now that you are thinking about sharing knowledge, consider what knowledge you have to share. Is there a new procedure that your hospital is doing? How you implemented a new restraints-free policy that is highly effective?

Who Will Read My Article?

Be clear about who the reader—the *audience*—is. You can read in Chapter 3 about researching the publication you're writing for. Knowing who reads a journal, magazine, blog, or book will make it easier for you to write an article that the publication's audience will find useful. For example, is the reader a clinical staff nurse? An advanced practice nurse? A researcher? An educator? Don't make the mistake of writing before knowing the answer; otherwise, you'll be spinning your wheels and will have to rework your writing—or your article will be rejected. For example, an article on managing multiple medications in older patients will be developed differently for an article intended for staff nurses as opposed to nurse practitioners.

What Interests Me?

What area(s) are you most experienced in? Are you an expert? What do you have an interest in? These questions are starting places for deciding what you could write about. Your experience, expertise, or interest in the topic will sustain you through planning, researching, writing, and revising. Otherwise, you could discover that creating an article is tough going.

Assessment

Why should I write an article?   _____

                                                  _____

Who will read my article?   _____

                                                  _____

What interests me?   _____

                                                  _____

What might interest others the most?   _____

                                                  _____

What can others learn from what I'm doing?   _____

                                                  _____

What is happening at work or in my specialty?   _____

                                                  _____

What writing style should I use for a topic?   _____

                                                  _____

What is the best timing for my article?   _____

                                                  _____

What publication is right for my article?   _____

                                                  _____

Figure 2.1   Writing assessment worksheet.

Editors often look for the voice of experience from an author, and experienced authors usually say that it's easier to write about a topic you know well, especially at the start of your writing efforts. Keep in mind, however, that you don't have to be widely published to be an "expert." If you have cared for hospice patients for 10 years, for example, you likely have developed expertise in particular areas, such as pain management, grief counseling, and managing end-of-life symptoms.

What Might Interest Others the Most?

Nurse editors and publishers spend a lot of time talking to nurses about what core topics interest them. Through polls, surveys, and personal contact, they have a good idea about what their audience wants to see. For clinical journals, those topics usually include drugs, cardiac and respiratory care, and emergency situations; actual clinical experiences or case studies on these topics are often sought after by editors. Other high-interest topics are diseases, treatments, nursing procedures, and diagnostic tests. These popular topics rarely change year to year, but you need to keep up on any new breakthroughs related to treatments and best practices pertinent to your topic of interest or to the publication you might be interested in writing for.

> **Q:** *I emailed an editor of a popular nurse's journal suggesting what I thought was a fantastic topic idea. She sent me a chilly reply saying they'd just run an article on the same topic. What should I do to avoid this in the future?*
>
> **A:** Subscribe to the journal (or other type of publication or website you are targeting) or access it online or at the library. Before you send off an idea (a query) to an editor, make sure you know what that journal has published in the past 6 months or more. Better yet, do an online search to see whether the journal has published an article on a similar topic and what the approach was. Then, modify your focus to include how your article will differ and pitch your idea accordingly.

As a first-time author, you might think that common topics aren't as interesting as uncommon ones, but that's not always true. Common topics involve the most prevalent disease states and treatments. Healthcare professionals spend the majority of their time caring for patients with these conditions, so interest is high for these topics by both readers and publishers. And don't forget hot topics that relate to patient safety and urgent situations, such as an emergency event or the latest disease epidemic.

From the Editor's Perspective

What makes a good idea? Thinking like an editor will help you choose a topic more likely to be accepted for publication. Here are some questions that an editor considers when evaluating your idea. Is your idea:

- New?
- Timely?
- Relevant to the publication's readers?
- Interesting?
- Consistent with the publication's mission?

What Can Others Learn From What I'm Doing?

Nurses often seek ways to improve what they're already doing. Perhaps your specialty is diabetes, and you have developed a detailed protocol for establishing dietary measures. Or maybe you fine-tuned a procedure for writing a business plan for managing community screenings or conducted a survey with interesting results. You might assume that your new methods or fresh discoveries are of interest only to those in your particular environment, but having your findings published can help others learn from you and build on your findings.

What Is Happening at Work or in My Specialty?

When you're looking for a journal article or research study topic, concentrate on the problems, issues, challenges, and trends that your colleagues speak of most often. Access your specialty organizations' websites for topics of interests; look for repeated comments or questions on discussion forums. While there, read the featured presentations for recent or upcoming meetings because these tend to present the latest developments in a field. Many national associations post abstracts from previous meetings online. Because there is a lag time between a new innovation and its publication in a journal, this information might help you discover a topic not yet published. Take note of the presenters, and consider one of them as a possible coauthor or mentor.

Don't ignore the general media when looking for trends and issues. *The Wall Street Journal* and *The New York Times* both frequently publish articles in print and online about new developments in healthcare.

Q: *I think I have an idea, but how can I research what others have written on it?*

A: Many excellent sources of nursing publications and literature are available, including CINAHL (Cumulative Index to Nursing and Allied Health Literature), Ovid, and PubMed. PubMed alone has more than 23 million citations from MEDLINE, life science journals, and online books. Citations can include links to full-text articles from PubMed Central and to publisher websites. You can access this site at http://www.ncbi.nlm.nih.gov/pubmed. Not all nursing publications are listed in this database, so look at other sources as well. Use general search engines such as Google (http://www.google.com) and Google Scholar (http://scholar.google.com) to supplement PubMed. Another option is an editorial reference manager system such as Mendeley (http://www.mendeley.com) or Zotero (http://www.zotero.org). You can learn more about finding information in Chapter 4.

What Writing Style Should I Use for a Topic?

After you decide on a topic, you need to know whether your topic, expertise, and writing style are best suited for a scholarly journal, a clinical how-to, a *soft piece* (a human interest story about a past experience), or a healthcare–related piece for consumers. If your expertise, for example, lends itself to a hands-on, practical article that focuses on useful information that helps readers deal with problems they face, then by all means plan to write a piece for the clinical or consumer markets. The specific tone of the article depends on the type of publication. For example, an article for *Nursing Research*, a scholarly journal, will be written in a different style than one for *Nursing*, which is clinically focused.

Regardless of the type of writing you decide to do, do not underestimate the value of preparation, and always keep in mind that the result of your writing doesn't have to please only you or your colleagues: It has to be good enough for your target readers to understand.

What Is the Best Timing for My Article?

If you are writing a blog post or an article that will be quickly published online, you need to be timely. For example, if your organization helped out in a major disaster, you would want to write about it quickly. Timing considerations apply in print, too. If, for instance, your operating room was one of the few sites doing an innovative procedure, you would want to get the word out before it becomes more common in practice.

The bottom line: No one wants to read about a topic that is dated.

What Publication Is Right for My Article?

In Chapter 3, you can read more about selecting the appropriate vehicle for your work. You need to know a specific publisher's mission, audience, types of articles published, manuscript format, and editorial process. Most journals have an editor who acts as the major decision maker for what is considered acceptable. Keep in mind that some journal staffs spend considerable time editing, rewriting, and copyediting. In these cases, it's your clinical knowledge and expertise that interest the publisher, not necessarily your writing ability. But others don't—meaning that some journals require a fairly well-written initial submission and will provide only light copyediting and proofreading.

Also keep in mind that some journals have mentoring programs for new authors (Mayer, Pieszak, & Amen, 2012). These programs pair or partner new authors with experienced authors who act as mentors—providing guidance through the peer review and publishing process.

Now that you have answered these questions, identify a topic that you want to explore further. Keep this topic in mind while you move to the next step—refining your topic.

Q: *Do journals and other publications publish lists of the topics that they are interested in?*

A: Check the publication's author guidelines to see whether they specify desired types of topics. You should also search for "call for manuscripts" or "call for topics" in journals—these alert you to what the editor needs for an upcoming issue with a special focus. One useful site for finding these types of items is Nursing Writing (http://nursingwriting.wordpress.com).

Refining a Topic

With a working knowledge of your topic under your belt, start doing your research or reviewing the literature. Before you can frame your topic, you will want to know what others have written. Reading articles related to the topic, especially those that are particularly interesting, factual, and well written, will help you better understand where your idea fits. While you're analyzing each article you read, check for the number of citations for your topic, which is an indication of the depth of coverage.

When your research is completed, consider how the article you want to write can provide information that fills a void or offers a new perspective. For example, if your idea is about administering medications safely, you might find quite a few articles on your topic. However, your article could focus on how an innovative technique developed through collaboration between nursing and pharmacy reduced medication errors in your hospital.

Don't despair if your search turns up several articles within your expertise on what you thought was a unique topic. You might be able to take the topic and refocus it to a more specific discussion, based on your own experiences. For example, if you look for articles on neurological assessment, the sheer number might deter you from thinking that this would be a good topic. But these articles might not include a more recently developed tool. Or, you might find that few articles on neuro assessment target a specific group of nurses, such as those in home health. Looking at popular topics from new angles provides you with the opportunity to revisit the topic of neurological assessment in a new light.

Narrow Your Topic

Just like your eyes focus on a detail of an image, you need to focus your topic. Writing about the patient with diabetes undergoing surgery could fill a book, but strategies for managing hypoglycemia in the patient about to undergo ambulatory surgery would be a topic that a standard journal article could accommodate (Saver, 2006). Sometimes focusing won't involve only narrowing your topic; sometimes you also have to turn it around a bit and focus on an aspect that is new, different, or unseen. For example, you could adjust the topic "the benefits/ advantages of manual chest percussion for the patient with chronic obstructive pulmonary disease" to "the benefits of manual percussion versus mechanical percussors."

Mind mapping is an excellent tool to use to narrow your topic (see Figure 2.2). It helps you identify and understand the structure of a subject and how the main topics fit together. Further, it taps into how your brain works by allowing your thoughts to flow freely. First, you start with a central idea or a main topic in the middle of a large sheet of paper (Mind Maps, n.d.). Then you add branches and sub-branches to further represent subtopics and your ideas. You can then look at relationships to see possible linkages.

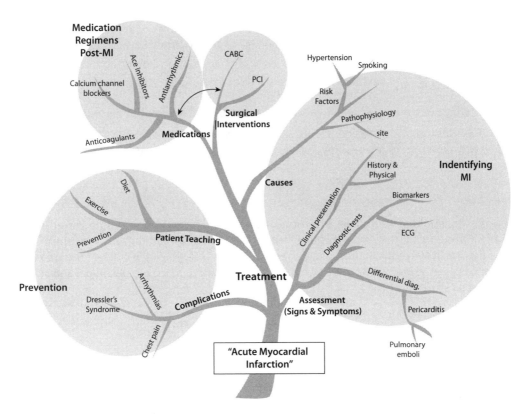

Figure 2.2   A mind map can help you visually analyze your topic and shed new light on how you might focus it.

When you examine your topic, remember that it's brainstorming time! Don't critique your thoughts—just write down everything related to your topic, including ancillary ideas and research. This step should be the fun part; use colored pencils or markers to stimulate your creativity or to prioritize subtopics.

For example, start with the broad topic of acute myocardial infarction (MI). The topic on its own is too large for a standard journal article, but when you use a mind map, you can develop several subtopics, including assessment, complications, and medical and surgical interventions. Now, narrow the topic even further by breaking down the subtopics. In this case, we (the authors of this chapter) broke down assessment into subtopics, such as clinical presentation, diagnostics, and differential diagnoses. Ultimately, it becomes clear that we might want to focus on identifying an acute myocardial infarction. Other topics to focus on could be preventing complications of an MI or managing medication regimens post-MI.

You might also try other techniques for creating a successful mind map. Use single words or simple phrases and then draw lines to show linkages. On a separate sheet of paper, keep track of new concepts you think of while looking at these relationships. You might even find a new phrase or name for a concept that provides a solid foundation for your paper.

If you're technology oriented, consider using a digital tool for your mind map such as Mindjet, Xmind, Coggle, Freemind, and MindNode (Lifehacker, 2013). Coggle and Freemind are free and allow you to download your map as a PDF so you can share it with others.

Confidence Booster

Nurses are taught to write short, brief notes, so making the transition to writing an article can be challenging. The next time you're feeling discouraged, read the bios for some of the authors in the publication you're targeting. Chances are, you'll see many of them come from work settings similar to your own. They found a way to make the transition, and so can you!

Write and Test a Summary Statement

After you have your topic sufficiently narrowed or you think you might be on the right track, you can see whether it works on paper. Write one sentence that summarizes the article. Think of your sentence like a goal statement in a patient care plan. The statement should include the purpose and target audience for the article (be specific). For example, consider some sample original summary statements and notice how the revised statements are more specific than the original.

> **Original statement:** This chapter covers how to pick a topic for an article.

> *Revised statement:* This chapter explains how a nurse new to publishing should choose, define, and refine a topic for publication.

> **Original statement:** This article will tell you how to identify a myocardial infarction.

> *Revised statement:* This article will tell you how to quickly identify a patient with an acute myocardial infarction by assessing their clinical presentation, analyzing their ECG and laboratory results, and ruling out any differential signs or symptoms.

After you write your own summary statement, test its effectiveness by answering the question: Does it pass the "So what?" test? Although you might know what you want to accomplish, you must be sure that nurse readers will be able to answer the question "So what?" with a response that has meaning to them in their professional or personal lives.

Q: *The peer reviewers for my manuscript for a general nursing journal said it wasn't relevant to clinical nurses. How can I refocus it?*

A: It sounds like you didn't fully answer the "So what?" question before you wrote your article. Double back and ask it again. Ask your target audience what is of interest to them and see how it could relate to your topics. Try writing statements to answer the "So what?" question. Soon you will be back on track.

Defining a Topic

Now that you have narrowed your topic, you're ready to further define it with specifications and an outline.

Determine Specifications

By now, you have determined what kind of article you're writing—research or how-to, for example—and what sort of publication you're probably going to target—say a general nursing magazine versus a research nursing journal. Next, you need to check the publisher's author guidelines for the publication you are considering. Author guidelines delineate and detail what the publisher expects to see in a submission, including length of your piece (in words or both words and pages), and will usually offer suggestions as well as expectations for other main features of your submission, such as case studies, tables, and illustrations. Following the author guidelines will increase the likelihood your article will be suitable for the publication you are targeting, which, in turn, increases the likelihood it will be accepted for publication.

Further, author guidelines usually provide explicit instructions about the article format and use of illustrations and tables. One of the most important things to look for is which editorial style the publisher uses. Many academic journals follow the *Publication Manual of The American Psychological Association* (commonly called *APA style*), while your city magazine might use *The Associated Press Stylebook*. It would be disappointing to put in so much work only to have your manuscript rejected because you prepared it incorrectly.

Most journal publishers will reject a manuscript if your submission doesn't conform to the basics:

- Importance, timeliness, relevance of the topic

- Adequacy of the rationale and/or literature review

- Logical organization of ideas and thoroughness of presentation

- Congruence between the questions or issues investigated and implications/conclusions stated

- Clarity and consistency of writing

- Adherence to the publisher's editorial style guide (such as the APA manual)

Having a clear focus on the specifics of your planned article will help you craft a more effective query letter and write a better article after your topic is accepted for publication.

Q: *Where do I find the author guidelines?*

A: Each publication has its own set of guidelines. The best place to start is with the individual magazine, journal, or book publisher's website. Look under Submissions, Author guidelines, or even Contact us. Typically, author guidelines are available in a PDF or other downloadable file. If you can't find them on the website, try a broader Google search or email or call the publisher's offices.

Draft an Outline

Your next step is to create an outline of your paper or article. The outline may seem like a throwback to junior high English class, but in reality, it will guide you through the writing process. Just like a care pathway is a plan for a patient, an outline is a plan for an article. At this stage, forget about rules, such as every Roman numeral I must have at least a Roman numeral II beneath it. Instead, organize your thoughts into broad categories, expanding on what you came up with in the mind-mapping exercise.

To begin, put your summary statement at the top of the outline to serve as a touchstone while you write. Make a rough outline of your topic, writing down each major section with a topic sentence. Include any tables, figures, or illustrations in each section as appropriate. After you have your major topics listed, you can organize them into an orderly flow of information by adding appropriate headings and subheads, helping the reader to understand each topic in a logical order.

Figure 2.3 shows a short example of an outline that you would flesh out as you considered how you wanted to develop your article.

Summary statement: This article tells nurses how to quickly identify a patient with an acute myocardial infarction (MI) by assessing clinical presentation, the patient's ECG and laboratory results, and ruling out any differential signs or symptoms.

   I. Introduction (Present a case situation.)

  II. Clinical presentation (How does the patient with an MI present?)

      Chest pain: type, location, and severity

      Respiratory: shortness of breath

      General: diaphoresis

      Atypical findings

 III. ECG findings (What are indications of MI on an ECG?)

      ST segment depression or elevation (STEMI)

      T wave inversion

  IV. Lab tests (What findings indicate MI?)

      Cardiac markers (CK, CK-MB)

      Others

   V. Differential signs or symptoms (What else could this be?)

      Gastrointestinal

      Psychosomatic

      Pulmonary embolism

      Other

 VI. Conclusion

      Take-home points

Figure 2.3   Sample outline.

The Value of a Good Idea

The most important aspect of writing is that you take time in the beginning to find a topic that you feel passionate about. Finding the right subject and approach will sustain you throughout the writing process. To narrow the topic, consider how long your article will be and the scope of what you want to cover. If you're working on a book proposal, your topic will guide you on the next steps of your journey. If you're preparing a journal article, it will help you choose a journal. And if you're submitting an idea to a magazine, an online-only publication, a blog, or a newsletter, you'll be ready to send a query letter to the editor.

The next few chapters provide detailed information about how to further organize your article, create good flow, and supplement or enhance your article with such tools as tables, graphs, and illustrations. Starting with a good idea, though, will give you the wings you need for a successful start to your writing career!

Write Now!

1. Identify an idea for an article.

2. Use a mind map to narrow the focus of your idea.

3. Write a summary statement.

4. Create an outline.

References

Lifehacker. (2013). Five best mind mapping tools. Retrieved from http://lifehacker.com/five-best-mind-mapping-tools-476534555

Mayer, D. K., Pieszak, S., & Amen, K. (2012). Mentoring new authors: *Clinical Journal of Oncology Nursing*'s Writing Mentorship Program. *Nurse Author Editor, 22*(3).

Mind Maps®. Mind Tools. (n.d.). Retrieved from http://www.mindtools.com/pages/article/newISS_01.htm

Saver, C. (2006). Finding and refining an article topic. *AORN Journal, 83*(4), 829–832.

"Writing is the best way to talk without being interrupted."

–Jules Renard

How to Select and Query a Publication

Cynthia Saver

3

When you choose a dressing for a wound, you carefully weigh the options to determine the best match for the patient. For example, you would never put a transparent film dressing on a wound with a lot of exudate—it just wouldn't do the job.

In the same way, you need to carefully select the publication, such as a journal, where you want your article to appear. After you decide that, you should see whether the publication editor accepts queries or reviews papers only after they've been submitted. If the editor is open to a query, your next step is to prepare a *query letter* (ironically, usually sent via email) to see whether he or she is interested in the article. But first, take a look at what goes into selecting the best publication fit for your idea.

Q: *Is the term* journal *limited to peer-reviewed, scholarly, text-heavy publications?*

A: Journals vary in "look" and tone. Some journals look more like magazines, even though they are publishing scholarly or evidence-based material. The term "journal" is a broad one, which means that more and more nursing information is accessible to more and more nurses. Although this chapter uses "journal" because most nurses are familiar with the term, the principles discussed also apply to other publications. For example, as you read, you'll see you can often substitute the words *publication*, *website*, or *newsletter* for the word *journal*. Don't be boxed in by terminology.

WHAT YOU'LL LEARN IN THIS CHAPTER

- To choose a publication for your article idea, consider the right audience, the right circulation, the right timing, the right review process, and the right impact factor.

- A query should promote both your idea and why you should be the one to write the article.

- Match the tone of the query to the tone of the publication.

Finding a Journal

The good news for authors is that there are more than 200 nursing journals in the United States, with hundreds more in other countries. This means plenty of opportunities for getting published. The easiest place to start is your own mailbox with the journals you currently receive and know the most about. You might also take a trip to your area nursing school's library—or, if you are fortunate to have one, your organization's medical library. But if you want to get a list of names, and do even more research, you can go online.

In addition to the resources listed in Chapter 2, try these additional sites for lists of nursing journals:

- **BioMed Central** (http://www.biomedcentral.com): Source of more than 250 open-access journals, although only a few are specific for nurses. Other sources of open-access journals are **PLOS ONE** (http://www.plos.org) and **ScienceDirect** (http://www.sciencedirect.com). For more information about open-access journals, see the sidebar later in this chapter.

- **Directory of Open Access Journals** (http://www.doaj.org): Search by entering "nursing" as a key word. Also try entering "nurse".

- **Cumulative Index to Nursing and Allied Health Literature (CINAHL**; http://www.cinahl.com): Lists of journals include the regular CINAHL database, CINAHL with full text, CINAHL plus, and CINAHL plus full text. You can download a PDF or Excel file or view in HTML. CINAHL is now accessed through EBSCO.

- **EBSCO Publishing** (http://www.ebscohost.com): Provides databases that users can access, but you need access to a medical library that uses it. (Check with your hospital or university.)

- **Nursing and Allied Health Resources Section Selected List of Nursing Journals** (http://tinyurl.com/85oa5o6): A list from the Medical Library Association that was compiled based on set criteria (NAHRS 2012 selected list of nursing journals, n.d.).

- **Nurse Author & Editor** (http://www.nurseauthoreditor.com/library.asp): Includes a directory of journals with editor contact information.

Once you have a list of journals, you want to select the one that is most appropriate for your topic idea.

Choosing the Right Journal

Choosing the right journal is just as important as choosing a partner for a project. Start by considering your goals. One goal of writing might be to reach the widest possible audience. Another might be to direct your information specifically at a narrow target audience of nurses. At the same time, you want to do everything possible to boost the likelihood an editor will be interested in your idea. That includes analyzing your possible journal (or magazine) selection with a critical eye.

Similar to the "rights of medication administration" (right medication, right patient, right dose, right time, right route, and right documentation), these "rights of choosing a journal" should help you make the best decision.

When selecting the right journal for your idea, ask yourself whether each potential journal has the right:

- Audience

- Numbers

- Timing

- Review process

- Impact factor

Completing this analysis will help you match your idea with the best journal.

Right Audience

Who are you trying to reach with your article? If you want to reach clinicians, Christine Webb (2009) recommends choosing a journal that appeals to them directly. Articles in these types of journals are typically shorter, include easy-to-read features—such as boxes and bullet points—and include a clear link of the information to clinical practice. If you want to reach researchers, scholarly journals, also sometimes called academic journals, might be more appropriate. *Scholarly journals* tend to have longer articles as well as a specific structure for research reports. They primarily reach nurses in academic and research settings. In some cases, nonscholarly journals will also publish research, just in a different format.

Know that these differences are a bit arbitrary. Clinicians read scholarly journals, for example, when they are working on evidence-based projects. And researchers read clinical journals to learn about latest innovations and application. The terms are simply a way of locating your primary target audience.

Sometimes you might have more than one audience for your article. Say that you completed a research study on a new suctioning technique for an intensive care unit (ICU) patient on mechanical ventilation. Those who would benefit from reading your study include critical care nurse researchers, critical care staff nurses, and critical care educators, among others. Immediately, you know that your article should appear in a critical care journal, but to target an editor, you need to narrow the options. If you want to reach critical care nurse researchers and staff nurses, a good choice might be *Critical Care Nurse* (*CCN*), a journal packed with research studies related to clinical practice. Another option might be *Dimensions in Critical Care Nursing*. One advantage of *CCN* is that it is from the American Association of Critical-Care Nurses, which gives you guaranteed access to members of the large specialty association.

What if your article relates to suctioning of ICU patients with heart failure? In that case, you might choose *Heart & Lung: The Journal of Acute and Critical Care*, the official publication of The American Association of Heart Failure Nurses. Although the audience for the latter journal is decidedly smaller, you are directly targeting the nurses who need your information the most.

Right Numbers

Publishing is partly a numbers game. For example, say that you narrowed your possible journals to three, all of which seem to fit well with your manuscript. Checking each journal's circulation number, typically found in the marketing materials for the journal on its website, gives you more information to help you make your decision.

Say that *Journal A* is published every month and has a circulation of 15,000 nurses—that's 180,000 possible readers. *Journal B* is published every month and has a circulation of 10,000 nurses—that means 150,000 annual possible readers. *Journal C* is published quarterly, with a circulation of 15,000, making the total possible hits 60,000. In this case, *Journal A* would give you the best opportunity for reaching the most nurses with your information and would be the best pick of the three journals that fit with your topic. Generally speaking, the more often the journal or magazine is published, the more likely that your article will be published because the editor must fill a certain number of pages.

However, there is another factor to consider—*reach*. Reach goes beyond the simple number of subscribers and includes all the people who read your article beyond the magazine's circulation. Does the journal publish all its articles online? And, more importantly, are those articles available to subscribers only or locked behind a pay-wall? If you publish in a bimonthly journal that allows only subscribers to access articles, you greatly limit the reach of your article. Keep in mind that most medical journals and many scholarly nursing journals limit access to subscribers; however, in some cases, the editors or the publisher may allow general access after a specific time period, such as 6 or 12 months. Your article might also be required to have nonrestricted viewing if any part of your research was funded by certain grants that require open access. Finally, some journals publish key research articles online ahead of print. Remember that after your article is published online, it is considered *published* and you can't make changes to it.

Another factor related to reach is how active the journal is in using other platforms for getting the word out about what has been published. For example, how active is the journal's social media? Do you see articles in the journal mentioned in other nursing publications or even the general media? Some journals offer authors the ability to do podcasts, deepening the article's impact. Others offer a service called "AudioSlides," which are short, webcast-style presentations that are shown next to the online article on ScienceDirect. This presentation lets authors talk about their research in their own words (Elsevier, n.d.).

Of course, numbers aren't everything. You should balance "who" with "how many." For example, you've completed a study on the financial impact of a program to retain new graduates and want to see it implemented in other hospital. A good journal choice might be *Nursing Economics*, read by nurse leaders who have the ability to green-light such a program in their own organization, as opposed to *Nursing*, which probably has more subscribers, but is read by a broader audience.

Open Access

Open access (OA) is a controversial issue in publishing. Traditionally, publishers make money when individuals and organizations (such as libraries) subscribe to a journal. Many journals also accept advertising. The full content in this type of journal is accessible only to subscribers, those who have access to the journal through paid databases such as EBSCO, and those willing to pay for an individual article, which can be costly.

OA breaks with tradition by giving everyone free access to journal articles as soon as they are published; these articles are also free of most copyright and licensing restrictions (Suber, 2012). For example, the Open Access Scholarly Publishers Association (n.d.) recommends publishers use the Creative Commons-BY license, which allows for unrestricted reuse of content, although the source work must be appropriately attributed.

Types of OA include the following (Campbell & Morgan, 2009; Scholarly Publishing and Academic Resources Coalition, n.d.; Suber, 2012):

- **Gold:** In this case, a journal provides the OA. The authors (or the authors' institution) pay the publisher to make the article OA and readily available. Most OA journals maintain rigorous acceptance standards and editorial boards.

- **Green:** In this case, articles are archived in a digital or an institutional repository. (You can search for OA repositories at www.opendoar.org.) Many universities (such as Harvard) now require faculty to deposit their research in the university repository, but in many cases, the article is embargoed until the publisher's version is printed. Many funders now also require that results must be published as OA. Traditional publishers worry that libraries will cancel their subscriptions because they can obtain articles through green OA.

There are now online journals—many on very narrow or specific topics—that are solely OA with no accompanying print version. These journals are subsidized by grants and other financial support, in-kind support, and fees paid by or on behalf of the author. Many institutions have signed the Compact for Open-Access Publishing Equity, which states that universities and funding agencies can support authors by paying fees in the same way they pay for subscriptions to journals (n.d.).

In some cases journals make content OA after a set amount of time has passed from publication; in other cases, the journal may offer the author a choice as to whether he or she wants to pay a fee for the article to be OA.

In a survey on OA (Taylor & Francis Group, 2013) that received more than 14,700 responses, respondents most commonly identified advantages of OA as provision of wider circulation compared to a subscription journal, faster publication times, and higher visibility than in a subscription journal. Interestingly, most respondents disagreed with statements about potential disadvantages, such as lower quality and low production standards. Nearly two thirds (65%) of respondents strongly agreed that publication of research "should not be limited by the ability to pay."

Traditional publishers resist OA, citing the need to recoup costs for developing content. And be aware that not all OA journals are created equal; some are simply fraudulent. Many articles on the blog "The Scholarly Kitchen," by Phil Davis, explain potential issues with OA.

Finally, check whether the journal is indexed in databases, such as EBSCO. These databases are used by healthcare organizations and schools, so they extend the reach of your manuscript. You can check the database directly, or the journal may list where it is indexed in the front part of each issue.

Q: *I've read about OA, and think I want to try that option. What else do I need to know?*

A: You can search for OA journals at the Directory of Open Access Journals (DOAJ; http://www.doaj.org). Remember to do your homework. Some publishers of OA journals prey on authors, getting them to publish in journals of low quality while cashing their checks. Verify that the journal is peer reviewed, that it's published by a reputable organization or publishing company, and that is adheres to editorial standards. Beall (n.d.) maintains a list of "potential, possible, or probable predatory scholarly open-access publishers" based on set criteria. However, even the DOAJ or Beall's list are not foolproof. A study in *Science* (Bohannon, 2013) found that a bogus paper was accepted by some DOAJ journals and rejected by some journals on Beall's list.

Right Timing

Timing might vary, depending on the type of publication, but editors generally plan their issues 6 months to 18 months ahead. For a magazine or for some journals, editors establish a general outline of the issue. Others, including more formal research journals, compile an issue based on the papers submitted, peer reviewed, and edited. And, still others have a "call for manuscripts" or "call for submissions," which alerts readers to an upcoming special issue, for instance, on diabetes or disaster nursing. The *Journal of Dermatology* might plan a special issue on psoriasis, or the *Journal of Radiology Nursing* might want to do a special issue on radiologic interventions for stroke. Sending a query in response to a call for manuscripts increases your opportunity for being heard above the background noise of a busy editor's day.

Q: *Where can I find calls for manuscripts?*

A: Calls for manuscripts are usually listed in the journal or on its website. Another good source is the Nursing Writing blog by Thomas Lawrence Long at http://nursingwriting.wordpress.com. You can also search for "call for manuscript" or "call for submissions" and "nursing" in search engines such as Google.

Keep in mind that many journals or magazines publish monthly, but others publish quarterly. It's worth examining which issue might be best. If you're writing about treatment protocols for H1N1 influenza, fall would be a better fit for your topic than summer, which is not flu season.

Timing of events can also affect your topic. For instance, when a major national disaster occurs, it often prompts interest in articles related to disaster response or prevention topics. Other events that receive widespread media coverage can also be a factor. For example, when singer Michael Jackson died, authorities disclosed that he had been administered *propofol*, a sedative delivered by IV infusion. Until then, the drug was primarily known only by ICU, operating room, endoscopy, and postanesthesia care unit nurses, but the incident prompted many editors to publish articles on the use—and abuse—of propofol.

Certain diseases or conditions can also be seasonal. If you have a manuscript on the care of heat stroke, most editors will want to publish it in the summer. As a general rule, start sending queries to editors about one year before you would like to see it published.

Don't forget about online publications. They often have much shorter lead times than traditional print publications, but they can be a great venue for your work. Many editors publish topics that they find of interest, and often your article can be published within a matter of weeks or days—not months.

Right Review Process

Most scholarly journals use a formal peer-review process (described more fully in Chapter 9). After your manuscript is fully finished and submitted, a panel of experts in your area will review it and offer comments or suggestions. Peer reviewers offer a journal a way to validate what you have written. If you are a faculty member required to publish for tenure, or even a graduate student looking for a prestigious outlet for your research, you will probably want a journal that uses peer review. Journals clearly state in the author guidelines whether the article will be peer reviewed or *refereed* (another term for the same process).

Right Impact Factor

If you are choosing a scholarly journal that includes a peer-review process, you might want to consider the journal's *impact factor* (IF), which is the formula of measurement based on how often articles in a particular journal have been cited in a particular year or period (Thompson Reuters, n.d.). The most commonly used IFs are those published in the *Journal Citation Reports* (JCR). The Institute of Scientific Information (part of Thompson Reuters) calculates a publication's IF, which is determined by "dividing the number of current year citations to the source items published in that journal during the previous two years" (Thompson Reuters, n.d.). Publishers and editors put great stock in IFs as a measure of how heavily their journal is used for research. Librarians, university researchers, and even corporations use IFs to choose which journals to subscribe to or advertise in. The IFs of the journals where someone publishes can play a role in tenure decisions for a faculty member or funding decisions for a researcher.

Here is the formula that would be used to calculate a 2014 IF:

> **A:** The number of times that articles published in 2012–2013 were cited in indexed journals during 2014
>
> **B:** The number of articles, reviews, proceedings, or notes that were published in 2012–2013
>
> 2014 IF = A/B

JCR also provides a 5-year impact factor, so that a broader effect can be seen.

You cannot access the list of IFs without being a subscriber to *JCR*; however, a medical librarian might be able to answer your questions. You can also check whether a specific journal is included in *JCR*'s master journal list by doing a search at http://science.thomsonreuters.com/mjl.

Just because a journal doesn't have an IF doesn't mean you should automatically strike it from your list as a possible option for publishing. As Webb (2009) notes, the journals without IF can still publish material as good as or better than those with an IF. Some journals are simply too new to have received a full assessment; others might focus on material less likely to contribute to an IF, such as case studies. Webb says that IF should "not be the only factor considered when choosing which journal to be published in" (Webb, 2009, p. 19).

Q: *Are there other ways to measure a journal's effectiveness beside an IF? What about measuring the effect of a single article?*

A: Because so much literature now appears online, and traditional techniques such as measuring citations require time to have passed so that citations can appear in future articles, experts are examining other ways to measure "impact" using what's called "alternative citation metrics" or "altmetrics" (Galloway, Pease, & Rauh, 2013; Kraft, 2013; Priem, Taraborelli, Groth, & Neylon, 2010). Altmetrics measures the impact of individual articles, rather than journals. It measures dissemination, checking how often an article is bookmarked, cited in a blog post, tweeted, or shared online (Kraft, 2013). Some researchers are studying the correlation between citation impact and altmetrics (Kraft, 2013). It's too soon to know how altmetrics tools will stack up against impact factors, but it's a development worth watching. Almetrics might prove to be especially valuable in tracking the impact of research in the realm of the general public.

IF is not without controversy. It was originally designed (in 1975) to measure a journal's influence in the broader literature, which is why citations were chosen as a determinant. However, McVeigh and Mann (2009) believe that it has erroneously become a surrogate for assessing the scholarly value of a work published in that journal. The San Francisco Declaration on Research Assessment, initiated by the American Society for Cell Biology (2013) calls for the elimination of journal-based metrics such as IFs in "funding, appointment, and promotion considerations" and provides recommendations for research assessment by funding agencies, institutions, researchers, publishers, and organizations that supply metrics. As of October 2013, 407 organizations and 9,492 individuals had signed the declaration; no nursing organizations have signed.

JCR has refined its system for analysis and added metrics over the years to try to address criticisms. One example is the Eigenfactor Score, which provides a way to assess the journal's prestige. Eigenfactor.org is an academic research project (Eigenfactor.org, n.d.). Other alternatives to JCR include the Reliability-Based Citation Impact Factor, which incorporates data over the journal's lifespan (Kuo & Rupe, 2007). Journals included in the Nursing and Allied Health Resources Section Selected List of Nursing Journals, from the Medical Library Association, must meet set criteria such as be listed in the nursing subset of CINAHL and be highly cited (n.d.).

It is wise to keep in mind that only a small percentage of nursing journals have an IF score, so it should be only one factor in your decision of where to publish your work. Polit & Northam (2011) suggest nurses "adopt a strategy of having a diversified portfolio of publications, with articles aimed at a range of academic and clinical audiences" (p. 26).

Key Steps to Making a Choice

In her 2009 article, "Avoid rejection: Write for the audience and the journal," Charon Pierson distills making the choice into three key steps:

- Read several articles from the journal you plan to target.

- Look at the table of contents for the issues from the past 2 years.

- Read the journal's mission statement.

Unfortunately, as Pierson says, "Regardless of how widely publicized this advice is, it is the exception rather than the rule that authors follow one or more of the suggestions" (Pierson, 2009). Whichever journal you choose, tailor your manuscript to that journal. For example, if you plan to write about how to assess pain in cognitively impaired older adults for a clinically focused journal, focus on the step-by-step process of assessing pain in clinical practice. However, if the journal is more scholarly, you might want to write a review of current pain-assessment tools for older adults and include recommendations for practice.

After you have chosen a journal, the next step is to see if the editor is interested in your idea.

Framing a Good Query

After you select your target journal, send a query letter to the editor to determine his or her interest in the topic. A query letter, which is typically sent by email, includes an overview of your article and the reasons why an editor should publish it. Some writers call this a *pitch letter*, a letter pitching your idea to an editor to see whether her publication would like to put it in the lineup.

The query can be in the bottom of an email or written as a letter and sent as an attachment. Keep in mind, however, that an email with an attachment sent to someone you have not previously corresponded with could end up in the person's spam folder. That's why it might be best to keep your query to the body of the email.

Q: *Do all editors accept queries?*

A: Some editors of scholarly journals do not accept queries. The author guidelines, available on the journal's website, usually state whether queries are accepted. If not, a simple note to the editor asking whether she accepts queries will get you the answer you need.

You want to query before you start writing because:

- You won't waste time writing if the editor isn't interested in your topic.

- The editor can give you feedback on your idea, helping you to tweak it to make it the most effective possible for the journal's target audience.

- You will feel more confident that your article will be published. An important note of caution, however: Editor interest in an idea does *not* equate with ensured publication (Saver, 2006).

A query letter is your opportunity to sell your idea to the editor. We nurses don't typically think of ourselves as sales people, but consider what you do when you teach patients—you have to sell them on why it's important to follow the prescribed treatment plan. What's more difficult can be the self-promotion needed to convince the editor that you should be the one to write the article.

Look at the elements of the query—addressing the right person/right journal, promoting your topic, promoting yourself, and wrapping up. To begin, look at the example of one nurse's letter (adapted from an actual email) and work on how to improve it for a makeover from a query that doesn't work to one that sells the editor on her article.

Here's what Kayla didn't do well—and why her query letter failed:

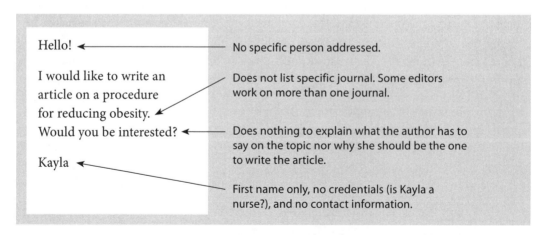

Think about how you would improve Kayla's query letter as you read the next section.

Addressing the Right Person/Right Journal

Be sure to address the correct contact person, which is typically the editor or editor-in-chief. This person's name will be in the author guidelines, which are usually posted on the journal's website. You can also check the journal's *masthead*, the section in the front of the journal that lists the names of staff members, editorial board members, and contact information. Always use the appropriate title with a person's name. For example, if the person has a doctorate degree, use "Dear Dr. Jones" instead of "Dear Mary." If the editor is also a dean, opt for "Dear Dean White." Err on the side of formality at first. Also be sure to get the name of the journal right. Surprisingly, this is a common mistake! It is frustrating for an editor to receive a query addressed to the wrong journal or with the wrong publication in the text.

 Can I use the same query for several publications?

 Sort of. That is, your query is too generic if you don't have to make a few small changes to appeal to one publication or another. Although it might seem many publications are the same, their editors and readers know the subtle differences. And no matter what, make sure you match the correct editor and title to your letter.

The subject line of an email should clearly state that you are inquiring about publishing an article. For example, which subject line do you think would generate more editor interest?

Staffing article idea for Journal of Nursing Administration

or

Journal of Nursing Administration: *Query for article on new technique for staffing off shifts that reduced costs*

You probably chose the second subject line. The word "new" will catch an editor's eye (just be sure what you are writing about is truly new), and the topic is not only clearly stated, but is also obviously something of interest to the journal's readers.

Unfortunately (and all too often), editors receive queries for topics that are not suited for their journals. An editor of *Nurse.com* (an informational magazine with news, coverage of issues, and a focus on immediate clinical application for nurses) received a query to publish a research article related to cellular changes in response to hypoxemia, clearly not something of interest to the publication's typical reader.

Q: *Can I submit my idea to two or more different journals at the same time?*

A: Editors, authors, and ethicists have conflicting viewpoints on this, but standard practice is that you should submit to one journal at a time. If you do submit to more than one journal or if your article is under consideration somewhere else, say so in your query.

Promoting Your Topic

Most editors don't sit around waiting for writers to contact them. They work their networks to get ideas and articles from readers, editorial board members, conference speakers, local and national media, social media (such as Twitter, LinkedIn, and Facebook), and more. Then they have to choose the topics that best fit the journal's mission and will interest the reader (Saver, 2006).

You have to help your topic stand out from the others first by clearly stating what your take on the topic will be. Again, which of the following statements will more likely get the editor's attention?

I would like to submit an article that would describe the results of a research study on how to reduce hospital readmissions.

I would like to submit an article that would describe the results of a research study showing how regular follow-ups from a nurse practitioner for patients with heart failure reduced hospital readmissions by one third.

The first statement certainly states the topic, but notice how the second tells the editor what the study found as well as the results that would make him or her want to read it. Next, explain why the topic is important to the journal's readers. Say that your article is about "hands only" CPR in people in the community. You might write something like the following:

> Cardiac disease remains the leading cause of death in the U.S., with many patients dying from acute myocardial infarction (MI) even before they reach the hospital. "Hands only" CPR provides a way to improve survival. The readers of *Home Healthcare Nurse* may encounter patients in cardiac arrest in the home, where state-of-the-art equipment is lacking, and all the nurse has to rely on is him- or herself.

Include statistics on how many people experience cardiac arrest in the home to strengthen your case.

Here is another example of how you might pitch an article—this one on childhood diabetes:

> The manuscript describes a new program for managing children with diabetes in an outpatient clinic. We conducted a survey of children and parents to determine unmet needs of the child, designed the program to address those needs, and then conducted a follow-up survey 6 months later. The needs we identified included management of diet in school and at parties, participating in sports, talking with friends about diabetes, and monitoring blood glucose.

> We found that our program, designed by a multidisciplinary team, increased overall satisfaction with care by 50%.

Note that the potential author provided a *hook* by telling the editor the program's effectiveness.

Depending on the publication, you can have a bit of fun with the opening of your query letter. Think about this when you skim through a magazine or journal. The first few lines can prove to be an important factor in whether you read the article. It's no different for the query letter. Here is a possible opening:

> In the midst of the nursing shortage, nurses struggle to deliver care with fewer numbers. What if they could count on an extra nurse on two of their three shifts? Better yet, what if the nurse didn't have to be paid?

> That's the situation at Anytown Medical Center, where we have a volunteer program for retired registered nurses. After an orientation, the

nurses work mornings and afternoons, helping out with morning or afternoon physical care, vital signs, and limited physical assessments. We now have more than 60 volunteers in our program.

An article on this program would be of interest to the readers of *American Nurse Today* because they would have the information they need to replicate the program in their own institutions and reap the benefits.

It's hard to imagine an editor turning down this request. However, the same idea pitched to a more scholarly journal would yield a much different letter. Match the formality of your query to the tone of the publication.

Describing the Article

Give the editor a short description of what the article will include so that he or she knows what to expect. This also gives the editor the opportunity to provide guidance as to the direction of the manuscript.

Here is an example of a query letter from nurse author Kristy Chunta, PhD, RN, ACNS, BC, CMC, that illustrates how to promote your topic (second paragraph) and the type of information about content that you should include (third paragraph):

I would like to write an article for nurse leaders entitled *Getting organized: Tips for taking control of email*. I feel that the article would be relevant for the Career Sphere section of *American Nurse Today*.

Nurse leaders are bombarded with email on a daily basis, and trying to handle this form of communication can be overwhelming at times.

This article will focus on how to review and handle email using an organized system. Suggestions for improving time management when reviewing email, especially when using multiple electronic sources (computer, iPad, Smartphone technology), will also be included.

This query ended in a published article: "Control your email before it controls you" (Chunta, 2013).

Selling Yourself as an Author

Your query letter is not the time to be shy. Tell the editor why you should be the one to write the article. For example, perhaps you want to write an article about how to more efficiently teach patients with asthma. You might write something like this:

> I have more than 20 years of experience working with children with asthma in inpatient and outpatient settings. Currently, I am a staff nurse in the asthma clinic at Anytown Medical Center, where we see an average of more than 500 patients every month.

Include any past writing experience. For example, "I have had three articles published in nursing journals, including the *Journal of Emergency Nursing*." If the topics were related to asthma, say so.

Q: *What if I have never been published? Is it more likely my idea will be rejected?*

A: Don't despair if you have not been published. Every writer had to start with one article. You might consider listing nonpublished writing experience. For example, perhaps you write your hospital's or clinic's newsletter. Even though the style of the article is likely to be different, it at least shows that you have an interest in writing. Another option is to choose a coauthor who has been published.

Closing Your Query Letter

Let the editor know when you could have the manuscript done: "I could have the manuscript ready by September 30, 2014."

If you have any flexibility with the date, change the sentence to read, "I could have the manuscript ready by September 30, 2014, or sooner if that better meets your needs."

Be honest when it comes to deadlines. Editors expect manuscripts to arrive on time. They might have even tentatively scheduled the article for a particular issue, pending peer review, so a late article disrupts the schedule.

If you can't write the article before September 30, don't say that you can. There is no faster way to take the gloss off the relationship between editor and writer than to miss your deadline. You can still see your article published (unless you miss the deadline repeatedly), but the editor will be more cautious about accepting ideas from you in the future. Take action if you know you will miss your deadline.

Q: *Another nurse in my department frequently writes for a nursing magazine. Recently, I had an idea accepted, too! But the deadline the editor gave me was much later than the one he gave my colleague. Why the difference?*

A: Some editors know which writers tend to miss their delivery dates and will sometimes give a false deadline (a date sooner than when the article is really needed) as a cushion.

What If You're Going to Miss Your Deadline?

Life happens, and editors understand that you might have to miss a deadline because of illness or a family emergency. Here is how to handle this situation professionally.

- **Notify the editor as soon as you know you will be late.** This sounds like common sense, but many authors fail to do this under the mistaken impression that they will somehow be able to salvage the project or because they simply don't want to admit defeat.

- **Give an estimate for a new deadline.** The editor may be able to simply reschedule your article for a later issue. If you are unable to commit to a new deadline, say so. That way, the editor can decide whether to pursue another author.

- **If possible, find a replacement author.** Ask your editor whether he or she wishes you to find a new author if you can commit to doing so. Depending on your topic, you might be able to find a colleague who is willing to pinch-hit for you. This will make you an instant hero with your editor. However, most editors understand that your circumstances will likely preclude you from finding a replacement.

The bottom line: Try to honor your commitment, but your health, family, and friends must come first.

To finish your letter, give your complete contact information, including full name, email and mailing addresses, and phone numbers, including which number is best for reaching you.

Q: *How long before I receive a response to a query letter?*

A: Some editors respond to query emails within one week, often sooner. Others do not. Keep in mind, however, that there is wide variation in these estimates. As a general rule, follow up 10 to 14 days after you send your email. In rare cases, you may have needed to mail a letter instead of sending an email; in this situation, follow up about one month after you send your letter. Be sure to attach the original query with your follow-up in case it was lost in transmission.

Finally, be sure to spell-check and grammar-check your query. This is your only chance to make a good first impression on the editor. A query riddled with typos could cause the editor to wonder whether you could handle the project.

Here is a "makeover" of the query letter from earlier in the chapter. The letter pitches the fictitious procedure *Adipose supra-ablation* (used in this letter for illustration purposes only) to a fictitious journal.

Kayla Lee, RN, MS, CNOR ← ──────────────────────── Addresses for sender and
1234 Woodlawn Ave. recipient would be omitted
Cleveland, OH 20345 in an email query.

February 17, 2014
Nancy Smith, PhD, CNOR
Editor-in-Chief
Perioperative Services Journal
PO Box 1111
San Antonio, TX 78229

Dear Dr. Smith, ← ──────────────────────────────────── Correct name of editor.

I would like to submit a manuscript to *Perioperative Services* ← ─ Correct name of journal.
Journal. The manuscript describes a new surgical procedure for
reducing obesity: Adipose supra-ablation. ← ──────────── Proposed topic.

Obesity is a leading cause of death in the United States, with
more than 25% of Americans classified as obese. Techniques
such as bariatric surgery have been used to treat patients who are
obese; these surgeries are associated with serious complications
and can be used in only a select patient population. Adipose
supra-ablation, a less extensive surgical option for those who
are obese, is associated with only minor complications and can ─ Explains why the article is
be performed in children and adults. My article would include important to readers.
indications for adipose supra-ablation, a description of the pro-
cedure, risks and benefits, and the perioperative nurse's role. ← ─ Briefly states what the
article will include.

I have more than 10 years' experience in the perioperative set- ─ Briefly explains why she
ting. For the past 3 years, I have been the nurse leader of our should write the article. If
perioperative team for adipose supra-ablation. Our surgeons per- Kayla has published any
form an average of 10 adipose supra-ablations each month, twice articles previously, she
the national average. ← ────────────────────────── should mention her writing
experience here.

I could have the manuscript ready by April 30, 2014. ← ───── States when the article will
Please call me at (555) 888-0000 or email me at be ready. If Kayla has some
k.lee@nowhere.com if you have any questions. ← ──────── flexibility with the date, she
should add that.

Thank you for your consideration. ── Provides several ways to
contact.

Sincerely,
Kayla Lee, RN, MS, CNOR ← ──────────────────────── Author's full name and
credentials.

*Adapted from: Saver, C. (2006). Choosing a journal and submitting your manuscript. AORN Journal, 84(1), 27–30.
(image on p. 29). Reprinted with permission.*

Choose Wisely

Choosing the right target publication journal requires careful thought and analysis. After you select your publication, write your query letter in an appropriate style and email it to the appropriate person. Writing an effective query will boost the likelihood the editor will respond positively, and you will be ready to start writing. Keep in mind that your manuscript will still need to be reviewed before it is accepted for publication.

Write Now!

1. Make a list of journals that would fit your idea for an article. Then narrow the list to three and rank them in order of best fit.

2. Write a query letter, including the topic, a brief description of the article, why you should write the article, and your wrapping-up information.

References

American Society for Cell Biology. (2013). San Francisco declaration on research assessment. Retrieved from http://am.ascb.org/dora

Beall, J. (n.d.). Beall's list: Potential, possible, or probable predatory scholarly open-access publishers. Retrieved from http://scholarlyoa.com/publishers

Bohannon, J. (2013). Who's afraid of peer review? *Science, 342*(6154), 60–65.

Campbell, R., & Morgan, C. (2009). The road to open access: Where are we now? *Nurse Author & Editor, 19*(1). Retrieved from http://www.nurseauthoreditor.com/article.asp?id=121

Chunta, K. S. (2013). Control your email before it controls you. *American Nurse Today, 8*(8). Retrieved from http://www.americannursetoday.com/Article.aspx?id=10648&fid=10604

Compact for open-access publishing equity. (n.d.). Retrieved from http://www.oacompact.org

Eignefactor.org. (n.d.). About eigenfactor.org. Retrieved from http://www.eigenfactor.org/about.php

Elsevier. (n.d.). AudioSlides. Retrieved from http://www.elsevier.com/about/content-innovation/audioslides-author-presentations-for-journal-articles

Galloway, L. M., Pease, J. L., & Rauh, A. E. (2013). Introduction to altmetrics for science, technology, engineering, and mathematics (STEM) librarians. *Science & Technology, 0*(0), 1–11.

Kraft, M. A. (2013). It's all about numbers: Factoring impact in the digital age. *AMWA Journal, 28*(3), 126–127.

Kuo, W., & Rupe, J. (2007). R-Impact: Reality-based citation impact factor. *IEEE Transactions on Reliability*, *56*(30), 366.

McVeigh, M. E., & Mann, S. J. (2009). The journal impact factor denominator: Defining citable (counted) items. *JAMA*, *302*(10), 1107–1109.

Nursing and allied health resources section of the Medical Library Association. (n.d.). NAHRS 2012 selected list of nursing journals. Retrieved from http://nahrs.mlanet.org/home/images/activity/journal_proj/2012introductionnahrsselectedlistnursingjournals.pdf

Open Access Scholarly Publishers Association. (n.d.). Frequently asked questions: Licensing. Retrieved from http://oaspa.org/information-resources/frequently-asked-questions

Pierson, C. (2009). Avoid rejection: Write for the audience and the journal. *Nurse Author & Editor*, *19*(2). Retrieved from http://www.nurseauthoreditor.com/article.asp?id=123

Polit, D. F., & Northam, S. (2011). Impact factors in nursing journals. *Nursing Outlook*, *59*(1), 18–28.

Priem, J., Taraborelli, D., Groth, P., & Neylon, C. (2010). Altmetrics: a manifesto. Retrieved from http://altmetrics.org/manifesto

Saver, C. (2006). Choosing a journal and submitting your manuscript. *AORN Journal*, *84*(1), 27–30.

Scholarly Publishing and Academic Resources Coalition. (n.d.). Open access. Retrieved from http://sparc.arl.org/issues/open-access

Suber, P. (2012). *Open access*. Cambridge, MA: The MIT Press.

Taylor & Francis Group. (2013). Open access survey: Exploring the views of Taylor & Francis and Routledge authors. Retrieved from http://www.tandf.co.uk/journals/pdf/open-access-survey-march2013.pdf

Thompson Reuters. (n.d.). Introducing the impact factor. Retrieved from http://thomsonreuters.com/products_services/science/academic/impact_factor

Webb, C. (2009). *Writing for publication: An easy-to-follow guide for any nurse thinking of publishing their work*. Hoboken, NJ: Wiley-Blackwell Publishing.

"If you don't have time to read, you don't have the time or the tools to write."

–Stephen King

Finding and Documenting Sources

4

Leslie H. Nicoll

WHAT YOU'LL LEARN IN THIS CHAPTER

- Authors need to find sources and then cite and organize them correctly to meet publishing standards.

- It's important to understand the different types of sources and when they are appropriate to use in a manuscript.

- You can apply tips in this chapter to keep your reference library organized, particularly if you plan to use a bibliography database manager to do so.

Whether you're writing a journal article, a book chapter, or an online education program, accurately documenting what you write is the gold standard of professional publication. Good sources help you develop and support the arguments and opinions you present in your article. In this chapter, you learn why references are important as well as how to find them, cite them, and keep them organized. Citations presented in the proper format will be one of the first things that an editor looks for in your submission—and one of the elements that are most often wrong or incomplete in a published paper. After all your hard work to write your article, paying attention to your references helps ensure that it isn't rejected for publication because of some careless errors.

Why Citations Are Necessary

In scientific writing, citations serve two important purposes. First, they document where you obtained the information you are reporting. Second, they provide the information that a reader needs to be able to find the original source material.

Q: *I recently wrote a chapter for a book on evidence-based practice. My colleagues told me that I wouldn't need to worry about completing my references because the publisher does it. Was I misinformed?*

A: Yes, you were. Furnishing a complete and properly styled reference list is *your* responsibility. A manuscript may be rejected because the reference list is incomplete or inaccurate. Although reviewers may pick up errors in the reference list, this usually happens because of their familiarity with the literature, not because they are expected to find and correct mistakes. The reference list is integral to the manuscript and is as important as the abstract and data that are reported. Knowing that it is accurate ensures you can stand proudly behind your own work.

By documenting where you obtained your information, you protect yourself against plagiarism and give credit to the original researchers for their work. *Plagiarism* is the practice of presenting another person's thoughts or ideas as your own. By providing a citation to the primary source material, you recognize the originators of the material and protect yourself.

Providing a reference to the source material is also important so that a reader can check the original report. A reader might want to verify that you interpreted the original source material correctly, or a researcher might also use your article and its associated reference list as a starting point for further exploration. (You can learn more about plagiarism and other publishing legal and ethical issues in Chapter 11.)

Finally, the references you cite provide a foundational basis for your conclusions. References show your peers, colleagues, and others interested in your topic the path you followed as you synthesized the literature.

If you fail to reference your material sufficiently, your professional reputation could suffer. Those with an interest in your subject area keep a close eye on what is published and may choose to send a letter to the editor if they see something not properly credited in a paper. Omission is a serious mistake, but falsifying references is worse and can set you up for professional failure. Falsified references can be the basis for retraction of a published article. If an editor is forced to retract something you have written, you will be banned from publishing in the journal. The journal world is a small one, so it is highly likely that you would find a cold reception at other journals as well. Depending on the circumstance, plagiarism, falsifying references, and retractions may prompt an editor to contact your employer to report the issue, which could have negative repercussions for your work situation as well. Prevent all of these problems by being thorough, careful, and accurate when referencing your paper. "I didn't know," is not a sufficient defense for plagiarism, falsifying references, or other ethical transgressions. If you are going to write and publish in the professional literature, you need to understand these issues.

Q: *Does the use of references vary by type of article?*

A: References cited within the text, and then listed in detail at the end of the article, are essential in academic writing, including articles for scholarly journals, school papers, and textbook chapters. Although formal references are not typically part of opinion pieces and certain online writing such as blog posts, you should still cite sources that support your points. Instead of using the citation method for academic work, in this case you can simply work the source into the text or, in the case of an online reference, insert a hyperlink to the relevant information. Magazine articles include references in more subtle ways, which may include statistics from well-respected organizations such as the American Heart Association or commentary by experts. For example, "Lori Stein, a nurse practitioner whose research on women and heart disease has been published in leading academic journals, says women often experience a heart attack differently from men."

Primary, Secondary, and Tertiary Sources

The three kinds of sources are *primary, secondary*, and *tertiary*. A *primary* source document is the original written report, such as a research report published in a journal like *Nursing Research*. Primary sources can also include letters, diary entries, data from patient records or surveys, and so on—essentially anything that serves as an original source for information.

Secondary sources are those citations that quote the primary source document—for example, textbooks or literature review articles.

Q: *If someone writes a journal article from his or her dissertation, is the journal article considered a secondary source?*

A: No. The dissertation is a report of research that has been done and is thus a primary source, but a report written for a journal is also considered a primary source, as that is also reporting the findings of the research project. Just as a journal has specific guidelines for authors as to length and format, so does a university for how a dissertation is to be produced. A dissertation would never be acceptable as a journal manuscript, so the author must rewrite the research report to conform to the journal's specifications. Thus the two documents are considered completely different (even though they are reporting the same research) and are both primary sources.

Tertiary sources are distillations of information from primary and secondary sources, such as almanacs, fact books, dictionaries, and encyclopedias. Tertiary sources can be handy to obtain a quick overview of a topic, but you should not cite them in your paper as an authoritative source.

As a rule, you should try to rely on and quote primary documents, from research papers to first-hand interviews. Sometimes, admittedly, this is impossible. For example, not many of us have access to Florence Nightingale's original letters—but you may read a letter in a secondary source. In this case, acknowledge both the letter and the secondary source in which it is cited. However, if you want to quote a study cited in a textbook, do the legwork to obtain the primary source document.

Q: *Can I use Wikipedia as a source? It claims to be the fifth largest source of information on the Internet.*

A: Wikipedia is a tertiary source that describes itself as an encyclopedia, so, in general, you should not use it as a source in an article or paper. Even Wikipedia acknowledges this on the page "Researching with Wikipedia," which states that Wikipedia should not be used for primary research ("Researching with," 2013).

References for Student Writing

Another key reason to provide citations illustrates the fundamental difference between a student paper and a paper for publication in a professional journal. A *student paper* is, essentially, a document that conveys to the faculty member what you learned. A paper in a professional journal conveys new information to readers, whether that information is a synthesis of the literature or a primary research report.

If you are a student, the references that you cite provide evidence to the faculty member that you collected information on a topic, read the associated articles, synthesized the data, and can provide a comprehensive analysis of what you have studied. This analysis should go beyond just a simple regurgitation of the articles that you read. The ability to analyze ideas and synthesize new ones is the core of critical thinking.

A student paper may contain information that would be appropriate for publication in a professional journal, but the paper, as written, most likely will not be suitable. You need to do the work to edit the paper to journal style and, at the same time, transform the content in such a way that it provides new information to the audience of readers. (You can learn more about how to do this in Chapter 17.)

The Essence of Documentation

How many sources should you document? That's an excellent question, and one that novice authors struggle with. Certainly, you want to be comprehensive and appropriately cite the sources that you have used. However, you want to find a balance and not over-cite references in an article for publication. Take a look at a couple of examples to help you find your own middle ground.

Many different organizations, such as the American Cancer Society and the National Cancer Institute, collect statistics on the incidence of breast cancer. If you quote a statistic, do you need to include two, three, or four organizational references to support it? No. One authoritative and up-to-date reference should be sufficient—and you should cite the actual source you used. Although this sounds obvious, different organizations report statistics in different ways, so you want to make sure the citation you use matches the data you report.

As another example, the SF-36 is a measure of health outcomes and quality of life that has been widely used and has well-established psychometric properties (Ware, n.d.). According to its developer, it has been cited in more than 4,000 articles. If you were using this instrument in a research study, would you cite all these articles? Of course not! You should include only the most salient, recent, and relevant citations that are illustrative of what you are doing to demonstrate how and why the instrument is appropriate for your study.

> **Q:** *What about common knowledge? Do I need to cite every statement?*

A: If something is common knowledge, it does not need to be cited. But what is considered "common knowledge"? It depends on your audience. If you are writing to clinicians, you can assume that they will know and accept certain things as facts, such as *Nursing is an art and a science* and *A diagnosis of breast cancer is a devastating moment in a woman's life*. On the other hand, even though it is widely stated and accepted as truth, the statement *One in nine women will be diagnosed with breast cancer during her lifetime* should be backed up with a citation.

Editors of journals are beginning to react to over-citation, and some editors have taken steps to limit the number of references allowed in an article (Nicoll, 2012). When you encounter this limitation, the number is firm. If the publication's information for authors or author guidelines lists a maximum of 50 references, that means 50—not 51 or 52. Even though you believe that every reference is absolutely essential, you need to delete some if you go over the limit. How do you do that? Remember the earlier example: It is not necessary to provide multiple citations to document a single statement. Read with a critical eye—you will see where references can be pared.

Also, consider how often you cite a single source. For example, say you have a five-sentence paragraph, and all of the ideas in that paragraph come from the same source. Write the paragraph to make the source of the information clear and then include the citation at the end of the paragraph. You do not need to cite the reference at the end of every sentence. However, if several sources contribute to the content of the paragraph, make sure to add citations appropriately so the reader will be able to follow your line of thinking and documentation.

Q: *How far back do I need to go in my literature search and citation of references?*

A: Certainly in your goal to master the topic area, you want to read thoroughly and deeply. How far back you go depends on your project. If you are writing a literature review, you need to seek out articles from a number of years ago in addition to more recent works. If you are writing an article on a quality improvement project or a clinical condition, you usually do not have to search back more than 3 to 5 years.

No matter how many articles you've read, you need to synthesize the literature and cite only those sources that are key to your presentation. So even if you have read articles dating back 20, 30, or 50 years, be selective in what you cite. Some editors ask you to only include references written in the last 5 years, unless it is a classic source that requires citation. This is particularly true for clinical articles where treatment and interventions change based on research findings. You want to make sure you have the most up-to-date information on the topic you are presenting.

Style Manuals

A *style manual* or *stylebook* provides a set of guidelines and standards for written documents. *Style* is an inclusive term that can encompasses everything from punctuation and capitalization to specifics for formatting citations. Style manuals include much more than directions on how to reference citations. They also provide guidance on how to structure your paper, writing style, preferred abbreviations, how to report statistics, and ethical issues related to publication. The idea is to standardize formatting issues for authors, editors, publishers, reviewers, and anyone else involved in the process of disseminating information through publication. Many newspapers (and some magazines) use *The Associated Press Stylebook and Briefing on Media Law* (2013). Another heavily used style guide—especially in mainstream book publishing—is *The Chicago Manual of Style*, first published in 1906 by the University of Chicago Press, and now in its 16th edition (2010).

The two manuals that are most widely used in nursing are the *Publication Manual of the American Psychological Association* (6th ed.), published by the APA (American Psychological Association, 2009), and the *AMA Manual of Style* (10th ed.), produced by the American Medical Association (AMA) (Iverson et al., 2007).

Q: *I've noticed that many style guides have new editions that come out every few years. I have an old edition. Can I use it?*

A: You should use the most up-to-date edition of the style guide that your publisher requires. Teams of editors carefully review styles every few years to ensure maximum usability and address changing times. For example, older editions of the APA manual don't address how to properly cite blogs, websites, or even electronic archives. Sometimes, new releases are controversial, so many editors and publishers won't always adopt a new edition right away. Make sure to verify which style manual and edition you should use before submitting.

Some journals use their own style manual for certain aspects of their articles, such as citing references, but differ in other areas of guidance. Thus, remember to carefully read the information for authors or author guidelines to understand what exceptions (if any) are expected, and then format your paper accordingly.

Q: *I am most familiar with APA because that is what we used in school. Therefore, I think I'll only consider journals that use APA style. Is that a good idea?*

A: No, because you are limiting yourself to a specific group of journals. Just as you learned APA, you can learn AMA (or any other style). If this seems like a big hurdle, consider asking a more experienced colleague for help, or perhaps hire a professional editor to assist you.

The most important issue, no matter which style manual you use, is to be complete and accurate in your citations. Check and double-check that you have authors' names spelled correctly; the correct year of publication; and complete citation information, including title of the article (or book), the journal where it was published, and volume, issue, and page numbers. The AMA and APA style manuals handle citations differently, and most editors are adamant that the guidelines be followed.

Anatomy of a Reference

When gathering citations, make sure to carefully document all the information related to the reference. When you compose the actual citation, some information may not be required, but it is easier to edit out information rather than search for missing information at the last minute.

In the past, authors kept track of citations on index cards. Now you can organize your references in a bibliography database manager, Excel spreadsheet, a table in Word, or another system that you develop. If you can import citation information from an online source, or cut-and-paste into your library or spreadsheet, do so. Errors caused by retyping are common and a major source of inaccurate citations.

Whatever method you choose, make sure your notes are complete. Essential elements include

- **Author(s)' names:** Include complete information for all authors: first and last names and middle initials. Even though the style might only require last name and first initials, you should have complete data in your notes. Double-check that you have spelled the authors' names correctly.

- **Title of article:** Include the complete title.

- **Title of journal:** Be sure you have the complete title of the journal. If the journal title is abbreviated, make sure you find the correct, full name. For citations in the PubMed database, you can click on the link of the journal abbreviation to obtain the full name.

- **Date of publication:** This is when the article was published, or in the case of online, posted.

- **Volume:** In general, the volume number changes each year; for example, the first year a journal is published is volume 1, year five would be volume 5. There are some journals that publish so frequently they may have two volumes in a year.

- **Issue number:** The issue number changes each time an issue is published within a volume; for example, the first issue of the year is issue 1, the second is issue 2, and so on. As a rule of thumb, if the publication is monthly, the issues match the months: issue 5 is May, issue 12 is December, for example.

- **Page numbers:** Include all page numbers even if an article "jumps" (finishes in the back of the journal). Check the appropriate style manual for the proper formatting of nonconsecutive page numbers.

- **URL or Uniform Resource Locator:** For online sources, you will need the complete URL and the date you retrieved the information. Some style manuals require the specific date you retrieved a source, such as October 30, 2014.

- **DOI or Digital Object Identifier:** The DOI is a unique code that is assigned to an article upon publication (whether online or in print) that enables a person to retrieve the article using the DOI in a search. Older articles may not have DOIs assigned to them; many newer articles (since about 2010) do. APA requires that you include an article's DOI in the reference citation when a DOI is available. You can check for a DOI number by using a free website such as crossref (http://www.crossref.org/guestquery).

Reference Formatting

When it comes to references, one major difference between AMA and APA is how they are cited in the text. AMA uses superscripted numbers that are consecutively numbered and listed in numerical order in the reference list. APA uses author and date citations in the text with an alphabetical reference list. The following examples illustrate what you might see in the text.

> AMA: Four studies reported that the treatment was effective.[1-4]

> APA: Four studies reported that the treatment was effective (Allen, White, Marcel, & Lee, 2012; Jones & Smith, 2013; Michaels, Hale, & Pierce, 2009; Peterson, 2008).

One thing to keep in mind is that reference lists in AMA are numbered in consecutive order of references appearing in the text; thus if you add a reference to the text, unless it's the last reference in the document, all the existing references need to be renumbered. If you are using Microsoft Word as your word processing program, you can use the software's auto-numbering feature to help with formatting. However, know that most journals won't accept manuscripts using the Word footnote feature. You will need to convert these citations to plain text before submitting your manuscript.

Q: *I read* The American Journal of Nursing *on my iPad. How do I cite something I've read electronically but not online?*

A: The rule for citation is that you should include the reference to the most widely and easily accessible version of the document. Currently, the gold standard for most publications is still print. So, even if you read an *American Journal of Nursing* article on your iPad, you should cite it as if you read the print version (include volume, issue, and page numbers) because that is (at present) the most accessible version of the journal for the majority of readers. If you read a PDF on your iPad, it should include the page numbers so you have this information easily available. If an article is available only online, you should cite that particular version, with complete citation information.

Remember, you provide citation information so a reader can go back to the same source you used for verification or further reading, so it important to be complete and accurate. Many journals now require that citations include DOI numbers, which allow a reader to quickly find the article online.

Q: *Can I cite fugitive literature in my paper?*

A: Fugitive literature, or *ephemeral literature*, consists of documents that exist outside of traditional, peer-reviewed publications. A common example is abstracts (or papers) published as part of a conference program and distributed only to conference attendees.

If you want to cite an abstract from a conference, your first step would be to check whether the presentation has been published as a paper. A published article would be preferable over citing the proceedings, as the latter would be hard for people who did not attend the conference to access. If there is no published paper, is something available online? Absent that, you can cite the materials that you have in hand. Keep in mind, however, that as your source becomes more difficult to access, it becomes less valuable to your reader. Obscure references are not necessarily better or more scholarly (although some people labor under that impression).

Databases as a Source of Reference

How do you go about finding references? Your first step is to find out what resources are available to you. If you are a student or if you work in a setting with a library, go there first. Health sciences libraries have access to online databases that include citations and, often, full text. Students and employees usually can use these resources at no charge. In addition, the librarians will be able to provide instruction on how to use these resources effectively. The top databases are licensed to institutions rather than individuals, and you should definitely take advantage of this resource if one is available to you.

PubMed

The most useful online database for health literature is PubMed from the National Library of Medicine (www.pubmed.gov). PubMed comprises more than 20 million citations that make up the MEDLINE database. The citations include complete reference information, abstract (when available), and keywords. Many of the citations include links to full-text articles. One note of caution: Not all peer-reviewed nursing journals are indexed in PubMed.

A number of tutorials are available to help you get started at PubMed, which you can find here: http://www.nlm.nih.gov/bsd/disted/pubmed.html.

Google Scholar

A resource that is not limited to the health science literature is Google Scholar (http://scholar.google.com):

> Google Scholar provides a simple way to broadly search for scholarly literature. From one place, you can search across many disciplines and sources: articles, theses, books, abstracts and court opinions, from academic publishers, professional societies, online repositories, universities and other Web sites. Google Scholar helps you find relevant work across the world of scholarly research. (http://www.google.com/intl/en/scholar/about.html, retrieved July 16, 2013)

As with PubMed, Google Scholar has tutorials and various levels of help to assist you with searching. An advantage of Google Scholar is that it searches a wider range of journals.

Search With Search Engines

Both PubMed and Google Scholar use similar search engines. You can search on any number of variables, including author name, words in the title, year of publication, keywords, volume, issue, and more. You can use operators, such as AND (narrow your search) or OR (expand your search). For example, you want to write an article related to diabetes in children. Using the terms "children" and "diabetes" would result in articles that are about children with diabetes, excluding articles that don't have both words in them. This search makes it more likely you will find articles related specifically to your topic.

Putting quotation marks around a phrase, such as "myocardial infarction" cues the search engine to look for the exact phrase.

Other Database Options

Other useful databases include the Cumulative Index to Nursing and Allied Health Literature (CINAHL), available through EBSCOhost, and ProQuest Nursing & Allied Health Source. Remember, however, that you need to access these resources through an institution such as a medical library. You can find open access journals by searching BioMed Central (http://www.biomedcentral.com) or the Directory of Open Access Journals (http://www.doaj.org). (You can learn more about open-access journals in Chapter 3.)

Some universities have their own open-access resource such as the Digital Access to Scholarship at Harvard (http://dash.harvard.edu). And professional organizations often have repositories like the Virginia Henderson International Nursing Library, from Sigma Theta Tau International, which shares nursing research and evidence-based practice materials (www.nursinglibrary.org).

Finding What You're Looking For

By now you have probably narrowed your topic and started your search for articles and data. Many people begin a search in a rather haphazard fashion, which is fine because it provides an idea of just how much information on a given topic is out there. For example, typing "breast cancer" in PubMed retrieves more than 264,000 citations—clearly more than you would ever need for a paper or could even read and synthesize.

The next step, then, is to begin to focus and refine your search. You might have specific aspects of your topic that you'd like to study, or you might want to use the suggestions many databases provide for you. Are you interested in breast cancer risk, or metastasis, or pain? You can narrow your results by year or discipline (nursing). As you begin to get a handle on your search, the results will become focused—and more manageable.

Track your keywords, which will help give you additional avenues for searching. Looking at reference lists on the articles that you retrieve is another trick that can help you to be comprehensive. Are there certain authors or articles that keep showing up? This might be a pointer to a *classic reference*—one that is essential in the literature and that you should be familiar with. Your goal through this process is to achieve a level of saturation where you feel you have found all the relevant articles that exist on a topic.

Q: *How can I be more efficient with my searching?*

A: Keep track of what search terms you use and the order in which you used them so that you don't repeat them. Also keep track of how many results you had and how you narrowed your search. What inclusion and exclusion criteria did you use to keep references in your search? Document all this information in your notes or reference library.

One thing to keep in mind as you move toward saturation: Narrowing your focus is easier than trying to read hundreds or thousands of articles on a given topic. It is better to be comprehensive within a narrow range rather than superficial and arbitrary, such as selecting random cutoff years or places where articles are published.

As you search, you will be retrieving as many as three things:

- Information for a complete article citation

- Abstract (that is, the short summary of the article, presentation, or document)

- Full text

Information for a complete citation has been discussed previously—see the box on "Anatomy of a Reference" earlier in this chapter. *Abstracts* are the summaries of full-text articles written by the authors and made available at no cost. They are useful for helping you determine whether it would be useful to retrieve the full-text of the research paper, chapter, presentation, and so on. Databases like PubMed include an abstract if it was published with the article. Certain types of journal articles—such as letters to the editor, editorials, and columns—do not include abstracts. You also won't often find abstracts for magazine articles, profiles, personal interviews, and so on.

Full text is what it says: the full text of an article. Just about everything published in scholarly journals is available online, but access to full text varies, depending on the publisher, the topic of the article, and the database in which it is maintained. Some articles are available at no charge; however, many require a fee, often called "pay per view."

Q: *How can I find out whether an article will be useful to me before I pay to access it online?*

A: Databases like PubMed, online libraries, and other databases give free access to abstracts (often provided by the journal publisher) with links to the full-text versions of articles online. Although some articles may be available at no cost, many publishers charge a fee. Even if you're on a budget, all is not lost. Your university, community college, or hospital library might maintain an institutional subscription to the journal for which you need access. Many databases like PubMed allow you to enter your school affiliation and then grant you access to any for-pay articles viewable to you through your school's subscriptions.

If you belong to a professional organization (like Sigma Theta Tau International), you might receive a journal subscription as part of your member benefits. You might also receive substantial discounts on other journals you'd like to receive. Your membership may give you access to full text online for free. Similarly, if you subscribe to a journal, part of your subscription may include online access to full text of the articles at no charge. Do a little sleuthing before pulling out your credit card to pay for access to an online full-text article.

Q: *Is it acceptable to just cite the abstract of a full-text article so I don't have to pay for the article?*

A: The abstract can help you determine how relevant it is to the topic about which you are writing. However, a standard of good scholarship is that for anything you cite, you should have read the entire article, not just the abstract.

Bibliography Database Managers

Strive to be accurate and organized with your references. For years, the hallmark standard was to use *bib cards* (short for *bibliography cards*), which were hand-written index cards with the complete citation, where it was obtained, notes, and even portions of the abstract. Bib cards have become an anachronism in modern scholarship, but the concept has not. They have just been replaced by software.

Many professional writers create their own systems, spreadsheets, or databases for references, but a different—and perhaps better—option is to use a commercially available bibliography database manager (BDM), such as Endnote, published by Thomson-Reuters. Other programs are available—free or for purchase—that work the same way, more or less. A detailed description of all the programs available is beyond the scope of this chapter. However, Wikipedia has a helpful comparison chart of many of the programs that currently exist, their cost (many are free), and whether the resource resides on your computer as software or is housed "in the cloud." You can access the information at http://en.wikipedia.org/wiki/Comparison_of_reference_management_software ("Comparison of," 2013).

Q: *What a minute! Earlier you said not to quote Wikipedia, but you just did. What's up with that?*

A: Good catch. Note that I said that Wikipedia is a tertiary source and thus a compilation of facts and information from many places. It should not be used as a primary source and in this case, I am not doing so. This particular table is a good synthesis of reference management software. Because information on Wikipedia is updated regularly, I have confidence that directing you to this source will be more accurate at the time this book is published versus listing all the information here in this chapter. As a tertiary source, summarizing information on BDMs, it gives you a starting point to learn more.

What Does a BDM Do?

A BDM provides a database to maintain your references by creating a *library*, or internal reference database, on your own computer or in the cloud, creating an electronic substitute for bib cards. You can attach notes and keywords to each reference so that you can easily sort and access information. You can also attach PDFs of the article, pictures, figures, and annotations. How much or how little you include depends on your need and writing. Nothing is required—although a citation without the minimum, basic information, as discussed earlier, is not going to be very useful.

BDM programs work in conjunction with your word processor, helping you format your references and making sure that they are presented correctly in your paper. Other functionalities vary depending on the software, but a good BDM also makes it easy to change between required styles, such as APA or AMA. For example, if you write a paper for *Journal A* that uses APA style and the paper is not accepted, you can easily revise the references in the paper to AMA style, which might be required for *Journal B*. Your BDM also helps keep your references numbered properly no matter how many references you move around in the course of editing and revising your manuscript.

After you get really comfortable with the program, whichever one you decide to use, you'll be able to work with online databases such as PubMed and Google Scholar, which have the capability to import references into a BDM. This can save you time because you don't have to retype the citation; more importantly, importing a citation increases the accuracy by ensuring that you won't mistype an author's name or the year of publication. By using this feature, you can also have a more complete citation in your library. For example, by default, PubMed includes abstracts, keywords, and medical subject headings, called *MeSH terms,* used for indexing by the National Library of Medicine. Citations from PubMed also include the DOI for an article. Many BDMs also enable you to search online databases from within the program and import citations directly into the program.

A new feature of BDMs is the capability to share and sync libraries among users. This makes collaboration among coauthors easier and is a major feature that has been warmly welcomed by those who use a BDM on a regular basis.

> **Q:** *I am writing a short article with maybe 10 or 12 references. But I have never heard of any of these programs. Should I take the time to learn how to use one in this case?*
>
> **A:** Probably not. Keeping track of 10 references is not hard to do manually. Keeping track of 100, however, is a challenge. It is up to you to decide when you want to make the investment in a BDM and begin to use the program.

BDMs have some drawbacks, too. Their disadvantages can include

- **Steep learning curve:** For many people, BDMs are not naturally intuitive and easy to use. They do require time to learn; and for some users, the learning curve is so steep that using one is not worth the effort.

- **Time:** Maintaining a library and using it effectively takes time. To really be useful, you need to keep it up to date.

- **Sloppy data entry:** If you put references into the BDM incorrectly, the resulting citation will be inaccurate. You will need to take time to edit as you go, correcting capitalization and punctuation and ensuring that journal titles are correctly entered.

If you are embarking on a project, particularly a project that is expected to encompass years of work (such as a dissertation), or you know that you will work in a specialty area for a significant time, a BDM can be the best way to maintain and organize your reference data. If you find that a BDM just doesn't work for you, you might try seeking out a resource person who can maintain your library for you and help you with the documentation process.

Tracking and Organizing Material

You can use online tools to keep track of what is being published in your area of interest (Saver, 2012). For example, aggregators such as Feedly (www.feedly.com) help you manage RSS (really simple syndication) feeds from various sources of published web content, whether they be blog entries, news headlines, or streaming audio or video. New content is aggregated and delivered, allowing you to quickly skim and select content of interest.

Free research database managers such as Zotero (www.zotero.org) allow you to add information to your personal library directly from your web browser. You can then add PDFs, images, audio and video files, snapshots of web pages, and other data so you can easily search one source for all of your information and share as needed with your collaborators (Zotero, n.d.).

Confidence Booster

So you are confident in knowing you have current information, remember the terms for your search, and run it once a month to retrieve anything new that has been published on your topic. Import the citations into your BDM. In doing so, you will always be up-to-date on the relevant literature.

Solid Researching

Now you know the usefulness of style guides, and how to find sources, organize them, and cite them appropriately. Just like writing, searching and managing your sources take practice. Your payoff is a high-quality article useful to readers—and isn't that your ultimate goal?

Write Now!

1. Conduct a search in PubMed and Google Scholar and compare your results.

2. Select three journals and identify the type of reference citation that each uses.

3. Here is a citation from PubMed. Format it correctly in both APA and AMA style:

   Leslie H. Nicoll. Nursing education enhanced by informatics. Comput Inform Nurs. 2011 Jun; 29(6 Suppl):TC81. doi: 10.1097/NCN.0b013e31822720ca. PubMed PMID: 21701275.

References

American Psychological Association. (2009). *Publication manual of the American Psychological Association* (6th ed.). Washington, DC: Author.

Associated Press. (2013). *The Associated Press stylebook and briefing on media law 2013* (46th ed.). New York, NY: Basic Books.

Comparision of reference management software. (n.d.). In *Wikipedia*. Retrieved from http://en.wikipedia.org/wiki/Comparison_of_reference_management_software

Iverson, C., Christiansen, S., Flanagin, A., Fontanarosa, P. B., Glass, R. M., Gregoline, B., et al. (2007). *AMA manual of style: A guide for authors and editors.* (10th ed.). New York, NY: Oxford University Press.

Nicoll, L. H. (2012). Length matters: References. *Nurse Author & Editor, 22*(2). Retrieved from http://www.nurseauthoreditor.com/article.asp?id=186

Researching with Wikipedia. (n.d.). In *Wikipedia*. Retrieved from http://en.wikipedia.org/wiki/Wikipedia:Researching_with_Wikipedia

Saver, C. (2012). Keeping practice knowledge current: Part 1. *The Nurse Practitioner*. Retrieved from http://www.zotero.org

University of Chicago Press Staff (Ed.). (2010). *The Chicago manual of style* (16th ed.). Chicago, IL: University of Chicago Press.

Ware, J. E. (n.d.). SF-36® health survey update. Retrieved from http://www.sf-36.org/tools/sf36.shtml

Zotero. (n.d.). Retrieved from http://www.zotero.org

"Clutter is the disease of American writing."

–William Zinsser

Organizing the Article

Mary Alexander

5

You gathered all your data from your research project. You implemented a novel idea to improve patient care. Or maybe you reviewed several articles on a single topic. What now? You need to disseminate this wealth of knowledge by writing an article for publication.

As you look to contribute to the body of nursing literature by publishing your research or sharing relevant clinical experiences, the articles that you write should be presented in a coherent and logical manner with evidence to support your conclusions. Organizing your content in a predictable manner allows the reader to follow your line of reasoning and makes understanding your message easier. Different types of articles lend themselves to different types of organization.

Although there is some flexibility in writing, following a structured format—or rather, a *template*—will assist you in including all the necessary components, thereby minimizing the chance of omitting an essential part of the article. Some authors believe that using templates can stifle a writer's creativity, but Graff and Birkenstein (2009, p. 11) state that "templates do not dictate the content of what you say, which can be as original as you want it, but only suggest a way of formatting how you say it."

WHAT YOU'LL LEARN IN THIS CHAPTER

- The type of article that you write will depend on the data you have and the key messages that you want to convey to the readers.

- Using a standard template to organize your content makes it easier for readers to follow your article.

- Each type of article has a different template.

This chapter explains types of articles and describes the typical format that each one should follow. When the content of an article flows in an organized way, your reader can easily follow your train of thought and better understand your message.

Basic Format of the Article

Your article should have a title, a beginning, a middle, and an end. When you follow this format, you enable the reader to understand and follow the logic of the information presented in your article. Writing an organized piece also keeps the reader engaged and more apt to read the entire article. Depending on where you'll be submitting your article for publication, you might also need to include an abstract.

Title

The style of your title might vary depending on whether you're writing an article for a nursing magazine or submitting to a scholarly journal. Either way, your title tells the reader about the information presented in the article by simply summarizing the main idea. Use key words that represent the content, and keep the title concise. For less-formal publications, you can be clever and create a title that draws readers' attention. However, for a scholarly work, your title should be fully explanatory on its own. The title should be longer and more descriptive so that key words in the title will come up when someone searches the literature for a particular topic.

Avoid overly general titles; however, you should avoid too much detail (AMA, 2007). For example, the following original title goes into too much detail for the targeted general nursing journal. The revised title is more concise.

> **Original title:** Management of the Patient with Phlebitis and the Nursing Interventions Needed to Treat the Problem After Assessing Needs: Utilizing the INS Phlebitis Scale

> **Revised title:** Effective Management of the Patient with Phlebitis

Although you'll want to do your best to give your article the right title, don't be concerned if an editor changes your title; this happens frequently to best fit the publication's style.

Beginning

Whether it's a paragraph, a section, or just a good opening line, the *introduction* sets the tone of the article. It tells readers what the article is about and entices them—formally or informally—to continue reading. Ultimately, the introductory statement should stimulate interest in the subject so that the reader will want to read the entire article (Saver, 2006a).

There are a number of techniques for writing a *lede*—writer parlance for that strong opening line or paragraph—but some examples you might use in an introduction include providing relevant background information, giving pertinent statistics, asking a provocative question, or defining a term used in your article (Troyka & Hesse, 2012). Your introduction should reflect the style of the publication, journal, or online resource. For example, in the *Journal of Infusion Nursing*, Moritz (2013) introduces the issue of electrolyte disorders that will be explained further in the article:

> The most common electrolyte disorders are those involving disorders in serum sodium, hypo-, and hypernatremia. Disorders in serum sodium are frequently iatrogenic, from improper fluid management; therefore, fluid management requires great care. The management of disorders in serum sodium can be quite complicated because therapy can vary significantly according to the etiology of the disorders. Nurses are on the front line of care for patients at risk for, or who have developed, a disorder in serum sodium. They therefore must be able to recognize and treat a disorder in serum sodium when it is occurring. (p. 270)

The introduction of this example from *OR Nurse* describes the considerations that the perioperative team must address in older adult patients to ensure safe care:

> On January 1, 2011, the first members of the Baby Boomer generation turned 65 years old. Every day for the next 19 years, 10,000 baby boomers will reach age 65. Older adults undergo several age-related physiologic changes that directly impact their perioperative courses. Older adult patients experience profound alterations in pharmacokinetics and pharmacodynamics, directly or indirectly affecting individual responses to surgery. It's imperative that all members of the perioperative team are aware of the physiologic changes associated with aging in order to provide safe and effective care (Garces & Wallace, 2013, p. 15).

Middle

The *middle* is the main portion of the article. To maintain the flow of the article, paragraphs and subtopics should address the points in your article outline. Each paragraph will have a "topic" sentence, which is the main point of the paragraph, with subsequent sentences supporting the main idea. Each separate distinct paragraph aids the reader, signaling a new step in the development of the subject (Strunk, 2013). The body of the paragraph might include examples, reasons, facts, and details directly related to the topic (Troyka & Hesse, 2012).

A paragraph can be as short as one sentence—for example, when you want to emphasize a point or make a dramatic change—but tends to be no more than four to six sentences long. The main point to keep in mind is that each sentence should relate to the topic sentence.

End

Regardless of whether you use a separate formal concluding section or not, all articles have a *conclusion* summing the key message(s) that you want your readers to glean from the article. The conclusion brings the discussion to an end and should flow logically while simultaneously reinforcing your message. Some options for endings include a summary of key points, a call to action, or suggested future directions for research.

You want to avoid introducing new ideas or facts in your ending that belong in the body of the article and also simply rewording your introduction (Troyka & Hesse, 2012).

The following conclusion of "Symptom Distress in Older Adults Following Cancer Surgery" effectively summarizes the key points of the article:

> We conducted a study to explore factors related to symptom distress over time in older adults undergoing thoracic, abdominal, and pelvic cancer surgery. Our analyses generated findings that showed symptom distress significantly decreased over 6 months after cancer surgery, reflecting a typical postoperative course. Factors related to increased symptoms distress following surgery were type of cancer, number of comorbidities, mental health, and function. Our findings also showed that patients 75 years or older experienced greater symptom distress over time than did those aged 65 to 69 years. Patients with a diagnosis of digestive or thoracic cancer who have increased comorbidity burden, report worse mental health, or experience decreased function should undergo heightened surveillance for increasing symptom

distress leading to morbidity. More research, though, is needed to clarify the relationship between age and symptom distress over time (Egleston, et al., 2013, p. 300).

Abstracts

Although not a formal part of the body of your article, for many publications (including scholarly journals), you will need to prepare an abstract. An *abstract* is a brief, comprehensive summary of the contents of an article, allowing the reader to survey the article contents quickly. A well-written abstract has become increasingly important in directing readers to articles of potential clinical and research interest (AMA, 2007). Readers frequently decide on the basis of the abstract whether to read the entire article, so it should be accurate, concise, coherent, and compelling.

For journals that require an abstract with a specific structure, the following headings are typically used: *Purpose*, *Design*, *Setting*, *Subjects*, *Measures*, *Results*, and *Conclusions*. Be sure to adhere to the word count for the abstract. Word count for an abstract varies from journal to journal, ranging from 150 to 300 words (AMA, 2007; APA, 2010). An unstructured abstract does not use headings, is written in paragraph form, and has a word count that typically does not exceed 150 words (APA, 2010).

Types of Flow

For the reader to understand and follow your train of thought, you must consider the flow of the article. In Chapter 1, you learned about these types of flow: how to, case studies, IMRAD (introduction, methods, results, and discussion), disease process, and chronology. Take a closer look at a few of these. Remember that you can use a single approach or a combination of methods to get your point across (Saver, 2006a).

How-To

Quality improvement projects and clinical tips can be best described in *how-to* articles. Using the nursing process, you can organize your article by writing about your assessment of the problem, plan of action, implementation, and evaluation of the process/procedure/practice. For example, you might write about how you implemented an in-service education program to address the problem of occluded central lines. Be sure to include "lessons learned" so that readers know what to avoid. (You can learn more about clinical how-to articles in Chapter 13.)

Case Studies

Case studies provide information on nursing practice and how that information can be applied to a specific patient problem. You may organize the entire article around the case study, or the case study may be part of a manuscript. The flow of this type of article typically includes a patient history, assessment, diagnosis, treatment, nursing interventions, and outcomes with implications for clinical practice.

IMRAD

Just as you learn the scientific method for research and experiments, you'll use IMRAD (introduction, methods, results and discussion) if you're writing a research paper. IMRAD is the standard flow for a research article, especially those that report on quantitative studies.

Disease Process

You may choose to organize your article according to the traditional topics for discussing a disease, including incidence, signs and symptoms, diagnosis, medical treatment, and nursing care. This format can be particularly helpful when you are writing an educational program about a specific disease.

Chronological

Time can serve as an organizing tool for an article, either as a timeline (what happened when) or as a process such as preoperative, perioperative, and postoperative.

Confidence Booster

Keep writing. Keep submitting your work. Some of the most well-known works of literature were initially rejected—multiple times. Among manuscripts originally rejected are *Harry Potter and the Sorcerer's Stone* by J. K. Rowling (rejected by 12 publishers), *Dubliners* by James Joyce (22 rejections), and *Gone with the Wind* by Margaret Mitchell (rejected by an amazing 38 publishers). Thankfully, these authors kept writing—and offering their work for publication.

Types of Articles

The kind of article that you write depends upon the topic you have selected and the message you want to convey. (The following sections provide an overview of these types. You'll learn more about each type in more detail in subsequent chapters.) The most common types of articles are:

- Research articles

- Quantitative and qualitative articles

- Evidence-based practice articles

- Quality improvement articles

- Clinical articles

- Literature reviews

- Case studies

- Nursing narratives and exemplars

When matching the style of article, you also need to consider the type of publication that you're targeting. Not all journals accept nursing narratives and exemplars, and an evidence-based practice (EBP) article, for example, wouldn't necessarily fit in some scholarly research journals. If you completed a study evaluating the effectiveness of saline versus heparin solutions to flush central IV catheters, you would write a research article that describes the statistical analysis and significance of your results. If the rate of occluded central IV catheters increased on your unit because of improper flushing techniques, a description of how you resolved this issue would be appropriate in a quality improvement article. Each category has a format, or template, that is useful in developing a concise, organized article that will generate interest for the reader.

Q: *There are so many types of articles. How can I pick the one that best fits my message?*

A: Some factors that you can consider are your specific message, who you want to read that message, how much information you have, and your general purpose. Realize that there isn't always one answer. For example, say that you just saw a patient with a rare disease in your emergency department. You might choose to present this as a case study, or perhaps provide a broader picture by writing about the disease itself and using the patient as an example.

Research Articles

Research articles are reports of original data, findings, and results. They summarize a study, its purpose, methods, and findings. Oermann and Hays (2011, p. 90) state, "Writing about research is similar to making a reasoned argument—the author's goal is to demonstrate to readers that the study was important to do and follows logically from previous research, the methods were appropriate for examining the problem, the findings are valid, and the implications for practice are consistent with the data."

The typical format for a research article is the IMRAD format—introduction, methods, results, and discussion. This format follows the stages of the research process, enabling the author to easily organize the article.

Introduction. The *introduction* should present the problem and gaps noted in the research. A *literature review*, or presentation of the existing research on the topic, can be part of the introduction or written as a separate section following the introduction. Stating the problem early in the introduction explains why particular concepts or theories were used to direct the research. A statement of the problem should be clear to readers in the beginning of the introduction.

Methods. The section describing your research methods should be written in subsections, which generally follow a specific order: study design, subjects, measures, procedures, and data analysis. The reader can easily follow the research methodology.

Results. The *results* section describes the findings of the study and should both address the purpose of the study and answer the research questions. Typically, you present the main findings first, followed by any secondary findings. Keep in mind that the data results belong in the "Results" section, and the *implications* of those results belong in the "Discussion" section.

Q: *Some of my results run counter to what I expected to find. Can I omit those results?*

A: No. All findings, even those that run counter to expectations, are to be reported. Uncomfortable results or those that do not support your hypothesis should not be omitted (APA, 2010). Reasons for those results can be explained in the "Discussion" section.

Discussion. In this section, the author interprets the results of the study and explains the findings in relation to the original hypotheses. Begin this section with a clear statement of support or nonsupport for your original hypotheses. Discuss whether this research is consistent with previous research. Acknowledge any limitations of your research, such as a small sample size. Describe the implications of the research for clinical practice. Remember that your statements and conclusions need to be supported by your data. Suggestions for future research can be included in this section. End this section with a clear, direct statement on the importance of your findings. (You can find more information on research articles in Chapter 14.)

Quantitative and Qualitative Articles

Research articles can be reported as quantitative or qualitative. *Quantitative* research papers typically follow the IMRAD format. When presenting results of quantitative studies, the findings and related discussion are organized according to the purposes, questions, or hypotheses. Quantitative research studies are used to test a theory or to build on one. They focus on measurement and statistical analysis of data to test a hypothesis with a goal of discovering relationships or cause and effect between variables. The data analysis is numerical (Saver, 2006b). Quantitative research methods include surveys and experimental manipulation of variables. These studies can include interventions between two or more groups, with one group acting as a control group (Saver, 2006b).

In comparison, a *qualitative* study concentrates on an individual's perspective and describes meaning rather than cause and effect. Research methods include verbal descriptions such as interviews, narrative analyses, and participant observation. Reporting patient perceptions can be included in a qualitative article (Saver, 2006b).

In a qualitative study, the format depends on the purpose of the research, the methods used, and the data obtained from the research. There is no one style for presenting qualitative research; you may use one of the following formats (Oermann & Hays, 2011):

- **IMRAD**
- **Time:** Findings are organized as they happen, or what was learned at different points in time.
- **Prevalence:** The most frequently occurring themes are presented first.
- **Concept:** Describe or test a theory noted in the study.

Evidence-Based Practice (EBP) Articles

Evidence comes from a variety of sources, including published and unpublished reports, internal quality-improvement project summaries, and expert opinion (Hagle & Senk, 2010). An evidence-based practice (EBP) article, or evidence report, includes knowledge synthesis, review, and documentation of how evidence-based practices are used in a clinical area. It can also include a discussion of the clinical relevance to a proposed change in practice (Benefield, 2002). The format for an EBP article typically includes the following sections:

- **Summary statement:** Succinctly describe the clinical question that is being addressed and what the evidence reports.

- **Analysis of the scientific data:** Describe the review of the published and unpublished reports, target populations that were studied, type of clinical interventions that were investigated, and the strength of the individual and/or collective study results.

- **Critical appraisal of the evidence:** Summarize the scientific reports, including the rank and strength of the evidence.

- **Practice recommendations:** Based on the cumulative information from the analyzed evidence, state the practice recommendations suggested for integration into clinical practice. Should a recommendation be suggested for implementation into practice, the benefits versus risks to the patient are discussed in this section (Benefield, 2002; Hagle & Senk, 2010).

Quality Improvement (QI) Articles

Quality improvement (QI) articles describe how to improve care or solve a problem. Like a research article, data are used to support the information presented in a QI article. However, some differences exist between a QI and a research article (see Table 5.1). A research article must put the study in context with prior research by including a comprehensive literature review. Research methodology tries to control the variables in the study, but there is less control over variability in a QI project. Also, the statistical analysis required for a research study is more rigorous than that used for a QI study (Saver, 2006b).

Table 5.1   Comparison Between Research and Quality Improvement Articles

Criterion	Quality Improvement	Research
Scope	Narrow (e.g., one nursing unit, one hospital)	May be broad (e.g., multiple health systems)
Built on a theoretical or conceptual foundation?	Not necessarily	Yes
Patients are representative of the population of interest?	No, convenience sample used	Yes
Variables controlled?	Not necessarily	Yes
Inclusion/exclusion criteria?	None or basic	Yes
Able to generalize?	No	Yes
Signed participant consent required?	Not necessarily	Usually
Statistical analysis	Sample size determined by convenience. Basic statistical tests (e.g., mean and standard deviation, percentages).	Sample size determined through statistical analysis. Basic and advanced statistical tests (e.g., tests of significant difference or correlation).

Adapted from Saver, C. (2006a). Determining what type of article to write. AORN Journal, 84(5), 751–57. Reprinted with permission.

All About Reporting Guidelines

Reporting guidelines exist to improve the consistency and usefulness of published information. The guidelines are typically developed with input from an expert panel.

For example, many journals require authors to follow the "Standards for QUality Improvement Reporting Excellence"—the SQUIRE guidelines—when writing quality improvement articles. The guidelines provide a framework for sharing quality interventions "closely, carefully, and in detail" (SQUIRE, n.d.). They were developed with input from an expert panel and public feedback. You can download the guidelines and an easy-to-use checklist at http://squire-statement.org.

lines include:

...solidated Standards of Reporting Trials) for randomized clinical
..., 2010). These guidelines comprise a 25-item checklist and a flow

- ......ed Reporting Items for Systematic Reviews and Meta-Analyses).
  These guidelines consist of a 27-item checklist and flow diagram (PRISMA, 2009).

- STROBE (STrengthening the Reporting of OBservational studies in Epidemiology). You can access checklists for cohort, case-control, and cross sectional studies (STROBE checklists, 2007).

- CARE (CAse REport). These guidelines are discussed later in this chapter (Gagnier, et al., 2013).

Use of these guidelines is expanding in the nursing literature, although they are far from ubiquitous in either nursing or medical publications. The publication's author guidelines will tell you if you should follow a particular reporting guideline for a certain type of article. Reporting guidelines help you organize your article. You can learn more about reporting guidelines through the Enhancing the QUAlity and Transparency Of health Research (EQUATOR) network (n.d.).

Clinical Articles

Clinical articles address topics that are relevant to clinical practice. They might present new skills or knowledge related to patient care, provide an empirically or clinically based review of a disease state or procedure, or analyze current literature related to a topic. Research findings, if available, should be included to support the rationale for recommended interventions (Saver, 2006b).

The format for writing clinical articles varies among journals. Unlike research articles, there is no specific format; however, some general guidelines are helpful as you develop your manuscript.

Begin the article with an *introduction*, which may be a brief presentation of a patient or situation that a nurse might experience. Describe the purpose of your paper, an overview of the topics, the relevance of the content for clinical practice, and the value of the article to the reader. Here, you tell the readers that the article will present useful information that can be applied to clinical practice.

In the *body* of the article, tell readers the key points. For example, if you are writing about a specific procedure, you might include a review of the disease or condition associated with the procedure, its incidence and pathophysiology, information about the procedure, and a care plan—and then conclude with a summary of information. If you are presenting a new procedure, discuss the steps in the order in which they occur (Saver, 2006b). Organize the content from simple to complex and from known to unknown. To help the reader understand your decision to recommend a particular intervention, provide sufficient background information and data. Describe the evidence and research that support the changes in practice. And remember the purpose of the article addresses nursing management of a patient's problem, not medical management, so your content needs to reflect your nursing interventions.

Each clinical article ends with a *conclusion* that summarizes the information presented. Although your conclusion might suggest areas of further study, do not add new information at this point. The conclusion for these types of articles should show the value to the nurse in clinical practice when a new intervention is implemented or a change in nursing practice is endorsed. (For more on clinical articles, see Chapter 13.)

Literature Reviews

One type of literature review is part of the research process, but a formal, written *literature review* is another type of article that you can submit for publication. This literature review is a critique and summary of current knowledge about a particular topic that has already been published. In meta-analyses, authors combine the results of multiple studies. By evaluating previously published literature, authors of literature reviews consider the progress of research toward clarifying a problem (APA, 2010). Clinicians often use review articles as guides for clinical decisions, so be sure that reviews are systematic, include relevant data, and aren't overly influenced by the opinions and biases of the authors (AMA, 2007).

Here is a handy format for writing a literature review:

Beginning. Begin with an introductory statement about the literature that you will present and its importance to the problem or purpose of the paper. This statement should not be too broad; keep it specific enough so the reader knows what literature will be discussed. A more-specific statement gives the reader a better idea of the content of the article. Compare these examples of too-broad and more-specific:

Not specific enough: The authors conducted a literature review of studies published on glycemic control in adults with type 2 diabetes.

Good overview: A systematic literature review of studies published between 2002 and 2012 was conducted to evaluate the impact of isolated telephone interventions on glycemic control in adults with type 2 diabetes.

Middle. In the body of the literature review, summarize previous publications to inform the reader of the state of the research. Highlight important studies and describe their significance to the research. Note classic studies and how they have contributed to the research. If you can't locate relevant literature about a topic, note the dearth of literature in your review as well as any relationships, contradictions, gaps, and inconsistencies that you identify in the literature.

End. In your conclusion, describe how the review closes a gap in the literature and extends existing research. Address how this work will contribute knowledge to the profession.

Case Studies

Case studies, or *case reports*, provide new information on nursing practice or patient care problems. Often found in less-formal venues like magazines, these articles don't necessarily follow the same rigorous format that original research articles follow. They can be used to describe patient care; illustrate how concepts, theories, and research are used in practice; present issues in a patient's care and strategies for resolving them; or apply information to a real or hypothetical case. Case studies illustrate a problem; indicate a means for solving a problem; and/or shed light on needed research, clinical applications, or theoretical matters.

Preserving Patient Privacy

When writing a case study about a real person, it's important to preserve patient privacy by not publishing identifying patient information, such as names, initials, or hospital numbers, without informed consent (ICMJE, 2013). Avoid any details that might make it possible to identify someone, such as writing about a patient with blunt chest trauma as a result of wrecking his car during a high-speed car chase through a rural town. The events are likely to have been published online and in print. You should simply state the patient was someone involved in a high-speed auto accident. Another option is to change the gender of the patient, if it isn't germane to the case study. To protect yourself, it's best to obtain the patient's consent before writing the article, although that's not always practical. (You can find more on privacy rights in Chapter 11.)

The case study article begins with why the case was selected and its importance to nursing practice. Then the article continues with a description of the patient and related care given. Case studies are used to promote clinical-judgment, decision-making, and critical-thinking skills. As previously noted, when providing illustrative material, be sure not to disclose information that would identify a specific patient by name (APA, 2010).

The CARE (CAse REport) guidelines contain a checklist for items that should be part of a case study (Gagnier, et al., 2013). You can use the following elements from the checklist as a guide when writing your article:

- **Introduction:** Provides a summary of the case and why it's important.

- **Patient information:** Includes demographic information; main signs and symptoms; and medical, family, and psychosocial history.

- **Clinical findings:** Presents the relevant results of the physician examination.

- **Timeline:** Includes key time frames.

- **Diagnostic assessment:** Provides information about diagnostic methods and reasoning.

- **Therapeutic intervention:** Describes medical, surgical, and nursing interventions, including modifications made as needed.

- **Follow-up and outcomes:** Tells what happened to the patient and what kinds of follow-up testing or visiting were done.

- **Discussion:** Summarizes the strengths and limitations of what was done and should include relevant literature and main "lessons learned" from the case.

If possible, it's also helpful to share the patient's perspective.

The CARE guidelines recommend obtaining informed consent from the patient even though he or she is not named. If the patient is unable to provide consent, the alternative is to contact a relative. If neither the patient nor a relative is available, the guidelines recommend obtaining consent from an ethics committee or institutional review board. The step of obtaining patient consent for a case study is an unusual requirement for nursing publications, particularly because authors are typically asked to make adjustments to protect patient privacy. However, it will be interesting to see if adoption of the CARE guidelines by journals affects future practice.

Keep in mind that in addition to being the entire article, shorter case studies can be used to illustrate key points in an article, as shown by this excerpt:

> Case examples can teach nurses new to the emergency department to have a heightened index of suspicion for signs and symptoms that appear to be one thing but are actually another.   — Introduction

> A 78-year-old man was brought to the emergency department by his family because his behavior had suddenly changed, and his family was frightened by the way he was acting. Upon awakening from a nap, he became very agitated and told his family that he wanted "those strangers who are talking to me out of my bedroom." Despite his family's reassurances that there were no strangers in the room, he was insistent that there was an entire family in the bedroom, and they were all talking to him.   — Description of the patient

> A comprehensive assessment of the patient's physical condition and consideration of potential side effects from a recently prescribed antidepressant medication were evaluated. Within 2 days after the antidepressant was discontinued, the agitation and hallucinations were gone, and the patient was "back to normal."   — Nursing care

> A thorough medical history and the appropriate laboratory tests can reveal that an apparent psychiatric patient is really a medical patient with psychiatric symptoms.   — Conclusion

> *Pestka E., Billman R., Alexander J., & Rosenblad M. (2002). Acute medical crises masquerading as psychiatric illness.* Journal of Emergency Nursing, 28(6): 535.

Nursing Narratives or Exemplars

If you are a novice author, a way to gain experience and confidence in your writing skills is to write a *nursing narrative* or *exemplar*, which is a personal account that describes outstanding examples of the actions of individuals in clinical settings that have enhanced patient care. A discussion of difficult interpersonal, ethical, or clinical judgments is the basis for these articles (Saver, 2006b). (You can learn more about this type of article in Chapter 19.)

Q: *I was recently invited to contribute to a regular department for a journal. What format should I use?*

A: Many publications include regular columns or departments. Departments make a good target for your ideas because they are published frequently and feature shorter articles.

You can usually identify the format by studying two or three past articles for the specific department. Stick to the same length, style, and tone—and if in doubt, ask the editor to verify that you're on the right track.

Organize for Success

As an author contributing to the body of nursing literature, the content must be written in a logical and coherent manner. Articles fall into many different categories, from lengthy research articles written in a formal style to an opinion piece not longer than one page. The type of article that you write will depend upon the data you have and the key messages you want to convey to the readers. Templates can help you organize your information more easily. When your article is written in a predictable pattern, the reader can more easily follow your line of reasoning. General characteristics of articles with corresponding formats exist, making it easier for the author to organize the information. Keeping in mind the elements of organizing, your article will add to your success as an author.

Write Now!

1. Choose a journal in your specialty. Read two to three articles and identify the types of articles you've read.

2. Identify three types of articles that you would like to write. For each one, create an overview of what you would include, using templates for those provided.

References

American Medical Association. (2007). *AMA manual of style: A guide for authors and editors* (10th ed.). New York, NY: Oxford University Press.

American Psychological Association. (2010). *Publication manual of the American Psychological Association* (6th ed.). Washington, DC: American Psychological Association.

Benefield, L. E. (2002). Evidence-based practice: Basic strategies for success. *Home Healthcare Nurse, 20*(12), 803–807.

CONSORT. (2010). The CONSORT Statement. Retrieved from http://www.consort-statement.org/consort-statement

Egleston, B. L., Ercolano, E., McCorkle, R., & Van Cleave, J. H. (2013). Symptom distress in older adult patients following cancer surgery. *Cancer Nursing, 36*(4), 292-300.

EQUATOR Network. (n.d.). Enhancing the QUAlity and Transparency Of health Research. Retrieved from http://www.equator-network.org

Gagnier, J. J., Kienle, G., Altman, D. G., Moher, D., Sox, H., Riley, D., & the CARE Group. (2013). The CARE guidelines: Consensus-based clinical case reporting guideline development. *Journal of Medical Case Reports, 7*, 223. Retrieved from http://www.jmedicalcasereports.com/content/7/1/223

Garces, J. & Wallace, B. (2013). Anesthesia considerations in the older adult patient. *OR Nurse 2013, 7*(4): 15–18.

Graff, G., & Birkenstein, C. (2009). *"They say/I say": The moves that matter in academic writing* (2nd ed.). New York, NY: W. W. Norton.

Hagle, M., & Senk, P. (2010). Evidence-based practice. In M. Alexander, A. Corrigan, L. Gorski, J. Hankins, & R. Perucca (Eds.), *Infusion nursing: An evidence-based approach* (3rd ed.). St. Louis, MO: Saunders/Elsevier.

International Committee of Medical Journal Editors (ICMJE). (2013). Uniform requirements for manuscripts submitted to biomedical journals: Ethical considerations in the conduct and reporting of research: Privacy and confidentiality. Retrieved from http://icmje.org/ethical_5privacy.html

Moritz, M. L. (2013). Case studies in fluid and electrolyte therapy. *Journal of Infusion Nursing, 36*(4), 270–277.

Oermann, M. H., & Hays, J. C. (2011). *Writing for publication in nursing* (2nd ed.). New York, NY: Springer Publishing.

Pestka, E., Billman, R., Alexander, J., & Rosenblad, M. (2002). Acute medical crises masquerading as psychiatric illness. *Journal of Emergency Nursing, 28*(6), 535.

PRISMA. (2009). The PRISMA Statement. Retrieved from http://www.prisma-statement.org/statement.htm

Saver, C. (2006a). Determining what type of article to write. *AORN Journal, 84*(5), 751–757.

Saver, C. (2006b). Ready to write. *AORN Journal, 83*(5), 1049–1052.

SQUIRE Standards for Quality Improvement Reporting Excellence. (n.d.). About SQUIRE. Retrieved from http://squire-statement.org/about

STROBE STrengthening the Reporting of OBservational studies in Epidemiology. (2007). STROBE checklists. Retrieved from http://www.strobe-statement.org/index.php?id=available-checklists

Strunk, W., Jr. (2013). *The elements of style.* Upper Saddle River, NJ: Longman.

Troyka, L. Q., & Hesse, D. D. (2012). *Simon & Schuster handbook for writers.* (10th ed.). Upper Saddle River, NJ: Longman.

"To be effective, communication must take place in an atmosphere of mutual respect and desire for understanding."

–Imogene King

Writing Effectively

Julie A. Goldsmith

6

After you choose a structure for your article, you are ready to begin drafting it. Armed with an understanding of flow, you want to concentrate on the elements of good writing. Good writing is a basic skill you use in practice and to communicate with patients and those external to the nursing profession. Consider this: The modern pioneers of nursing believed so strongly in communication that patient education remains central in the science and art of healing.

Language Tools

Just as you use many basic tools on the job—your stethoscope, a sphygmomanometer, and so on—there are some tools related to language skills that will help you write more effectively. These include voice, bias-free language, cultural sensitivity, technical language, acronyms and abbreviations, parts of speech, and transitions.

Voice

Voice can refer to a grammatical construction with verbs in the active or passive voice, or the author's personality. Voice can also refer to how sentences are constructed and deliberately presented to craft your message.

Verbs have an active or passive voice. *Active voice* occurs when the subject drives the action with a verb; conversely, *passive voice* occurs when the subject receives the action through the verb.

WHAT YOU'LL LEARN IN THIS CHAPTER

- Language tools, such as voice and bias-free writing, enhance your communication.

- You can sharpen your writing technique by using variety and by revising and editing your work.

- Your writing style can be adapted for print and digital media.

Sportswriters plunge readers into highly descriptive texts to recapture the physicality of a game; their active voices reach beyond the nature of scientific explanations. Passive voice is appropriate for clear definitions and emphasis on a subject instead of an object. The best voice for the verb depends on its purpose in a sentence. The following examples show how you can easily change passive voice into active voice.

- **Passive:** The neurologic check was performed every 2 hours.

- **Active:** The nurse performed the neurologic check every 2 hours.

- **Passive:** The unique function of the nurse is to assist the individual, sick or well.

- **Active:** The nurse assists the individual, sick or well.

Use active voice when possible because it is more direct and more dynamic. You see active voice in general nursing publications, websites, and educational tools. However, scholarly or research articles that describe results tend to use passive voice.

Authors express personality through their choice of words. Nurses may write in a variety of voices, including empathy, strength, or support. An essay on health policy might be dispassionate; or, it might be political, cutting, and caustic. Nursing articles in lay publications might contain overtly expressive and colloquial phrases that in a scientific journal would be considered subjective. Even the most scientific articles bear traces of personality, if only—and importantly—the author's values. Match your voice to the tone of the publication or website.

Confidence Booster

You can enhance your confidence by heeding advice from experienced authors. One of America's most popularly read authors advised writers to be direct:

"I notice that you use plain, simple language, short words and brief sentences. That is the way to write English—it is the modern way and the best way. Stick to it; don't let fluff and flowers and verbosity creep in. When you catch an adjective, kill it. No, I don't mean utterly, but kill most of them—then the rest will be valuable. They weaken when they are close together. They give strength when they are wide apart. An adjective habit, or a wordy, diffuse, flowery habit, once fastened upon a person, is as hard to get rid of as any other vice.

–Mark Twain, March 20, 1880, in a letter to D.W. Bowser

Bias-Free Language

Researchers have long agreed that public discourse can marginalize a person or group in society through the use of stereotypes or stigmas (Allport, 1954; Biernat & Dovidio, 2000; Goffman, 1963). The most frequent stereotypes include generalizations about a person's age, race, sex, or religion. Writers often struggle to find gender-neutral nouns and pronouns that help avoid sexist stereotypes. Try to be aware of unintended meanings when writing about a disease or disability. Don't define anyone by a deficit, such as "the blind person." Instead, choose a more descriptive reference, such as "the individual with a visual impairment." Your decision to describe a person by an impairment or disease, of course, would be based on the relevance to your other content.

Sometimes, bias is just as hard to see as it is to repair in your text. Here are some strategies for averting bias:

- Change a singular noun to plural, if appropriate and factual, to eliminate feminine and masculine pronouns. For example, change

  *How can a nurse respond in a disaster, when **he** or **she** has no emergency kit?*

  to

  *How can **nurses** without emergency kits respond to a disaster?*

- Evaluate pictures for bias, incorrect characterizations, and nonfactual or harmful depictions.

- Assess whom and what are included or excluded in the texts and images.

- Vary anecdotes for diversity and use them only if they represent the content. Avoid outliers, which address rare occurrences instead of representing the majority population.

- Use humanistic language that treats a person as an individual, not a category, and does not inadvertently embarrass or humiliate.

Q: *I thought I'd eliminated bias from a recent paper for a contributed book, but the editor returned it to me asking for a rewrite. What can I do to better learn to spot this problem?*

A: When in doubt, have a colleague give your writing a read to see whether he or she can spot biases or prejudices you might have inadvertently added. Eventually, you'll be able to spot them while you're writing—and fix them as you go.

Cultural Sensitivity

Nurses with diverse cultures, languages, and backgrounds will have access to what you write. Consider whether your content will be clear for those unfamiliar with your culture. For instance, colloquialisms in informal articles may add a friendly tone of familiarity and casualness, but they remain culturally specific and may produce confusion. In the following example, the colloquial "hats off" has been replaced with a more common word.

> **Draft:** Hats off to Pauline Sato....

> **Revision:** Congratulations to Pauline Sato....

Cultural sensitivity is—particularly in social networking—an important tool for expanding your audience. When communicating through social media, avoid culturally specific language or words known only in a region or population. The use of scientific and professional jargon is appropriate for a specialty group, but not for broader populations. (You can learn more about writing for social media in Chapter 12.)

Technical Language

Scientific definitions serve a critical purpose for members of the same discipline, but if you're writing for a general audience, technical language will put off readers. Who comprises your general audience might not always be obvious and will vary from publication to publication. For example, a blog for a website targeting new mothers or a health column for a local newspaper will be written in lay language. However, as savvy Internet users, these readers will likely survey the health literature and expect and accept some scientific terms if terse translations are included. The following examples show how you can succinctly provide definitions for scientific terms:

- a myocardial infarction, or heart attack,

- circadian rhythm—a person's physiological time clock—

Proper names can be just as arcane as technical terms. Unless you're writing for a small group of readers who all know each other, explain in a few words the relevance of the person or organization that you cited. Here is an example where the author clarified the organization:

> Mary Tolle Wright, one of seven founders of Sigma Theta Tau International, the honor society of nursing, traveled to India, Liberia, Nepal, and Afghanistan.

Remember that a paragraph full of proper names or unfamiliar terms and numbers will slow down the reader. Give facts and unfamiliar terms some breathing space by intermixing explanations and familiar prose. A few new words can be captivating, but too many will increase anxiety. In short, avoid fact-packing and jargon-junking.

Acronyms and Abbreviations

Acronyms (pronounced like they look: *HIP-AA*, for Health Insurance Portability and Accountability Act of 1996) and *abbreviations* (pronounced by their letters, as in *F-D-A*, for Federal Drug Administration) can be one of the most confusing style issues to conquer. On first reference, as a general rule, include the complete title of a proper name before reducing it to letters. However, many nursing acronyms are the same, or similar, such as the American Association of Critical-Care Nurses (AACN) and the American Association of Colleges of Nursing (AACN). Find every opportunity to refer to an organization by its common purpose. For example:

> ANCC, the world's largest nurse credentialing organization, is a subsidiary of the American Nurses Association. (In this case, you would have already defined ANCC as the American Nurses Credentialing Center.)

Q: *I understand that what I write needs to be accurate, but how important is it really to adhere to the minutiae of grammar?*

A: Grammar rules are annoying and sometimes confusing, but without them, chaos can creep in. When your communication is both accurate and grammatically correct, the content is easy to read, and its purpose is easy to understand. You have met your goal to communicate your information. Good grammar and a consistent style are the foundation that makes your content work; readers should not be aware of either grammar or style while they read. If they become aware, which can occur when grammar and style have been compromised, you have either lost them or lost the information you wanted to convey.

Parts of Speech

Sometimes even the best writers need to brush up on their grammar. You know the basics of grammar, but sometimes the basics are worth revisiting to help you gain confidence in your ability to arrange words in sentences to sharpen their meanings.

A basic sentence consists of:

- A noun (actor) as the subject
- A verb (action)

  Example: I ate.

That's it: a basic sentence. Of course, such simplicity doesn't give you much information. You're undoubtedly familiar with a more complex sentence that also contains the following:

- A verb as predicate and often a *direct object* (receiver of the action)

  Example: I ate lunch.

  and maybe

- An adjective and/or adverb (qualifiers)

  Example: I ate a light lunch.

Exceptions might include a subject or predicate that is understood but not written: for example, the command (sometimes called an *imperative*) *Go!* The subject is understood to be *You*, so what you're really writing is *You go!* In a broader context, the subject might be a specific person.

Subject-verb-object word order is the easiest and most basic sentence form to understand. For example: *The nurse filled the syringe with saline.*

The key functions in a sentence convey some or all of the following information: who, did what, to whom/what, what kind, why, when, and how. Consider the following example and see how to break it down into the parts of speech:

> On Tuesday, a nurse administered crushed aspirin through the patient's nasogastric tube and observed for signs of bleeding.
>
> - **When:** On Tuesday = prepositional phrase
> - **Who:** (a) nurse = subject
> - **Did what:** administered = verb
> - **What kind:** crushed = adjective (for aspirin)

- **What:** aspirin = direct object

- **How:** through the patient's nasogastric tube = prepositional phrase

- **Did what:** observed = verb

- **What:** signs = direct object

- **Why:** of bleeding = prepositional phrase

(See Appendix C for more parts of speech.)

Transitions

Transitional words and phrases link thoughts between sentences and paragraphs, interpret the relationship of two parts of the text, and offer information about the next idea. Transitions can also be ordinal (first, second, third) or cardinal (1, 2, 3), repeat a key word or thought, or paraphrase a thought with the addition of new content. You can use certain words to cue the reader that you are making a transition.

Here are examples of transitions and what they convey:

- **Conclude:** as a result, consequently, finally

- **Contrast, subtract:** although, however, nevertheless

- **Compare, add:** also, by comparison, in addition

- **Impart a sense of time:** just as, meanwhile, then

- **Show:** for example, such as, to demonstrate

Pick out the transitional words in this excerpt:

> Cigarette smoking is the highest risk factor for developing chronic obstructive pulmonary disease (COPD). In addition, inhaled pollution, whether indoor or outdoor, can contribute to COPD.

> With emphysema, a type of COPD, alveolar septa are destroyed, resulting in a smaller surface area for gas exchange.

> Corticosteroids reduce inflammation; however, they are not that helpful in COPD.

The transitional words are *in addition*, *resulting*, and *however*.

 Q: *What else can I do to make my writing effective?*

A: Seek out workshops and continuing education courses on writing for publication, some of which are specifically geared for nurses. Joining a writing group is another way to learn. Form a writing group; your colleagues might also want to improve their writing skills. You might also want to try online writing tutorials if they are from reputable sources such as universities or professional associations.

Sharpening Your Writing

In addition to the tools just discussed, you can improve your writing through variety, accuracy, revising, and editing.

Online Writing

Leslie Nicoll, PhD, MBA, RN

The basic principles of good writing apply to both print and online. However, it's worth focusing on some unique principles of writing content that will primarily appear online.

People tend to "read" differently online. There is a need for text that can be easily searched and cataloged, which also changes how people write. You need to adapt your writing so that it best meets the needs of online readers.

A few hints: Break up your text into chunks to make it easier for readers to follow the material. Use lists and short paragraphs rather than multiple unbroken lines of text. A sentence should not contain more than 20 words, and a paragraph should not contain more than six sentences, according to the U.S. Department of Health and Human Services' Research-Based Web Design and Usability Guidelines (2013).

Graphics and multimedia features (such as audio and video) are excellent tools for illustrating your points, but should be used appropriately to provide useful information instead of distracting the reader. The main image should be given dominance, with the others available through links within the text.

For more success, try the following tips for writing for online publications (Research-Based Web Design and Usability Guidelines, 2013).

- Avoid jargon and use abbreviations sparingly.
- Define any acronyms and abbreviations used.
- Use conventional capitalization of sentences.
- Keep sentences and paragraphs short.
- Use active voice.
- Make the first sentence in a paragraph descriptive because readers tend to skim these sentences when scanning text.
- Don't overdo graphics. Some writers have the mistaken impression that online readers only look for visuals. In fact, they will read text if it is of interest to them.

Note that many of these tips, such as using active voice, and defining acronyms, are important when writing for print, too.

Variety

One easy route to sharper writing is through the use of diverse sentence structures and word choice. Although subject-verb-object order offers the greatest clarity, varying your writing by using independent and dependent clauses helps as well. (See Appendix C for examples of dependent clauses.)

Also, vary the first word in consecutive paragraphs to add fresh words to new thoughts. As you proofread, check whether your paragraphs start the same. The words in the last sentence of a paragraph should differ as much as possible from the words in the first sentence of the next paragraph. To freshen your vocabulary, create a lexicon of words that you like from your own readings and include at least one new word each time you write. Finally, don't forget to use tried-and-true reference works, such as a dictionary and thesaurus, many of which are available online. A quick and easy search with an online thesaurus can make your writing sing.

Accuracy

Provide sources for your data to strengthen your credibility, prevent errors, and credit other authors. Correct information trumps all other aspects of writing. Double-check facts for accuracy and relevancy. When introducing data, place facts in a separate sentence or paragraph from the opinions and interpretations. Over-citing isn't a substitute for real substance—and can cause its own problems—but a fair number of citations to back up your research and facts will make your paper a reliable and trusted source.

Separating Facts, Opinions, and Interpretations

Clearly separate your facts from your opinions and interpretations to enable readers to know the difference.

- *Facts* convey information attributed to the sources.

- *Opinions* place value judgments on people, places, things, or institutions.

- *Interpretations* connect the facts to provide understanding based upon the best knowledge available. The art of interpretation *must* be obvious to be scientifically valid and responsible.

You can set off opinions and interpretations with such words as *discussion, explanation, I believe, we think, based upon the best evidence, this evidence leads me to consider the possibility, these facts suggest,* and so on. Opinions suggest a heavy use of value judgments and perspective. The interpretation needs to be set in a separate paragraph before or after the facts. You can also expand on your interpretations in a Discussion section. Interpretation can follow a list of clinical procedures to explain why you chose such methods. Making distinctions in the facts, opinions, and interpretations requires your highest levels of consideration.

Here is an example:

> **Opinion:** When I entered the hospital room and introduced myself, the child wouldn't look at me. He was angry.

> **Fact:** When I entered the hospital room and introduced myself, the child did not look at me or respond.

Or

> **Fact:** When I entered the hospital room, the patient winced and said that his pain was unbearable.

> **Interpretation:** The child's lack of interaction with me and his repetitive twisting with his blanket may suggest autism or another cognitive impairment. Our inability to know how he feels concern us.

Revising

While you write your first draft, don't be too critical of your work. After the draft is done, go back and question everything, revising as needed to make the text clearer to the reader. Revising is the most challenging part of writing. Try to be objective and see your words as if for the first time. This is an excellent time to get feedback from others.

Editing

After you revise your article, the next step is editing. Editing is like polishing a gem until it shines. You can take your writing to the next level with good editing. For example, vague and nonessential words in a sentence can obscure the main idea and tire your readers. The choice of the vague pronoun *it* at the beginning of a sentence can leave a reader wondering who or what *it* is. For example, the first five words of the following draft sentence offer little information, and the subject remains undefined—who or what is the actor? And *it* does not make decisions. The revision places the key information at the beginning of the sentence.

> **Draft:** It was decided that the teenager's body mass index was the primary determinant of the nurse selecting to use a 25-millimeter needle for giving an intramuscular injection at the patient's deltoid site.

> **Revision:** The teenager's body mass index guided the nurse's decision to use a 25 mm needle for an intramuscular injection at the deltoid site.

> **Draft:** Such as it is, when a patient hopes to psychologically return back to the phase preceding the accident, this is so very unfortunate, because that situation will never be able to be repeated again.

> **Revision:** A patient may hope to reestablish the same lifestyle that preceded the accident, but unfortunately, his physical abilities will never be the same.

For a quick edit, look for redundancies (for example, *returning back*, or *repeating again*) and extra words or fluffy phrases (*such as it is, so very unfortunate, needless to say*) without meaning. Here are some examples of fluffy modifiers, nonessential phrases, and common redundancies. In the case of phrases, the words in italics are unnecessary.

> Merely, simply, surely, very, truly, just, most *ever*, the best *ever*, as it were, such as it is, originally *began*, during *the course of*, my *personal* opinion, entered *into*, off *of*, the *end* result, *over*-exaggerate, mutual regard *for each other*, *still* continues, bridges *across*, examines *with scrutiny*

Q: *I spent last semester working on an article for a journal, only to have it returned to me with a note from the editor asking that it be revised to house style. What is house style?*

A: Publishers adhere to a broad style guide for references and general structure, such as the American Psychological Association (APA) or American Medical Association (AMA) stylebooks, but they likely also have additional clarifications for their own organization, considered *house style*. For example, APA style, the style guide for all Sigma Theta Tau International (STTI) journals and books, specifies a particular order for academic degrees and titles. However, house style for STTI requires that professional credentials should always be published as the individual submits.

Before submitting an article, request information about the style to use and any house style specifics.

The grammatical structure and content of a sentence depends on a consistent language pattern, referred to as *parallelism*. For example, if writing about an occurrence in the present, do not switch the tense to a past or future verb within the same sentence. See the following examples:

Draft (tense)

Janet Sanchez, RN, was named Nurse of the Year and is a community health practitioner.

Revision 1

Janet Sanchez, RN, community health practitioner, is Nurse of the Year.

Revision 2

Mercy Hospital presented the Nurse of the Year Award to Janet Sanchez, a community health practitioner.

A series or pattern based on one part of speech also needs to continue with the same form.

Draft (active/passive verb)

The researcher collects sensitive data, is assessing it, and stores it outside the building.

Revision

The researcher collects, assesses, and stores sensitive data outside the building.

Proofreading

After you revise and edit your work, you are just about ready to submit! Before you do, whether electronically or via *hard copy* (paper), the final step of editing is proofreading. Use this checklist to ensure that you take care of every last detail. If you can answer *yes* to these questions, your content is ready for publication.

☐ Are the facts and characterizations of all people, groups, and institutions presented accurately and without bias?

☐ Are the references accurate and formatted in the appropriate style?

☐ Are your meaning and purpose clear?

☐ Do the visual content and captions work?

☐ Do you have all legal and ethical consents? (Refer to Chapter 11 for more information on legal and ethical issues.)

☐ Have you checked for spelling and grammatical errors? (Remember to always run the spell-check and grammar-check in your word processing program. However, such tools don't replace a keen eye. For example, a spell-check won't pick up the error in this sentence: *There [instead of Their] anxiety over the drug's recall grew rapidly.*)

☐ Have you confirmed the spelling of proper titles/names with primary sources?

☐ Have you read for and corrected any potential, unintentional harms or insults?

☐ Have you verified the accuracy of statistics and all numbers in the text?

☐ Is your wording concise?

> **Q:** *I used to think writing was easy until I tried to write a brief information sheet for home care after one of our treatments. My writing wasn't clear and raised more questions than it answered. At that time, someone more skillful rewrote the information, but I would like writing to be one of the ways how I contribute to patient care. What do you suggest?*

A: It's trite, but true: Practice, practice, practice. Writing is a skill that can be learned but then also needs practice. Through practice, you can improve your writing skills and increase your comfort level with disseminating health information through writing.

Communication as a Tool

The modern pioneers of nursing believed that communication held a pivotal role in managing disease and improving health. Consequently, nurses arrived in the Information Age understanding the art of interpersonal communications for the benefit of patients. The opportunities for extending a nurse's effectiveness with traditional media and online media tools remain limitless, when the meaning of words are clear and without figures of speech, colloquialisms, or flowery language.

Write Now!

1. Think of a somewhat complicated message that you want to convey to a colleague. Take no more than 3 minutes to write, and then stop. Did your writing convey your message clearly and concisely? If yes, congratulations! If no, go back to see how to make your message more clear. Perhaps unnecessary words are muddying the message.

2. Select a small health-related topic and then write about it for two audiences. One audience is the general public, and one is a peer-reviewed journal.

References

Allport, G. (1954). *The nature of prejudice*. New York, NY: Addison-Wesley.

Biernat, M., & Dovidio, J. (2000). Stigma and stereotypes. In T. F. Heatherton, R. E. Kleck, M. Hebl, & J. Hull (Eds.), *The social psychology of stigma*. New York, NY: The Guilford Press.

Goffman, E. (1963). *Stigma*. Englewood Cliffs, NJ: Prentice-Hall.

King, I. M. (1971). *Toward a theory for nursing: General concepts of human behaviour*. New York, NY: John Wiley & Sons.

King, I. M. (1981). *A theory for nursing: Systems, concepts, process*. New York, NY: John Wiley & Sons.

Twain, M. (1880). Retrieved from www.marktwainquotes

U.S. Department of Health and Human Services. (2013). Research-based web design and usability guidelines. Retrieved from http://guidelines.usability.gov

"One picture is worth a thousand words."

–Fred R. Barnard

All About Tables, Figures, Graphs, Illustrations, and Photos

7

Susanne J. Pavlovich-Danis

WHAT YOU'LL LEARN IN THIS CHAPTER

- Eye-catching graphics call attention to key points in your manuscript.

- Graphics should be labeled using standard conventions.

- You'll want to style the graphics in your manuscript to match those of the publication you are submitting to.

- To hold readers' attention, balance text with graphics.

You envision that every word in your manuscript will captivate readers. The truth is many readers will skim an article or book chapter, focusing on the introduction, graphics, and summary to determine the key points. If you omit graphics or insert ones that don't emphasize your take-home points, you decrease your chance to make a lasting impression.

This chapter provides technical guidance for authors wanting to include graphics in their manuscripts. *Graphics* is an inclusive term for tables, figures, graphs, illustrations, and photographs. When carefully selected, graphics provide visual enhancement, clarification, and an opportunity to stress significant points in your manuscript. Visual learners require them, and most readers appreciate how graphics break up text and allow better content comprehension. Combining words and images improves your manuscript and can enhance greater retention of your key points.

Q: *In an article I recently wrote, my editor cut many of the graphics I included. What can I do to ensure they make it in next time?*

A: Make sure that your graphics are directly related to the content of your paper. Space—especially printing space—is valuable, and editors are careful about what they use to fill it. Try this test: Does your paper make sense without the graphic? If so, then the graphic might be unnecessary. If your paper makes better sense with the image, table, or photo, you can justify its inclusion.

Language of Graphics

Using graphics requires more effort than simply using an Insert Table, Insert Picture, or Copy/Paste command in a word processing program. There are some key points authors must consider, including the purpose, number, and style of graphics:

- Graphics should captivate reader attention and solidify key points.

- Use graphics to supplement—not completely replace, duplicate, or overshadow—your text.

- Use eye-catching graphics to draw in readers.

- Limit graphics to no more than one-third of your manuscript.

- Position graphics to provide readers with a visual break from reading text. Even in scholarly journals, readers expect to find graphics.

- Do your homework. Carefully study the format of the publication you are preparing your manuscript for and design your graphics in a similar fashion.

- Refrain from describing graphics in the first person unless you are an expert describing your own research or have been asked to provide an expert opinion.

- Avoid biased wording when describing your graphics. For example, "This graph clearly identifies the inferior wound care product."

Q: *Are graphics really necessary?*

A: This depends on where the manuscript will be published, space limitations, and the intended use. Some publications don't use graphics at all. Short features rarely accommodate graphics, but larger features might require them to be considered for publication.

Q: *I want to include graphics, but I notice the publication rarely includes them. What should I do?*

A: Review the publication's specifications and contact the editor in advance if possible. Specify in your cover letter or early communications with editors that you can provide graphics and then follow their cue.

You must learn the language that editors use for graphics. Editors generally identify graphics by using standard conventions and numbering them consecutively: for example, Table 1, Table 2, and so on; Figure 1, Figure 2, and so on. Use this standard naming convention to identify the files that correspond to your graphics: for example, table1.pdf, figure1.jpg, figure2.png. Note that each graphic in this example tells the editor the kind of file by its *file extension*: those three or four letters after the file's name (.pdf, and .jpg, for example). An accurate file name, complete with its extension, helps you and the editor keep track of all graphics. For created graphics—such as in Photoshop or Illustrator—the file extension also tells an editor the host program. Bottom line: Check with the editor for what file types are accepted.

Q: *Can I submit my manuscript first and describe graphics I will create if my work is accepted?*

A: This typically isn't a good idea unless you already have a working relationship with a publication and your editor has approved your plan. Ideally, you should submit a manuscript for consideration in its entirety with all graphics provided for review. It's hard for an editor or a peer reviewer to complete the review without being able to see the graphics that accompany the text.

Before you submit your paper, article, or book chapter, consult the publication's guidelines. Some will ask you to go one step further and include a placement identifier for the book or article or even chapter. For example, in this book, Figure 2 for Chapter 7 is named Fig 7.2. Your editor will guide you if you have any questions.

You also want to be consistent in how you refer to your graphics in your manuscript. Will you refer to the graphic in text as shown in the following example?

> The studies supporting the effectiveness of telephone triage are summarized in Table 1.

Or, will you note it in parenthesis after the statement it supports?

> Many studies support the use of telephone triage (Table 1).

Whatever you decide to do, follow the publication's guidelines and author instructions—and make sure you apply them consistently.

> **Q:** *If I don't include graphics in my manuscript, can the editor add them later?*
>
> **A:** This varies by publication. Some have graphics departments, and others don't. Keep in mind that if a publication has to use resources locating graphics that authors should have provided, the likelihood of the manuscript being accepted and published may decline.

If you are working on a book, larger publishers with in-house graphic design departments might (but not always) be able to assist in creating images to accompany your manuscript. Be prepared to provide guidance or an example of what you want to depict.

After you decide that you will use graphics, the next step is to decide which type to use. Explore some of the unique graphic options available to enhance your manuscripts.

> **Q:** *I was so excited to write my first book chapter, but it was sent back as rejected. I copied my figures and pasted them into my Microsoft Word document, but my editor called these embedded figures and said they are a no-no. Shouldn't the editor be able to handle a common usage of Word?*
>
> **A:** It's not quite that simple. Your manuscript files will most likely be styled in a sophisticated template with all kinds of codes the publications uses for everything from layout programs to

e-books. Figures inserted in text don't necessarily convert—*compute*, if you will. Most editors will want you to submit all graphics separately so they can be assessed and redrawn if needed. Make sure to follow their instructions, or your submission might be sent back.

Tables

Tables, which are often used to compare data, comprise rows and columns. Tables are also useful for emphasizing numbers rather than trends. Use tables when you want to show relationships or convey detailed information about specific data. Tables enable you to present raw data or statistical analysis that would otherwise require a lengthy narrative explanation (Saver, 2006).

Word processing programs make table creation easy. Take a minute to review the table shown in Figure 7.1 to see the key parts of a table, including the title, column headings, row headings, body or data fields, and footnotes.

Title → **TABLE 1   Gender Difference in Subjective Burden (Step-wise Binary Logistic Regression)**

	B	p	Adjusted OR	95% CI
Step 1: Gender (exposed: woman)	0.681	.013	1.98	[1.15, 3.39]
Step 2: Previous step plus: duration of caregiving	0.634	.022	1.89	[1.10, 3.24]
Step 3: Previous step plus: amount of care per week	0.662	.018	1.94	[1.12, 3.35]
Step 4: Previous step plus: number of ADLs assisted	0.601	.033	1.83	[1.05, 3.17]

Column headings → (B, p, Adjusted OR, 95% CI)

Row headings → Step 1: Gender (exposed: woman)

Body Text →

Note: OR = odds ratio; CI = confidence interval; ADLs = activities of daily living. The OR of each step has been adjusted for the variables in the previous steps.   ← Footnote

Source: In R. del-pino-Casado, et al., "Gender differences regarding informal caregivers of older people." (Table 4) *Journal of Nursing Scholarship*, 44(December, 2012), 354.

Figure 7.1   Sample table, including its key parts.

Keep these tips in mind for creating a table that works well for the reader:

- Avoid long table and row heading titles.
- Align and justify column content.
- Insert adequate spacing between columns for easy reading.

Two common types of tables are text and tabular tables:

- Text tables showcase information only in words.
- Tabular tables showcase figures or a combination of words and figures.

Text Tables

A text table can feature information that summarizes key points, which can help reduce the word count of the main body of the manuscript. You can also display comparisons, descriptions, and instructions. For example, a text table can list items on a tool used to survey nurses regarding compliance with hand washing and standard precautions (see the table shown in Figure 7.2). Note that this table has a title, column headings, data fields, and a footnote, providing any necessary explanations the reader will need to understand the table and the data it represents more clearly.

TABLE 2 Definitions of Common Methodologies Used in the Study of Metabolic Syndrome ← Title

Type of Study	Description ← Column headings
Linkage analysis	Traces patterns of inheritance in large, high-risk families to locate a disease-causing gene mutation by identifying traits that are co-inherited with it
Genome-wide association studies	Search the genome for small variations, called single nucleotide polymorphisms (SNPs), that occur more frequently in people with a particular disease than in people without the disease
Epigenetic studies	Search for changes in the regulation of the expression of gene activity without alteration of the DNA sequence
Proteomics	Study the complete complement of proteins (proteome) of organisms

(Data fields)

Note: Definitions adapted from Genetics Home Reference (http://www.ghr.nim.nih.gov/) ← Footnote

Figure 7.2 Sample text table, including its key parts.

Tabular Tables

The tabular format features data sorted and compared by specific characteristics. The table shown in Figure 7.3 reports the sociodemographic background variables among a group of nurses. Note that this tabular table also features a title, column headings, data fields, and a footnote.

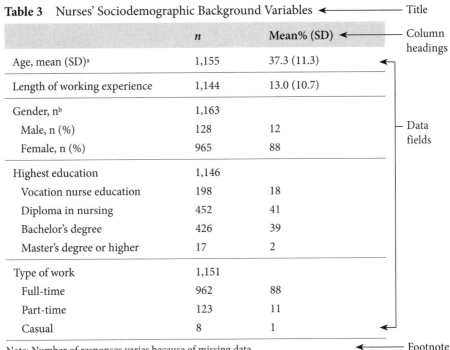

Table 3   Nurses' Sociodemographic Background Variables ⟵——— Title

	n	Mean% (SD) ⟵
Age, mean (SD)[a]	1,155	37.3 (11.3)
Length of working experience	1,144	13.0 (10.7)
Gender, n[b]	1,163	
Male, n (%)	128	12
Female, n (%)	965	88
Highest education	1,146	
Vocation nurse education	198	18
Diploma in nursing	452	41
Bachelor's degree	426	39
Master's degree or higher	17	2
Type of work	1,151	
Full-time	962	88
Part-time	123	11
Casual	8	1

Note: Number of responses varies because of missing data.
Source: In E. Idvall et al., "Nurses' Sociodemographic Background and Assessments of Individualized Care." (Table 2) *Journal of Nursing Scholarship*, 44(September 2012), 288.

Figure 7.3   Sample tabular table, including its key parts.

Figures

Figures is a collective term that includes all other graphic images—other than tables—you can include in your manuscripts. Figures can be graphs; charts; diagrams; illustrations; photographs; and diagnostic images, such as X-ray and ultrasound images. Here are some tips for using figures:

- Unlike tables, titles for figures are placed under the image.

- Don't describe visual images; describe the data. For example, do not say that the lines or the bars went up. Instead, explain what the line or bar changes represent.

- Avoid using shorthand—*chart speak*—abbreviated nursing language used for documenting in medical records when describing graphics. Use full sentences.

Here is a closer look at some of the most common types of figures used.

Graphs

Graphs quickly draw attention, providing the visual impact that tables usually lack. They provide information about the relationship or frequency of specific variables. Use graphs to display how two or more sets of data are related. Select a graph based on the point you are trying to make. For example, if you want to show how patient satisfaction levels fluctuate during the year on three different patient care units, a line graph works well. If you want to compare the percentages of actual patient satisfaction levels on each of the individual units, using a table might be best. Keep reading to see the different types of graphs you can incorporate into your manuscript.

Choosing a Graph Format

You must select the appropriate graphic for the key point you want to highlight.

For example, look at the same information presented in two different graphic formats: first as a table (see the table shown in Figure 7.4) and then as a line graph (Figure 7.5). Each quarter, a different staffing pattern was implemented on three intensive care units. Note the table focus is on detailed data and scores. The line graph emphasizes trends in patient satisfaction over time.

However, the line graph does not enable the reader to appreciate the actual quarterly percentage scores for each of the units. Therefore, in the main text of your article, you need to briefly describe the graph and summarize what it depicts. For example, Figure 7.2 reveals the highest satisfaction scores during the fourth quarter with a patient-to-nurse ratio of 1.75:1, which is not mentioned on the graph, but is what the data describes. All units experienced increases in satisfaction scores as nurse: patient ratios decreased. Do not describe the entire graph; just highlight the main or most significant points and allow readers to explore the graph and arrive at their own conclusions.

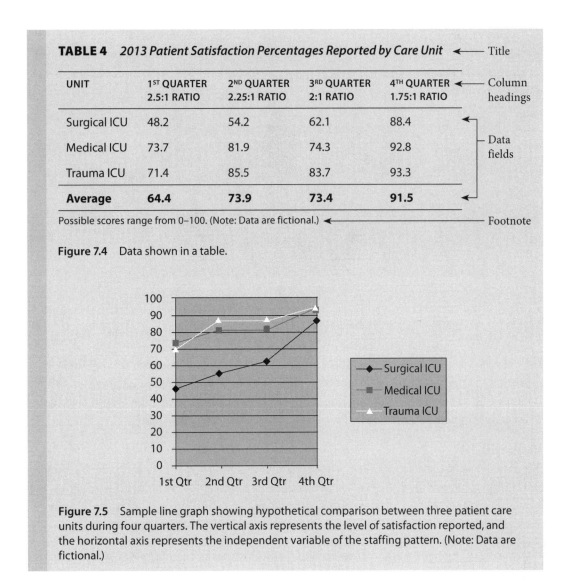

TABLE 4   *2013 Patient Satisfaction Percentages Reported by Care Unit* ←——— Title

UNIT	1ST QUARTER 2.5:1 RATIO	2ND QUARTER 2.25:1 RATIO	3RD QUARTER 2:1 RATIO	4TH QUARTER 1.75:1 RATIO
Surgical ICU	48.2	54.2	62.1	88.4
Medical ICU	73.7	81.9	74.3	92.8
Trauma ICU	71.4	85.5	83.7	93.3
Average	**64.4**	**73.9**	**73.4**	**91.5**

Possible scores range from 0–100. (Note: Data are fictional.) ←——————— Footnote

Figure 7.4   Data shown in a table.

Figure 7.5   Sample line graph showing hypothetical comparison between three patient care units during four quarters. The vertical axis represents the level of satisfaction reported, and the horizontal axis represents the independent variable of the staffing pattern. (Note: Data are fictional.)

Line graphs

Use *line graphs* to show the effect that an *independent variable* (the variable manipulated in the study) has upon a *dependent variable* (the variable being evaluated for response to the independent variable). For example, you can use a line graph to evaluate the effect of medications or placebo on pain levels or how staffing patterns affect patient satisfaction.

Independent variables are plotted on the horizontal (x) axis, and dependent variables are plotted on the vertical (y) axis. Data points are plotted along the corresponding x and y axis. Use a legend to describe what the data points represent. Figure 7.6 depicts the key features of a line graph.

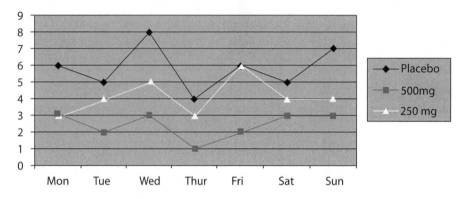

Figure 7.6   Pain Level Sorted by Medication Administered. (Note: Data are fictional.)

Line graphs are created by entering data into a corresponding table, which displays data as points on the line graph along the corresponding x and y axes. Connecting data points allows the reader to see upward or downward trends, or the absence thereof. Line graphs clearly show trends in data and can allow the viewer to speculate on future trends.

Pie graphs
Pie graphs, also known as *pie charts*, are circles divided into segments (see Figure 7.7). You'll find this graphic useful for displaying percentages of a whole. Pie charts must be clearly labeled, and those with many segments requiring excessive labeling may also have a corresponding legend.

Pie charts can misrepresent information when all components are not provided. For example, if a value is omitted, the values of remaining parts can be altered inappropriately. Figure 7.7 would inaccurately represent data if five vacancies in oncology and three vacancies in pediatrics were not reported in the pie chart.

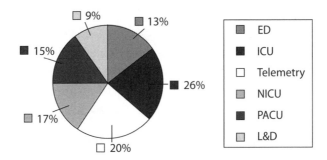

Figure 7.7   Sample pie graph showing hypothetical vacancies on nursing units at a hospital. (Note: Data are fictional.)

Bar graphs

Use *bar graphs* to compare individual groups of data that are discontinuous or categorical or classifying in nature, for example, RN or LPN. Bar charts are divided into columns that provide a visual comparison between two or more variables (see Figure 7.8). They can be displayed in horizontal or vertical orientation.

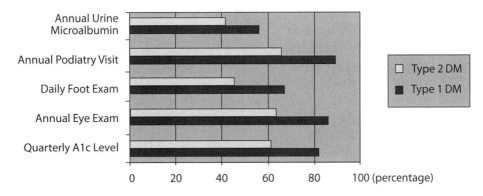

Figure 7.8   Sample bar graph comparing hypothetical compliance with diabetes care measures among samples of individuals with Type 1 and Type 2 diabetes. (Note: Data are fictional.)

Scatter plots

You can use a *scatter plot*, also known as a *scatter gram* (see Figure 7.9), to show the relationship between two variables. This relationship is described as a *correlation*. These images are similar to line graphs in that they allow comparison along vertical and horizontal axes to determine a relationship (*positive* correlation), an opposite relationship (*negative* correlation), or no relationship. The x axis represents the independent variable, and the y axis represents the dependent variable. A perfect positive correlation on a scatter plot is from the origin to high values on the x and y axes (bottom left to top right). A perfect negative correlation on a scatter plot is from a high value on the y axis to a high value on the x axis (top left to bottom right).

How close the points on a scatter plot come to these ideal imaginary directions depicts correlation strength. For example, in Figure 7.9, the data points that represent homocysteine levels for non-Hispanic Whites are clustered more closely together along the line representing the correlation for the group, and the data points that represent levels for Mexican Americans are farther from the correlation line for that group. This tighter clustering results in a stronger correlation for non-Hispanic whites.

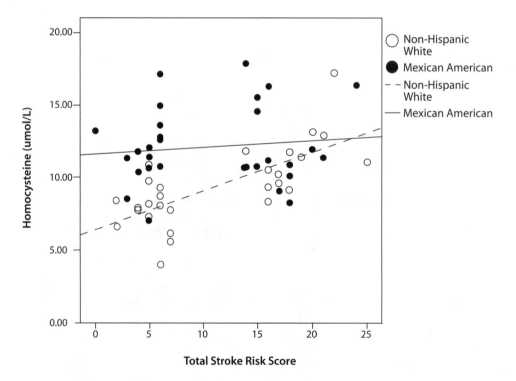

Figure 7.9 Sample of a scatter plot. In C.M. Baldwin et al., "Differences in Mexican American and Non-Hispanic White Veterans' Homocysteine Levels," (Figure 2). *Journal of Nursing Scholarship 39* (September 2007): 240. Reprinted with permission from Wiley-Blackwell, Hoboken, NJ.

Illustrations

There are different kinds of illustrations, including flow charts and diagrams, photos, videos, and created art or images.

Flow Charts and Diagrams

Flow charts or diagrams are also useful ways to visually capture complex information, highlight relationships, or provide instructions (see Figure 7.10). Flow charts that include decision points are also called algorithms.

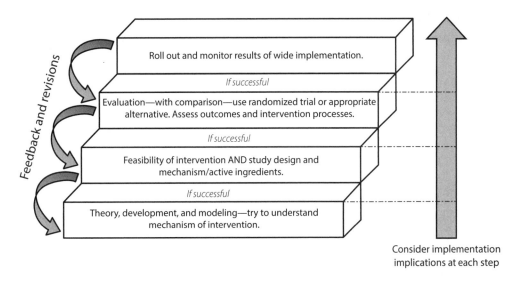

Key steps in developing and evaluating EoLC interventions. Although it is possible to begin at any step in the ladder, it is important to progress development with successful interventions. EoCL, end of life care.

Figure 7.10   Example of a flow chart.

Use illustrations when you want to depict an image for which a photograph might not be suitable or space won't accommodate—for example, if you want to review the anatomical structure of the heart or visually depict the necessary steps to gather a blood sample.

Photographs

Photographs offer an additional dimension that tables, charts, and graphs don't provide. For example, say you want to compare melanoma lesions found among samples of adults in different areas of the country. A chart or table can feature size and stage data, but photographs can show discoloration, margins, and surrounding skin tone. Visuals can also provide information about variables that weren't included in an original study or observation but would be of note to suggest for future studies. Use photo captions to highlight what you want to emphasize. If measurement is important, include a ruler with the illustration.

Here are some tips for photographs that you should keep in mind:

- Pictures should not reveal patient identity.

- Even if the person cannot be identified, you must comply with federal privacy laws (the Health Insurance Portability and Accountability Act [HIPAA]) and institutional policies—don't assume you have the right to take and use images in any clinical setting; doing so puts you and your employer at risk of a HIPAA violation.

- Obtain consent from all subjects in your photographs. You will need to use a special photo consent form provided by the editor. (For more information about copyright, refer to Chapter 11.)

- Obtain permission to use any photographs you didn't personally take. Ask early and plan an alternative in case your request is denied.

- Most publications prefer high-resolution digital images for printing.

- If hard copy photographs are accepted (many publications do not), they must be of high quality.

- If you scan a photograph, follow the software and author guidelines to ensure your file is of high enough quality for printing.

Digital Image Quality

Image quality is crucial. Your photos should be well lit, tightly cropped, in focus, and only include the important objects being discussed (Saver, 2007). Images taken with instant-print cameras (Polaroid) and cellular phones typically have low resolution and aren't acceptable. (Polaroid was once associated only with cameras that instantly produced photographs. However, the company now offers digital cameras that produce high-resolution images acceptable for publication.) You don't have to invest hundreds of dollars in a digital camera, but digital is the most common format today.

High-resolution digital cameras often yield a large file size but the best quality images. Larger image files may pose a problem when submitting them as an email attachment so you may be asked to upload them at a designated website.

Dots per inch (dpi) defines how sharp the resolution of an image is. Images with low resolution will appear distorted or pixilated (have a box-like appearance with jagged edges for text or color transitions instead of smooth lines). Photographs must have at least 300 dpi resolution for the final layout. If images are enlarged, their resolution changes. You can calculate minimum image requirements by multiplying vertical and horizontal size in inches by 300. For example, if an image is to appear in a 3 x 4 inch space, it must have a resolution of at least 900 x 1200 pixels. If you have a 2 x 2 inch space for a photo, it must have a resolution of 600 x 600 pixels. (Resolution requirements for online use of photographs are not as strict.)

Common formats include Tagged Image File Format (TIFF), Joint Photographic Experts Group (JPG/JPEG), and Photoshop Document (PSD). Portable Network Graphics (PNG) and Bitmap (BMP) files are sometimes used in place of JPG/JPEG and TIFF images. Identify the publication's preferred format(s) before sending image files.

Created Images

Graphics can be created in a variety of programs including Adobe Illustrator, Adobe Photoshop, CorelDraw, Microsoft PowerPoint, and Microsoft Excel. Before choosing software for creating the graphic, check to see if it will be acceptable to the publication. Most editors will want you to send graphics in the original file format of the program you used to create it or as a portable document format (PDF) file. Saving PDF documents requires you to have software (usually Adobe Acrobat) installed on your computer.

Technical Tips for Using Images

Here are some tips for using images:

- Publication requirements differ significantly. Check online for author or manuscript guidelines and review graphic requirements *before* you create or identify images you want to use. Ask for a copy of written guidelines if a publication does not post them online.

- Study the publication to identify whether certain colors or color schemes are customary—and then design your photographs to conform.

- For publications printed in black and white or in grayscale, design your graphics to emphasize differences with various shading or fill options. Again, study the publication first to detect any preferences.

- Images may be used in alternative venues. For example, you want to include color images of a wound with a journal article but you discover that it is published in black and white. An online version, however, includes color images. You might be asked to submit the images for the online version. You could alert the reader to additional online content with a callout, such as "To view an online version of this article and all images in color, go to http://www.*sitenamehere*.com."

- Images abound on the Internet, but beware that the vast majority of them are not considered in the public domain. For formal publication, you must find the owner and obtain permission to use any online image within your work, even if you properly cite the source. Some images can be purchased for a fee, but you must pay attention to what permissions are granted. For example, you might purchase an image to use in your manuscript only to find out that you are granted only personal use that does not allow for publication or commercial reproduction in an article or a book.

- Become familiar with sources for free images, including the Public Health Image Library (PHIL) (http://phil.cdc.gov/Phil/home.asp) and the National Institutes of Health (NIH) photo galleries (http://www.nih.gov/about/nihphotos.htm). Although the images are free, you should still credit the source.

- Some content will require you to seek permission through a copyright clearinghouse, an independent company that handles the copyright permission requests for a specific journal, publisher, or organization. Many clearinghouses require a fee to grant permissions, so it is best to seek guidance before you submit a request and pay.

- Keep a sample request template on hand to quickly customize a request (see Figure 7.11).

Q: *I want to include a graphic but have not yet received permission to use it in my manuscript. Should I include it and let the editor know that I'm seeking permission?*

A: Yes, you should let the editor know you have not yet obtained permission. The editor might also be able to suggest a replacement graphic that could be designed by the publication's staff, although this occurs less frequently than in the past because of resource limitations.

Dear Permissions Editor:

RE: Figure 4.1 appearing in Smith, R: *Journal of Nursing History*

I am preparing an article titled "Nursing a Century After Florence Nightingale" ("the Article") shortly to be published in *Nurse.com*, the magazine by Gannett.

I request your permission to reproduce or, if it is necessary, to redraw or modify the material listed below within the article. Permission is requested in any form or medium, in all languages, for distribution throughout the world. Full credit will be given to the original source.

Material requested:

> **Author:** Smith, R.
> **Journal or Book Title:** *Journal of Nursing History*
> **Volume No.:** 24
> **Article Title:** The birth of modern nursing
> **Details of illustration or other material required:** Image of Florence Nightingale caring for soldiers
> **Page No.:** 214
> **Publisher and Year of Copyright:** Sage Publications, 2012

Please insert any preferred credit line.

Sincerely,

Susan Danis, RN
sauthor@internet.com

Figure 7.11   Sample permission email text (or letter).

- Learn how images should be credited and whether permission to use a graphic also allows any manipulation or changes. For example, some images must be displayed with specific verbiage under them and must not be cropped or enhanced in any way whereas others may be displayed as the author chooses. The restrictions depend upon what the owner of the image will allow.

- Don't embed text or insert lines–*callouts*—on your photos. Use a computer program, such as Illustrator or Photoshop, to create an additional layer that contains your descriptions or labels, or simply describe to the editor what you need. Send the unlabeled image along with the labeled image in case adjustments are needed.

- Lastly, you may be asked to provide an image of yourself. Carefully review the style of the publication to determine what type of photograph should be submitted. Most publications prefer a head-and-shoulders image with a solid background and professional attire. Others may accept less-formal images depicting the author in familiar or article-appropriate surroundings. For example, if your article is about nursing on a cruise ship, an image taken in the ship's clinic may be a perfect choice.

Video/Audio

If you're writing for an online publication that incorporates videos or animations, you should consult with the editor for any specific submission requirements for media footage or clips you wish to include with your manuscript. If you are creating or providing information to a site that supports your publication, make sure that you clear the source and permissions for videos you use. Remember that the same rules that apply to photographs also apply to media clips: You must have permission to use them, and you must also have releases from individuals who appear in the media clips.

You may also want to consider video or audio clips for your PowerPoint presentation. The files can be embedded for easy access during your talk.

Q: *What if the publisher granting permission for the figure or table I want to use in my manuscript charges a fee? Who pays?*

A: This varies by publication, so seek guidance before you pay any fees or include the graphic in your manuscript. Some publications prefer to create their own graphics using their design staff rather than pay for outside graphics; others expect the author to pay the fee, which in some cases, may be costly.

Choosing the Right Graphic

It's important to match the graphic to the purpose. Table 7.1 can help you select the right graphic based on the purpose you want it to serve.

Table 7.1   Selecting the Right Graphic Based on Purpose

	Compare data	Provide detailed information	Emphasize numbers	Emphasize trends	Show relationships	Display percentage of a whole	Summarize key points	Provide descriptions	Provide steps or instructions
Table	✓	✓	✓		✓		✓	✓	✓
Line graph				✓	✓				
Pie graph						✓			
Bar graph	✓								
Scatter plot					✓				
Flow chart		✓			✓		✓	✓	✓
Diagram		✓						✓	✓
Photo or video								✓	✓

Combining Figures

Sometimes, you can combine different types of graphics to stress two points in the same space. For example, you can use an image as a background for a text table that provides the steps to complete a procedure. Figure 7.12 combines the data from a table depicting the increase in portion size and calorie count for different snack foods with drawings of those foods to emphasize the increase over time.

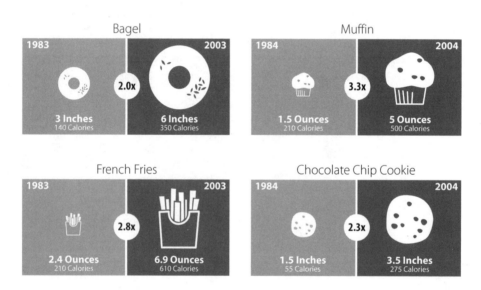

Figure 7.12   Sample mixed media image combining the data from a chart and images of snack food. This image is from a government document in the public domain (Healthy People 2010 – National Heart Lung and Blood Institute (NHLBI).

Q: *Can I embed my graphics in the Word file of my manuscript?*

A: Don't embed graphics within the word processing file of your manuscript. This can reduce image quality, make the file size too big, and eliminate editing options. As discussed earlier in this chapter, remember to use standard naming conventions and also save each graphic as a separate file.

Saving and Submitting Images

Here are some tips to keep in mind when saving and submitting images.

- **Format.** When possible, save your graphics in a format that can be adjusted if necessary for color, shading, size, and font to accommodate style and space limitations. If your graphics can't be edited, your images might not be included or might display with reduced quality.

- **B&W.** Save images containing lines—such as tables, charts, graphs, and drawings—in black-and-white format, not grayscale.

- **Grayscale.** Save images or photographs that contain shading as grayscale format, not black and white.

- **Creation program information.** The more information you provide to a publication about your graphics, the better. Specify what software you used to create the graphic, including the operating system (PC or Mac) and its version, as well as the program name and version. You can often locate this information by clicking the top navigation bar of most programs and selecting Help and then About.

- **Online source quality.** If you plan to use graphics from online sources, contact the publisher or the author of the online source for high-resolution, editable files. Images displayed online are typically inadequate for press-quality publication.

- **High resolution.** It's typically best to make your graphics large and of the highest resolution. Your graphics will be scaled to fit during the journal production process. Enlarging smaller graphics can result in a loss of image quality.

- **Publication guidelines.** Review the publications graphic file size limit (usually found in the Author Guidelines) and don't exceed it.

- **Online storage.** If you routinely send large files or graphics, consider subscribing to a virtual storage service that allows you to upload and share large data. As a last resort, store large images on a portable media device (burning to a CD or DVD, or saving on a data card or flash drive) and mailing them.

Making the Most of Graphics

By including relevant eye-catching graphics in your manuscript, you'll enhance your work and give readers a break from excessive reading. Tables, figures, graphs, illustrations, and photographs enhance communication with fewer words. As with every step of the writing process, it pays to be prepared.

Write Now!

1. Choose a research article and analyze the effectiveness of the graphics.

2. Choose a clinical article and note how the graphics differ. Are they effective?

References

Saver, C. (2006). Tables and figures: Adding vitality to your article. *AORN Journal, 84*(6), 945–950.

Saver, C. (2007). More strategies for enhancing your message. *AORN Journal, 85*(1), 131–134.

"The difference between the right word and the almost right word is the difference between lightning and a lightning bug."

–Mark Twain

Submissions and Revisions

Tina M. Marrelli

Having worked hard on your research, flow, structure, and journal choice, you smile with satisfaction as you click the Save button. Your article is done; your blood, sweat, and tears have been poured into this manuscript submission. Now you're ready to submit this manuscript to the journal editor you met at a conference last year. Or to the colleague who asked you to write a chapter for his or her book. Or to the journal you've carefully researched and chosen. What can you do at the submission stage to be successful?

Or maybe you're at the point where you have already submitted to a prestigious nursing journal and just received the peer reviewer comments on your manuscript. After taking a deep breath, you wonder how you're going to revise the article to boost your chances of final acceptance—when a submission or manuscript becomes an accepted article.

This chapter describes how to successfully navigate any of those scenarios and explains how the submission and revisions process works. Even though the process covered here is typical for peer-reviewed journals, the overall submission and revision process is similar for print and online magazines and books.

WHAT YOU'LL LEARN IN THIS CHAPTER

- It's important to follow the journal's author guidelines when you submit your manuscript.

- Your manuscript will be revised by an editor(s), as well as possibly peer reviewers.

- You'll need to make requested revisions on time and clearly indicate how they were made.

- If you have questions about requested revisions, make the editor(s) your resource.

First Impressions Count

At this point, it's unlikely you have been toiling in a vacuum. You have most likely talked to or corresponded with the editor of the publication you are submitting a manuscript to. In fact, most editors prefer that authors send an email query before a manuscript is submitted. And although the editor has been careful not to guarantee that the journal will publish your manuscript submission, he or she has probably been supportive.

Chances are also high that the editor or publications staff has also referred you to their specific Publisher's Guidelines or journal Author Guidelines. Strictly adhering to the rules within this document is the best way to make your submission shine. Editors want to help prospective authors get published. An easy way to get rejected, though, is when an author obviously didn't take the time to read the guidelines and/or proofread the paper one last time before submission. Think of a submission like a job interview: First impressions do count.

Author guidelines vary from publication to publication, but each have a few common elements you should look for: page count or word count, double-spacing and formatting guidelines, submission requirements for figures and data, and which editorial style guide to follow.

Word Count

Make sure to double-check the word count your article should be—minimum and maximum. For example, say that *Journal A's* guidelines specify that your article be no more than 3,500 words. If your submission is 6,000 words, the editor is faced with either trimming your manuscript to fit the requirements or returning it. Unless you are submitting the seminal research study on a cutting-edge technique, the editor will likely return it to you for editing—or, in the worst-case scenario, simply reject it. If you believe that you must have (a few) more words, first discuss this with the journal editor.

Alternatively, don't shortchange your chances for acceptance by turning in a manuscript far less than the desired word count. The peer reviewers will likely find your article lacking in substance and depth.

 Will an editor really reject my paper just because it's too long?

 Considering the sheer number of papers that most journal editors see, as well as the demands on their time, editors often make the easy decision to eliminate a paper based on length or other formatting error. Editors might assume that you'll give it another try—saving them valuable time—while they move on to another opportunity. And think of it this way: You don't want to give them any excuse to say no.

Properly Styled References

Be sure that your references or citations are current (typically 5 years old or newer unless you're citing a "classic" reference such as a seminal research study), accurate, and complete. Researchers have found inaccuracy rates for references ranging from 22.9% (Oermann & Ziolkowski, 2002) to 41.6% (Oermann, Cummings, & Wilmes, 2001). In the latter study, errors in the titles of articles, chapters, and books were the most common type of mistake, followed by errors in authors' names. More recent research related to nursing journals isn't available, but studies in other healthcare fields have found similar results. A study of five orthopedic journals found an error rate of 41% (Luo, Li, Molina IV, Andersen, & Panchbhavi, 2013).

All journals have a preferred editorial style, with the most common styles being American Psychological Association (APA) and American Medical Association (AMA) style. You can research all style rules simply by searching online by the name of the style. For specific referencing components in APA that may appear challenging, consider consulting "Writing and Reading with American Psychological Association Style" (Marrelli & Stamey, 2013).

Make sure that you're using the preferred style specified in the guidelines and check that each reference has the elements required by the journal's reference style: typically, author name(s), title of article, journal title, year published, volume, issue number, and page numbers. One of the most common mistakes is not including page numbers when citing a chapter within a book. Another common mistake is not including quotation marks on direct quotes.

Tables and Figures

The way in which figures, tables, and data are handled varies from publication to publication. A book publisher might want you to submit these elements as separate graphics with inserts in the text where they go. Online publications might want figures embedded. And journals usually require authors to put tables at the end of the manuscript, with one table on each page. Figures and tables are often created in Microsoft Word, Excel, or PowerPoint. Excel is also often used to create graphs. (You can learn more about figures and tables in Chapter 7.) The most important component from an editor's perspective is that the figures and tables be "called out" in the body of the manuscript submission—for instance, "A partici-patory leadership style increased nurse retention by 20% (Table 2)," or "Figure 3 shows the internal workings of the digestive system."

Submission Checklist

Here are key questions to answer before submitting your article.

Content

- ☐ Am I within 5% to 10% of the requested word count?
- ☐ Did I proofread and spell-check the final submission? (See Appendix B for a proofing checklist.)
- ☐ Is my math correct (for any calculations included)?
- ☐ Does the article support my purpose in writing it?
- ☐ Is the organization logical?
- ☐ Is the tone appropriate for the readership of the journal?
- ☐ Did I correct simple grammar mistakes?
- ☐ If this is a continuing nursing education (CNE) submission, does the content have the depth and specific information needed?
- ☐ Did I give the manuscript to a trusted colleague to read with "new eyes"? And, did I make changes in the areas identified as needing improvement or have a rationale for not making a change?

References

- ☐ Are statements cited in the text as needed?
- ☐ Did I use the correct reference style?
- ☐ Does each reference entry have complete information per the style?
- ☐ Is each listed reference also mentioned in the text?

Tables and figures

- ☐ Are my figures in the correct electronic format for submission?
- ☐ Do the numbers for tables and figures match what is called out in the article?
- ☐ Are the figures complete?

Format

- ☐ Did I write an abstract or summary according to the journal's format (if requested in the Author Guidelines)?

- ☐ Did I include a cover letter or cover email?

- ☐ Have I included a title page with author names and contact information, but omitted names or other identifying information in the actual manuscript?

- ☐ Have I double-checked the correct spellings, credentials, and affiliations for all of my coauthors?

- ☐ Is the manuscript formatted properly according to the author guidelines?

Formal Submission

Not too many years ago, *formal submission* included sending a perfectly double-spaced, printed hard copy of your paper, article, or chapter to an editor. Your piece would be returned to you, sometimes many months later, marked in blue pencil; and then you'd revise, retype, and resubmit it.

Today, the process is much easier because electronic submission has become the norm for most publishers. You can submit electronically a number of ways—and, yes, the Author Guidelines will tell you about those ways.

Most book publishers, magazine publishers, and online publications want their text submitted by email to the editor or managing editor. They will note which word processing program file types they accept. (Microsoft Word is by far the most common.) Figures, tables, and other additional pieces can usually be emailed as well.

Use caution when attaching your files to an email; your Internet service provider (ISP) probably has a limit of how large an attachment can be. If what you attach is too large, your email transmission will fail. As a workaround, use a compression program to "bundle" your files in a tidy, smaller package that your email program can send. You can also use websites that allow you to post your document at no charge; you then enter the email address of the person you want to send the article to. That person receives the notification and downloads the file.

Many healthcare and academic journals require you to submit your manuscript online through an electronic editorial management system. If the journal is published (or co-published) with a major publisher like Elsevier, Wiley-Blackwell, or Lippincott, Williams, & Wilkins, you'll find yourself using a standardized system that enables authors, reviewers, and editors to work with manuscripts online from all over the world.

After creating an account in the electronic management system, you upload your title page, manuscript, abstract, signed copyright transfer agreement, digital artwork, permission for any materials you are using from another source, and other requested items.

Some authors find online submission a little daunting at first, but if you work through the process step by step, it begins to make sense. If you get stuck, chances are that the journal has a staff person who can help you along. The greatest advantage of these automated systems is that you can track the progress of your manuscript submission throughout the review and publication process.

Whether submitting by email or by an electronic editorial management system, know that more publications now require you to submit the following items in addition to your manuscript:

- Title page, including the name of the manuscript, author names and affiliations, and contact information for the corresponding author.

- Signed transfer of copyright agreement.

- Completed author profile form (so that the editor has the correct information for your byline and bio statement at the end of the article).

- Conflict of interest form. (You can learn more about conflict of interest in Chapter 11.)

Many scholarly publications require completion of a form that outlines the areas of responsibility for each author. For example, the author guidelines for *Clinical Simulation in Nursing* state:

> The cover letter should include a statement detailing the work each author contributed to the work. This may include: (1) conception and/or design of the study, acquisition of data, or analysis and/or interpretation of data (2) drafting or revising the manuscript. All contributors who do not meet the author criteria as defined should be included in the acknowledgements section (*Clinical Simulation in Nursing*, n.d.).

Not all publications include an acknowledgments section.

> **Q:** *I just sent my article to the publisher, but I see a passage that I need to revise. Can I resubmit?*
>
> **A:** Check with your editor. It's best to avoid this situation. Submitting multiple manuscripts—or even revised passages, piecemeal—can cause confusion. Keep track of any correction you need to make in a file. Then, when you begin the revisions process, you can make all your changes at one time.

Editorial Review

Editorial workflows vary from publication to publication and from editor to editor. Some like to thoroughly read all submissions right away, and others read quickly to determine if the article is suitable for the next step, then wait until after peer review for a more detailed reading.

If your submission was to a book, magazine, or online publication and won't be peer reviewed, the editor to whom you submitted your work will tell you about the next step. He or she will most likely read through your work, edit it, and then send you notes and the text to revise. Your editor will also give you a deadline and a publication date when your piece might be likely to publish, run, or appear.

Peer Review

When you're submitting a manuscript to a journal that uses peer review, the process is a bit more formal. After an initial evaluation, the editor will usually send your manuscript out for peer review. During the peer-review process, experts evaluate your manuscript against specific criteria such as logic, accuracy, and consistency with the journal's purpose.

Reviewers provide an invaluable and volunteer service to journals, editors, publishers, authors, and readers. A good reviewer clarifies information, identifies missing content, identifies problematic references, suggests revisions when needed, adds headers for clarification, helps connect the dots for readers, and generally improves the manuscript. The primary role for reviewers is to focus on content, which is another reason why manuscripts should be carefully proofread before submission. Reviewers should not have to copyedit or wordsmith your work. You want them focused on the information—not on typos, non-sentences, poor sentence structure, and so on.

In essence, reviewers are another help on your way to being published:

- Peer reviewers are chosen for their expertise in the content area.

- Usually the review is *double blind*: that is, neither author nor reviewer is identified to each other.

- Peer reviewers are either volunteers or paid a small stipend.

- Peer review usually takes about 4 to 6 weeks, depending upon the journal and the reviewers.

- Journals have two to three peer professionals reviewing any one paper.

Q: *What do I do when two reviewers give conflicting information?*

A: Receiving varying comments can be a tough situation. Sometimes, reviewers have different priorities as to what is important for readers. For example, one reviewer might say to expand a section, whereas another says to shorten it. In this case, you have to make a decision as to what you think is best for the reader. If you are unsure, consult your editor. However, reviewer disagreement can also be a sign that your intent is unclear. Think about the possibility of a broader question—What's causing the confusion?—and revise accordingly.

Most peer-reviewed manuscripts need some revision. As succinctly put by Patricia Becker, "Most of us live with a manuscript for so long in the preparation phase that we do not see inconsistencies or omissions that are apparent to a blind reviewer. A primary value of the review process is feedback that assists the author(s) in producing a concise and logically crafted manuscript" (Becker, 2004, p. 379). You can learn more about peer review in Chapter 9, but here are some common questions reviewers are asked to answer:

- Does the manuscript have relevance to clinicians?

- Is the topic timely? Does it have a new or unique slant?

- Is the organization clear and logical?

- Are references used when needed? Are they current?

- Is the manuscript developed in adequate depth?

- Are illustrations, figures, or tables appropriate?

- Was the manuscript interesting to read?

- Is the manuscript innovative or does it provide a better presentation of what is already in the literature?

- Is the title relevant and does it explain the topic?

- What are the manuscript's positive points?

- What are areas for improvement?

The Revision Process

After peer review, the editor reviews the comments and then places your manuscript into one of several categories:

- **Accepted**: The editor might ask for minor corrections, but the paper is ready to publish. It is rare that your manuscript will be completely accepted at this stage.

- **Accepted Pending Revision**: The revisions required are a bit more extensive, but the editor would like the author to address them so the paper can be accepted for publication. This is more common than simply having an article accepted.

- **Revise and Resubmit (R&R):** The author needs to address issues on a broader scale, but there's merit in the research and information. R&R means if the author can address the editors' concern, the editor would like the paper to be reviewed again.

- **Rejection:** Rejection doesn't mean failure. Perhaps the paper isn't a great fit for this particular journal. Make sure to review the notes to see what concerns reviewers and the editor had. Note that not all journals share peer review comments when an article is rejected.

Your editor might use slightly different names from these, but the intent is the same. Sorting manuscripts by category helps keep them flowing back to authors while the editor can still compile an issue based on what is available and ready to publish.

If you have been asked to make revisions, don't give up. It's an exciting day when your editor tells you that the peer reviews are back and then asks you for revisions; if the revisions are satisfactory, you will be in print!

In the case of minor revisions, you will likely be asked to make them after the article is edited or when the article is laid out and ready for publication (sometimes referred to as "page proofs"). If you're making page proof edits, you'll be asked to make your corrections electronically, using a PDF markup program. Don't worry about this part of the process, though; your editor or journal will give you instructions for accessing your pages, making your corrections, and returning them. If you have questions, a production editor or other staff person is typically available who can answer your questions on the phone or via email. Some journals continue to use hard copy page proofs, and not all journals send page proofs to authors. In that case your final review will be when you see the edited copy.

In the case of more detailed revisions (far more common), the editor will send you copies of the actual review forms or a summary of the comments for you to use in making revisions. If you're working in a journal's electronic manuscript management system, you'll receive an email notification that your manuscript is ready for you to log in and "pick up" for revision. Comments might also be embedded in the manuscript. The editor also may call you to discuss the revisions.

Confidence Booster

If you have an idea for a manuscript or a book, don't let someone else talk you out of it! Sometimes you just need to find the right publisher. I (Tina Marrelli) wrote my first book and knew it was needed as I had already shared it with my home care team and some others. It clearly explained many of the complex rules related to home healthcare, and there was nothing else like it at the time. One publisher told me "There's no market for this book." … 25 years later the "Handbook of Home Health Standards: Quality, Documentation and Reimbursement" is in its 5th (2012) revised edition. Since then, I have written more than 10 books and have been the editor of three peer-reviewed publications. The moral of this story: Know your market, keep your passion for what you know and love, and don't let anyone who may not "know enough to know" stand in your way—you can do it!

Consult the publication's author guidelines if you have questions on how to make your revisions, especially if you're asked to make revisions electronically. After you're finished, you're ready to resubmit your work to the editor or through the electronic manuscript submission website.

Make every effort to adhere to the requested due date for revisions. If you know that you cannot make the date, notify the editor as soon as possible. Identify the date when you will resubmit the paper—and then honor that deadline. Editors are working with many issues of journals at any one time. Your manuscript might have been tentatively scheduled (assuming that revisions are accomplished and the article can be accepted) for a certain issue. Journal issues and article "line-ups" are scheduled months in advance for production reasons. Courtesy and ongoing communications are keys for effective author and editor workloads as well as for maintaining positive relationships.

The Emotional Side of Reviews

Reviewer comments should seek to improve papers. Reviewers do this by identifying positive aspects of the submitted article and by listing recommendations that would improve the paper in the revision stage.

That does not mean it's always easy to read the reviewers' comments. The positive ones make your heart soar; negative ones make it plummet to your toes. It can be an emotional roller coaster. And, unfortunately, not all reviewers are as tactful as they should be.

First-time (and even experienced) authors can get discouraged and never make the suggested revisions. That's too bad because being asked to revise—instead of receiving a rejection—is a good sign that the editor is interested in publishing your article.

After you read through the reviews, put them away for a day if you feel frustrated. Then look at them with fresh eyes. The good news is that because you have not read the article for a while, you, too, might see areas for improvement. Put aside your ego and remember that the article is not about you—it's about delivering great information to readers. Think of yourself as part of a team that includes you; the editors; and the peer reviewers, who are experts in the subject matter of the article. Each of you brings a unique perspective, and your article can be improved when you consider these various points of view (Saver, 2006).

Requested Revisions

Making your revisions can include rewriting, reorganizing, adding content, or deleting content (Saver, 2006). Address each comment from the editor (a *query*). If you believe that there is a sound reason not to make a revision or address a query, provide the rationale, preferably evidence-based, to the editor. Remember, however, that you should make changes requested by the reviewers unless you have a good reason not to. Be sure that's the case instead of you just not liking the fact your words were changed. Here are a few examples of the types of comments you might receive:

- Correct or update references.

- Clarify information.

- Check information that the reviewer thinks might be inaccurate.

- Define terms.

- Suggest how the organization of the article could be improved.

- Add a patient case scenario (particularly for clinical journals) or other illustrative examples.

- Note gaps in information (for example, no patient education tips in a clinical article on a surgical procedure).

- Strengthen a paper by adding tables, figures, tools (for example, assessment tips), or more examples.

Most editors will ask you to enter your comments directly into the text, and sometimes, a publication or editor will want you to summarize the changes in a table or in your note back to the editor.

Figure 8.1 shows an example of how to organize your manuscript revisions as a table. Note that the location of each revision is noted.

Request Revision	Revision Made
Explain why you choose to use the Spearman correlation (page 1, 3rd paragraph)	Added rationale for using this text (page 1, 4th paragraph)
Change "24 hours" to "24 to 48 hours" (page 3, 1st paragraph)	Change made
Add a section on Jones' research to the background section (page 3, 3rd paragraph)	Section not added because of word count restraints and because Smith, whose study is already cited, found similar results in a more recent study
Suggest moving signs and symptoms from the text to a table (page 5, 2nd paragraph)	Created table

Figure 8.1   Organizing manuscript revisions using a table format.

Q: *I have really been struggling with revisions to a paper. They seem unclear. I was so excited, but now I'm completely bogged down. What should I do?*

A: Talk with your editor if you're struggling with revisions. Some editors will match a mentor writer with a prospective new author if there is a topic or manuscript that they believe is particularly noteworthy. These mentors might be members of the publication's editorial board or are experienced writers and reviewers who are willing to take the time needed to help a new author navigate the process. Or better yet, seek out a writing mentor of your own: A published colleague might be willing to help you.

About Editorial Boards

Most journals and websites that publish health information have editorial boards, also called editorial advisory boards (EAB). These are experts in the field(s) covered by the publication. Typically the EAB includes members from different geographic regions of the country, practice settings, schools, and so on. They advise the editor on trends in the field and serve as peer reviewers.

When you complete your revisions, ask someone else to read through the manuscript again and use the original submission checklist to be sure that you haven't overlooked anything. Include a cover letter (or a note in the body of an email) that tells the editor how you organized any revisions and any major areas that you did not change because you disagreed with a reviewer. Also put the title of your manuscript in the subject line of the email. If you are using an electronic submission system, follow the instructions for uploading your manuscript.

If you made major revisions to your manuscript or were asked to resubmit, you might have to go back through a second peer review and additional editing. Second round reviews usually occur if more substantive changes were made, including major revisions in the structure, length, organization, style, and/or research/scientific content.

Final Edits

After your article is accepted, the publisher will edit it to fit the publication's style and tone and return it to you for review before or after it is formatted for publication. There might be a few minor queries for you, and your editor will include instructions on how to submit corrections. Scholarly journal editors usually do less major editing than ones working with clinical journals. As with the peer reviews, seeing these changes can be a shock. However, the people who edit your article are experts in what they do and are most familiar with the style and tone of the journal, as well as readers' preferences. They respect you as a content expert, so respect them as editorial experts. Try not to change their edits unless clinical errors have been introduced or your intent has clearly been changed. Once again, it's important to meet your deadline for review.

Q: *My article was accepted a year ago. Today, I got the edited version back with a request to return in 2 days. Isn't this unreasonable?*

A: Ideally, you should have at least 1 to 3 weeks to make revisions. Preferably, you will be told when your article is scheduled so that you have some notice. However, journal schedules change, or, perhaps, your topic has suddenly become a hot issue in nursing. You will be a hero to your editor if you can turn around your reviewed article quickly. But do not be discouraged if your scheduled article gets "held over" at the last minute. This can happen for a variety of reasons within the publishing company and has nothing to do with the quality of your article or the editor's desire to publish it. Page proofs are much more time sensitive; if you're asked to return them in 24 to 48 hours, make sure you do so.

If you feel that your article has been unfairly edited, contact your editor immediately to express your concerns in a calm, rational manner. By maintaining a professional composure, communication channels will likely remain open for a productive dialogue and resolution of the issues.

Q: *When my article is sent to me for a final review after it has been formatted as it will appear in the journal, can I make changes?*

A: After an article is formatted and you see it (in PDF form), it is essentially ready for publication. You should correct only any typos, formatting issues (for example, the items in a table are not lined up correctly), or clinical errors that might have been introduced during the editing process. Not all journals have authors review the formatted version of the article.

Early Online Publication

Most journals now have the capacity for publishing articles online ("online first") before they appear in print, also commonly referred to as "publish ahead of print" or "publish before print" (Sage Journals, n.d.). A significant advantage of early online publication is that information can get out into the professional community sooner—this is of particular importance in the case of cutting-edge research.

When the article is made available online, it is considered "published" because it typically receives a Digital Object Identifier (DOI) number, which registers the article with the DOI Foundation (American Psychological Association, n.d.; Sage Journals, n.d.). This means you cannot make changes to the article, although, of course, corrections can be noted. The article may or may not be subsequently published in the print version of the journal.

Open-access journals also consider manuscripts published once they are posted online because there is no corresponding print copy.

Be Persistent

Everyone who writes started somewhere. To get off to a good start, submit your article according to the journal's guidelines. Use the reviewers' and editors' comments to get your manuscript to the level it needs to be accepted. Don't be discouraged; be persistent.

As stated by Hawkey, "writing is an exacting and exciting activity. Although frequently difficult to get started, it can become addictive with practice. Nursing is in great need of a new generation of challenging authors who are prepared to shake off the shackles of caution and timidity in so many current publications. Writing is a weapon of empowerment as well as a medium for communicating ideas" (Hawkey, 2001, p.66).

Write Now!

1. Pick a journal where you are interested in publishing and review its submission guidelines.

2. To learn more about peer review, visit Elsevier's reviewers resource information page at http://www.elsevier.com/wps/find/reviewershome.reviewers.

References

American Psychological Association. (n.d.). Frequently asked questions about online first publication. Retrieved from http://www.apa.org/pubs/authors/online-first-publication-faq.aspx

Becker, P. T. (2004). What happens to my manuscript when I send it to *Research in Nursing & Health? Research in Nursing & Health, 27*(6), 379–381.

Clinical Simulation in Nursing. Author guidelines. Retrieved from http://www.nursingsimulation.org/authorinfo

Hawkey, M. (2001). Joys, frustrations and concerns of a journal peer reviewer. *Journal of Nursing Management, 9*(2), 65–66.

Luo, M., Li, C. C., Molina, D., IV., Andersen, C. R., & Panchbhavi, V. K. (2013). Accuracy of citation and quotation in foot and ankle surgery journals. *Foot & Ankle International, 34*(7), 949–955.

Marrelli, T., & Stamey, B. (2013). Writing and reading with American Psychological Association Style. *Home Healthcare Nurse, 31*(7), 349-351.

Oermann, M. H., Cummings, S. L., & Wilmes, N. A. (2001). Accuracy of references in four pediatric nursing journals. *Journal of Pediatric Nursing, 16*(4), 263-268.

Oermann, M. H., & Ziolkowski, L. D. (2002). Accuracy of references in three critical care nursing journals. *Journal of Perianesthesia Nursing, 17*(2), 78-83.

Sage Journals. (n.d.). Online first. Retrieved from http://online.sagepub.com/site/sphelp/SageColl_PAP.xhtml

Saver, C. (2006). Decisions and revisions. *AORN Journal, 84*(2), 183-84, 188.

"I love science. I hate supposition, superstition, exaggeration and falsified data. Show me the research, show me the results, show me the conclusions—and then show me some qualified peer reviews of all that."

–Claire Scovell LaZebnik

Writing a Peer Review

Cindy L. Munro

Amazingly, peer review of scientific journals dates back to the 1700s (Lovejoy, Revenson, & France, 2011). Peer reviewers have a crucial role in the publication process. Think of them as watchdogs; they help ensure that published clinical and research articles, which guide nursing practice, are accurate, timely, and useful to readers.

Whether or not you're a published author, consider becoming a peer reviewer. Editors of scholarly journals often depend on peer reviewers for assistance in evaluating and improving manuscripts. Peer reviewer comments influence the editor's decision about whether to accept or reject a manuscript, and provide recommendations about changes required before acceptance.

This chapter gives you the information you need to know for you to feel confident about serving as a peer reviewer, including the role and responsibilities of reviewers and the steps to follow in conducting a review. Don't stop reading if you're an author, but have no plans to become a reviewer. Understanding the perspective of a peer reviewer helps you anticipate potential questions in your manuscript and makes you a better writer.

WHAT YOU'LL LEARN IN THIS CHAPTER

- Peer reviewers are important contributors to the publication process.

- Being a peer reviewer has many benefits and is a skill that can be learned.

- Preparing a review is easier if you go about it systematically.

- A well-done review provides objective, honest, constructive, and specific comments to authors and editors.

Roles and Responsibilities of Peer Reviewers

Editors decide what articles will be published in their journals, and the decision-making process differs among journals. Scholarly or academic journals have traditionally required manuscripts to undergo peer review, and many clinical and other types of journals now require the same. Other types of writing, such as magazines and book reviews, typically don't require peer review. Although the value of peer review has been debated, the process allows the manuscript to receive what the International Committee of Medical Journal Editors (ICMJE, 2013) refers to as "a fair hearing" among the scientific community.

Peer Review Panel

There are many types of expertise, for example, clinical, procedural, methodological, statistical, health system, and very few people are experts in every area! Multiple peer reviewers with a variety of expertise are assigned to the same manuscript so that editors can adequately evaluate the manuscript as a whole. Each reviewer has expert knowledge important to assessing that manuscript. For example, a manuscript on a research study of an intervention to improve the quality of life for patients on dialysis might include a panel composed of reviewers with expertise in research methodology, quality of life, and chronic renal failure. The editor can then read each peer review and evaluate the manuscript as a whole.

The number of reviewers assigned to each manuscript differs among journals, but two to four reviewers per manuscript is most common.

Peer reviewers act as advisors to the editor, and the editor carefully considers their comments, concerns, and recommendations in making a final decision about the fate of a manuscript. As a peer reviewer, your most important role is to help the editor evaluate a manuscript's quality, relevance, and importance.

Peer reviewers provide feedback to authors as well. Editors vary in how they make peer reviewer comments available to authors. Some editors provide the full text of original reviewer comments, whereas other editors prepare a summary of the reviews for the authors. Comments and suggestions made by peer reviewers help authors improve the content of the manuscript. In a study of three nursing journals, 73.8% of authors agreed that peer review provided constructive guidance (Shattell, Chinn, Thomas, & Cowling, 2010).

Benefits of Being a Peer Reviewer

Most journal peer reviewers serve as volunteers, and payment for reviews is not common. Even so, being a peer reviewer benefits the nursing profession and your career (Chichester, 2011; Fulton, 2011).

As a peer reviewer, your expert knowledge helps to improve the quality and accuracy of the articles published, strengthening the *nursing profession*. Your critique enables journals to provide trustworthy and useful information for nursing practice. If you are an author who expects peer reviewers to be available for your manuscripts, or a clinician who values high-quality information in nursing practice, you should be prepared to contribute to the publications process as a peer reviewer.

Selection as a peer reviewer for a highly respected journal is a recognition of your expertise, which can enhance your *career*. List peer review activities on your curriculum vitae or resume to document your service to the profession. Preparing peer reviews hones your ability to critique, and your own writing will benefit from your suggestions to others about how to improve content and clarity of presentation.

How to Become a Peer Reviewer

Editors use a variety of methods to identify potential peer reviewers. Your publications or presentations demonstrate that you are an expert in a topic, so many editors search publication databases, such as PubMed and the Cumulative Index of Nursing and Allied Health Literature (CINAHL), and specialty conference proceedings to find new reviewers. Some editors permit authors to suggest names of potential reviewers, usually in the case where only a small number of experts have knowledge of the information.

Q: *What if I want to be a peer reviewer, but no one has contacted me?*

A: You don't have to wait for an editor to "discover" you; you can volunteer! Connect with editors at professional conferences or by email to let them know you're interested in volunteering as a peer reviewer. Briefly describe your expertise and why you think you are a good match for the journal. And be sure to provide a curriculum vitae or resume documenting your experience and accomplishments.

Most journals maintain a list of qualified individuals who have expressed interest in serving as peer reviewers. If the editor invites you to register in the journal's reviewer database, do so. When you register, you'll be asked to identify in what content and methodological areas you are an expert. Choose carefully, as editors will use these categories to match your expertise to submitted manuscripts for review assignments. It's better to choose fewer categories where you have in-depth expertise, rather than many categories where you have less depth of knowledge (Lovejoy, Revenson, & France, 2011). Be certain that all of your information is correct, complete, and reflects your true abilities. Don't be dismayed if you do not immediately get an invitation to perform a peer review; it may be some time before a submitted manuscript matches your qualifications as a reviewer.

Considering an Invitation

You'll typically receive an invitation to be a peer reviewer by email. The invitation will give you some information about the manuscript (usually the title and abstract or a description of the article). The full manuscript is usually provided only after you have agreed to review. The invitation will also provide the timeline for submitting your review. Although journals vary in the time allotted for peer review, 2 to 3 weeks is a common deadline. You'll be asked to reply, either accepting the invitation or declining, within a relatively short deadline; if you cannot serve, the editor will need to quickly invite others.

Consider two questions when deciding whether to accept the invitation:

1. **Do I have the expertise to do a comprehensive and fair evaluation of the submission?** To answer this question, read the abstract or description included in the invitation to determine whether you have the expertise needed to fairly evaluate the paper. Is the topic something you know a lot about? Is there a particular aspect that is similar to your interests and experience? Remember that you don't have to be an expert in every aspect of the topic. If you don't think your expertise is a good match, decline the invitation. If you aren't clear about why the editor thought you would be the right expert to review the submission, you can ask for clarification before you accept or decline.

2. **Can I return the review within the time allotted?** Consider realistically whether you can meet the requested deadlines. Delays on your part will extend the entire length of the review process, which will be frustrating for both editors and authors. If it's unlikely you can complete the review on time, you should promptly decline.

Editors will appreciate your honesty if you cannot take on a review assignment, and it will not deter them from inviting you in the future.

Preparing to Be a Peer Reviewer

As you prepare to be a good peer reviewer, you establish ground rules for your behavior. Strive to be objective, honest, constructive, and specific. Be respectful and compassionate in composing your final comments—commit to writing reviews that you would want to receive if you were the manuscript's author.

 What resources can I use to prepare myself to be a peer reviewer?

 No matter where you fall on the continuum of peer reviewer expertise (reviewing your first or 101st article), consider tapping into resources available to help peer reviewers improve their skills. These include

- The Committee On Publication Ethics (COPE, www.publicationethics.org)
- Enhancing the QUAlity and Transparency Of health Research (EQUATOR, www.equator-network.org)
- Online tutorials from journals and publishers
- Workshops at professional conferences

Being *objective* demands that you focus on the manuscript you are reviewing and look at it on its own merits. Make a commitment to give every manuscript a fair chance and to keep your review fact based. Objective peer reviewers do not make assumptions about the author, do not let perceptions about the authors influence their judgment, and do not make any hostile, personal, or derogatory comments about the author (Garmel, 2010).

Do your best to be *honest* in your evaluation, identifying both the positive and negative aspects of the manuscript. As you review a manuscript, it may be tempting to think, "If I had tackled the problem this manuscript describes, I would have done things differently." You need to focus instead on what the author reports. The author's approach might be an acceptable alternative to how you would have done things. If you think the work is flawed, say so, but resist the impulse to redesign a project that has already been completed or suggest revisions that can't be accomplished without time travel.

Make your comments *constructive* and *specific*. Providing constructive comments doesn't mean ignoring problems, but where possible, offer potential suggestions for correcting the deficiencies. The more specific your comments are, the more helpful they will be to editors in evaluating the manuscript and to the author in improving it. In the following example, most authors would find the revised comment to be more helpful than the original.

> **Original comment:** Add more information about the educational intervention.
>
> **Revised comment:** Additional information about implementation of the educational intervention should be presented to help readers better evaluate the outcomes of the intervention; it is also critical to replication of the study or adoption of the strategy in clinical units. How were unit champions chosen? Did the PowerPoint presentation have accompanying audio, or did it consist of slides only? Was technology for viewing the PowerPoint easily accessible in all units to all nurses? What degree of saturation was achieved with the PowerPoint presentation (proportion of staff who saw the presentation)? How frequent were the "regular" inservice sessions, and were they conducted on all shifts?

Ethics of Peer Review

Ethics in peer review are just as important as ethics in nursing practice. The COPE Ethical Guidelines for Peer Reviews (2013) provide a good overview of ethical principles related to peer review.

As a peer reviewer, you will see unpublished material that is entrusted to you with an ethical obligation for confidentiality. Never share a manuscript you are reviewing with anyone (ICMJE, 2013). You must never use information you obtain during peer review for your own (or anyone else's) advantage nor against anyone. You must not reveal any details from the manuscripts before the journal releases the information, and you must not discuss peer-review details with anyone (COPE, 2013; Council of Science Editors, 2012; ICMJE, 2013).

Types of Peer Review

Although the process can vary slightly from journal to journal, this section describes the basics of peer review. Journals have different approaches to anonymity of authors and reviewers during the peer-review process. Concealing identities during the review process is known as "blinding." Levels of blinding include double blind, single blind, and open review (Elsevier, n.d.).

Double Blind

In a double-blind review, which is the most traditional approach, neither reviewers nor authors know each other's identities. Any information that could identify the author is removed from the manuscript that is sent to reviewers, and the author's name is not revealed to reviewers. Conversely, authors are not told names of the peer reviewers, and reviewers must be careful not to inadvertently or intentionally reveal who they are to authors. Double-blind review is designed to minimize any positive or negative bias reviewers might have if they know the author's identity, to encourage frank critique of the manuscript, and to maintain the editor's control over the review process by preventing authors from directly engaging (or challenging) reviewers.

Single Blind

In single-blind reviews, information that identifies the author is permitted so reviewers can include an assessment of the author's qualifications and past accomplishments in evaluating a submission. The identities of the peer reviewers for the submission are not shared with the author. Single-blind review is often used in evaluating requests for funding, where details about the investigator and environment are critical to the appraisal of the project, but it's not commonly used in peer review of journal manuscripts.

Open Review

An open review is just what the name implies: Reviewers know authors' identities, and authors know who the reviewers are. Reviewers may be asked to sign the review, and some journals publish comments by the reviewers alongside the author's paper. Proponents of open review believe it holds reviewers more accountable for their remarks than the blind-review process does. Journals may select open review to promote intellectual exchange and discussion between authors, reviewers, and readers. Open review is uncommon in nursing publications, however.

As a peer reviewer, you'll want to know the level of blinding that governs the review process for the journals you serve. You can usually find this information in the Author Guidelines and Reviewer Guidelines that the editor will send you, or you can it find online at the journal's website.

How to Conduct a Peer Review

You have received and accepted your first invitation to be a peer reviewer. Now what? First, mark the due date on your calendar and plan adequate time to complete the review! Then read the journal's instructions to reviewers and familiarize yourself with any review forms the journal requires. Many journals now use web-based editorial management systems; if you will need to submit your review electronically, test your username, password, and ability to access the system, and complete any web-based system training needed to learn how to navigate the system. Now you're ready to begin.

Confidence Booster

"I never thought of myself as an 'expert.' Then one day I received an email from the editor of a national nursing journal. She had found my name because I spoke on repair of ruptured aortic aneurysms at my specialty association's national meeting and wanted me to review a manuscript on aortic aneurysms. I wasn't sure if I could do it, so I asked for the guidelines. They seemed clear enough, and I had the time, so I did the review. Several months later, I saw the article in print! Even though I couldn't tell anyone I was the reviewer, I felt proud. I did a couple more reviews, and the next thing I knew I was writing my own article. And…it was published!"

–A published nurse author

First Steps

After providing you with reviewer instructions and information on accessing the web-based editorial management system, the editor will provide you with access to the full manuscript in an electronic file. Begin by reading the manuscript straight through, from start to finish. Your goal in this first reading is to get a general impression of the manuscript; you don't need to take any notes or write any comments at this point. As you read, consider the writing style, tone, and readability of the manuscript. Is it written similarly to recent articles that the journal has published? Do you think it fits with what the journal's readers expect? Assess the overall presentation and readability of the manuscript. Does it make sense? Is it understandable? Is it interesting?

On rare occasions, as you read through the full manuscript, you may discover that there is some reason you should not be a peer reviewer for this particular manuscript. For example, you may realize that you provided consultation on an earlier draft. If you think you have potential conflicting interests, or any other concerns about your ability to review the manuscript objectively and honestly, seek advice from the editor. If at any time during the review you have ethical concerns about the manuscript (for example, it has substantial similarity to a published article, or you suspect misconduct may have occurred), you should immediately tell the editor. The editor will investigate the situation; even if you can identify the author, you should not personally investigate.

Critique Positives, Problems, and Potential Improvements

Now, return to the manuscript and use a systematic approach to critiquing specific sections. As a rule, manuscripts of any type have three broad sections: an *introduction* that provides background information, a *body* that has specific information the author wants to convey, and a *discussion*. Use these broad headings for the overall organization of your notes about the manuscript.

These three sections will differ depending upon the type of article. For example, research articles usually have a background section, a methods section, a presentation of results, and a discussion. The format for how-to clinical articles and for case studies varies from journal to journal. In your notes, add subheadings for the section titles specified by the journal to your main sections of introduction, body, and discussion.

Start with the introduction, and leave the abstract for last. You will be better able to judge how accurately the abstract portrays the manuscript if you complete your critique of the introduction, body, and discussion beforehand. As you read each section carefully, make three groups of notes about each section: *positives*, *problems*, and *potential improvements*. The following includes examples of questions you might ask as you take notes on each section of the manuscript.

Evaluate the Components of a Manuscript

These questions can help you evaluate each component of a manuscript.

> **Introduction.** The introduction should prepare the reader to understand the body of the manuscript.
>
> - Does the background set the stage for the rest of the story?
> - Does everything in the introduction relate to what comes after?

- Is there any unrelated or unneeded information?

- Is the literature current and concisely synthesized so that the importance of what has already happened is clear?

- Is the purpose of the manuscript clear?

Body. The body of the manuscript should be the main focus of the article, and is the section where the author conveys new information.

- Is the body complete and understandable to the reader? Tailor your assessment to the specific subheadings of the journal.

For articles that describe activities the author conducted, such as research, quality improvement projects, or case studies, ask the following:

- Is it clear why the activities were done, and what the expected outcomes were?

- Are the concepts and variables identified and defined?

- Is it clear what was done, and how?

- Were the methods described appropriate to the clinical or research problem, and are the reliability and validity of the methods discussed?

For how-to manuscripts, ask the following:

- Are the procedures and underlying rationales clearly presented and completely explained?

- Are indications and contraindications stated?

After you have answered the questions about what was done and how it was done, proceed to review what happened next.

- How were decisions made about whether the activities were successful or not?

- Were statistical methods used, and if so, were they appropriate for the data?

- Are the clinical or research results understandable?

- Do the figures and tables help you to understand the manuscript?

- Are figures and tables clear, and is all of the information necessary?

- Is the body of the manuscript aligned with what you expected to find based on the introduction?

Discussion. The discussion should summarize the major points of the manuscript and put the new information in context.

- Is the new information placed in the context of what is already known?

- Are the conclusions valid?

- Are limitations identified and discussed in enough detail?

- Are the implications for clinical practice discussed?

References. Now that you have reviewed the article, turn to the references.

- Are they current and appropriate?

- Are there too few or too many?

- Are any important references missing?

Depending on the journal, the editor might tell you that you should evaluate a manuscript based on specific reporting guidelines that have been developed by a national consortium. This occurs more commonly with research or quality-related manuscripts. For example, CONSORT (Consolidated Standards of Reporting Trials) guidelines are used for reporting randomized clinical trials (CONSORT, 2010), and SQUIRE (Standards for QUality Improvement Reporting Excellence) guidelines are recommended for reporting quality improvement projects (SQUIRE, 2008).

Wrap-Up

After your step-by-step review of the positives, problems, and potential improvements in each section, return to a more general assessment. Based on your initial reading and your detailed review of each section, is the manuscript likely to be of interest to the journal's readers? Does it address an important topic? Does it provide new information? Is it well reasoned, well written, and well organized? Are there any ethical issues?

You began your journey with this manuscript by reading the title and abstract in the invitation to review. Return there to finish your notes about the manuscript. Ask the following:

- Does the information in the abstract match what the journal requires in an abstract?

- Does the information in the abstract match the rest of the manuscript?

- Does the title accurately describe the content, and would the title help you find this content if you were searching for it?

You're now ready to use the notes you've taken on the positives, problems, and potential improvements for each section to write your review.

Write Your Review

Begin with an opening paragraph that gives a short, two- to three-sentence synopsis of the manuscript. Then, give your overall opinion of the manuscript, based on the notes from the general assessment you did following the step-by-step review of sections.

Summarize the major positive aspects. State the most important problems you've identified, how serious you think they are, and whether it's possible for the author to fix them. Major problems that cannot be fixed are fatal flaws—be objective and honest in identifying them and explaining why you think they are unfixable.

Here is an example of how a well-written review starts:

> This manuscript reports results of an educational intervention for nurses to increase backrest elevation in ICU patients, using a pre-intervention comparison to aggregated unit data. The manuscript is likely to be of high interest to the journal's international readership, and the topic is well matched to the journal.
>
> While the manuscript is generally well done, I have several major concerns. First, the researchers do not carefully explain the limitations of the pre- and posttest design used. Second, there are instances in which literature central to the manuscript is not correctly or completely cited; I believe this is a critical problem that must be addressed in a revision of the manuscript. Third, additional information about the educational intervention will be crucial to readers. Fourth, the discussion should include alternative explanations for the findings.

Next, summarize your notes for each section of the manuscript; you can present your positives, problems, and possible improvements as bullet lists under each section heading. Address any suggested changes to improve figures and tables.

Before you submit your review, read it carefully—and check for spelling and grammar errors. The author may receive your comments exactly as you wrote them. The written comments should be consistent with the ground rules for peer reviewer behavior—objective, honest, constructive, and specific.

Submit Your Review

You are now ready to submit your review! The written critique you've prepared is submitted as your comments to the author. Don't put recommendations about acceptance or rejection in the comments to the author; remember that the editor may share these comments in their entirety with the author. Some journals will also ask you to give a numerical score for each section of the manuscript and for the manuscript overall; in that case, the journal will provide information about how to use their numerical scoring system.

Q: *After reviewing the manuscript, I have some comments for the editor that I do not want to be shared with the author. What's the best way for me to send these?*

A: In addition to the comments to be shared with the author, you may provide confidential comments to the editor; these confidential comments will not be shared with the author. You do not need to repeat anything you have already written in the comments to the author, as the editor already has those. If the journal uses an electronic submission process for reviews, there is usually an area for submission of confidential comments to the editor on the submission website. If not, you can simply email the editor confidential comments that expand on your impressions or specific concerns. Be sure to note in the email that you do not want the comments shared with the author.

Also, you should indicate your recommendation regarding publication. You can include this recommendation in the confidential comments to the editor. Publication recommendations are usually given in one of these categories:

- **Accepted**. No modifications are needed. This is the rare case of a perfect manuscript with not a single problem identified or suggestion for improvement. The manuscript will still undergo editing before publication, and the author will need to respond to editorial queries.

- **Accepted Pending Revision**. A few improvements are suggested, but the changes are not essential.

- **Revise and Resubmit**. More substantial revisions are needed. (Many journals combine conditional accept and revise into "accepted pending satisfactory completion of revisions" or "revisions needed before a publication decision can be made.")

- **Rejection**. The manuscript has fatal flaws, or the problems are too extensive to be fixed by a revision.

Instead of writing a peer review, some editors have you complete a review form that asks you to respond to questions. Instead of yes or no, you might be asked to respond based on a rating scale.

Sample questions include the following:

- Is the information relevant for the readers of the journal?

- Does the manuscript provide new information or insights?

- Is the information accurate?

- Is the information current?

- Is the information complete?

- Is the manuscript well written and organized?

- Are figures and tables clear and useful?

- Are references included as needed?

- Are key references missing?

- Are the clinical applications of the manuscript described clearly?

Additional questions for a research study might include these:

- Does the introduction and background identify the problem and review the literature sufficiently?

- Are the methods appropriate for the research question and are they explained?

- Are the results clearly presented in the text or supporting tables or figures?

- Does the discussion section explain why the results are important and where they fit in the literature?

- Are study limitations included?

You also will usually have a space to provide general comments.

Feedback

It's always helpful to get feedback to improve your performance as a peer reviewer. After the editor has made a decision about the manuscript, the other peer reviewers' comments may be shared with you. You can see how congruent your assessment of positives, problems, and possible improvements was to the other reviewers, and learn from positives and problems they identified that you might have missed. If your comments differ from theirs, however, do not assume that you did not do a good review. Reviewers' comments routinely differ when their areas of expertise are different, and editors welcome a variety of perspectives to inform editorial decisions.

You can also ask the editor to provide you with feedback; some journals provide reviewers with annual evaluations of their performance. The most positive evidence of your peer review skills is an invitation to do another review!

Write Now!

1. Make a list of the three topical areas where you are an expert and provide evidence of your expertise in each area (for example, certification, presentations, publications, clinical experiences).

2. Contact the editor of a journal that publishes articles in your areas of expertise and ask about serving as a peer reviewer.

References

Chichester, M. (2011). Peer review: A service to your profession. *Nursing for Women's Health*, 15(6), 535–538. doi: 10.1111/j.1751-486X.2011.01686.x

Committee on Publication Ethics (COPE). (2013). COPE ethical guidelines for peer reviewers. March 2013, v.1. Retrieved from http://publicationethics.org/files/Ethical_guidelines_for_peer_reviewers_0.pdf

CONSORT. (2010). The CONSORT statement. Retrieved from http://www.consort-statement.org/consort-statement

Council of Science Editors. (2012). CSE's white paper on promoting integrity in scientific journal publications. Retrieved from http://www.councilscienceeditors.org/i4a/pages/index.cfm?pageid=3639#232

Elsevier. (n.d.). Peer review. Retrieved from http://www.elsevier.com/reviewers/peer-review

Fulton, J. S. (2011). In praise of reviewers. *Clinical Nurse Specialist*, 25(5), 215–217.

Garmel, G. M. (2010). Reviewing manuscripts for biomedical journals. *The Permanente Journal, 14*(1), 32–40.

International Committee of Medical Journal Editors (ICMJE). (2013). Recommendations for the conduct, reporting, editing, and publication of scholarly work in medical journals: Roles and responsibilities of authors, contributors, reviewers, editors, publishers, and owners: Responsibilities in the submission and peer-review process. Retrieved from http://www.icmje.org/roles_c.html

Lovejoy, T. I., Revenson, T. A., & France, C. R. (2011). Reviewing manuscripts for peer-review journals: A primer for novice and seasoned reviewers. *Annals of Behavioral Medicine, 42*(1), 1–13. doi: 10.1007/s12160-011-9269-x

Shattell, M. M., Chinn, P., Thomas, S. P., & Cowling, W.R., III. (2010). Authors' and editors' perspectives on peer review quality in three scholarly nursing journals. *Journal of Nursing Scholarship, 42*(1), 58–65.

SQUIRE Standards for Quality Improvement Reporting Excellence. (2008). SQUIRE guidelines summary. Retrieved from http://squire-statement.org/guidelines

> *"The skill of writing is to create a context in which other people can think."*
>
> *–Edwin Schlossberg*

Publishing for Global Authors

10

Susan Gennaro

In the global world of the 21st century, we can communicate easily across geographic boundaries and time zones using everything from phone calls to text messages. Although time and space no longer curtail our ability to communicate, global authors for whom English is a second language still face publication barriers (Belcher, 2007).

Certainly, many native English authors wish to publish in international journals of different languages. However, most articles in the hard sciences are published in English, and more than 50% of all articles published globally in the health sciences are in English (Guardiano, Favilla, & Calaresu, 2007). In this chapter, you learn the implications of English as the language of science, the barriers to publication for nonnative English–speaking authors, and strategies for breaking down those barriers.

English and Science

English is the common language of the scientific community. The number of scientific articles disseminated in English has increased over the past 10 years in English-speaking countries, such as the United States. English has been adopted by the scientific community in the European Union; increased numbers of journals globally

WHAT YOU'LL LEARN IN THIS CHAPTER

- Global authors make a particularly important contribution to science.

- Global authors face unique challenges in selecting appropriate journals and in understanding ethical international standards.

- Language barriers are expensive for authors and journals alike. They not only increase time to dissemination as well as cost for authors who must obtain language help, but they can also cause difficulty for editors.

now publish in English, and there is a global increase in the number of students learning English as a second language (Kaplan, 2001).

Although English language predominance in science has some disadvantages, including the likelihood that dissemination of scientific findings in non-English journals is slowed (Stolerman, and Stenius, 2008), English is currently the language of science just as Greek, Arabic, and Latin were historically the language of science (Castillo, 2009).

Q: *How did English come to be accepted as a global language of science? It doesn't seem fair.*

A: World War II hastened the transformation of English as the common language of science because some of the victor nations (notably, England and the United States) were English speaking. Some strong non-English-speaking countries with deep backgrounds in science (such as Germany) had longer recovery periods. The growth of computers and computerized databases in English-speaking countries in the latter half of the 20th century helped spur the growth of English. Is it fair? No. But it is a reality of getting your research published.

Having a common language for science makes it easier for scientists to communicate with each other and to build on the work of others around the world. Multilingual authors can enrich global science by making important scientific work available to English-only journals (Flowerdew, 2008).

The problem is that too many journal reviewers (and some editors) have difficulty reading a manuscript for the quality of its *science*—not the quality of its *language*. Instead of focusing on the science, they are too easily distracted by grammatical issues resulting from writing English as a second language. Grammatical problems with language should not be the focus because they can be addressed in the review process. Problems with the actual science of your manuscript are less easily fixed but do not result from language barriers.

Whether the fact that English is the language of science in the 21st century is positive or negative for the future development of science has been much discussed (Tardy, 2004), but the dominance of English as the language of science isn't likely to change anytime soon. Certainly, reviewers and editors need to do more to be supportive of nonnative

English–speaking authors, but you can also improve your publication success rate by understanding the global barriers that you can control. You might find your work rejected by English-language journals for any of the following reasons:

- Misinterpreting a journal's mission and/or submitting your paper to the wrong journal
- Language barriers
- Value differences in the scientific newsworthiness or significance of your research
- Lack of a common understanding of scientific rigor and methodology
- Technology barriers such as outdated versions of word processing programs, making it difficult for editors and authors to exchange files

This chapter discusses how to overcome these barriers, helping both you—as an author—and editors of English-language journals understand some of the differences inherent to global authors and their work.

Fitting Your Work to a Journal's Mission

It has become increasingly easy for an international author to submit a paper to a journal in another country. Author Guidelines that clearly state a journal's preferences regarding manuscript style and length are readily available online, and most journal editors are easily accessible by email. You can read the Author Guidelines to find the type of topics of interest to the editor, and then simply send an email to inquire about possible publication. Most manuscripts are now submitted either by email or through electronic editorial management systems.

However, you won't get to manuscript submission unless you do some upfront research and consider how the mission of a journal fits with your topic.

Examine the global literature before submitting your idea to an editor. Develop excellent search strategies; look for databases that yield references of a global nature; and, in short, develop a thorough understanding of the global state of knowledge on a topic. This research will help you cast the topic in a global light, thus making it more likely to be published. There's an added benefit: You will learn about journals that might previously have been outside your scope of reading.

> **Q:** *There have been no articles published on my topic of interest in my country although research has been done on this topic in other countries. Would a manuscript on this topic be of interest to an international journal?*
>
> **A:** Publishing articles on knowledge that is already widely accepted globally might be of interest to journals in that specific country but are generally not of interest to global journals.

You'll usually find the journal's mission printed in its first few pages and on its website. For example, the mission of the *Journal of Nursing Scholarship* is

> ...to advance knowledge to improve the health of the world's people. We are therefore, most interested in receiving manuscripts that provide new knowledge designed to improve nursing practice globally. (Author Guidelines, 2013)

That mission tells you what would—and would not—interest that journal's readers. Take a look at some examples.

> Smoking cessation in African-American inner-city youths in California
>
> Social support and perceived health quality of life among Turkish women

The mission refers to "the health of the *world's* people" and "knowledge designed to improve nursing practice *globally*." Both sample topics seem to address regional, not global, issues, so they might not be a good fit.

However, if the manuscript on smoking cessation in African-American inner-city youths provides new information about a novel intervention to improve smoking cessation that can be used by nurses in other countries, the article is much more likely to be published than is a study that provides knowledge that can be used only in the United States or that can be used only for a specific population.

Authors need not only to know about the mission of a journal, but must also consider the quality of a journal. The advent of open-access journals has created many more avenues for publishing scientific work, but not all journals are of equal quality. It may be difficult for global authors to assess the global reputation of a specific journal, but bibliometric indices (which help determine the impact of a particular journal), circulation numbers, and information about the electronic databases in which journals are indexed are all measures of quality.

Although journal impact factors are not the only measure of quality, it's one important indicator as to whether your manuscript is being published in an English language journal that other scientists actually read (Baron, 2012). Ensuring that your work is being published in a journal that is indexed in electronic databases such as MEDLINE or Cumulative Index to Nursing and Allied Health Literature (CINAHL) makes your work accessible to other researchers—if others can't find your work, the impact of that work will be severely limited. (You can learn more about selecting a journal in Chapter 3.)

Q: *I keep getting emails from journal editors asking me to submit my work to their journal. It makes sense to me to submit to a journal that wants to publish the work of scientists for whom English is not a first language. Is there any disadvantage in publishing in one of the journals that has contacted me?*

A: Check if the journal is listed in reputable indices such as CINAHL or in the *Journal Citation Reports*, which lists the impact factor (a measure of the number of times articles in a specific journal are cited by others based on the number of articles published by the journal). If a journal to which you would like to submit is listed, you are safe in proceeding. Not being listed doesn't mean the journal isn't high quality, but it signals that you should be cautious and explore a bit more. Ask about the number of subscribers, or, in the case of online journals, the frequency of article viewings; the peer review process; and the organization funding the journal. Note that it takes a few issues before a new journal can be indexed.

Writing in a Second Language

For authors who use English as a second language, the burden of needing to read as well as to write in English is a barrier in global dissemination of knowledge (Belcher, 2007).

An important strategy for overcoming this barrier is to avoid writing first in your native language and then translating to English (Svavasdottir, 2008). Writing in English from the start supports clarity of the flow of ideas, and the syntax and the construction of your points are more likely to be understood by an English-speaking audience. For authors who use English as a second language, language nuances and stylistic differences—more than grammatical differences—can result in authors not making effective arguments.

Poor word choice, for example, can be distracting to reviewers and create problems with reviewers understanding the science in a particular article. Some examples of inappropriate word choices include essence of life (quality of life), conscious consent (informed consent), and initial prevention (primary prevention) (Rezaei-Adaryani, 2012). Here are ways you can decrease problems with translation and poor word choice:

- Compare word choices in your manuscript with word choices from your references.

- Choose someone to translate who is experienced as a translator and who translates medical or nursing text.

- Have a native English speaker who is familiar with word choices read your manuscript (Rezaei-Adaryani, 2012).

Another option to improve communication in scientific writing is to include scientists who are native English speakers as part of your research team. It's not always possible to have a native English speaker who is geographically close, but with current technology, it has become increasingly possible to belong to a scientific community that is not geographically bound and in which some members of the community have better facility with English and can serve as coauthors and help with developing a manuscript in English (Belcher, 2007).

Q: *I have had no luck publishing in English-language journals. Reviewers do not mention language issues in discussing my manuscripts, but they often speak about idea flow. I am not sure what they mean.*

A: There are cultural differences in logic and how ideas are presented to make a scientific case. Try reading a lot of different articles from the journal to which you plan to submit and outlining how logical flow is developed. Use this outline of logical flow in developing your own outline for your manuscript. Reading for style, use of subheadings, and length is also helpful in developing a polished manuscript.

Other factors that authors writing in a second language need to consider are value differences, scientific rigor and methodology, technology barriers, and ethics.

Tips for Authors

Here are some tips for nonnative English–speaking authors:

- Work with a native English speaker to develop an outline for your manuscript.

- Set your word processing program preference to English so that you can use the spell check and grammar check features.

- Ask for peer review from others before you submit your article. Some universities have programs where English-speaking students who engage in peer review for authors whose native language is not English can get extra credit in course work (C. Pottsdaughter, personal communication, October 16, 2009).

- Find grammatical help, if possible. Although it can be difficult to locate and expensive, some authors can find resources, such as English tutors, at their local universities.

- Choose the journal where you would like your article published. Before and while you write, review several articles from that journal to get a sense of style, flow, and word choice. Following the same general style of subheadings, length, and flow will help you write an article that is more recognizable (and, therefore, more easily reviewed) by reviewers and editors.

- Check with the editor whether he or she provides any additional support for authors who have English as a second language. For example, the *Journal of Nursing Scholarship* provides copyediting support for particularly promising manuscripts. *Nursing Research* provides a list of vendors providing language editing services, but does not endorse them and encourages authors to seek out other vendors (n.d.). Some publishers supply language editing services for a fee; search online using the term "English language editing" services.

- Work with colleagues who are native English speakers to develop an outline for the manuscript. Often, there are cultural differences when presenting scientific arguments. Native English speakers can help to ensure the points that need to be made are placed in the manuscript in a way that is understandable to English speaking readers and that points are made with a proper degree of forcefulness to ensure they are understood by the global scientific community.

- Use web-based services, such as online dictionaries (oxfordonline.com) and online translation services (cucumis.org). As with all translation services, the expertise of the translator in terms of knowledge of the language and the science impacts excellence. Translation services are best used for small numbers of words.

Understanding Global Value Differences

Significance in research is the understanding of the real meaning of a research study. Defining significance means getting beyond the simple facts and understanding *why* the research is important and the potential impact it could have. Globally, nurses are conducting significant research, but explaining that significance is often challenging. Cultures can see these values differently. A nurse from Russia might see a different relevance than a journal editor or peer reviewer from the United States. Until one can understand what an English-language journal audience finds relevant, this value difference can cause a barrier to publishing for foreign authors.

Try supporting the significance of the study you're writing about by explaining how global leaders—such as the World Health Organization or the Institute of Medicine—have framed the topic. Understanding it in global terms can help a reviewer understand the significance of a problem that might not be common in the geographic area in which they live.

In a study of editors, Flowerdew (2001) found that *parochialism* (viewing your topic too narrowly in your geographical area) was a barrier for multilingual scientists that kept them from getting published. If you do not describe the significance of your work beyond your local context, peer reviewers will likely not find the work you do to be significant. To combat parochialism, define the global significance from conceptualization of your research project, long before you've thought of where you'll publish. Communicate with international colleagues with an interest in a similar area of research, and examine how your study will fit into the needs of the global community. These international conversations are key components in developing quality research projects and will also help ensure that the significance of a study is framed so that multiple communities understand its value.

Q: *What specific help do journals provide to authors with English as a second language?*

A: Resources vary by journal. For example, the *Journal of Nursing Scholarship* has a list of writing resources available on its website, including those available through the journal's publisher. Journals often work closely with editorial board members around the globe to identify local resources where they exist, some with global pools of reviewers who are also helpful in reading for science, not language. Others can spend additional editing resources on particularly promising manuscripts before they are resubmitted for further review.

Scientific Rigor and Methodology

Another difference stemming from global cultures can have to do with scientific methodology. Flowerdew (1999) suggests that qualitative research might be harder than quantitative for nonnative English speakers to publish in English. The nuances of meaning used to analyze qualitative research can be much more difficult for nonnative English writers to convey.

In either case, you need to understand standards of scientific rigor. Scientists have developed "gold standards" for research methods and data analysis. If these aren't used, reviewers often raise questions about the adequacy of a manuscript (Kaplan, 2001).

In nursing, the areas of scientific rigor most likely to be omitted are:

- Information in support of sample size and sample selection

- Information about how design is most appropriate to answer research questions

- Information about the validity and reliability of data collection methods (quantitative studies) or the trustworthiness of data collection and analysis (qualitative studies)

To ensure that reviewers understand the rigor of a particular study, include specific information that justifies sample size and sample selection and provides information about the rigor of the methodology and the appropriateness of the design to answer the research question. (Refer to Chapter 14 for more information on writing a research article.)

Overcoming the Technology Barrier

For scientists in less-developed countries, technology can provide its own barriers by the lack of consistent function or lack of availability. As Salager-Meyer (2008) points out, there are more phone lines in Manhattan than in sub-Saharan Africa; and in some areas of the world, electronic submission processes are exclusionary (rather than inclusionary) because they make it difficult or impossible for those with technologic barriers to contribute manuscripts.

The reality is that journals are increasingly migrating to online-only submission platforms and online content management systems. These systems cut down on turnaround time and errors as editors in diverse geographical locations can work on multiple issues at once.

The accessibility of technology should continue to improve for developing nations. Partnerships with colleagues at universities who can assist around the world may be one way to overcome these issues.

Ethics in Publishing for Writers With English as a Second Language

Ethics in publication do have some cultural determinants, so it's helpful for authors to periodically read the guidelines of the Committee on Publishing Ethics (COPE), which are available at http://publicationethics.org/resources/guidelines. Although there is universal agreement about the dishonesty of falsifying data, an area that might be a more significant ethical consideration for authors with English as a second language is duplicate publication.

Almost all journals have access to software that provides information on how much of a manuscript is word for word the same as other online sources. Writers for whom English is a second language might find that duplicating the language of other scientists in their field improves clarity. However, too often words are copied and the source of these words is not identified. If authors are going to use the words of others, they need to use quotation marks and adequately reference these words. If duplication between a submitted work and the work of others is found by an editor, the manuscript is likely to be rejected or the ethics of the author are likely to be questioned. (You can learn more about the ethics of publishing in Chapter 11.)

Confidence Booster

In all disciplines the numbers of manuscripts from nonnative English speakers being submitted and being published is rising (Annual Meeting Reports, 2008). Your manuscript might be one of those rising numbers; taking into account the concepts in this chapter will increase the likelihood of your success.

Pathway to Success

Communication within the scientific community is key for the success of global authors. When English is your second language, you can help ensure your paper's success by building teams of scientists with different strengths and abilities, including facility with different languages. After your study begins, pay attention to what journals might be a good fit for dissemination of your findings.

When you begin writing a manuscript, use some of the tips in this chapter to help you through the process. Research and submit your work to journals where editors and reviewers are likely to understand the importance of global scientific diversity.

Writing in English takes additional time for nonnative speakers and costs additional money. Many nonnative English speakers have difficulty making claims for their science with the same authority that native English speakers do. The resulting differences in language construction in manuscripts might make a difference in how reviewers judge the work of nonnative speakers (Guardiano, Favilla, & Calaresu, 2007).

The need for nonnative English speakers to publish in English-language journals isn't likely to change soon. Just remember that persistence is a necessary attribute for all authors who are ultimately successful in being published (Uzener, 2008). When English is your second language, that same persistence can result in the satisfaction of seeing your name in print and sharing your information with the world.

Write Now!

1. Identify a topic for a current article. Then go online and identify global publications on this topic.

2. For your next upcoming project, identify global scientists who could help you plan the project so that global considerations are met.

References

Annual Meeting Reports. (2008). English-as-an-international-language authors (formerly non-native-speaking authors) in science deserve programmatic assistance. *Science Editor, 31*(5), 152.

Author Guidelines. (2013). In *Journal of Nursing Scholarship*. Retrieved from http://onlinelibrary.wiley.com/journal/10.1111/%28ISSN%291547-5069

Baron, T. (2012). ABC's of writing medical papers in English. *Korean Journal of Radiology, 13*(Suppl 1). S1-S11.

Belcher, D. (2007). Seeking acceptance in an English only research world. *Journal of Second Language Writing, 16*(1), 1–22.

Castillo, M. (2009). English as an international language: Web-based help. *American Journal of Neuroradiology, 30*, 857–858.

COPE guidelines. (2013). Guidelines. Retrieved from http://publicationethics.org/resources/guidelines

Flowerdew, J. (1999). Problems in writing for scholarly publication in English: The case of Hong Kong. *Journal of Second Language Writing, 8*(3), 243–264.

Flowerdew, J. (2001). Attitudes of journal editors to nonnative speaker contributions. *TESOL Quarterly, 35*(1), 121–150.

Flowerdew, J. (2008). Scholarly writers who use English as a second language: What can Goffman's stigma tell us? *Journal of English for Academic Purposes, 7,* 77–86.

Guardiano, C., Favilla, M. E., & Calaresu, E. (2007). Stereotypes about English as the language of science. *AILA Review, 20,* 28–52.

Kaplan, R. B. (2001). English: The accidental language of science? In U. Aamon (Ed.), *The dominance of English as a language of science: Effects on other languages and language communities* (pp. 9-20). Berlin: Mouton de Gruyter.

Nursing Research (n.d.). Language editing services. Retrieved from http://journals.lww.com/nursingresearchonline/_layouts/1033/oaks.journals/editservices.aspx

Rezaei-Adaryani, M. (2012). Letter to the editor: Advice for non-English authors writing for international nursing journals. *International Nursing Review. 59*(1), 4.

Salager-Meyer, F. (2008). Scientific publishing in developing countries: Challenges for the future. *Journal of English for Academic Purposes, 7*(2), 121–132.

Stolerman, I., & Stenius, K. (2008). The language barrier and institutional provincialism in science. *Drug and Alcohol Dependence. 92,* 1–2.

Svavasdottir, E. (2008). Publication for authors with English as a second language. Paper session presented at the meeting of the Sigma Theta Tau Research Congress, Singapore.

Tardy, C. (2004). The role of English in scientific communication: Lingua franca or Tyrannosaurus rex? *Journal of English for Academic Purposes, 3*(3), 247–269.

Uzener, S. (2008). Multilingual scholars' participation in core/global academic communities: A literature review. *Journal of English for Academic Purposes, 7,* 250–263.

"Writing is thinking on paper."

–William Zinsser

Legal and Ethical Issues

Nancy J. Brent

Writing an article, chapter, or textbook, and then seeing your work in print is an exciting experience. Although not nearly as exciting, you also must be aware of legal and ethical issues related to writing, just like you are aware of legal and ethical issues in your daily practice, for example, ethical issues surrounding end-of-life care. The most important legal concern for an author is compliance with United States copyright law. Ethically, consistency with established ethical principles for writers is essential. In some cases, such as confidentiality and plagiarism, legal and ethical issues overlap.

This chapter gives you an overview of copyright law and selected ethical issues you need to know to make your writing experience as easy as possible, while keeping a steady eye on your legal and ethical responsibilities.

This chapter is not intended to be legal or other specific advice. Should the reader need specific advice, he or she should seek guidance from a professional.

WHAT YOU'LL LEARN IN THIS CHAPTER

- When using another's work in your work, you need to obtain the proper permission.

- When you write, don't plagiarize, and avoid intentional redundant writing of any kind.

- If necessary, declare to your editor any conflict of interest that might affect the published work.

- In your work you should take care to maintain the privacy and confidentiality of all individual information used.

- Regardless of the publication you are writing for, always adhere to publishing ethics.

Copyright and Permissions

New—and even experienced—authors often have questions about copyright. Although copyright law can be complex, some basic information will help you sort out what you need to know.

What Is a Copyright?

Generally, a *copyright* is a legal protection for original "works of authorship fixed in a tangible medium of expression, whether published or unpublished" (U.S. Copyright Office, 2006). This legal protection allows a creator of a work of art, literature, or other work-like ideas the right to control how that work is used (Fishman, 2011). Creators can be authors, photographers, artists, poets, and even nurse researchers. The U.S. Copyright Act of 1976 protects artwork, photographs, novels, sculptures, computer software, magazine articles, book chapters, songs, and more. Remember that copyright refers to works that are in print, online, or in any other format.

Establishing a copyright grants the author certain rights. Defined as a recognized and protected interest, a violation of which is unlawful (Garner, 1999), copyright rights protect your work from unauthorized use, including duplication rights (copying the work), economic rights (selling the rights, receiving royalties), and rewriting or adapting the copyrighted work in some way (Fishman, 2011).

A copyright protects a work against *infringement,* which occurs when someone uses the work without the expressed permission of the creator, like incorporating a table from a copyrighted article into another article without the permission of the copyright holder.

This United States Act does not protect everything. For example, facts, ideas, systems, or methods of operation are not eligible for copyright (U.S. Copyright Office, 2008). However, for writers, the Act protects what is important: namely, the words with which a writer expresses ideas and facts (Fishman, 2011).

How Do I Obtain a Copyright?

In most cases, you don't need to file for copyright after your work is created. In short, a work is protected after it is written down, typed into a computer, or dictated.

Q: *Do I need to copyright my work before I submit it to a publisher for publication?*

A: No. If your work is accepted for publication with a journal, magazine, or book publisher, your publisher will have you sign a transfer of copyright from you to the publisher, but you do not need to formally obtain copyright ahead of time. Obtaining copyright beforehand can cause problems with the contract and possibly your pay rate. If you are publishing the work, for example, on your blog, you may want to consider identifying your copyright parameters through Creative Commons, a nonprofit organization.

Q: *My publishing contract says that my article is "Work Made for Hire" and that the publisher owns the copyright. Can I reuse any of the material?*

A: Work Made for Hire is work that the publisher has contracted from you. Upon completion and acceptance of your work, the publisher owns it—and can, in fact, edit it, repurpose it, and even republish it. Depending on the type of work, writers may sometimes earn more for creating this sort of content because they can't reuse it. Bottom line is that writers who enter into this type of arrangement will not retain the copyright, and they will have to contact the publisher to obtain permission to reuse the material.

In some instances, a creator of a copyrighted work might want to independently register his or her work with the Copyright Office (U.S. Copyright Office, 2006): for example, when the author wants to make the public aware that he or she is indeed the holder of the copyright. Registration can take place with the use of hard copy forms or through the U.S. Copyright's Office online at http://www.copyright.gov/eco. The eCo Online System is fast and available 24 hours a day (U.S. Copyright Office, 2013).

Registration of the work also opens the door to allowing attorney's fees and statutory money damages under the Act if the work is infringed upon and the creator decides to sue.

Q: *I wrote a nursing story about my experience as a student nurse and then shared it with a colleague. Imagine my disappointment when I saw my words appear as part of an article that she published in a student magazine. Do I have any recourse?*

A: Your options can be discussed with you when you consult with an attorney who practices Intellectual Property Law, which includes Copyright Law. The attorney can provide specific advice with an evaluation of the exact way in which your words appeared in the published article. Anytime someone uses your words without your permission, you should seek legal advice to protect your work. Remember, too, that before sharing any work with another, your copyright designation should be placed on the writing.

Do I Need a Copyright Notice on My Work?

A copyright notice on any work is optional for works created after March 1, 1989 (Copyright Clearance Center, 2005b), but many authors include a copyright notice, especially when distributing their material to an audience during a presentation or to the public under other circumstances, for example, as an online blogger.

The copyright notice consists of three elements and can be used in any of the following forms (Bitlaw, 2013):

Copyright 2014 Jane Smith.

Copr 2014 Jane Smith.

© 2014 Jane Smith.

Unfortunately, some people erroneously believe that if it's online, it's in the public domain, which, of course, is not true. In fact, materials online, whether in the form of a blog, an article, or research findings, are protected by copyright law. The Digital Millennium Copyright Act and its Title II, the Online Copyright Infringement Act (OCILLA), was passed by Congress in 1988 to apply copyright law and infringement to online materials (Mabelson, 2012). Through its establishment of, among other things, safe harbors for Internet providers who "transmit, cache, store or index" online content and procedures for the identification and removal of online material that is an infringement of a copyright owner's exclusive rights, courts have used OCILLA to protect Internet providers and exclusive copyright holders of their materials (Mabelson, 2012).

In short, you must obtain permission for text, artwork, photographs, figures, and any other created content, whether online or in print (U.S. Copyright Office, 2012). In addition, if you are unsure, you should assume that work published after March 1, 1989, is protected under the Copyright Act.

Q: *What are copyright rules related to social media such as Facebook?*

A: It's important to note that copyright law applies to Facebook entries. When you upload material to Facebook, for example, you retain the copyright to your material and grant Facebook a license to use and to display it. You can learn more about your intellectual property rights and responsibilities when using Facebook by going to its Statement of Rights and Responsibilities at https://www.facebook.com/legal/terms and its Intellectual Property page at http://www.facebook.com/legal/copyright/php.

Twitter is also regulated by copyright law through the application of Title II of the Digital Millennium Copyright Act discussed previously. Twitter's Help Center contains information on its Rules and Policies and guidelines concerning copyright law at http://support.twitter.com/articles/15795-copyright-ind.dmca-policy#.

The world of social media changes quickly, but keep in mind that if new tools supplant Facebook and Twitter, you still need to be aware of copyright issues.

Individual copyright holders and publishers may specify how the permission should be listed. Publishers always include a copyright notice on the copyright page of a book or journal, such as Copyright © 2014 by Sigma Theta Tau International.

Q: *How do I find the publisher of a book or an article?*

A: For a book, look on the copyright page, which should follow the title page in the front of the book. In the case of a journal or magazine, this information might be located on the back of the Table of Contents page of the specific issue or on the inside of the front or back cover of the journal.

Many publishing houses and authors also place on the published work an additional caveat to the reader. The warning is another way to alert the reader that the work is copyrighted and should not be infringed upon. An example of such a caveat is

> No part of this work may be reproduced or transmitted in any form or by any means, electronic or mechanical, including photocopying, recording, or any storage and retrieval system, without the express permission in writing of _____ .

Q: *I recently used photos for a presentation that I found on the Internet under a Creative Commons license. These were OK to use, right?*

A: Not necessarily. Creative Commons is a nonprofit organization that gives individuals and organizations a way to grant copyright permission to their creative work. The creator can choose from six main licenses, ranging from "all rights reserved" to "some rights reserved" to "no rights reserved" (in the public domain). Typically you will be able to click a logo, button, or icon (see Figure 11.1) to access the copyright parameters, or you can review the parameters on the Creative Commons website (Creative Commons, n.d.).

Figure 11.1   An example of a Creative Commons logo.

Copyright and Publishing

After you sell or release your work to a book or journal publisher, you may retain your copyright. However, in most cases, you will be asked to transfer the copyright of your work to the publisher. To do this, you must guarantee the publisher in writing that you have the right to transfer that copyright in its entirety. The two types of copyright transfer are *exclusive* and *assignment/all rights transfer* (Fishman, 2011).

An *exclusive* copyright transfer occurs when one or more rights of the copyright holder are transferred while others are retained (Fishman, 2011). For example, you may transfer to *American Nurse Today* the exclusive right to publish your article on a new relationship treatment option for the first time in the United States and Canada but retain the right to republish that article as one of the chapters in your doctoral thesis. *American Nurse Today* owns the specific right to publish the article; you, as the author, retain remaining rights, such as republishing or creating a derivative work, not transferred to the journal (Fishman, 2011).

In contrast, an *assignment* or *all rights transfer* occurs when you, as the copyright owner, transfer all your rights of the copyright to a single publisher (Fishman, 2011). The publisher then owns all rights of the copyright; you, as the author, no longer hold any of the rights of the copyright. This is the more typical arrangement in nursing publication, including books.

Regardless of the type of transfer, the holder of the copyright can exercise its options with the manuscript in print form or electronic form. As a result, *American Nurse Today* can print your article in its journal or on its online publication.

Q: *How long does copyright protection last?*

A: Copyright protection doesn't last forever; the copyright exists for the life of the author plus 70 years. There are lots of exceptions and caveats to the rule, but the copyright could outlive you! Copyright is considered an asset and can even be assigned to your heirs as part of your estate.

Some authors are hesitant to relinquish copyright to a publisher because they don't understand why the publisher needs it. Consider that the publisher provides services such as editing, design, production, distribution, marketing, and sales. The copyright protects the publisher's assets. In addition, the copyright transfer usually includes a statement that the author's name will always be associated with the work.

The Scholarly Publishing and Academic Resources Coalition (SPARC, n.d.) has published an addendum that authors can consider asking the publisher to add to the traditional author agreement. The addendum is designed to help authors retain certain rights to articles. Based on anecdotal reports at this time (no formal information is available), publishers are resisting this initiative, so it's unclear how widely the addendum will be used, particularly in nursing literature.

As an author, before signing a transfer of copyright, you might want to have it reviewed by a nurse attorney or another attorney with a concentrated practice in intellectual property.

Some publishers will also license the copyright over a period of time, such as the life of the book. When the book is out of print, you might be able to request that your copyright be returned to you if you'd like to republish the book or repurpose the content. Check your book contract for more details.

Noncompete Clauses

Publishing original works can result in a financial windfall for publishers. Publishers also want to decrease, insofar as possible, any competition with these works. As a result, many publishing houses are now requesting that authors not only transfer all copyright rights to them but also include in the publishing agreement a covenant not to compete (Gerhardt & Kjervik, 2008). Many of these covenants are quite broad, and, in theory, they can last as long as the length of the copyright the publisher owns upon transfer by the author (Gerhardt & Kjervik, 2008).

In the nonpublishing world, covenants not to compete are often challenged due to their broad scope and the length of time mandated by the covenant. As an example, let's say a nurse employee was hired as a vice president of clinical services at Hospital A. The employment agreement at Hospital A includes a provision that the nurse employee not compete with Hospital A by taking the same or similar job at a competitor's facility for 10 years and in a geographic locality within 50 miles of Hospital A. Such a restriction on the right of the former nurse employee to seek and obtain employment would not be upheld by most courts. Although there may be a reasonable restriction on where the former nurse employee can work for a reasonable amount of time, an overly broad restriction on his or her right to continue employment is seen as preventing lawful competition.

Unfortunately, challenges to publishing agreements that contain overly broad and overly restrictive time frames are not as common. As a result, publishing houses are fairly free to craft a covenant not to compete to suit their specific interests and at the expense of those of the author.

As a prospective published author, read any covenant not to compete carefully, and, if possible, negotiate with the publisher to make it more "balanced" (Gerhardt & Kjervik, 2008). Although one purpose of being a published author is to have your work widely disseminated, an objective shared by the publisher as well, you don't want to foreclose future publishing opportunities (Gerhardt & Kjervik, 2008).

Also important to determine is what state law will apply if there is a challenge to the covenant not to compete? Most often the "choice of laws" provision in any contract will state which state law will be used if there is a challenge to the covenant or to any other provision of the publishing agreement. Some states have no statutes or case law governing covenants not to compete whereas others have strict requirements that are reviewed if a covenant is challenged. Knowing what the law is in the selected state where the laws will be applied is essential.

If you think you are not able to handle the negotiations to obtain a more balanced covenant not to compete, consult with a nurse attorney or another attorney whose practice is in intellectual property.

Permissions and Citations

What happens when you're writing, and you want to use and credit copyrighted material from another work? The most common form of attributing copyright ownership in a writing product is through a citation of the material. A citation should include the author's name, the date of publication, the name of the work, the city where published, the publisher's name, and specific page numbers. The permission of the author or publisher is not needed when citing another's work this way.

If, however, a large part of another's work is needed in your article, or you want to include a form developed by a nurse researcher in your commentary on the article, then you must obtain the permission of the original author to include the material.

To do so, contact the copyright owner. If the owner is a publishing house, you can check the publisher's website for a permission request section where such requests are handled automatically. Many publishers now use a third-party company, such as the Copyright Clearance Center (http://www.copyright.com), to process requests. If you can't find the information, contact the publisher by email or telephone and ask for the permissions department.

Most often, publishing houses have specific online forms that are used to grant permission to reprint portions of an article or a table, and the forms contain clear directions as to how the credit for the article section or table must appear in your article. You'll be notified by email whether your permission request has been granted or denied. Be sure to save that email as evidence that you have obtained permission.

If the publisher does not have an automated system for permission requests, simply send a request that includes the specific information as shown in this example:

Sample Permission Email Text (or Letter)

Subject line (or at top of letter): Permission request for *Today's Nursing Journal* ◄—— Immediately state the purpose of your communication.

I am requesting permission to use Figure 1, Nurses Who Are Self Employed, which appeared in the May 2013 issue (Volume 5, Number 5) of *Today's Nursing Journal.* ◄—— Give complete citation information.

The figure will be included in an article I am writing on the self-employment of nurses for *The Nurse Entrepreneur.* ◄—— Explain how the information will be used.

If you agree to extend permission, please sign below and fax this letter to me at [fax number] or sign electronically and return to me via this email.

If you have any questions, I can be reached at 555-811-1212 or s.brown@somewhere.com. ◄—— Give multiple ways you can be reached.

Sincerely,

Shirley Brown, MSN, CCRN

—— This is an example of what you might have the person granting permission sign with hard or electronic signature.

I/we hereby grant *The Nurse Entrepreneur* permission to reprint and adapt Figure 1, Nurses Who Are Self Employed, which appeared in the May 2014 issue (Volume 5, Number 5) of *Today's Nursing Journal.* ◄——

—— Some publishers want the source to be referenced in a specific way, for example: From *Today's Nursing Journal*, May 2014. Copyright Name of Publisher. All Rights Reserved.

Please insert any preferred credit line: ◄——

Approved (print and sign name)/date: ◄——

—— You may not always receive signed permission. In that case, save the email in your files; the publisher will want to see documentation that shows you have permission for the reprint.

If the owner is an individual, you must contact the person and obtain written permission. You might be able to find his or her contact information in the written document (e.g., Professor of Nursing, University of XYZ), or you might have to find the person through public sources. Two such resources are the Author's Registry (www.authorsregistry.org) and the University of Texas searchable database WATCH (Writers, Artists and Their Copyright Holders, http://tyler.hrc.utexas.edu) (Fishman, 2011). Of course, you can also simply search for the author on a major search engine such as Google. In today's highly connected world, chances are you will be able to find the person.

Here are some other things to remember about permissions:

- The publisher might have restrictions on how the permitted use occurs. For instance, it might grant permission only for the first edition of a textbook, or permission might not extend to electronic forms of the textbook.

- The publisher might charge a fee for use of the material. Check the author guidelines or with your editor about who is responsible for the fee. Unfortunately, in response to the chronic problem of people using material without permission, fees have increased in recent years.

- Individuals who own copyrighted material may also use their own forms for granting permission to use their work. Many of the same aspects of these forms are similar to those used by publishing companies.

Fair Use and Public Domain

Two major exceptions to the requirement of obtaining permission to use another's work in one's own include the *fair use doctrine* and those works considered to be in the *public domain.*

The *fair use doctrine* identifies various purposes for which the reproduction of a work can be considered fair. Included in the list are news reporting, teaching, research, criticism, and comment (U.S. Copyright Office, 2009).

The fair use doctrine (U.S. Copyright Office, 2009) also describes four factors that a court considers in determining whether a use is fair:

- The purpose and character of the use, including whether the reproduction is commercial or for a nonprofit educational purpose

- The nature of the copyrighted work

- The amount and essential nature of the portion used in relation to the copyrighted work as a whole

- The effect of the use upon the potential market for, or value of, the copyrighted work

Fair use, then, is most often a short excerpt of a work and proper citation to the author is essential (Warnock, 2012). However, what is and is not fair use is not always easy to determine. Therefore, always seek permission from the copyright holder if you have any doubt whether the copyrighted material fits into this doctrine.

Copyright and Copying

Teachers, speakers, or others may not copy articles and/or distribute them in any way, including electronically, for students in their courses without obtaining the permission of the holder of the copyright. This prohibition includes "coursepacks " composed of required reading materials for a particular course. Courts have held that such duplication and distribution is not "fair use" under the Copyright Act.

Q: *It's considered fair use as long as it's fewer than 500 words, right?*

A: The 500-word-rule is a common misconception regarding fair use. In fact, a short sentence could be considered an infringement if it were so important that it would preclude anyone from referencing or purchasing the original work. Song lyrics, movie lines, and poetry are also problematic from a fair use standpoint. Avoid their use when possible—and when in doubt, request permission.

A second exception to the requirements of obtaining permission is the *public domain doctrine,* which states that any work not protected by copyright is in the public domain (Fishman, 2012). Public domain works include any works for which the copyright is lost, has expired, or was not renewed. It also includes anything published or funded by the government. Because there is no copyright protection, the public can use the work in any manner it chooses. You still need to properly cite the work.

Q: *My study was funded by the National Institutes of Health (NIH). How does that affect copyright?*

A: Investigators who are funded by the NIH must submit an electronic version of their final, peer-reviewed manuscript to the National Library of Medicine's PubMed Central upon acceptance for publication. The full text of the article will become publicly available no later than 12 months after publication in a journal (Stanford, n.d.).

Note that there are several ways to identify works in the public domain. All governmental publications are public domain works, for example, the Medicare and Medicaid website (http://www.cms.gov) lists the publications of this federal agency. Such agencies also place on the publication the fact that it is a public domain publication and can be reproduced and copied without permission but must be properly cited.

Nongovernmental publications in the public domain can be found in many sources, including Public Domain websites, such as www.publicdomainresource.com. A comprehensive resource is Stephen Fishman's (2012) *The Public Domain: How To Find And Use Copyright–Free Writings, Music and More.* The text includes chapters on "The Internet and the Public Domain" as well as "The Public Domain Outside the United States."

A Few Words for Teachers

Although not an exception to the Copyright Law in the same way that fair use and works in the public domain are, The Technology, Education and Copyright Harmonization (TEACH) Act, passed in 2002, provides a balance of the perspectives of the copyright owners and users, in addition to providing guidance for how accredited, nonprofit educational institutions and some governmental agencies use copyrighted material (Copyright Basics: The TEACH Act, 2005).

The TEACH Act's purpose is to allow the presentation and display of copyrighted materials for distance education by any enrolled student wherever the student is located. To allow an enrolled student access to copyrighted material that can be stored, copied, or digitalized by that student, the institution must adhere to specific requirements, some of which include:

- Be accredited.

- Be nonprofit.

- Use the materials as part of mediated instructional activities.

- Limit use to a specific number of students enrolled in a particular class.

- Use the material only for "live" or asynchronous class sessions.

- Do not transmit textbook materials, class materials "typically purchased by students," or works developed explicitly for online uses (Copyright Basic: The TEACH Act, 2005a).

TEACH does not allow for commercial document delivery and does not extend to coursepacks. In addition, the Act does not supersede the doctrines of fair use or existing digital licensing agreements (Copyright Basics: The TEACH Act, 2005a).

A full list of the requirements of the TEACH Act can be accessed at www.copyright.gov/legislation/archive/.

Ethics of Publishing

Ethics can be defined as rules of conduct recognized in a particular group or class of human actions (Ethics, 2013). Ethical principles govern every aspect of researching, writing, and publishing your original work. Two ethical areas of concern are authorship and conflicts of interest.

Authorship

Although the concept of authorship sounds straightforward, in the real world of publishing, it is not. Authorship makes explicit both the credit and the responsibility for the content of published articles (International Committee of Medical Journal Editors [ICMJE], 2013; World Association of Medical Editors [WAME], Policy Statement: Authorship, 2007).

Authorship should include all those who have made a substantial contribution to the article (WAME, 2007). ICMJE's "Recommendations for the Conduct, Reporting, Editing, and Publication of Scholarly Work in Medical Journals" (2013), which are used by many medical and nursing journals, recommend authorship be based on these four criteria:

- "Substantial contributions to the conception or design of the work; or the acquisition, analysis, or interpretation of data for the work; AND

- Drafting the work or revising it critically for important intellectual content; AND

- Final approval of the version to be published; AND

- Agreement to be accountable for all aspects of the work in ensuring that questions related to the accuracy or integrity of any part of the work are appropriately investigated and resolved."

In short, authorship presents an honest account of what took place during the development of the article, chapter, or research (WAME, 2007).

There are two main ways a person or persons can falsely state authorship. The first is listing names of individuals who took little or no part in writing the article (*gift authorship*). The second is leaving out the names of those individuals who did take part in the writing of the article or having one individual compose the entire article with the author having no input (*ghost authorship*) (WAME, 2007). Most publications prohibit ghost authorship, where the person who wrote the article is not acknowledged. All contributors should be acknowledged, including biomedical writers or editors who may help you craft your manuscript (American Medical Writers Association [AMWA], 2003).

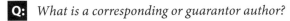 *What is a corresponding or guarantor author?*

A: Although all authors involved in a work take responsibility for the accuracy and integrity of a completed manuscript, the corresponding or guarantor author deals with correspondence with the editor and publisher and with issues that might arise after the work is published. This author's name usually appears on the published work as the corresponding author with a statement that any questions be directed to that individual. You should choose a corresponding author before writing begins.

If you're working with others to develop and write the results of your research or to draft an article for publication, avoid potential authorship issues by discussing the issues of credit for the work before you begin and then documenting your decisions in writing. For example, who will be the lead author? How will the authors be listed? Who, if anyone, needs to be acknowledged for his or her help with the finished product, even though they are not contributing to the actual writing? All authors should agree that there will be no gifting of authorship or any type of ghost authorship. If you have any doubt about who should or should not be listed as an author on your manuscript, consult with your editor.

Some publications ask authors to list the contributions of each author for a manuscript, with some publications listing the contributions in print.

Conflicts of Interest

In the world of publishing, a *conflict of interest* exists when a divergence occurs between an individual author or authors' interests (competing interests) and his or her responsibilities to scientific and publishing activities so that a reasonable reader may question whether the author's published product—for example, chapter, blog, or article—was motivated by that competing interest (ICMJE, 2013; WAME, 2009). Conflicts can be personal, financial, commercial, political, religious, or academic (WAME, 2009).

For example, say that you are writing an article on a new model of nursing that has gained wide acceptance. You detail its many accomplishments in terms of staff morale and patient care. You do not disclose to the publisher, however, that you received financial support for developing the model. When this fact is discovered, the entire article, your credibility, and the publisher's integrity are brought into question.

It is essential, then, to declare a conflict of interest—or even a *possible* conflict of interest—to the publisher when submitting an article for publication. Most, if not all, publishers require this written declaration and have a form—often called Conflict of Interest or Disclosure statements—for the author to fill out with the submitted article.

A general rule is helpful here: If you're in doubt about a conflict, declare it. The editor or publisher can then decide whether it truly is a conflict and how to proceed with the article.

If a conflict of interest exists, its presence doesn't necessarily mean that the article or manuscript for a book will not be accepted and published. Depending on the conflict, the publisher may simply note it when the work is published. Publishers must be careful to avoid even the appearance of presenting biased information without disclosure. Typically statements related to conflict of interest include sources that financially supported the work (such as a research study funded by a pharmaceutical company) and the role of the sponsor, if any, in steps such as study design, data collection and analysis, and writing and submitting the report (ICMJE, 2013).

Similarly, if there is no conflict of interest, some publications routinely state that in the published materials.

Confidentiality and Privacy

Often, when nurses publish an article, a book chapter, or a textbook, the contents deal with patient information or patient care issues that illustrate the theory or information presented. As a result, one overriding legal *and* ethical practice that a nurse author must adhere to is maintaining the privacy and confidentiality of the patient information presented in the written manuscript. Both the privacy and confidentiality must be safeguarded because an invasion of privacy and a breach of confidentiality are two separate legal and ethical concepts.

Invasion of Privacy

An *invasion of privacy* occurs when one intrudes upon the *private affairs* of another. In regard to publishing, this could occur in several ways. One way is if you include in your article the patient's name or likeness (photograph) for your commercial advantage (the selling of the text) without the patient's consent (Dobbs, 2001).

Another example is if the patient's information meets the requirements for a public disclosure about private facts of the individual. In this type of invasion of privacy, the information disclosed must take into account the following (Dobbs, 2001):

- *Private* information about the patient is made public: For example, the book is sold and contains detailed private facts about the patient.

- Any person of *ordinary sensibilities* would be offended by the disclosure.

- The information disclosed is the type that the public has no legitimate interest in knowing.

As a potential author, you can avoid these allegations by simply obtaining the written permission of the patient to include his information or likeness in your written article. The patient may provide you with full information or ask that certain information not be used. Likewise, the patient may request that you not use his or her real name and that some of the facts about the illness or treatment discussed in the manuscript be changed to further safeguard privacy.

Protecting a patient's privacy is in keeping with a nurse's ethical obligations (Fowler, 2010). The CAse REport (CARE) guidelines for case reports state that authors have an "ethical duty" to obtain informed consent (Gagnier et al., 2013). If consent can't be obtained from the patient or relative, the guidelines recommend authors seek permission from an institutional review board. Because these guidelines are relatively new, it's unknown how many journals will adopt them.

You would do well to develop your own release form for obtaining a patient's permission to use his or her information in your written work. There are formbooks available for you to review, such as *Publishing Forms and Contracts* by Roy Kaufman (2008). You can also consult with a nurse attorney or another attorney in your state who can develop a form for your use.

If you have any questions about protecting patient privacy that aren't covered in the Author Guidelines, contact the editor.

Confidence Booster

You may be feeling overwhelmed by all the information in this chapter. Know that the editor of the publication is a good resource for answering questions. Take a break with this confidence booster (Literature Fun Facts, n.d.).

Did you know that J.K. Rowling had great difficulty finding a publisher for her first Harry Potter book? When she finally did find one, the publisher, Bloomsbury Press, would only print 500 copies because it was concerned the book would not sell. Bloomsbury also requested that J.K. not use her first name, Joanne, because it feared young boys would not read a book about wizards if written by a woman. Because Rowling did not have a middle name, she chose "K" for Kathleen. J.K. Rowling sounded more masculine to the publisher.

Today, the first edition of *Harry Potter and the Philosopher's Stone* is worth thousands.

Breach of Confidentiality

The protection of patient information shared within a patient–healthcare provider relationship is a unique protection that requires the healthcare provider, including a nurse, not to share the information with a third party unless the consent of the patient is obtained. Although there are exceptions to that overall mandate (e.g., in an emergency, when there is a danger to the patient or to others), the nurse is obligated, again both legally and ethically (Fowler, 2010), to maintain the confidentiality of the information shared.

Legally, this protection lies in state laws on patient privacy, including state mental health codes and patient privacy laws. If confidentiality is breached, the patient can sue for a breach of confidentiality *and* an invasion of privacy.

As in the case of protecting patient privacy, you can avoid allegations of a breach of confidentiality by obtaining the written permission of the patient to use information obtained during the care and treatment of the patient. Changing some of the facts or circumstances about the patient can help further secure his or her confidentiality.

If you are developing a hypothetical case study based on your experiences with multiple patients, you do *not* need to obtain permission because you should not be providing the level of detail needed to identify a particular person. Too often, nurses veer from including real-life experiences for fear of violating confidentiality. However, the true-life experiences are often what can help drive home a point to a reader. An easy-to-follow guide when writing case studies and protecting patient privacy at the same time is Marla DeJong's *Case Studies: Strategies To Protect Patient Privacy* (2012).

State laws that protect patient confidentiality often require that specific content be included in a written release by a patient. As an author, you need to review any law in your state for required forms and use them as you write your manuscript. You can also seek a consultation with a nurse attorney or another attorney whose practice includes confidentiality issues to identify and obtain copies of those forms.

Any permission forms obtained should be submitted with the manuscript, which is most often required by the publisher. You should also keep a copy of any permission forms you submit.

Misconduct in Research

Conducting and publishing research in nursing is an essential part of nursing practice. Indeed, findings from such research have improved clinical outcomes for many patients. When the results of a research project are published, it is vital that the publication is honest, clear, accurate, complete and balanced, and should avoid misleading, selective, or ambiguous reporting (Wager & Kleinert, 2011).

Be careful not to condone, participate in, or allow any conduct that compromises your research project and that violates any ethical codes, including the Code for Nurses (American Nurses Association [ANA], 2001) and the Code of Ethics and Professional Practice (Association of Institutional Research, 2013). Possible violations identified can include allowing research funders or sponsors to veto findings that do not support their product or position, not crediting proper authorship of the research study, not obtaining proper informed consent from participants in a research protocol, and ignoring an inappropriate risk or burden to the participant (Working Group for the Study of Ethical Issues in International Nursing Research; Chair Douglas P. Olsen, 2003).

Plagiarism and Redundant Publishing

Plagiarism is both a legal and an ethical issue. Copyright infringement can result in a federal court case involving monetary damages and other legal remedies, but plagiarism is another serious violation with equally frightening legal ramifications.

Plagiarism is a significant violation of truthfulness (King, n.d.) and occurs when one takes another's work, copyrighted or not, and passes it on as his or her own (Fishman, 2011). If a plagiarist steals only works in the public domain, he or she is not a copyright infringer because the Copyright Act provides an exception for works in the public domain. Even so, there are always potential, additional legal consequences to plagiarizing another's work.

For example, when you submit an article for consideration for publication, you often must *warrant* (guarantee) that the work is original. If that is not the case, despite your saying the work is original, the publisher or owner can file a breach of contract action and/or a case alleging fraud against you. In the world of academics, plagiarizing another's work can result in loss of a job (if a teacher) or ramifications from violating a student code of conduct (e.g., probation, dismissal from the program). In the world of publishing, such a breach clearly results in a loss of integrity and honesty that follows the author for the rest of his or her professional career. In fact, many publishers now routinely use software programs to check for possible plagiarism before sending the manuscript for peer review.

Q: *If I sign the copyright transfer, may I still write another article on the same topic?*

A: The transfer of the copyright does not mean you cannot compose another article about the same topic. Rather, what will need to be done is to ensure that subsequent manuscripts are substantially different from the one transferred (Saver, 2006). Many publishers ask authors to submit any articles that have been published before the second work is submitted for publication so that the editor can evaluate the differences between the two works.

Redundant or *duplicate publishing,* which can be equally problematic, occurs when an author publishes a work that significantly overlaps with another work already published (Saver, 2006). This conduct is also referred to as "self-plagiarism" (King, n.d.). The practice is unethical because it makes the author appear to be prolific when, in fact, he or she simply rehashes already published material. And, if the already published material is copyrighted or licensed to a publisher, the author is guilty of copyright infringement.

Some journals address the problem of redundant publication by asking authors who submit a manuscript to also submit previously published papers or those that are currently under review related to the topic of the manuscript under consideration (Office of Research Integrity, 2013) or require that a manuscript not be considered if it has been submitted elsewhere until a rejection letter is received from the first publisher, which is known as a "single submission policy" (King, n.d.).

A form of duplicate publishing, informally called *salami slicing,* occurs when an author breaks up portions of a whole work into different works and submits them to several publishers rather than submitting the entire work to one publisher for consideration (Elsevier, n.d.). The ramifications of salami slicing are many, including an unfair inflation of the author's published works and, in the case of a research-based article, a skewing of the data reported because it appears to be from more than one research project (Elsevier, n.d.).

A good risk management approach for avoiding redundant publication and salami slicing is, first and foremost, to disclose to the editor any previous dissemination of the material. That includes an article in another journal, a conference presentation, or material posted online (Office of Research Integrity, 2013). Yes, you can publish for other journals with other audiences on the same topic, but you must have a new focus and new information. Cite the previously published article on the topic and get permission to use content from Article 1 in Article 2 if you are using information from that publication.

Q: *How do I handle the methodology section when reporting on different aspects of a research project in different journal articles?*

A: Give a copy of Article 1 to the editor/publisher of Article 2 to discuss what to include in Article 2. Possible options include picking up the content by asking permission from the first publisher and then putting the methods in a sidebar in Article 2, crediting the original source and noting permission granted or referring the reader to Article 1 for the methodology.

Satisfaction in Print

You have learned about several legal, ethical, and other issues related to protecting your own work and the work of others. Follow the basic guidelines—and consult with your editor when in doubt—to navigate the publishing waters. There are many challenges to publishing an original work, but after those challenges are met and you see your work in print or online, it is indeed worth all the effort spent getting to the point.

Write Now!

1. Practice writing a permission letter to a journal, requesting the use of a figure from an article.

2. Download and read the *American Journal of Nursing* Authorship, Responsibility, Disclosure, and Copyright Transfer form at http://www.editorialmanager.com/ajn. Note the sections on financial disclosure and the authorship statement, which addresses qualifications for authorship and copyright transfer.

3. Review other agreements and compare and contrast them for consistency and differences.

References

American Medical Writers Association. (2003). AMWA position statement on the contributions of medical writers to scientific publications. *AMWA Journal, 18*(1), 13–16.

American Nurses Association (2001). Code of ethics for nurses with interpretive statements. Silver Spring, MD: Author.

Association of Institutional Research. (2013). Code of ethics. Retrieved from http://www.frontrange.edu/About-Us/Institutional-Research/About-IR/DMS-About-IR/CODE-OF-ETHICS.aspx

BitLaw. (2013). Copyright notice and registration. Retrieved from http://www.bitlaw.com/copyright/formalities.html

Copyright Clearance Center. (2005a). Copyright basics: The Teach Act. Retrieved from http://www.copyright.com/Services/copyrightoncampus/basics/teach.html

Copyright Clearance Center. (2005b). Copyright basics: What is copyright law? Retrieved from http://www.copyright.com/Services/copyrightoncampus/basics/law.html

Creative Commons. (n.d.). About and About Licenses. Retrieved from http://creativecommons.org/about/ and http://creativecommons.org/about/licenses/

DeJong, M. J. (2012). Case studies: Strategies to protect patient privacy. *Nurse Author & Editor*, *22*(4). Retrieved from http://www.nurseauthoreditor.com/

Dobbs, D. (2001). *The Law of torts* (Vol. 2, pp. 1197–1213). St. Paul, MN: West Group.

Elsevier. (n.d.). Salami slicing. Ethics in research & publications. Retrieved from http://www.elsevier.com/__data/assets/pdf_file/0009/163719/ETHICS_SS01a.pdf

Ethics. (2013). In *Dictionary.com*. Retrieved from http://dictionary.reference.com/browse/ethics?s=t

Fishman, S. (2011). *The copyright handbook: What every writer needs to know* (11th ed.). Berkeley, CA: Nolo.

Fishman, S. (2012). *The public domain: How to find and use copyright-free writings, music and more* (6th ed.). Berkeley, CA: Nolo.

Fowler, M. (Ed.). (2010). *Guide to the code of ethics for nurses: Interpretation and application.* Silver Spring, MD: American Nurses Association.

Gagnier, J. J., Kienle, G., Altman, D. G., Moher, D., Sox, H., Riley, D., & the Care Group. (2013). The CARE guidelines: Consensus-based clinical case reporting guideline development. *Journal of Medical Case Reports*, 7, 233. Retrieved from http://www.jmedicalcasereports.com/content/7/1/223

Garner, B. A. (Ed.). (1999). *Black's law dictionary* (8th ed.). St. Paul, MN: Thomson West.

Gerhardt, D. R., & Kjervik, D. K. (2008). Protect your right to write again: Tips for assuring that your publication agreement is a comfortable fit. *Journal of Nursing Law*, *12*(3), 124–126.

International Committee of Medical Journal Editors. (2013). Defining the role of authors and contributors. Retrieved from http://www.icmje.org/roles_a.html

Kaufman, R. (2008). *Publishing forms and contracts.* New York: Oxford University Press.

King, C. (n.d.). *Ethical issues in writing and publishing.* Retrieved from https://www2.ons.org/Publications/CJON/AuthorInfo/WritingSupp/Ethics

Literature Fun Facts (n.d.). J. K. Rowling. Retrieved from http://www.bestfunfacts.com/literature.html

Mabelson, C. J. (2012). *DMCA handbook for ISPS & website content creators, copyright owners.* Phoenix, AZ: Brooks Press.

Office of Research Integrity, U.S. Department of Health and Human Services. (2013). Redundant and duplicate (i.e. dual) publications. Retrieved from http://ori.hhs.gov/education/products/plagiarism/14.shtml

Saver, C. (2006). Legal and ethical aspects of publishing. *AORN Journal*, *84*(4), 571–575.

Scholarly Publishing and Academic Resources Coalition (SPARC). (n.d.). Author rights: Using the SPARC author addendum to secure your rights as the author of a journal article. Retrieved from http://sparc.arl.org/resources/authors/addendum

Stanford (n.d.). National Institutes of Health (NIH) public access law in a nutshell. Retrieved from http://elane.stanford.edu/laneconnex/public/media/documents/NIHPublicAccessLaw-in-a-Nutshell.pdf

U.S. Copyright Office. (2006). Copyright in general. Retrieved from http://www.copyright.gov/help/faq/faq-general.html#what

U.S. Copyright Office. (2008). What does copyright protect? Retrieved from http://www.copyright.gov/help/faq/faq-protect.html

U.S. Copyright Office. (2009). Fair use. Retrieved from http://www.copyright.gov/fls/fl102.html

U.S. Copyright Office. (2012). Copyright registration for online works. Retrieved from http://www.copyright.gov/circs/circ66.pdf

U.S. Copyright Office. (2013). eCo Online System. Retrieved from http://www.copyright.gov/eco

Wager, E., & Kleinert, S. (2011). Responsible research publication: International standards for authors: A position statement developed at the 2nd world conference on research integrity, Singapore, July 22–24, 2010. Available as Chapter 50 in: Mayer, T., & Steneck, N. (eds.). (2012). *Promoting research integrity in a global environment* (pp. 311–319). Singapore: World Scientific Publishing.

Warnock, C. (2012). *What every writer should know: Copyright.* Author.

Working Group for the Study of Ethical Issues in International Nursing Research; Chair Douglas P Olsen. (2003). Ethical considerations in international nursing research: A report from the International Centre for Nursing Ethics. *Nursing Ethics, 10*(2), 122–137.

World Association of Medical Editors (WAME). (2007). Policy statement: Authorship. Retrieved from http://www.wame.org

World Association of Medical Editors (WAME). (2009). Conflict of interest in peer-reviewed medical journals. Retrieved from http://www.wame.org

*"Without promotion,
something terrible happens…nothing!"*

–*PT Barnum*

Marketing Yourself and Your Work

12

Renee Wilmeth

One of the biggest challenges for authors is promoting and helping sell their own work. Many authors dream of publishing to great fanfare with a whirlwind book tour, an appearance on national television, and skyrocketing book sales, but the reality is that you must shoulder a large portion of the responsibility for making your published book successful. It's the same with your published research articles. No one will notice your work if you don't tell them about it.

If you have published a book, your book publisher might help with a few basic marketing ideas. However, marketing budgets for publishers are tight, which means that authors have become increasingly responsible for their work's success.

Just as you are increasingly responsible for the successful outcome of publishing projects, the same sentiment applies to your academic career, consulting business, or personal path. You alone are likely the one most vested in your success. If that success means gaining recognition for your research by publishing in a journal, networking to make coauthor connections, or using social media to establish yourself as an expert, you need to become comfortable with the idea of self-promotion and promoting your work.

Fortunately, many tools are available to help you get the word out about your publishing success and also to help you establish your broader reputation to generate more business or professional

WHAT YOU'LL LEARN IN THIS CHAPTER

- It's important to understand why goals are important for writing projects. Do you want to get a book published? A grant? A promotion? What are you hoping to achieve?

- To market your publication, determine the right tools for the job—then use them.

- Marketing yourself isn't a bad thing. These days, it's a necessity.

- When marketing yourself, create a plan. Analyze what makes you special. What is your personal brand?

opportunities. The most important tool is your own mind-set. You must first establish a platform and then use it as a jumping-off point for your writing work. This means beginning to think of yourself and where your work and career fit in your field. Are you just staring out? Are you an experienced dean? Do you write as first author or second? Are you—and your projects—known to colleagues in your field? Once you think about your position within your area of expertise, then you can think about how you can help market yourself.

Q: *I was so excited to have my book published by a major textbook publisher! However, sales have been disappointing, and my editor said the book would have to succeed or fail on its own. What can I do to help salvage its success?*

A: Nothing can be more frustrating than hearing your publisher say that it can't support your work. After all, the publisher believed in your book enough to publish it, right? Bottom line: You have to take control of your own success—and your book's success, too. Talk to the publisher to find out what you can do to help. You will have to create your own marketing plan and execute it. You'll find that self-promotion will benefit you in many ways and help sell your book.

What Is a *Platform*?

Two nurse authors decided to write proposals for topics and see who could get their books published first.

Nurse A graduated top of her undergraduate class, has been successful in her job at a major hospital, has participated in management training courses, and was recently accepted into a prestigious research program. However, she rarely attends conferences or speaks publicly, even though she's an expert on bedside leadership and evidence-based nursing with more than 10 years of clinical experience. She is having difficulty getting a publisher interested in her book proposal.

Nurse B graduated from a less-prestigious school and had trouble landing a job. However, she capitalized on her down-time by attending conferences; networking with well-known leaders in nursing; submitting abstracts; and speaking on new nurse issues, bedside leadership, and reflective practice. She even did some consulting projects for organizations to build her resume. She became active in the online nursing world through Twitter and started a blog exploring issues faced by new nurses in the field. Her blogging, social networking, and speaking brought her to the attention of a publisher, and she is now writing her first book. She also just accepted a leadership position with a nationally known medical facility.

Do you have any ideas on why Nurse B was more successful than Nurse A in attracting the attention of a publisher? The answer is that Nurse B knows how to market herself.

If you want to be noticed, you need an author platform. Your *platform* is who you are: the sum of your bio, expertise, base of contacts, and work. Your platform is how a publisher or editor defines who you are relative to others in your area. In addition, many of the components of a platform make it easy to market your work, which is why publishers want you to have one. Your platform includes your built-in ability to support your work and promote it through your contacts.

Nurse B has less experience, but she is more successful presenting herself as an expert—and backing up that claim by speaking and writing on the topic. She has active ways to get the word out about her projects—and an upcoming book. People follow her and listen to what she has to say. Nurse A, no doubt, has many successful journal articles ahead of her, but without the ability to toot her own horn, she might find herself at a disadvantage when it comes to demonstrating that she's more of an expert than her colleagues.

Why Build a Platform?

Success begets success. If you are an expert, you must be able to sell yourself as an expert. When others see you as that expert, they'll continue to come to you. More importantly, people will listen to what you have to say. If you are an expert and can build a following, that following is valuable in marketing terms.

A platform helps you build your following by showing your expertise. Sure, you want to showcase your articles, research, books, and experience, but a platform also gives you a chance to make your voice heard. A platform isn't just what makes you a reliable source: It's what makes you *the* reliable source. A platform gives you the power to notify followers—by blog, Twitter, or your favorite journal—that you have something to say. Venues that crave an expert author or source include:

- Books: For a book deal, platform is a must.
- Magazines
- Online journals

- Conference speakers, both those to which you've submitted an abstract and those at which you've been invited to speak.

- Speakers' bureaus

- Recruiters

- Grant funders: Grant funders like professionals with a platform because they have more opportunities for disseminating information.

Once you know the value of a platform, the next step is to build one.

How Do You Create a Platform?

Your platform is all about how credible and well known you are in your area of expertise. You need to get to know everyone of importance in your specialty—and have those people know you. There are a number of great ways to develop your own voice and share your expertise and views. Here are some ways you can achieve visibility:

- Get certified

- Present webinars

- Create a podcast

- Try a vlog (a video blog) and create a YouTube channel

- Obtain another degree or credential

- Take classes

- Create a website

- Write a blog

- Teach

- Volunteer

- Lecture

- Travel

- Network

- Become active in a society related to your profession or specialty

Setting Goals

When it comes to creating your platform, goals play an important part in planning how to build your platform. Ask yourself what you want. Do you want a promotion? A better job? To be the best in your field? Do you want to be a published author? Do you need to publish for tenure? Do you want to learn from or teach the best in your area of expertise?

Whatever you want to accomplish, a solid author platform will help you get there. With a goal, you can define *strategy* (the framework of where you're going) as well as *tactics* (how you're going to get there). And if you're worried that you don't have the time to build a platform, setting goals can help you prioritize—and priorities help you make the time.

Tools for Creating a Platform

A platform isn't just about promoting yourself by tweeting (on Twitter), blogging, or posting your profile on a professional networking site like LinkedIn. Establishing a platform is about having something relevant to say—and saying it. To take a leadership role in your area of expertise, you need to use the right tool for the job. If your specialty is extremely narrow, you might not have as much success establishing yourself by using Twitter or Facebook. If you are focused on reaching new graduates or younger nurses, a blog or online presence is the perfect tool for the job.

Q: *Recently, I spoke to a book publisher about submitting a proposal for a book. I know a lot of people in my field and can bring together an excellent group of contributors. However, the proposal asked for a marketing plan. Where do I start? I would hate for good research to be lost because I'm not a marketing expert. What do you suggest?*

A: In today's world, being an author requires more than just bringing colleagues together for a contributed book. A marketing plan is merely a chance for you to let your publisher know what you can do to help promote your book. It's a chance to explain your platform—and how you plan to leverage it! List organizations you're involved in, meetings you plan to attend, presentations you will be giving, and people you know in your field who you can enlist for help. Don't forget your university magazines or organizational websites. It's a chance for your publisher to better understand the overall chances of success for the book. So, get creative!

You need to consider your goal—for example, getting published, creating a consulting practice, changing direction in your career, or becoming the top researcher in your field—and then examine how you can best reach your audience. Some venues for building your platform include:

- Your university

- Your hospital/medical facility

- Libraries/repositories

- Journals

- Books

- A website

- Social networking tools

- Discussion groups and forums

- Conferences and meetings

- Professional and scholarly society chapters

- Book or journal clubs

If you already use some of these tools, your next step for building platform is to assess where you started and where you want to go.

Building Your Personal Brand

Your platform is all about building your personal brand, or *Brand You*, as author and consultant Tom Peters (1999) calls it. In addition to what you know, your platform helps you communicate your passion of and commitment to your subject matter or area of expertise. If you bring your heart to your platform, your readers—and editors—will notice.

Becoming comfortable promoting yourself is not always easy. Some nurses will never be completely comfortable tooting their own horns. However, when you look at your goals and how to accomplish them, you'll ultimately become more comfortable telling editors what you know, why you are the best expert, and why you should be the one to share your knowledge with readers.

Confidence Booster

Marie is a nurse researcher of baby boomer age who has little experience with social media. She consults with Jennifer—a nurse from generation Y who is not a researcher but is an expert at social media—about how she can build her platform. Together, they create a plan that gradually increases Marie's online presence. After using a template to create a simple website, Marie starts accounts on Twitter, Facebook, and LinkedIn. After following the conversation in a researchers' group on LinkedIn, she starts to participate. Next she begins sending one tweet a day, including "retweeting" (sending tweets from other people to those who are following her). She starts posting more often on her Facebook page. She works closely with Jennifer throughout the process. By devoting just 5 minutes a day to her social media presence, Marie reaps significant benefits, and 6 months later she is asked to present at a national meeting. Follow Marie's example and work with those who are expert at social media to gradually increase your presence.

Here are some practical ways to create a personal brand for promoting your work:

- Think up a brand name. If you were a company, what would you be called?

- Title your blog. What would your blog posts cover?

- Register the URL for a website.

- Create a mission statement. What do you stand for?

- Register for Facebook, Twitter, and LinkedIn.

So Many Excuses

Authors can come up with many excuses to avoid something they're not comfortable with—in this case, self-promotion. Ultimately, if you have a clear set of goals and are working toward them, you'll be able to find reasons why so many of these excuses are just reasons to learn how to overcome them! See whether you've caught yourself saying one of the following statements:

"I'm not comfortable promoting myself or my work."

"My work should speak for itself. People should be coming to me."

"I only have so much time each day to spend in front of the computer, and I don't want to spend it in online discussion groups and social media sites."

"I get it, but where I am I supposed to find the time?"

> "If I were going to participate, I wouldn't want to do it for the sole purpose of promoting myself and my name."
>
> "I don't know about blogs, YouTube, Facebook, Twitter, and all those sites."
>
> "I wouldn't know where to start building my own website."
>
> If you want to achieve your goal and your goal involves having a more successful book or getting a top writing project, you'll find that some of the obstacles you thought were challenges will become priorities. Finding time, expanding your comfort zone, learning new technologies, and even starting a blog become important when they will help you reach your goals.

Q: *I understand that I need to take the time to create my own brand and gain followers, but I'm a social media novice. What's the best way to start?*

A: As with most new skills, the key is to start small. Begin by creating accounts and learning to use the most common social media platforms like LinkedIn, Facebook, and Twitter. These sites have easy-to-use templates for creating your profile, and they're easy to navigate. You can also find online tutorials, books (such as the *Nurse's Social Media Advantage* [Fraser, 2011] and *The Nerdy Nurse's Guide to Technology* [Wilson, 2013]) and blogs (like thenerdynurse.com) to help!

Promoting Your Work

Understanding the concept of having a platform and having an idea about personal branding will increase the likelihood writing opportunities will open up to you. And after you have that book deal in hand, have landed a column with a major nursing magazine, or published a series of articles on a key issue such as the importance of civility, it's time to promote your writing.

You are probably wondering at this point where you should start. "But," you're thinking, "I don't know anyone. How can I possibly have the contacts to help promote my work or pay attention to what I have to say?" The answer is that you know more people than you think you do.

If you don't already have a personal mailing list, you should begin to build one. Whom do you notify when you have a big success? Friends? Family? What about business and academic colleagues? Think of these contacts as your biggest fans. And your fans want to know about what you're doing to succeed. They will be most likely to comment on your online writings, send reader reviews to online retailers, and share your journal articles around to their own lists of contacts. Before you know it, you—and your work—have gone viral! Welcome to promotion in today's connected world.

> **Q:** *I recently published an article in a prestigious nursing journal. Imagine my surprise when the editor emailed me to ask me for the contact information of several top researchers in my field. She wanted to send them a copy of my article bringing their attention to my work. I was a little uncomfortable sending her the information, but was pleasantly surprised when one of the most respected researchers in my field emailed me to congratulate me on my paper! Why would an editor help me in this way?*
>
> **A:** What a smart journal editor you have! By personally sending your article to several of your top colleagues, your editor is accomplishing several things. First, she is hoping researchers will cite your article, which will increase the journal's impact factor. (You can learn more about impact factors in Chapter 3.) Additionally, she is making a connection between you and a top colleague and an introduction for you. Also, she is building awareness of her journal with top researchers so they will think of it as a place to find relevant papers. And lastly, she is establishing her journal as one to which you will want to submit again. In helping build her journal's platform, she is helping you to build yours. What a win-win!

Promoting Your Book

Books require special marketing attention. Refer to Nurse B in the example at the beginning of the chapter. Several months in advance of her book's publication, her editor begins asking for some key information, including:

- Author bio and photo
- Cover "blurbs" or advance praise, which are positive comments from well-known experts to whom readers would be likely to respond
- Conferences/appearances
- Any travel plans she has that might provide promotion opportunities
- URL for her website and blog

- Press contacts with her university and hospital

- A list of editors and columnists she knows

- How many Twitter followers she has; how many Facebook friends/fans

- Whether she is active on LinkedIn

- Whether she is comfortable working in an online environment like a Facebook thread or a Twitter chat

- Whether she has presented live webinars

- Whether she knows how to use basic Internet video and audio software like Skype or GotoMeeting

The publisher is going to want to know what you can do to help promote your project and expect that you can use all these items as promotion avenues. Without them, the publisher's sales and marketing materials will be less robust—whether it's a book you've authored or a special issue of a journal you have guest edited.

Creating a Marketing Plan

Next, start building your own marketing plan that goes beyond what the publisher can do. Remember that the book you've written is part of your larger Brand You plan. Yes, your publisher has a marketing plan for the book, but you'll want to build your plan based on everything else you're doing. Stuck for ideas? Try some of these:

- Make a contact list of people you know—and want to know!

- Populate your blog roll and exchange guest blog posts.

- Try your hand at a video for YouTube.

- Submit abstracts to conferences.

- Learn to record and produce podcasts.

Keep in mind that these strategies are also effective for marketing works other than books. Speaking at a national meeting on your series of articles about civility might lead to more opportunities and even a research grant.

If you're a little uncomfortable with the idea of sticking your hand out to meet total strangers, look for a book on the basics of networking and marketing. If you're attending a conference, review the attendee list in advance and make a list of people you want to meet. A good book on business communication or networking will also give you techniques to help you feel more comfortable with introducing yourself to strangers or approaching a speaker after a session. For inspiration, order new business cards, complete with your URL, book title, and cover so your audience can find you.

Most importantly, think creatively. Depending on your area of expertise, you'll find alternative venues for your work and discover leads. Of the many components of a plan for marketing and promoting your work, three of the most important are your website, social media networks, and reviews.

Self-Publishing: Going It Alone

As you research potential publishers, you will find you have many to choose from. Scholarly presses, professional publishers, commercial houses, and even society publishers may all be interested in your project, but what's right for you? These days, you can't make a choice based on the financial package because for many authors there might be only a tiny advance (or none at all) and a net royalty rate. You might also be wondering about self-publishing and whether it might be a better use of your time and money.

Consider your goals for your writing project and your platform when deciding whether to self-publish. If you are targeting a highly specific readership and have a built-in distribution network for that readership, self-publishing might work for you. For example, let's say your book is designed for new nurse managers. You have a successful blog for new nurse managers and a large following on Twitter. In addition, you speak at many meetings to this audience and consult with hospitals to deliver special programs for new managers. Your connections will help you in marketing the book; however, keep in mind that you will be totally responsible for all aspects of publishing, including the costs of editing, printing, production, and sales.

That responsibility is why you might find that it's worth it to go with a more traditional publisher, who will take care of the editing, proofreading, layout, book design, sales, distribution, and even marketing. Having access to the resources a publisher brings to the table allows you to focus on larger goals you have for your career and not be bogged down in details.

Another self-publishing option can include primarily digital options with Print on Demand (POD) copies available. Keep in mind that platforms like Amazon Digital Publishing offer great reach, but limited options, because Kindle is still a proprietary format. Some self-publishers also allow you to serve up PDF copies, but working to protect your copies from theft can be tricky. Finally, POD is a great option to save on a large printing investment, but can ultimately be much more expensive and eat into your profit margin. Self-publishing might be a great option, or it might be an expensive mess. Do your research and ensure you're prepared for whatever choice you make!

You'll want to develop a marketing plan whether you go it alone or work with a larger publisher. And even if you get a terrific book deal, a larger publisher is still going to want you to use your contacts to get the word out about your book. Whether you self-publish or stick with a professional house, promotion and platform is the name of the game. Ultimately, it's probably best to start with a traditional publisher so that you better understand the publication process before attempting to go it alone.

For some authors, a marketing plan seems like a strange thing to include in a book proposal, but the old adage, "It's not what you know, it's who you know," is truer now than ever. A publisher is going to assess your work not just on your knowledge and expertise, but also on your list of contacts and your stature in the field. That standard might not always seem fair, but in today's business climate editors and publishers are looking for every angle to sell books. For example, if you know the chief nursing officer at a major healthcare organization then you should be prepared to have your publisher ask you if he or she would be willing to buy a bulk order of your book.

When you're creating a marketing plan that is part of a book proposal, bear in mind that your editor is hoping to get an idea of who you know and how creative you can be when thinking of how to effectively spread the word about your book. Focus on strategies and tactics. Set your goals and then consider adding strategies such as:

- **Business strategy:** How can your organization or business promote the book?

- **Personal marketing strategy:** How will you personally promote or market the book?

- **Online presence.** What is your online strategy with tactics including email, websites, and social media?

- **In-person strategy.** What are your regular appearances, speaking engagements, and signing opportunities? Make sure you're clear about what you are planning to do. This isn't a place for suggestions for what you would like your publisher to pay for.

- **Sales strategy.** What is your strategy for helping sell books, including tactics for any bulk sales, institutional sales contacts, book signing sales, and sales via your website and contacts?

- **Publicity or PR strategy.** Are you willing to hire a publicist? Can you work with your university on a joint press release?

As you begin to explore these ideas, create a simple document and—voila!—you have a basic marketing plan. Include it with your book proposal and you might discover that your publisher finds your project a solid bet.

Building a Website

Considering the wide range of tools at your fingertips for promotion, building a website is the single most important thing you can do to promote yourself. It serves as your base of operations and a starting point for your audience. It will help your audience contact you and help you point them to your other work. A website is the base of a good platform.

On a website, you can include:

- Blogs
- Photos
- Videos
- Podcasts
- Ads or affiliate ads, which are ads that allow companies to promote their products but they only pay you under certain conditions, usually pay-per-click, pay-per-lead, or pay-per-sale
- Contact information

When you begin planning a website, keep a few things in mind:

- **Choose a name/URL:** If you're planning a website for a book, choose a URL that makes sense with the title, but is still short and easy to remember and spell.

- **Pick your branding/concept.** If you're planning a website as a base of operations for your writing, speaking, and even consulting or other research, think of an overall brand or name that can easily become your platform identity. Design your graphics accordingly.

- **Ask for help.** No one expects you to be able to host, build, or design a website. Educate yourself, but ask for help. Hundreds of books for every level of user are on the market on how to build websites.

- **Use links.** As you build your social networks and as your book or writing becomes available, create links to reviews, sites to purchase, colleagues, websites you like, and your pages on social media sites. Help your audience find you. You can also use links to send readers to your Twitter feed, subscribe to your podcasts, or watch your YouTube channel.

- **Do it yourself.** Podcasting software is readily available and a snap to use. If you have a computer, a microphone, and speakers, you can easily create a podcast for your fans on a regular basis. Looking for a model? Try looking at TED Talks (http://www.ted.com/talks), which are 20-minute, meaty, insightful educational podcasts that are setting the standard these days. Then set up an account or channel on iTunes so listeners can subscribe to your podcasts and receive automatic updates.

When your website is up and running, you'll also want to make sure you request a few items from the publisher to beef up your site and marketing materials:

- Book or journal cover

- Marketing plan/launch call (a call that includes your editor and the publisher's sales and marketing teams to discuss plans to promote your book)

- Advance order link (a link to where those interested in purchasing the book can place their order before the book is printed)

- Signing schedule (a listing of any book signings or author appearances the publisher sets up for you or you plan and set up for yourself)

- Press release

Writing for Social Media

"Why would anyone care about my project?" The key to writing for Facebook, Twitter or other short-form social media sites isn't to overly promote your book, project, or speaking engagement. The trick is to give your followers real content—a nugget of advice, a personal thought, or a tip. If you give them real content they can use, they'll remember—and value—you for what you can teach them. If you overtly promote your work again and again, they will "unfollow" you. You are only as good as the value you bring to your readers.

Promoting your work via social media outlets is all about using the right tool for the job. It's also about writing in a short, pithy style and an informal tone. Think about what you find fun to read online.

Facebook is more conducive to active discussion threads so it might be fun to ask colleagues what they thought of a paper or controversial issue in your field. Twitter is a way to broadcast a thought or pointer (to another article or resource) but remember your tweets must be short. LinkedIn is great for using the member forums to answer (or pose) questions based on your professional expertise.

Blogs lend themselves to longer posts and mini-essays, but beware of lengthy, multi-page posts. Try to keep your blog posts approachable, thoughtful, and shorter than 1,000 words. References generally aren't needed in blog posts, but links to outside work (instead of lengthy excerpts) are great ways to build traffic and establish a context for your thoughts.

Marketing on Social Media

Social media networks can be terrific ways to build your personal brand. They're also creative ways to expand your *reach*, or number and type of people in your audience. Many new social media networks pop up with special interest areas, but the big ones remain Twitter, Facebook, and LinkedIn. The following are some great social media strategies:

- Create *handles* or user IDs for your social media networks that are the same, if possible, and relate them to your website or personal brand strategy. You can even make your profile photo an iconographic logo or image that reinforces your brand. Extend this branding to slides for presentations, email signatures, note cards, and more.

- Take advantage of URL-shortening sites, such as TinyURL (http://tinyurl.com) and bit.ly (http://bit.ly), to create truncated links to your articles and blog posts. Some Twitter applications like TweetDeck (www.tweetdeck.com) will do this automatically for you. Others will automatically post your tweets to your Facebook status or page.

- Create a Facebook page for your book or business. You can gather followers as well as message them about speaking engagements, book signings, conferences you'll attend, and even new blog posts or website updates.

- Follow colleagues on Twitter and create lists so you can target the right folks to spread the word about your projects.

- Use hashtags (identifiers that begin with the symbol "#") and cross-post to friends and followers often. Although social media sites like Twitter don't seem to lend themselves to conversations and two-way communication, use hashtags, retweets, and cross-posts with followers when you can. Everyone likes a shout-out now and then!

- Answer questions on LinkedIn and other professional forums. Lend your voice and expertise to helping others, and you'll establish your expertise with entirely new communities.

- Investigate whether any professional associations or scholarly societies you know have their own social networking sites. Today, associations are creating their own social networking platforms so members can more easily network and share ideas.

- Choose a few of the most credible areas for your expertise and establish yourself as an expert. Remember that online forums are communities, and you want to spend a little time getting the lay of the land just as you do when you move to a new neighborhood. But after you feel like you can contribute, do so!

With the advent of new social networking sites, more advanced technologies, and ubiquitous devices like smartphones and tablet computers, new ways to participate and build a platform are cropping up each day. With more practice, you can assess what venues are right for you from style and tone to getting the most "bang for the buck."

A Few Words From the Lawyers

The online world has the same legal pitfalls as the offline world—and then some. The ease and speed of communication via the Internet can offer almost instantaneous mass distribution and sometimes massive headaches (including legal ones.) Although you are unlikely to encounter a legal problem, it's useful to educate yourself.

Areas of special legal concern include:

- **Collection and use of email addresses for marketing purposes:** Be sure that you are using addresses with permission, that you aren't sending spam, and that you are offering your email list members a chance to opt-out.

- **Online sweepstakes and contests:** Special rules can vary by state, so make sure you do your research first.

- **User-generated posts, chat rooms, bulletin boards, and blogs that may contain potentially defamatory or infringing content:** Make sure to clearly post usage and comment policies.

- **Copyright/permissions clearance for third-party property:** Don't forget to obtain permissions for photos.

- **Agreements for web-based design and other services:** Be sure to have signed formal agreements with anyone providing services such as hosting your website.

- **Use of testimonials/endorsements:** Obtain permission first.
- **Conducting e-commerce involving online sales:** If you're selling anything through your site, make sure you're fulfilling orders properly and charging sales tax if needed.

Law firms with established Internet communications practices offer e-newsletters and websites summarizing legal developments in these and other areas of legal risk. However, for specific legal question or claims, neither this book nor other pre-packaged information is an adequate substitute for personal consultation with legal counsel knowledgeable about the law of Internet communication (Penguin Group, 2008).

Generating Reviews and More

In addition to your website and your newfound social media skills, you want to concentrate on an old-school technique for promoting your book: reviews, email notifications, personal contacts, and generating word of mouth.

Online retail may be the primary way your book is sold in today's book market. It's rare that profession-specific books, like those on nursing, make it on to bookstore shelves. Online presence of your book is important because more and more readers find books using search engines like Google. Because your readers may be assessing your material online, it's important that you work with your publisher to ensure the online description and blurbs are posted. It's also important that you ensure your book has positive reader reviews.

Reviews can fall into three categories:

- Those you ask for from colleagues and big names in the field, such as cover blurbs or endorsements

- Those that come from third-party sources, such as nursing publications and journals that publish book and literature reviews

- Those that come from readers who post on sites such as Amazon.com or your publisher's book page

Often, your publisher will ask for your assistance in obtaining cover "blurbs" and endorsements before your book's publication. The strongest ones—from the biggest names—can be included on the book's cover or in its *front matter*, which consists of the material in the front of the book such as the title page, table of contents, foreword, and preface. You can work with your publisher to obtain a prepublished version of the manuscript, often called a *galley* or an *uncorrected proof*, to share with early endorsers.

Finding endorsers can be a great opportunity for you and your platform. Not only do you get to mine your database for your strongest contacts, but you should also create a wish list of people you might not know but would like to build a relationship with.

After your book is published, you'll want to work with your publisher's marketing team to ensure that review copies are sent to your best media contacts as well as theirs. You should include on your list any editors, columnists, or writers you know who work with publications that might review your book. If the publisher can't afford to send out as many copies as you'd like, use your free copies or author discount to purchase copies for mailing. After a book review appears in print, make sure to bring it to your publisher's attention and add a link from your website to the review. Work with your publisher to ensure he or she posts an excerpt from the review (with permission, of course) to the book's online catalog page.

Lastly, the most important kinds of reviews are those generated by readers themselves. *User-generated content* (reviews written by readers who have purchased and read the book) carries a great deal of credibility with potential purchasers.

Q: *I was so excited when reviews for my book showed up on Amazon, but then someone wrote a negative review, and I was devastated! What can I do?*

A: You can't counteract a negative review of your product unless it's a blatant personal or professional attack. The best thing to do is move it to the bottom of the list after more positive or helpful reviews. Mobilize your network of friends and colleagues and ask for them to post their own reviews with a more positive perspective on the work.

It's easy to focus only on Amazon, but don't forget that your book is available for sale in multiple online venues. Make sure to check and populate reviews at the publisher's website, other major retailers' websites (such as B&N.com), and venues that focus on nursing books.

Measuring Results

An important part of setting goals is measuring your success. When it comes to building your platform, online tools make it easy. When you're working hard to network—both online and in person—you'd like to see the results. Even more importantly, if you write for magazines or research journals, you should know who is citing your work. You might find some interesting new colleagues.

You'll want to track a variety of measurements, but the most basic will include some sort of analytic and statistics data from your website. You can use inexpensive web analytics services or a free one, like Google Analytics (www.google.com/analytics). Either way, you want to be able to measure any increase or decrease in traffic including users, page views, and site visits. Depending on the package you choose, you'll even be able to see where your primary traffic is coming from and originating countries of the world.

You can gather other information from an analytics toolset. For example, you can track your primary referral sources to see if your own cross-promotion is working. When you publish a blog post and then cross post it to Facebook, LinkedIn, and Twitter, you can see which posts generate the best results. When your friends on Facebook or followers on Twitter click through to read your post, you'll see their traffic. Over time, you'll get a feel for which types of cross-postings are the best use of your time.

If you track international traffic, an analytics tool will also give you good information on countries of origin, types and versions of web browsers your readers are using, issues with readers being bounced from a page, or ways readers are finding your blog or site via particular search terms.

Another way to measure results of your marketing efforts is to track who's talking about you and your projects. Try using a simple tool like Google Alerts (www.google.com/alerts). To set up a Google Alert, you simply include the search string to use (such as your name or book title, for example) and how often you'd like to receive updates. When the search engine finds a reference to the terms in your alert, you'll receive a note about it. If you set up a Google Alert for, say, your blog title, you'd see each time someone linked to you or made a reference in text. Use this handy tool to see just how far your conversation and platform can go.

Don't forget the most obvious tracking measurements, such as your number of fans (for your Facebook page), followers (on Twitter), and number of likes on your posts. Also look at the number of times an article is shared or retweeted. Your platform grows only as more people read what you have to say and share it!

Q: *I know self-promotion is important, but realistically, I have limited amounts of time. How can I collect all this data about my social media posts more easily?"*

A: Try setting up an account at Klout.com, a website that helps consolidate your shared posts to track your influence across the Web. Your Klout score can show you which strategies are most successful for you.

Getting Comfortable

When I was speaking on the topic of platforms at a large conference, I asked how many nurses, researchers, nurse leaders, and managers in the room were uncomfortable tooting their own horns. Half of the hands in the room went up. Chances are you might feel the same. It's difficult to move out of our own comfort zones. Learning new technologies and techniques for promoting yourself can be frustrating. In today's world, though, you are the only one who can build your platform. Your career isn't going to manage itself. You are your own best marketer—and, possibly, your *only* marketer.

The more you become part of the conversation, the more confidence you'll gain. You'll be successful before you know it.

Write Now!

1. List your top three goals and describe how building an author platform can help you achieve them. Remember to state your objective clearly with a deadline and, if possible, a way to measure your success.

2. Write three tweets that you might send to announce your publication of an upcoming paper. Remember that tweets must be 140 characters or less, and you should include a link to the journal's website or the paper's abstract.

3. Create a marketing plan for a project you want to propose. Think of your strategies and tactics, and then discuss how and when you would execute them.

References

Fraser, R. (2011). *The nurse's social media advantage: How making connections and sharing ideas can enhance your nursing practice.* Indianapolis, IN: Sigma Theta Tau International.

Penguin Group (USA). (2008). *Penguin author's guide to online marketing.* Retrieved from http://us.penguingroup.com/static/pdf/misc/penguin_authors_guide_to_online_marketing_summer_2008.pdf

Peters, T. (1999). *The brand you 50: Fifty ways to transform yourself from an 'employee' into a brand that shouts distinction, commitment, and passion!* New York, NY: Knopf.

Wilson, B. (2013). *The nerdy nurse's guide to technology.* Indianapolis, IN: Sigma Theta Tau International.

"If it reads nice and easy, chances are it took hard work. If it's wordy and complicated, chances are it was very easy to write."

–William Zinsser

Writing the Clinical Article

Cheryl L. Mee

Because you're likely most familiar with clinical articles, they make a great starting point for you to write. Clinical articles are read by all types of nurses and are published in many types of nursing journals. Formats can vary from journal to journal, but underlying all clinical articles is a discussion of a disease or health issue affecting a particular patient population. Clinical articles help nurses understand not only a particular disease or health concern; they also place the health concern in a context that helps readers understand how their patient population might present, how the illness might progress, what interventions should be considered, and how the patient may be managed, along with potential complications and outcomes.

Some clinical articles might also include patient-teaching information and medication information (either a medication summary or an in-depth review) depending on the journal or the author/editor preferences. Ultimately, a well-written clinical article will paint a picture for the nurse reader of the patient's presentation and progression, helping nurses better comprehend patient needs and care—thus providing better care for their patients.

This chapter will help you craft an effective clinical article. First, however, let's take a look at how a clinical article differs from a scholarly or research article.

WHAT YOU'LL LEARN IN THIS CHAPTER

- Planning and preparation usually take longer and require more work than actually writing a clinical manuscript.

- It's best to gather more information than you think you need on your topic.

- Multiple manuscript edits are essential to good writing.

- Developing a time schedule for researching, preparing, and writing your article will help you stay on task and on track.

Clinical and Scholarly Articles

Clinical articles target the nurse clinician: a nurse in clinical practice, caring for patients at the bedside, who wants useful take-away information that can be readily applied to day-to-day work. Clinical articles focus on patients, their clinical presentation, and how they might progress as nurses work with them on a day-to-day basis through a plan of care. Clinical articles can include opinion from expert clinicians, and also might cover clinical applications, such as how to do a procedure or an innovative way to put a new program in place.

Scholarly articles are geared toward nurses in research, science, and academia. This is not to say that researchers don't read clinical articles or that clinicians don't read research articles; that is indeed not the case. Many nurse researchers are also practicing clinicians, and clinicians read scholarly articles for evidence-based practice efforts.

However, compared with clinical articles, scholarly journal articles typically include a more in-depth review of the literature, contain more information related to the data collection process and new research, and focus more on the science of nursing and less on the clinical hands-on application of the content or expert clinical commentary. Scholarly articles are written to build the science and literature base of the profession, share new research and insights, and encourage more research related to the topic.

With the profession's focus on evidence-based practice, the line between clinical and scholarly articles is blurring as more clinical articles include more data and evidence, and research articles include more discussion of the clinical application to practice. Some overlap exists, but in general, clinical articles are more immediately relevant to practicing clinicians.

Writing Process

Nurses should write clinical articles to share their expertise and knowledge in a particular subject area. Don't be deterred by imagined barriers.

For example, consider writing a clinical article on a topic in your clinical setting with which you are familiar. This doesn't mean that you must be *the* specialty expert on this topic.

Q: *I'm not sure I have the experience to write a clinical article, but I think I should try. Do you have any advice for me?*

A: Unfortunately, some nurses shy away from writing because they believe they don't have enough expertise or credentials in a particular area—that they aren't good enough or knowledgeable enough. This lack of confidence holds nurses back from writing when, in fact, they can develop a well-done, well-researched clinical article that journal editors value for their publication. If editors waited for only the top experts and gurus in a particular field to write, we would have little nursing literature with few perspectives.

Additionally, some nurses hesitate to write clinical articles because they assume the topic is already well covered in the nursing literature. Others believe their perspectives on the topic are nothing new. Journal editors look for journal articles on topics with fresh clinical perspectives from nurses who provide care and improve outcomes. A special case study or your particular perspective on caring for a specific patient population can be the fodder for a new clinical article.

Writing a strong clinical article is within your grasp if you take a step-by-step approach.

1. Develop a clinical topic and focus.

2. Select a journal for publication.

3. Choose an appropriate format.

4. Gather information.

5. Write using active voice.

6. Edit your manuscript.

7. Submit!

Here is a closer look at each step.

Develop a Clinical Topic and Focus

Think about good clinical articles you have read. They usually don't cover too much: The focus is tight, the topic is well covered, and the article is not too long. Journal articles aren't like textbook chapters; they are typically more focused. So instead of writing on a general, broad topic—such as "diabetes in the home care patient"—narrow your topic to "reducing pain from frequent home blood glucose–monitoring." Explore the current literature in your topic area to help you develop and refine the topic niche you want to cover. Note the topics covered in your area of interest and consider what new perspective you can bring to an article. Keeping a tight focus helps keep you from writing too much on a broad topic and also helps you maintain better control of manuscript length. It's important to match the length of the manuscript to what is requested in the Author Guidelines.

> **Q:** *I know I'd like to write, but I'm not sure what to write about. Where do I start?*
>
> **A:** Consider writing in content areas where you have a passion. Think about patient care experiences where you had a great interest or particularly rewarding experience. Use your passion to fuel your topic idea list. Selecting a topic and an article focus takes time and energy, so this step can be a roadblock for some new authors. But if you take the time to delve into the literature and work to develop a topic that is relevant to the audience and important to you, you'll lay a foundation that supports your writing efforts and keeps you energized about the project.

After you select a topic, create a simple article outline. It's usually best to develop a topic by covering about four to six key areas. Make a list of these ideas. As you gather resources and references on the topic, refine this list (remembering to keep it focused). Use this outline as a guide when writing to help keep you from drifting from the list. The following example is a simple clinical article outline:

Patient Teaching to Improve Outcomes After Coronary Bypass Surgery

Preparing the patient and family for the postoperative experience

The basics: What to expect

Patient mobility and managing pain

Medications, diet, exercise: Helping patients with a timeline

Use this list in your query letter to the editor to describe the proposed content of your article. A topic query with specifics makes an impression on the editor and helps him or her come to a decision more quickly.

Editors may accept your idea and then work with you to refine the topic for their particular journal. (For more information on topic refinement, see Chapter 2; and for editor queries, see Chapter 3.)

Select a Journal for Publication

Chapter 3 discusses selecting a journal in great detail. Just as you would when submitting any article, review the aims, scope, and mission (or purpose statement) of the journal. Remember that the editor is the gatekeeper of the content. If you are working toward the same goal as the editor in developing the manuscript, you will have a stronger chance of manuscript acceptance. Consider talking with nurses in the specialty areas related to your topic to learn which clinical journals they typically read; you can also get their feedback on your topic idea.

All About Columns

A good place to target your article is a journal's columns, also called *departments*. Columns, which are typically shorter than feature articles, run regularly in multiple issues throughout the year. These pieces are intentionally developed to be shorter reads and mix with longer feature articles in a journal issue. The topic changes, but the theme remains the same. For example, some nursing journals have a regularly occurring legal column with changing topics each month such as "Consent" or "Malpractice." Note that these are highly focused because of the limited word count for columns.

Sometimes columns have a regular contributor, but often, they are open to any writer with a good idea. Editors are often challenged to develop topics for columns because they are published frequently. They are also always looking for new "takes" on common topics. For example, a regularly occurring column on documentation might be a good place for you to write about your work with a new time-saving documentation process. Follow word counts carefully and be concise in your writing. If you can come up with an innovative way to write about these "evergreen" topics, editors will usually accept your idea.

Choose an Appropriate Format

Review your target journal's clinical article formats to determine what might work for your manuscript topic. Clinical article formats can vary, but some standard elements are found in general clinical articles in most nursing journals. Refer to the journal's Author Guidelines for more details.

Elements of Clinical Articles

A nursing journal clinical article might include all or some of the following elements. Always read recent issues to see how these are handled in the journal that you are targeting.

- **Etiology:** The cause or the origin of the disease. The detail included here varies from journal to journal, with some providing in-depth information.

- **Pathophysiology:** The changes in physiology that occur in the disease. This elaborates on the etiology and helps the reader better understand the disease process. Note that some journals may use artwork and design elements to provide a visual representation. If the journal you are writing for uses art for pathophysiology, you might consider including suggestions for artwork. If you use art from another source, you need to obtain permission from the copyright holder. (Chapter 11 covers permissions in detail.) Refer to the journal's Author Guidelines for more details on artwork and permissions.

- **Incidence:** The frequency at which a disease presents in a particular population. Prevalence, which is similar, is the number of cases present at a particular point in time.

- **Clinical presentation:** What signs and symptoms the patient might have that are key parts of the nursing assessment.

- **Differential diagnosis:** Especially important for nurse practitioners because it provides clinical information about similar diseases or illnesses and how they differ.

- **Diagnostics:** The diagnostic tests, along with normal and abnormal values, that are relevant to the topic.

- **Treatment/interventions/medications:** Journals handle this content differently. Some might include detailed tables and charts on various medications, dose, nursing considerations, and so forth, and others might list only general medication categories. Again, refer to your target journal Author Guidelines and current similar articles for examples.

- **Patient education:** Some journals include a patient education handout written for patients at a specified grade level. Others might only include a few sentences on important patient education considerations.

- **Prevention:** Note that prevention might be wrapped into the patient education section.

- **Nursing implications:** Be sure to include nursing implications and considerations. In some clinical articles, you may become more focused on medications or medical management, but remember that nursing journals require implications for the nurse. Some editors call this the "So what?" Be sure the reader will finish the article and understand the application to their practice. Does the reader take away information that is relevant to patient care and readily applicable to practice?
- **Case studies:** A case study may be woven through the manuscript describing a particular patient and his or her presentation and progression through the illness and response to care. This is a great way to help nurse readers understand the topic as it helps present an image of a patient whom the nurse might care for.

Case studies. Formats for clinical articles can include case studies and "how-to" articles. *Case studies* are usually developed from real-life cases with the patient's identity concealed. Concealing identity in a real case study report can be difficult, so you should seek patient permission (refer to Chapter 11 for more information). Case studies can also be fictional, but they should be based on real-life cases from your experience. You might pull together a fictional case study based on your experience from caring for multiple patients. This method helps you demonstrate various aspects of patient care, for example, a fictional case might emphasize multiple potential complications at various time frames.

The case study serves as an example that helps the reader take the pieces of the clinical article and fit them into a patient scenario, helping the readers better understand the content. Case studies help readers visualize a real patient as they might care for them and help bring the article to life for the reader. Readers can relate to the case study, and the knowledge they gain from reading the article becomes more memorable. The case study may be presented followed by other sections of the clinical article (pathophysiology, results of key studies, nursing care), or the case study may be interwoven throughout the article. Here is an example of a case study that opens an article:

> A 16-year-old male presents to the nurse practitioner (NP) with a 2-day history of sore throat, swollen glands, and fever. He took over-the-counter analgesics/antipyretics with some relief but was awake all night with sweating, delirium, and weakness, according to his mother. He has not been drinking fluids because he cannot swallow. He is allergic to amoxicillin and takes no medications on a regular basis. He

has a history of "strep" throat and 2 years ago was hospitalized with Lemierre's syndrome. His girlfriend and her younger siblings recently had "strep" throat.

The patient appears very ill and lethargic. His tympanic temperature is 102.8°F (last dose of acetaminophen was 10 hours ago), and his skin is warm and moist. His apical rate is regular with no murmurs at 100 beats per minute. Respirations are 30 per minute with nasal flaring. Blood pressure is 100/60 in his right arm (sitting) and SpO_2 is 95% (room air). He is unable to open his mouth for adequate visualization. His neck is supple but has limited range of motion because of significant tender cervical lymphadenopathy.

As the NP, are you prepared to care for this patient? Most NPs would say "absolutely," yet how many are familiar with Lemierre's syndrome and what effect this prior diagnosis may have on the young patient's treatment? (Nicoteri, 2013)

This case study article then continues with a discussion of the common causes of pharyngitis in young adults and highlights life-threatening complications along with new guidelines and treatments. The case study method helps to pull the reader into the "real-life story" of a patient and his or her care.

How-to articles. *How-to* articles may focus on skills, procedures, interventions, or processes. For example, how-to topics from past issues of *Nursing* include caring for patients with hearing aids, changing an ostomy appliance, performing infant cardiopulmonary resuscitation, and using tissue adhesive for wound repair. These articles usually follow a progression of steps; carefully review each journal's published how-to articles to determine the fit with your topic.

To ensure how-to articles have the most value for practicing nurses, don't make them a step-by-step guide that you might find in product-use literature. Keep the focus on important aspects for the nurse that surround the use of the product, such as teaching tips, key infection control practices, or valuable nursing interventions. The writer's work is to help the reader understand the concept with clear, concise writing.

How-to articles may look simple to write, but depending on the topic, they actually take a great deal of effort along with a tremendous focus on details. Photos or artwork may accompany this type of writing along with carefully edited descriptions of the figures.

Gather Information

Even if you are well versed in a particular topic area, gather more resources than you think you need, including articles and books in nursing. Also look at the literature in other disciplines, such as medicine, psychology, social work, and pharmacy. For example, in an article titled "Identification and Management of Factitious Disorder by Proxy," published in the *Journal for Nurse Practitioners,* the author referred to literature not only from nursing, but also from psychology, psychiatry, sociology, neurology, pediatrics, and emergency medicine journals (Dye, Rondeau, Guido, Mason, & O'Brien, 2013).

If you read a great deal on the subject in a wide array of literature, you become immersed in the topic; when you start writing, it will come more quickly and naturally. You might want to keep all your sources in a big folder that you can easily access for reading and reviewing. Or consider an electronic bibliography database manager that helps you organize references and, in some cases, allows you to attach annotated PDFs of articles. (Chapter 4 has more details on these programs.)

Also read the lay literature to get a perspective on what the public is reading on the topic. Lay press articles usually include interesting statistics gleaned from primary sources. Always seek out primary sources and reference them in your manuscript.

 What is a primary source?

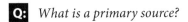 The *primary source* is the original article that an article, as a secondary source, is citing. Use primary sources in your article.

For example, if *The New York Times* quotes statistics from the Centers for Disease Control and Prevention (CDC) pertinent to your manuscript, get the CDC original document for your files. In most cases, you can download government documents at the agency's website. Note that using information from government websites is considered "public domain," and no permission for use is required, although it must be properly referenced.

It's a good idea to read all the articles and information you gather once as an overview, without worrying about highlighting or taking notes. Then read them a second time, highlighting key areas and making notes in the margins for the manuscript (or making notes in the electronic copies). Reread the content a few times. As you read, think about the clinical applications of the content to your work experience and how you can use your experiences in practice in your writing. You'll start to develop a list of key aspects of patient care that you want to be sure to emphasize for the reader. This helps you create an original manuscript based on your experience combined with current evidence—the ideal article.

Prepare to Write

Notice that a lot of effort is spent on preparing to write—selecting a topic, focus, and journal; gathering information; and immersing yourself in the literature. If you do your homework and prepare well, the writing process should be easy. Start by paying careful attention to the author guidelines for your target journal. It's important to follow these guidelines closely to be sure your final manuscript adheres to all specifications. Remember that an editor reads and writes all day long and will immediately identify manuscripts that don't adhere to the guidelines—so your first impression really counts! A polished manuscript shows you did your homework.

Some writers start writing in the middle of the manuscript, not worrying about grammar and punctuation. Their first writing sessions are focused on getting the main points, ideas, and key elements on paper. Then they build on each section, adding more information and periodically reorganizing. They continue writing until the manuscript starts to take shape, referring to the outline as a guide to help stay on track.

A helpful hint: Don't cut and paste from other documents when writing, even if your intention is to rewrite the information and use it only as a reference or "idea holder" in the manuscript. You can accidentally plagiarize the content by not eliminating the content as planned. Your writing *must* be your own unless you are quoting another source; in that case, cite the source as a reference.

Q: *Is it acceptable practice to use online references in a clinical article?*

A: Yes, but carefully select these resources, as you should do for print resources. If the article is from a well-respected source— for example, an article from a peer-reviewed journal—you may use it. Some reputable peer-reviewed journals are available today only as an online version. On the other hand, an online source such as Wikipedia doesn't belong in a clinical article. Always be sure to follow the appropriate style for referencing the article.

A Word About References

Carefully cite appropriate statements with references according to the journal's Author Guidelines. Guidelines and formats vary. Two common reference styles are the American Medical Association (AMA) and the American Psychological Association (APA), but note that many journals use a modified style that takes pieces of one style that is modified based on editorial team preferences and feedback from journal readers.

Refer to relevant references from recent years. Many journals prefer references from within the past 5 years. That doesn't mean you can't use older references; just be selective. For example, when writing about pressure ulcers, the groundbreaking work by Barbara J. Braden on predicting pressure ulcers may be relevant, and many articles on this topic are older than 5 years. Be sure that older references are relevant and look for more up-to-date information that augments the findings. As you work on your manuscript, continue to check for new relevant literature at least monthly, so you incorporate the most recent literature.

Don't reference every line of clinical article content. Too much referencing is difficult to read and not necessary. Much information in clinical articles can be considered common knowledge, and a source isn't necessary. Use your best judgment and remember to make the writing your own. Mix referenced content with your own experience and knowledge, and you should have the right blend of referenced original material in the article. If you are ever in doubt about whether material needs to be referenced, take that as a sign that you should probably include a source.

Use Authoritative and Active Voice

Writing from clinical experience and writing for a clinical journal requires you to be authoritative in your writing. Getting your perspective and experiences on patient care into the manuscript helps the nurse reader visualize that care experience. Remember that for clinical articles, it's acceptable to put yourself into the writing: Your experience and knowledge in the area are valuable. It's acceptable to be authoritative, to speak about your interpretations, and to voice an opinion.

Traditionally, as students of nursing, we are taught to make our writing in medical records objective and to state only the facts. This is important from a legal and a clinical perspective, but we often carry this concept into our professional writing. Nurses may be uncomfortable with authoritative writing because we are familiar with writing objectively in our daily work. Think back on some of your favorite articles, though. The authors might not have only described what happened, but they may include their perspectives as well. Do comply with the journal style and with the kinds of writing you find in current issues of your targeted journal, but don't be shy. Be bold and state what you believe and have experienced in practice. What editors are looking for in clinical articles is not just a statement of the facts, but for experience and confidence that makes for strong, compelling writing. Editors and readers can sense that strength and authority in your writing, which makes for more interesting reading.

Active voice adds to this concept and speaks directly to the reader. See Chapter 6 for a more information, but here is a simple example:

- Passive voice: The patient was assessed by Jane.

  In passive voice, the subject doesn't execute the action; the subject is acted upon. So the patient is the subject, and he is being acted upon (assessed) ("Active and passive voice," 2011). The word "by" is a tip-off that the sentence is in passive voice.

- Active voice: Jane assessed the patient.

  Jane is the subject of the sentence, and the subject executes the action described in the verb. In this case, Jane assessed (the action) ("Active and passive voice," 2011).

An important difference between active and passive voice is that active voice uses fewer words. Think about active voice as speaking directly to the nurse reader in direct language. Visualize a straight line from the author to the reader in the communication (see Figure 13.1). Passive voice, on the other hand, is less direct. Imagine passive voice as circling around the issue instead of in a shorter, straight line. Passive voice takes the longer indirect path to describe the concept and uses more words (see following sidebar).

Length of Passive and Active Voice

Passive: Endorsement of the candidate is being considered by the association. (10 words)

Active: The association is considering endorsing the candidate. (7 words)

Passive: The prescription was lost by the patient. (7 words)

Active: The patient lost the prescription. (5 words)

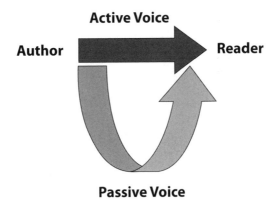

Figure 13.1   Active voice speaks directly to the reader about an issue. Passive voice is indirect and circuitous.

Active writing brings you and your clinical experience into the article and also helps readers connect with you. Think of it as painting a picture. The nurse can see the patient-nurse interaction and imagine the clinical care. Again, consider some of your favorite reading material. You like it because you can feel and see the story in your mind. In good writing—even in professional publications—you can use active voice to tell a story and describe care. Note that in formal research, writing in active voice may be used in the abstract, the introduction, and discussion sections that reflect on the relevance and interpretation of the results.

Finally, the last step is usually to write the lead paragraph (or lede) and title. After you have a well-developed manuscript, the lead paragraph and title should be easier to write. Also, try to add a value proposition. What value will the reader get from the article? Why should they read the article? Include this information in the title if possible. If not, get this information in the first paragraph and the abstract. Here are some examples of journal titles, with what might have been their original titles.

Finding the Best Title

Original title: Medical Management for Depressed Employees

Improved title: Prescriptive Guide for Getting the Depressed Employee Back to Work (Timm, Swanton, Asp, Miller, & Ring, 2013)

Original title: Preventing Industry Influence in Practice

Improved title: "There is No Free Lunch": Strategies to Prevent Industry Influence (Panther-Gleason, & Schaffer, 2013)

Edit Your Manuscript

Editing polishes your manuscript. After reading and editing the manuscript for flow and organization, start to dig and read and edit *every word*. As you read each sentence, you can probably eliminate one or two unnecessary words and make each sentence clearer. Again, think back to the editor reading all day long. If you can eliminate 200-300 words and say the same thing in a clinical article, your writing is tighter and more concise. Readers will find the work more interesting because they are not working as hard to glean the information. Continue this process, honing and rewriting sentences for a few rounds.

Read your manuscript out loud, and you'll immediately hear the extra words and problem sentences. Or have someone read your manuscript out loud to you. You might be surprised at the writing problems you hear that you didn't recognize in your earlier edits. A minimum of three edits is a good target. You'll likely get bored from reading the same information multiple times, but it is worth the effort as your manuscript becomes more polished.

Seek feedback from experts and nonexperts on your work. Have someone who knows the topic well, such as a well-respected colleague, critique and edit your manuscript. Provide an electronic and a hard copy (so they have a choice of how to submit their comments) and instruct your reviewers to provide valuable, constructive feedback of your work. You don't want them to just be polite and say that the work is good: You want a critical review (see following sidebar).

Additionally, share your paper with a novice in the field to gain more insights. Novices can provide feedback about the level of content if you made leaps that skipped over essential information or if they can understand the manuscript.

Getting Good Feedback

Here are a few questions you might ask colleagues to address when they review your manuscript:

- Is the clinical content valuable and accurate?
- Is content missing?
- Does the content flow well, or are there gaps?
- Is it organized?
- Is the work current and relevant?
- Can you comment and make suggestions for edits?

Long uninterrupted text is difficult to read (and boring!), so be sure to use subheads throughout the manuscript. A subhead breaks up the text and defines a section of the article. It also acts as a step for the reader when skimming an article. Reading a 4,000-word article with 10 subheads helps the reader understand the organization of the article and its steps; not having subheads leaves a long narrative section, which can lead to reader fatigue.

Use other elements such as charts, graphs, tables, figures, bulleted lists, or boxes with text. These elements attract readers' eyes as they skim the journal, which makes them popular with editors. They also may cut down the length of the narrative in the manuscript. For example, a clinical article with 4,000 words can be shortened if a section concerning common medications, their drug classes, nursing considerations, and so forth were pulled from the narrative running text and listed in a table.

Scan the journal you are targeting to see how it uses these elements. Additionally, your use of elements described here gets an editor's attention and is a sign of an experienced writer.

When you are finished with your article, you are ready to submit! (See Chapter 8.)

Confidence Booster

You have followed these guidelines, put a lot of time, energy, and passion into your work, and submitted your manuscript. You receive an email after the editor has sent the manuscript through the review process, and she is requesting revisions. You're frustrated because you already did your very best in writing the manuscript!

Don't give up; do the edits! The journal editor liked your manuscript enough to invest time in it and send it for review. But the editor and peer reviewers may have made recommendations for you to improve the manuscript. Change your feeling of defeat into recognition of the comments as a gift. The editorial suggestions will most likely make your final article better.

Some nurse writers stop here and give up, but don't. You have a high chance of acceptance if you make the suggested edits and revisions.

Setting a Timeline

Allow time for each step in writing a clinical article. Topic and focus development may take 2 weeks, journal investigation another 2 weeks, query and planning the content another 2 weeks, and so on.

Try using your bulleted topic outline to help you plan your writing. Give yourself a week, for example, to write a specific number of words for each bullet on the outline, based on the total suggested manuscript length in the author guidelines. Break up the time to write each section; don't plan to write for 8 hours straight. Some prolific writers can write all day, but many novice writers get fatigued after a short time (an hour or two at most), so plan breaks and short goals. Walking away and thinking about the work brings a fresh perspective and new ideas for writing, and also helps keep the creative juices flowing.

Remember: You are not just writing clinical facts. You want to write an interesting piece that draws in readers and holds their attention. Crafting and editing take time.

Keep It Simple

Now you know the steps for writing a clinical article. Simply follow these steps to keep your writing simple and straightforward, and you will soon find you have a finished manuscript ready to submit.

Write Now!

1. List three possible ideas for a clinical article.

2. Write a sentence in passive voice, and then rewrite it in active voice.

3. Choose a format for an article on a clinical topic of your choice and describe how you will approach the article.

4. Go on a treasure hunt: Find the subheads in this chapter.

References

Active and passive voice. (2011). In *The OWL at Purdue* (2013). Retrieved from https://owl.english.purdue.edu/owl/resource/539/01/

Dye, M. I., Rondeau, D., Guido, V., Mason, A., & O'Brien, R. (2013). Identification and management of factitious disorder by proxy. *Journal for Nurse Practitioners, 9*(7), 435–442.

Nicoteri, J. L. (2013). Adolescent pharyngitis: A common complaint with potentially lethal complications. *Journal for Nurse Practitioners, 9*(5), 295–300.

Panther-Gleason, R., & Schaffer, S. D. (2013). "There is no free lunch": Strategies to prevent industry influence. *Journal for Nurse Practitioners. 9*(2), 71–76.

Timm, B. J., Swanton, C. L., Asp, K. M., Miller, S. K., & Ring, D. L. (2013). Prescriptive guide for getting the depressed employee back to work. *Journal for Nurse Practitioner, 9*(7), 458–465.

"Writing is the kind of thing you get better at as you do it; you have to practice to improve."

–*Margaret McClure*

Writing for Scholarly and Research Journals

14

Shaké Ketefian

WHAT YOU'LL LEARN IN THIS CHAPTER

- Typically, include an abstract when writing a research report.

- Prepare your research report so that other researchers will be able to replicate it or include it in systematic reviews.

- It's important to approach the review of literature critically.

- To write systematic reviews, (meta-analysis and meta-syntheses), completed reports of original research are needed.

- Qualitative research methods are more flexible and naturalistic than quantitative research methods.

With the increasing emphasis on evidence-based nursing practice, the opportunities for conducting—and reporting on—research have increased as well. Today, the nursing profession has more journals than ever that publish reports of research. Some publish research in specialty areas, and others publish research of general relevance for nursing.

This chapter explains how to write publishable articles on quantitative and qualitative research and how to report your original research so that systematic reviewers and those conducting replications can include your study in future reviews or meta-analyses. The chapter also gives you practical advice on how to review and synthesize the literature, and how to best report your statistical results.

Anatomy of a Research Article

Typically, a report of quantitative research includes these elements:

- Abstract

- Introduction with an overview of the literature (also called *background and significance*)

- Methods

- Results

- Discussion

Not all journals use this exact structure, so be sure to read the Author Guidelines for the journal you've targeted. Read some recent issues, too, so you have a good sense of how to present your report. Find an article with a design similar to yours and use it as an example when formatting your article. The article you select doesn't have to be on the same topic as yours.

Also, check the Author Guidelines for any reporting structure requirements. For example, some journals require randomized controlled trials be reported according to Consolidated Standards of Reporting Trials (CONSORT) guidelines. You can access the guidelines at http://www.consort-statement.org.

Reporting Quantitative Studies

Quantitative research "is a formal, objective, systematic process in which numerical data are used to obtain information about the world. This research method is used to describe variables, examine relationships among variables, and determine cause-and-effect interactions between variables" (Burns & Grove, 2005, p. 23).

Abstract

Potential readers are likely to learn of your article by finding your abstract during an online search, so pack as much punch as possible in the few words that an abstract allows. Your abstract should communicate the highlights of your study and make readers want to read the whole article.

Some journals want abstracts organized by headings. Others want abstracts without headings. Be sure to follow the journal's Author Guidelines. In the following abstract, the authors complied with the guidelines of the *Journal of Nursing Scholarship* by including a clinical relevance section, which is a feature that most journals do not have, and reporting the information using subheadings. Note the brevity and precision with which the authors communicate the essential features of their work. Also note the international context and sample of this study, which have become a common feature of our publications, a salutary development that should enable cross-cultural collaboration and comparisons in many areas of research and healthcare.

- **Purpose**: The main purpose of this study was to describe the level of experienced burden among Taiwanese primary family caregivers (PFCs) of patients with colorectal cancer (CRC). Another purpose was to explore the relationship between demographic variables, perceived social support, and caregiver burden.

- **Design**: A cross-sectional study.

- **Methods**: This cross-sectional study included 100 PFCs of postsurgery colorectal cancer patients (CCPs) in one teaching hospital in the Taipei area of Taiwan. The research instruments included the Caregiver Reaction Assessment and the Medical Outcome Study–Social Support Survey.

- **Findings**: The caregivers' total burden mean was 3.00 (SD=0.50, range=2.00-4.19). Social support demonstrated a significant relationship with family caregiver burden (impact on health: r=-0.48, $p < .01$; impact on schedule: r=-0.58, $p < .01$; impact on finances: r=-0.44, $p < .01$; lack of family support: r=-.054, $p < .01$; and impact on total scale: r=-0.64, $p < .01$). Higher perceived social support reported by caregivers predicted lower caregiver burden. Multivariate analysis identified social support as a significant independent influence on caregiver burden after controlling for key demographic variables. Social support accounted for 33% (R^2 increment=0.33, $p < .001$) of the variance in caregiver burden.

- **Conclusions**: The study highlights the importance of social support on caregiver burden in this population. Future interventions should include social support to help alleviate caregiver burden in CCPs following surgery.

- **Clinical Relevance**: Results of this study emphasize the important role of social support to enable healthcare professionals to become more effective while caring for caregivers of the patient with CRC who has undergone surgery. The findings of the present study may facilitate cross-cultural comparison and cultural-oriented management of caregiver burden.

Reproduced with permission. Shieh, S-C., Tung, H-S., & Liang, S-Y. (2012). Social support as influencing primary family caregiver burden in Taiwanese patients with colorectal cancer. Journal of Nursing Scholarship, 44(3), 223–231.

Introduction/Background

Your introduction sets the stage for your research report by answering these questions:

- What is your study about (research problem or question)?

- What is the incidence of the problem you address?

- Why is the study important?

- Why did you conduct the study (purpose of the study)?

- Which relevant studies have preceded your study?

- What theoretical formulations or frameworks support your work?

This section draws on the literature review you conducted before embarking on your study, supplemented by additional reviews you make to help you put your results in context.

Preparing to Write the Research Article

You can prepare to write your article even as you begin your research. For example, as you analyze and synthesize the literature, you'll be making comparisons of the reports and the bend or biases that particular authors show. Start thinking about how what you are reading fits into the different sections of the research report. For example, you might find some items useful in the introduction of your paper, others for the literature review, and still others might help you frame the theoretical rationale for your study, or in shaping the methodological approach you take. You'll be writing about all these in your manuscript, so this preparation will serve you well.

You can choose from various methods to organize your review. For example, you might choose to use *chronological* order for research with a historical element, or you could discuss various *themes* related to a topic such as medication reconciliation.

If you are writing a research manuscript, focus on empirical and research literature. You can develop subsections around critical concepts in your study, and where possible, around relationships of your predictor (independent) variables to your dependent variable; in this manner, you display what is known, and at the same time, make a case for your own hypothesis.

Here are more tips for writing the review:

- Rely on paraphrasing authors' ideas and your own syntheses rather than listing quotations from others or simply describing them in a few sentences.

- Illuminate the concepts and relationships that are central to your study.

- Include what is known and identify gaps, making the case for your own study.

- Consider organizing the review about relationships rather than isolated concepts, as research is primarily about establishing relationships.

- Discuss the theoretical rationale that supports your own approach. You might use a framework that is well known in the field, an aspect of which you tested in your study, or one that you formulated in view of what you synthesized from the knowledge that is known.

- End the review with a paragraph summarizing the highlights of the section.

If you're new to the process, read the literature section of experienced investigators. When you have a draft, ask a colleague or a mentor to read it and provide constructive suggestions for improvement.

Q: *How can I improve my ability to write a research article?*

A: Sharpening your analytical skills makes you a better writer. Try this exercise: Identify two research articles from a journal on a topic of interest to you published in the same year by different authors. Read the significance, literature review, and theoretical rationale sections. Compare and contrast the approaches the authors took. Consider how successful they were in conveying to you as the reader their grasp of the issues, how they analyzed and synthesized the work of different authors, and how they presented their theoretical rationale to justify their study. Ask questions such as, "Was the research problem clearly stated?"; "Does the information set the tone for the rest of the article?"; and "Am I interested in reading more?" Then apply what you've learned to your own writing.

Methods

In addition to helping readers to evaluate the strengths and weaknesses of your study, the methods section plays a role in scientific advancement. Investigators who want to replicate or include your study in a meta-analysis will depend on your description of the specifics in the methods section. Typically, this section of a research article includes these elements:

- Design

- Sample

- Setting

- Procedures

- Ethics

- Instruments

- Data analyses approach

Design. Describe the design in specific terms. For example, if you used a quasiexperimental design, clarify whether it was a posttest only or both pretest and posttest. Also, note the number of comparison groups and any number of variations in quasiexperimental designs. This information prepares the reader for what follows. Sometimes, investigators use both quantitative and qualitative elements to enrich understanding of the phenomena under study (referred to as *triangulation*).

Sample. State the number of participants and spell out the inclusion and exclusion criteria. For example, note whether the subjects were healthy or they had a specific condition. State whether you used a random sample or convenience sample. Include the relevant characteristics, the number initially included, the number that dropped out, and any subjects you excluded, as well as your reasons for excluding them.

Setting. Describe the setting where the research was conducted, such as a community health setting or inpatient hospital units. Provide details as to the type of institution or organization so readers can better put the study into context. For instance, were the ICU patients you studied based in large teaching hospitals or small, rural hospitals?

Procedures. Describe the steps you took during the research process to ensure the internal validity of the study, such as how you controlled potential extraneous variables and what you did to ensure consistency in obtaining data and administering treatment to all subjects. If your study has an experimental design, describe the nature of the intervention in this section. If you used research assistants, describe how they were trained, and provide any relevant information, such as on their qualifications for the task.

Ethics. Describe the safeguards you used to protect the subjects from harm and ensure their rights. That includes approval from the relevant institutional review boards (IRBs), which is now mandatory for research on human subjects. IRB review is required by the Department of Health and Human Services (DHHS), and differs from any administrative or collegial reviews that may occur either to improve the quality of the project or to secure access to research subjects.

Seeking Consent

You'll have to obtain permission to conduct the research from your institution and the institutions where your subjects are located. For studies with human subjects, you'll need approval from the IRB, which ensures subjects' rights are protected. In your letter requesting permission or IRB approval, or in writing the informational letters to subjects, describe the following:

- The nature of the study

- The subjects' expected involvement

- The risks to the subjects

- The steps taken to minimize risks

- The subjects' rights to withdraw from the study at any time

- The subjects' rights to anonymity and/or confidentiality

- The need for written consent

Some studies may warrant more detail than others, depending on how intrusive the procedures are and how much risk the subjects face. IRBs have established levels of review, their intensity depending on the actual or potential risk involved for subjects.

Instruments. Describe the structure of the instruments, the purpose for which the instruments were developed, and the types of subjects that the instruments were tested on. Also, include these characteristics of the instruments:

- Number of items that each instrument has and the level of data it will generate

- Validity and reliability information and relevant statistical values

- Any modifications that you made and their possible effects on the psychometric properties

- Purpose and results of the pilot study, if appropriate

The reader needs to know that the instruments were appropriate for measuring the study variables for your subjects. Remember that a study is only as good as the measures you use. If you used several instruments, consider providing a table to present complex information concisely.

Data analyses approach. State your hypotheses or research questions and explain how you tested each one. Include these specifics:

- How the measures were scored, coded, and used

- Whether analyses were treated as continuous or categorical variables

- Whether you used instrument subscales or as a single, total measure

The type of data being collected depends on the research question and the type of measurement being used, which in turn determine the types of statistical tests that you can use to analyze the data.

At the early phases of knowledge development, statistics can enable *description and clarification of concepts,* providing summarization of data and exploration of any deviations. Examples of such descriptive tests are frequency distributions, measures of central tendency (mean, mode, median), and dispersion (range, variance, and standard deviation). At the next level of scientific advancement and data quality, statistics can enable the *examination of relationships* such as correlational analyses and some factor analytic techniques. Finally, at the highest level of science, statistics can be used to *predict phenomena* through various types of multiple regression analyses and other advanced procedures. Predictive research promises to have great value in nursing research and in healthcare. For example, finding out the extent to which age and illness severity—individually as well as together—might predict length of hospital stay would have wide ramifications for developing health-promotion programs for certain age groups and for health policy related to availability of hospital beds, cost, staffing, or alternative arrangements (Grove, Burns, & Gray, 2013).

This conceptualization doesn't account for every situation. For example, much research is conducted to measure differences across groups in both descriptive and experimental designs, or the research might be in the category of providing explanation and insights into phenomena of interest to nurses and nursing. Tests such as t-tests and analyses of variance are used to measure differences; tests used for prediction might also be appropriate for research at this level. I would place research for explanation of phenomena before predictive research, as the third level, following description and exploration of relationships, with prediction being the highest level of science.

Confidence Booster

Like some nurses, you may view statistics with trepidation. Few nurse researchers cast themselves in the role of statistical experts. Instead, they've learned from taking classes, reading books, and working with mentors. Most importantly, they know that they are part of a team that includes statisticians who can help with data analysis. Ask another researcher for suggestions. Above all, don't let your fear of statistics hold you back from conducting research.

You decide which statistical test is used on the basis of the assumptions that underlie a test, as well as the type of data being generated from the research. There are four levels of measurement:

- *Nominal*, the lowest level, where data can be placed into categories, such as in the case of gender or race.

- *Ordinal*, where data are ranked but the intervals between the ranked data are not equal, such as levels of pain.

- *Interval*, in which data yield numerical information and where the distances (in numbers) in a continuum of numbers are equal. For example, the distance between 30 and 40 degrees Celsius and the distance between 10 and 20 degrees Celsius, are equal, but because there is no zero point (a zero Celsius does not mean the absence of temperature), the absolute amount of the variable being measured can't be determined.

- *Ratio*, which is the highest level of measurement, and meets the rules of the previous three levels. Ratio data have absolute zero, as in the case of weight or distance measures.

Grove, Burns, and Gray (2013) have diagrammed the rules of measurement for these four levels in the following way: Nominal is the lowest level, where data can be organized into exclusive and exhaustive categories. Ordinal data have the same rules as nominal data, but in addition categories can be ranked, although the intervals between the ranked categories are not equal. In addition to the rules for the first two levels, interval data have the intervals between points on a scale numerically equal. Ratio level of measurement is the highest level, where absolute zero is present, in addition to having all the rules of the previous levels of measurement.

Statistical tests can be grouped into parametric and nonparametric. The *parametric* tests are thought to be more powerful, as they enable inference "to the parameters of a normally distributed population" (Grove et al., 2013, p. 542), and further, they meet certain assumptions. Typically, interval and ratio data lend themselves to inferential statistical procedures, which are parametric. Data that do not meet the assumptions for parametric statistics will require the use of *nonparametric* statistical tests.

More recently, various data management procedures have been developed for use in qualitative research (see, for example, Table 12-4 in Grove et al., 2013).

Q: *My advisor says I've included too much data in my article. What do you recommend to better present the information?*

A: If you have too much detail, consider creating tables and figures. This approach allows you to present your information clearly and concisely. There's no need to repeat tabular information in your running text. Just provide the highlights in your text and refer your readers to the table. Some journals will permit appendices of additional tables online. (You can learn more about how to use tables and figures in Chapter 7.)

Results

Begin the results section with descriptive information on your variables, providing means, standard deviations, or other relevant descriptive numbers in tables. The same concept applies in describing the sample. Some authors also include a correlation matrix across all variables before getting into the results of tests used for each hypothesis or research question.

Polit and Beck (2012, p. 687) have offered a number of guidelines for statistical tables; here are a few that the beginning researcher might find helpful:

- Tables are numbered sequentially and are assigned headings that give a good description of what they contain.

- You can arrange data in a way that reveals patterns.

- Be consistent in presentation; for example, you need to decide on the level of precision desired for reporting data, and whether you want to report your data to one or two decimal places. Whichever you choose, be consistent throughout.

- Each table should stand alone, should augment what is in the text, and should have clear labels for columns.

- Indicate probability levels and units of measurement (in table or footnote).

- Use footnotes to clarify any unit of measurement or for abbreviations.

Similar principles apply in preparing figures. If well used, tables and figures can facilitate the narrative so the reader doesn't get lost in numbers. Many journals have word-count limits for articles and the number of tables and figures they allow, so take these realities into account when writing. If you are writing a special report for your institution, or a thesis, however, you can prepare many more tables and place those with secondary importance in your appendix.

You're now ready to report on the results of your hypothesis tests. You can restate each hypothesis, and report on results, referring to tables if indicated. Do not add comments or interpretations; save those for the discussion section of your report.

Discussion

The purpose of the discussion section is to interpret your results and explain their implications for the area of scientific study. Tie your findings to your theoretical framework and the literature. Do your results support existing conceptions and theories? Or do they indicate a different view of the phenomenon? In either case, what explanations can you offer? Use the literature you have reviewed in your explanations and discuss how you would modify your theoretical framework in either case. If your research does not support your hypothesis, explain the possible reasons why. Be sure to include limitations of your study, such as the subjects being from one particular area of the country. At the end, provide implications for the relevant area of nursing and indicate the next steps for further research.

Balancing Internal and External Validity

When you make choices about how to control variables with your selections of subjects, settings, and procedures, you enhance the internal validity of your study. The more controls you exert, the stronger the internal validity.

However, more controls can weaken the external validity of the study, or the extent to which your findings apply to other populations and settings. So how do you make decisions that strike a balance between internal validity with external validity? Base your decisions on the reason why you are doing the study, *not* on the research question you are asking. For example, if you are more interested in a single population, you might decide in favor of strong internal validity. If, on the other hand, you envision broader applicability of your study to different populations, you might want to include a variety of subjects drawn from multiple kinds of settings, which will enhance your ability to generalize more broadly.

Systematic Reviews

Nurses' interest in systematic reviews as a tool for generating evidence useful for practice has grown. Systematic review has been described as "a structured, comprehensive synthesis of the research literature to determine the best research evidence available to address a health-care question" (Grove et al., 2013, p. 472); these same authors have provided specific steps for conducting systematic reviews and for evaluating such reviews from the literature (see Grove et al., pp. 473-482).

Writing a systematic review is similar to writing a research article; include the standard sections such as introduction, methodology, and results. Be sure to cover these elements:

- The question you identified—for example, "How often should the dressing for a peripherally inserted central catheter (PICC) site be changed?"

- What criteria you used to select studies or other information to include. For example, articles within the past 5 years, articles published in peer-reviewed journals, adult patients, patients with a particular diagnosis, and so on

- The specific key words that you used and what databases you searched

- What you found—for example, types of articles and research methods used

- The quality of the studies—for example, were sample sizes generally adequate?

- Implications of what you found—for example, recommended frequency of dressing changes based on study results and guidelines found

Remember, for a systematic review you need to use a specific protocol when selecting material so that others could reproduce your work.

Given the value of meta-analysis and its increasingly common use in research, it's worth discussing it in more depth.

Types of Reviews

It's easy to get confused by the terms systematic review, meta-analysis, and integrative review because many people incorrectly use them interchangeably. Here's what you need to know.

A *systematic review* answers a specific (usually clinical) question. The researcher uses explicit methods to identify, select, and analyze studies to arrive at an answer (The Cochrane Collaboration, n.d.).

A *meta-analysis* is a statistical analysis of *quantitative* studies (but not always), concerned with the effects of a specific intervention, and usually having randomized controlled trials as their design. A *meta-synthesis* is a synthesis of *qualitative* research on a given topic. However, it's possible to treat review of quantitative studies descriptively, which can make the report a meta-synthesis (as opposed to meta-analysis). In this case, the distinction is in the treatment of the identified studies, not in the studies themselves.

An *integrative review* casts a wider net than a systematic review, which helps to more fully understand concepts and phenomena.

Meta-Analysis

No one study can provide the basis for patient care. That requires multiple studies of the same phenomenon, including replication studies. However, multiple studies on the same topic tend to discover different kinds of results and relationships among variables, including contradictory findings. Different authors use different methods, measurements, types of subjects, and settings.

Integrating such research so that investigators can derive policy or practice implications requires meta-analysis. Typically, meta-analysts use a variety of statistical techniques and employ the effect size as a crucial metric. Even if the selected studies use different methods and measures, meta-analysis is possible—as long as the studies deal with the phenomenon of interest (your dependent variable), and use the same variables as predictors. It's also necessary that the original researchers report sufficient information to enable meta-analysts to carry out the required statistical procedures.

Meta-analysis requires the computation of a common metric, the most common of which is the d index. The d is computed by dividing group differences in the means by the standard deviation for the groups, pooled. Alternative methods exist for computing the d; other indexes can be used as the common metric as well. You'll need to determine which values are feasible and available in your research, and provide that information to the reader.

When reporting a meta-analysis, identify the sample as the studies selected for analysis. Include these characteristic of your literature search:

- Research problem/variables of interest

- Databases used

- Time period covered

- Journals searched

- Keywords used for searches

- Inclusion and exclusion criteria

- Types/qualities of studies selected

- Number of studies in the sample

The meta-analysis report should also include descriptions of the instruments, analyses, and results.

Meta-Analysis Instruments

To extract relevant information from the studies, most meta-analysts develop an instrument for recording substantive, methodological, and descriptive characteristics. This instrument enables them to check and report reliability across the different raters who reviewed the studies. If the quality of the studies is rated, the article must describe the scoring method because these scores can be used in analyses, yielding useful information.

Meta-Analysis Analyses and Results

Describe the measures used in your sample studies to operationalize the variables of interest, using descriptive statistics. Some meta-analysts choose only studies that use the same measures to increase confidence in the results. However, this approach limits the usefulness of the results, and in effect, defeats the purpose for which meta-analysis has proved so useful. The best way to convey descriptive information on all aspects of the sample of studies is to present them in table form; create columns for each piece of information, such as authors, title of study, research question the study dealt with, sample and measures used, and results. Enter the relevant information for the selected studies.

Describe the data analyses and the results. The effect size (*d*) is a critical statistic in meta-analysis, so you must describe how the *d* statistic was extracted or how some other statistic was used to compute the *d* as the effect-size estimate for each study and relationship. Analyze and report the results and overall conclusions for your research question. Some authors also analyze the relationship between quality scores and the effect sizes.

Present an interpretation of the findings, covering these points:

- Conclusions that can be drawn

- Implications for practice or policy

- Recommendations for next steps in research

- What gaps in knowledge were addressed through this study and what further work may be indicated

Quantitative research provides valuable insights, but so does qualitative research. So that readers gain the most benefit from qualitative research, you need to carefully consider how you report the results.

Reporting Qualitative Research

Qualitative research methods are more flexible and naturalistic than quantitative research. They aim to capture, document, or explain phenomena as they exist. Examples of these research methods are

- Phenomenological research

- Ethnographic research

- Philosophic research

- Critical theory research

The approach to reporting depends on the features of the type of study. Compare the features and the reporting of two specific types of qualitative research: the grounded theory and historical methods.

Grounded Theory Research

Grounded theory research was proposed in the 1960s to develop theory from data—which is to say, to develop theory inductively. Typically, the grounded theory method results in middle range theory development at a substantive level (Glaser, 1978). Grounded theory foundations include symbolic interactionism and pragmatism (Wuest, 2007). This type of research is typically done to understand phenomena about which little is known.

Reports on this research are not guided by the literature, although an investigator may use related research literature to inform the process during data analysis or interpretation of the results. The report includes these elements:

- Background of the research problem

- Circumstances under which the problem occurs

- Effects on specific populations

- Need for the study

In some cases, study objectives can replace the research problem.

This research process is iterative, and your report should take this into consideration. After presenting the problem, describe the sources of data, such as observation, individual or group interviews, or examination of documents. You will need to obtain human subject committee approval, unless you are examining old documents only.

Egan (2002) describes the steps of grounded theory research as:

1. Initiation of research

2. Data selection

3. Initiation and ongoing data collection

4. Data analysis and interpretation

As researchers collect data, they analyze the data with the constant comparative method to determine emerging concepts, categories, and themes. Data collection is complete when no new themes or categories emerge. In reporting the research, you need to describe the steps, detailing the data analysis process, including the completion of data collection, and the results. The analysis process moves from the concrete (naming, comparing) to categories and their properties, which "involve conceptualization of some essential elements or features" (Egan, 2002, p. 286).

The written report should document the evolution of categories "around a main story line" (Egan, 2002, p. 286). Egan describes this process as follows:

A structural framework is developed through the clarification of associations between the central (or load-bearing) categories and the supporting categories and properties. Grounded theory building establishes a foundation that bounds the theory, a description that elaborates on the structure and design of the theory, and an inventory that establishes the data-based building materials that compose the theory. (pp. 286–287)

Relationships among concepts and categories emerge, enabling the investigator to formulate the grounded theory along with propositions that can be tested in the future. This research approach can also be used to develop recommendations for policy at institutional or national levels. The following example illustrates these points eloquently.

Tregunno, Peters, Campbell, and Gordon (2009) conducted a study in Ontario, Canada to "examine the barriers and challenges internationally educated nurses experience transitioning into the workforces after they achieve initial registration in their adopted country" (p. 182). The researchers conducted semi-structured interviews with 400 nurses educated in 20 countries. Five themes emerged from their analysis of the interviews, and each theme had multiple components.

A central theme was that nurses found the expectations of them and the roles of patients and families to be different than in their home country. The authors made policy recommendations to address post-licensure transition issues as an area for intervention with these nurses.

Historical Research

Historical research is now widely accepted within nursing as an important area of scholarship, and nurses are studying and using historical methodology, known as *historiography*. The method is rigorous, with its own rules and conventions. It has been defined as "a process of examining data from the past, integrating it into a coherent unity, and putting it to some pragmatic use for the present and the future" (Sarnecky, 1990, p. 2). In reporting historical research, you need to outline the steps used.

The steps of historical research are the following:

- Identifying a problem area

- Specifying the sources of data to determine their adequacy

- Collecting data

- Testing the data for validity and reliability

- Analyzing and interpreting the data

- Writing the research report

Testing validity and reliability in historical research differs from other types of research and can pose challenges for the historiographer. *Validity* is established through external criticism, and is concerned with the authenticity of the data or documents. *Reliability* is determined through internal criticism, and has to do with "the meaning inherent in the content of the document and its trustworthiness as a source" (Sweeney, 2005, p. 69).

In this process, the researcher considers the following:

- Sources of evidence

- Question of whether the evidence is primary or secondary

- Types of corroboration sought before a datum can be accepted as fact

The data collected need to be organized and analyzed into an integrated whole in a coherent manner. Finally, the researcher applies what has been learned from the past to elucidate events in the present and the future. Typically, historical research does not require human subject review, but if you are interviewing people who might have participated in the events of interest, such review is warranted.

> In a published historical study, Traynor (2007) explores what he views as a tension between utilitarianism and empiricism on the one hand and a faith in transcendent values, which he believes nursing embodies, developed in 19th-century Europe. The author's analysis suggests that such a tension exists today in debates about practice and evidence. Specific themes that Traynor discusses include:
>
> - Women, social cohesion, and nursing
>
> - Moral talk and scientific talk as a dilemma

- Nursing identity, managerialism, and evidence-based practice
- Nursing, research, and development
- Controversy in medicine
- Nursing and evidence-based movements

Whether you are presenting quantitative or qualitative research results, follow a set structure to make it easier for the reader to understand those results.

Spread the Knowledge

Writing a research article or report can be intimidating. It's worth considering what will happen if you don't share your results: What you have learned will languish, depriving researchers and clinicians the opportunity to benefit from your work. Ultimately those who lose the most are the patients who could benefit from what you learned. Take that important final step as a researcher: Share your results.

Write Now!

1. Read a published research article without reading the abstract. Then, write your own abstract.

2. Read the results section of two research articles and note how the authors have used tables and figures to supplement the article. Critique the two papers in how well they presented their results and the extent to which tables and figures helped you understand what the authors were trying to convey. What would *you* do differently?

3. Read several systematic reviews from recent literature and describe their characteristics; compare similarities and contrast differences, and develop a table format with labeled columns into which information can be entered if you were actually conducting such a study.

References

Burns, N., & Grove, S. K. (2005). *The practice of nursing research: Conduct, critique, and utilization* (5th ed.). St. Louis, MO: Elsevier/Saunders.

The Cochrane Collaboration (n.d.). Glossary. Retrieved from http://www.cochrane.org/glossary

Egan, T. M. (2002). Grounded theory research and theory building. *Advances in Developing Human Resources, 4*(3), 277–295.

Glaser, B. (1978). *Theoretical sensitivity*. Mill Valley, CA: Sociology Press.

Grove, S. K., Burns, N., & Gray, J. R. (2013). *The practice of nursing research: Appraisal, synthesis, and generation of evidence.* (7th ed.). St. Louis, MO: Elsevier/Saunders.

Polit, D. F., & Beck, C. T. (2012). *Nursing research: Generating and assessing evidence for nursing practice.* (9th ed.). Philadelphia, PA: Lippincott Williams & Wilkins/Wolters Kluwer.

Sarnecky, M. T. (1990). Historiography: A legitimate research methodology for nursing. *Advances in Nursing Science, 12*(4), 1–10.

Sweeney, J. (2005). Historical research: Examining documentary sources. *Nurse Researcher, 12*(3), 61–73.

Traynor, M. (2007). A historical description of the tensions in the development of modern nursing in nineteenth-century Britain and their influence on contemporary debates about evidence and practice. *Nursing Inquiry, 14*(4), 299–305.

Tregunno, D., Peters, S., Campbell, H., & Gordon, S. (2009). International nurse migration: U-turn for safe workplace transition. *Nursing Inquiry, 16*(3), 182–190.

Wuest, J. (2007). Grounded theory method. In P. L. Munhall (Ed.), *Nursing research: A qualitative perspective* (4th ed., pp. 239–271). Sudbury, MA: Jones and Bartlett.

Reporting the Quality Improvement or Evidence-Based Practice Project

15

Jo Rycroft-Malone
Christopher Burton

WHAT YOU'LL LEARN IN THIS CHAPTER

- To know what to include in your report, start with the Author Guidelines.

- In your report, provide details, including the context of the project, to help readers gain practical insights that might have relevance to their own work.

- Using a variety of formats and media fosters dissemination by getting key messages out to different audiences.

Closing the gap between what nurses should be practicing and what actually happens in practice is a thorny challenge and a political imperative. Few would disagree with the idea of making changes in healthcare practice and service delivery that have the potential to lead to better patient outcomes, better system performance, and better professional development (Batalden & Davidoff, 2007).

Although there are some distinguishing features between projects labelled as "quality improvement" (QI) or "evidence-based practice" (EBP), such as the role that evidence plays and the types of interventions implemented, both have the same goal—providing patients with the best and safest care possible (Rycroft-Malone et al., 2004). These activities are the foundation for professional nursing practice and the responsibility of the entire healthcare team.

This chapter guides you through how to write articles about QI and EBP projects. Although similar to the process for writing a research article, these projects require the use of unique techniques. Using these techniques helps ensure that readers gain the most from your work and increases the potential for the wider community to learn from your improvement practice and research.

Common Questions About QI and EBP Projects

The answers to a few common questions about writing about QI and EBP projects will help prepare you to write.

What Is the Difference Between a QI or EBP Project and a Research Study?

Some people say that QI and EBP projects are not as rigorous as a full-scale research study, but this is not necessarily the case. All types of projects—research, QI, or EBP—can be conducted with more or less rigour. In fact, the quality and safety movement has been championing the need for more rigorous methods and transparent reporting.

Others say that QI and EBP projects tend to be local and focused on particular patient populations; however, you probably have read reports of research studies that have been conducted in a particular context with a specific patient group. And, you only need to read articles in the journal *Quality and Safety in Healthcare* to see that many quality projects can be large scale and fully funded by external agencies.

The one characteristic that differentiates QI and EBP projects from research projects is that they are consistently concerned with attempting to demonstrate and evaluate ways in which care, service delivery, or practice can be improved. These projects may be local, and some may be small scale, but they should be no less rigorously conducted than traditional research.

What Are the Challenges of Writing About Quality Improvement Work?

A growing body of research (Chen, 2005) indicates that using evidence in practice is a complex and multifactorial process. Consequently, improvement interventions rarely rely on one ingredient. It's likely that you'll have used a number of different strategies and interventions to effect change at different organizational levels, including with coworkers, managers, and potentially including patients and family caregivers. Unpacking the active ingredients, how they relate to each other, and how much of each is required presents considerable methodological and design challenges. A good article on QI will make sense of the active ingredients, carefully describing the reality of what was done and why.

Who Reads About Improvement?

Three main groups seek information about improvement projects. *Clinical nurses* who are developing their own projects or improving the safety, reliability, quality, and effectiveness of clinical practice might be particularly interested in rich, practical insights that could have relevance for their own work. *Project staff*, including individuals with improvement as part of their everyday work and those who have been assigned to support particular projects, will be interested to know what approaches or techniques seem to be helpful in delivering a successful improvement project. *Researchers* will be interested in what theoretical perspectives have been used, and how the methodologies used to evaluate the impacts of projects have generated new insights.

The publication where you choose to publish your work will have a target readership, which should drive the style and content of your writing. Although your work will most often appear in nursing publications, remember that there is now interest in learning whether knowledge of "what works'" in improvement can be transferred to other professional fields, potentially extending your readership. Follow these steps to increase the reach of your report:

- Understand the needs of the audiences you are writing for.

- Within the constraints of your chosen medium, adopt as rich and descriptive a writing style as possible.

- Include information on both the theory and practice of QI.

- Pay attention to the use of jargon, avoiding it where possible and clarifying it when it's necessary.

- Tease out the findings that may have relevance for a non-nursing audience.

Researchers are increasingly adopting a more collaborative approach to the design and conduct of improvement studies (Van de Ven, 2007), which is thought to increase the likelihood the findings will be used. In this spirit, consider consulting with key stakeholders from your target audience to see how you might increase the impact of your writing.

Start Writing

There has been a call for minimal standards for reporting on research about implementation, where the subject matter is concerned with closing the gap between what we "know" and what is practiced (Rycroft-Malone & Burton, 2011).

One commonly used set of standards for the QI project is the Standards for Quality Improvement Reporting Excellence (SQUIRE, n.d.). These guidelines provide a framework for sharing the knowledge acquired through both the practice and research of implementing improvement interventions systematically and in detail. They are useful because they encourage you to clarify your thinking, verify your observations, and justify your inferences.

Q: *Are the SQUIRE guidelines the only ones I need to consult?*

A: No. Depending on the approach you've taken for your improvement interventions and the requirements of the publication where you are submitting, you might also need to refer to other reporting standards. The Consolidated Standards for Reporting Clinical Trials (CONSORT, 2010) apply to randomized clinical trials and the Consolidated Standards for Reporting Qualitative Research is a 32-item checklist for qualitative research involving interviews and focus groups (Tong, Sainsbury, & Craig, 2007). In 2013, EBP Process Quality Assessment (EPQA) guidelines were released (Ching Lee, Johnson, Newhouse, & Warren, 2013). The guidelines can be used to guide and evaluate EBP projects.

The following sections draw primarily on the SQUIRE framework to help guide you through the issues that are important to pay attention to when writing your article.

Title

Busy readers need to understand the heart of your article quickly. They will use your title and abstract to make decisions about the relevance and importance of your paper. Titles should also contain key words that signpost your article so those searching the literature can easily find it and understand how it is similar to or different from other articles. SQUIRE points to three components of a title that will provide clear reference points that you should signpost to the reader.

How quality is considered within the study. Quality can be considered in different ways, including patient safety, clinical effectiveness, patient-centeredness, timeliness, efficiency, and equity of care. In addition, the way that improvement work in nursing is organized and practiced can also reflect different traditions, including:

- Quality improvement—for example, the use of PDSA Cycles (Langley, Nolan, Nolan, Norman, & Provost, 2009)

- Process design and evaluation—for example, lean technology (Ohno, 1988)

- Process variation and safety—for example, Six Sigma (Harry & Schroeder, 2006)

- Practice development (McCormack, Manley, & Garbett, 2004)

- Evidence-based practice (Sackett, 1996)

- Implementation (Rycroft-Malone et al., 2002)

Where possible, the inclusion in the title of one of these terms or phrases that describes your approach to quality will be a helpful signpost to readers.

The aims of the intervention. The title should provide a clear focus for the improvement activity. For example, were you attempting to change a process of care such as a patient's length of stay? Or were you focused on the reliability of care processes rather than a change in the process itself? You might be also interested in impacts for patients, staff, and other stakeholders.

The specifics of the study methods used in the improvement work. The methods that researchers use to evaluate improvement initiatives are broad. Providing some details in the title that show the methods used in your project will help to orient readers to your article early on.

Here is an example of an effective title:

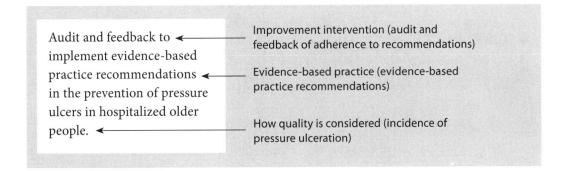

Abstract

Most publications require an abstract, which is a summary of your study in 250 words or less. Different publications have different requirements, but typically abstracts include four sections: a background that sets out the challenge and aim of your improvement; the methods used in implementation and evaluation; your findings; and the conclusions, which include clinical relevance. Often it's easier to write the abstract after the main article is nearly final because by then you have a much clearer idea about what issues are significant.

Introduction

In this section, explain to the reader why you undertook the project. Include a summary of current knowledge about the problem you tackled, and a detailed description of the context(s) in which the project took place. This will require you to report on the existing evidence about the topic—including, as appropriate, policy and practice and research literature—as well as drawing on your knowledge about the locality.

Your introduction should answer the following questions:

- **What is currently known about the topic?** For example, if the focus of your article is on a project to improve the care of peripheral intravenous lines, introduce what the policy, practice, and research evidence shows about best practice in this area, and how others have previously improved practice or service delivery.

- **What prompted the need to attend to this issue?** For example, was there an incident or safety event that identified the need for an intervention around the care of peripheral intravenous lines?

- **What is the gap or current practice or situation you are attempting to improve?** For example, "An audit of documentation found that information about why peripheral intravenous lines were being inserted and subsequently managed was poorly recorded." Clearly articulate the gap between what is currently happening in practice and what should be happening—this is the improvement gap.

- **What is the improvement-related question?** After you've identified the gap, clearly and specifically state the main and secondary questions you were addressing within the project. Include what you were expecting to see change and how.

- **What is the context of improvement?** The implementation of improvement interventions is contingent upon the context in which they are being implemented, so a detailed description of the context is vital. This is described in the SQUIRE guidelines as the "canvas upon which improvement is painted," which is a useful metaphor for the level of detail required. It's not enough to describe just the physical context; readers must understand the details of the structures, processes, people, and patterns of care of the setting(s) in which the project took place. In the earlier example of implementing an evidence-based approach to reducing the risks of pressure ulcerations, factors such as nurse-to-patient ratios and the profile of patient comorbidities might mediate successful implementation, and should be highlighted to readers.

After the introduction, the next step is to discuss the methods used.

Methods

The reader needs to understand the decisions you made in designing your improvement project. This should include a consideration of any ethical issues that you felt were relevant, the setting in which you were working, the interventions you selected, how you planned to study implementation, the measurement of effects, and the analysis of data. Untangle the focus of improvement activity (in the example, evidence-based practice in pressure ulcer prevention) and the improvement interventions (audit and feedback of nursing performance) designed to address the quality issue. The SQUIRE guidelines provide a useful framework for doing this and for writing an effective methods section.

Ethical issues. Any change in clinical practice might have implications for patients, family caregivers, staff, and other professionals that warrant critical review from an ethical perspective. If you sought approval from an ethical review committee for your work, it's important to make that explicit. However, simply stating that ethical review was obtained tells the reader little about the potential ethical issues that you faced in the study. Specific issues you might want to discuss include the following:

- **The protection of patients' well being:** Was there any risk that care could be compromised through the project?

- **The protection of staff:** What support was provided to ensure members of nursing staff were prepared for any changes?

- **Clinical governance:** Were any changes sanctioned by the appropriate hospital committees?

Also, you need to state how you addressed any ethical concerns—for example, obtaining consent from participants.

Setting. Your description of the study setting includes more than geography. You should also include those aspects of the context that were anticipated to influence improvement. The best way to highlight this is in the following example of a study improving the management of poststroke swallowing:

> **Example of a poor description of setting:** Implementation of a guideline for nurses' assessment of patients' swallowing function was tested on a 12-bed acute stroke unit.

Example of a good description of setting: Implementation of a guideline for nurses' assessment of patients' swallowing was tested on a 12-bed acute stroke unit. In the most recent national audit, the unit's organizational quality score was in the upper quartile, and the staffing profile was consistent with national recommendations. The unit was integrated within a regional service model with strong ethos of multidisciplinary working and service development. Within 3 years there had been engagement in a range of QI initiatives, including process mapping, audit and feedback, and networking with other services as part of a national improvement programme around benchmarking. This profile of organizational experience and external evaluation indicated that the quality of baseline clinical practice would provide a credible context for testing guideline implementation.

In this example, the reader is pointed to aspects of the history of organizational change, baseline performance, and experience with improvement, all of which were anticipated to positively influence the effects of guideline implementation.

Confidence Booster

If you're writing an article for the first time, consider asking someone who has been published before to help you. In the case of a QI article, tap into the expertise of stakeholders who were involved in the original project. You might want to include one or two of them as coauthors. Just be sure that you decide up front who will be the lead author and what responsibilities each author will have. You might also ask a trusted friend for encouragement as you move through the different stages of writing.

Planning the intervention. Quality improvement work can include two types of interventions:

- The new nursing practice or intervention that you have implemented as part of your QI project

- The implementation interventions that you have used to support staff in their use of the new nursing practice or intervention

Fully describe both, considering the following questions:

- What are the component parts of the intervention? Who completed the activities, and how were they prepared and supported? What would another team need to know to be able to reproduce what you did in their own clinical work?

- What was your justification for selecting the intervention? You might make links to your analysis of previous work outlined in the introduction section, but pay attention to their fit with the local contexts where your improvement work was completed.

Implementation Taxonomy

A good strategy in writing about your implementation intervention is to use words from a published taxonomy such as the Cochrane Effective Practice and Organisation of Care Review Group (2011) taxonomy, which includes four major types of interventions (see Table 15.1).

Table 15.1   Types of Implementation Interventions

Types of interventions	Examples
Professional	Distribution of educational materials, local consensus processes, audit and feedback, reminders
Financial	Fee-for-service, incentives
Organizational	Revision of professional roles, skill mix change, patient involvement, changing documentation systems
Regulatory	Management of patient complaints, peer review

The following provides an example of how use of the SQUIRE guidance adds meaning to your writing:

> **Non-SQUIRE Guidelines:** The new dietetic referral system included a nutritional screening assessment, which was completed by ward staff as the basis for prioritizing patients. Referrals were then coded as urgent, important, or routine, and managed by the service administration staff.

SQUIRE Guidelines: The new referral system included a screening assessment (see Appendix E), which registered nurses completed as the basis for prioritizing patients. The nurses coded referrals as urgent, important, or routine. Service administration staff then managed the referrals. All registered nursing staff completed 2 hours of education on how to complete the screening assessment, which included a test of reliability (threshold 90%). To promote successful implementation:

- A working group that included members of the unit team who would be completing the screening developed the assessment.

- The screening assessment was embedded within the electronic health record for all patients admitted to the unit.

Monthly audits of the timely completion of screening, referrals, and patient outcomes were provided and shared with staff to support ongoing review and development of this quality assessment.

Planning the study of the intervention. Your improvement project will be expected to have a number of consequences, or effects, for different stakeholders. These effects may relate to individual impacts (for example, changing thinking, changing behavior), care processes (such as length of stay), and patient outcomes.

The following points will help you comprehensively describe the study effects:

- How will you know that your interventions have been implemented sufficiently? You may consider how many of different intervention components are delivered within the study (dosage).

- You'll have a good idea as to how you anticipate the intervention working. Is there a chain of events or certain changes that your intervention will cause? If so, you might consider what data you could collect to test whether these changes are taking place.

- What is your overall study design to identify these changes? What are the most important outcomes that you want to consider? You should consider what strength your study design has to support any assertions about the effects of your intervention that you might want to make.

- Your study will not have happened in a vacuum. Were there any events either within the project, or in the wider organization, that might influence your findings?

Once you have described how the project was done, the next step is to describe how it was evaluated.

Methods of evaluation. Report the quality of any measures used within the study, paying attention to issues of validity and reliability. If you used standardized measures, have they been evaluated in previous studies? If you are relying on local data, such as clinical performance, how have you ensured that these data are credible? You may also want to describe any education in data collection techniques that members of project staff have completed as part of your project.

Analysis. Finally, your analysis section needs to provide an overview of how your data were managed and analyzed. How have quantitative data been summarized and how has variation between key variables been assessed? You can summarize qualitative data using appropriate codes, which you can in turn link through overarching themes that have the potential to explain what occurred within your project.

Results

Your results section should include two key sections: the nature of the setting and the improvement intervention, and changes in processes of care and patient outcomes.

Check the author guidelines for the publication you are targeting for more information on how different types of data should be presented. The following provides an indication of what you might like to include in each of these sections:

- Revisiting your description of the study setting in light of your experiences of the study will highlight those elements that provided an important context for the study. For example, how did the relationships between leadership, staffing, and resources affect buy-in to the project? This information provides a useful reference for findings related to the actual course of the intervention, the degree of success of implementation, and any lessons learned.

- In addition to summarizing impacts on processes and patient outcomes, pay attention to any unexpected findings. Inevitably, focusing attention on one aspect of clinical care in an improvement project means you're paying less attention to something else. Carefully describe any adverse events that others might need to watch out for.

It's not enough to simply report your results; you need to put them in context for the reader.

Discussion

The discussion section of the article gives you the opportunity to put the findings of your project into a wider context, highlight some of the successes and challenges that were experienced during your research, and consider the implications from your work.

Follow these tips to ensure your discussion section is effective:

- Give the reader a short digest of the main findings of the project before going on to discuss how these relate to the broader literature. Try to boil down your findings to three or four main points; you can also share these points through social media such as Twitter to encourage wider dissemination of your findings. Remember that your findings should be published before you share them on social media.

- Focus most of the discussion section on how the findings of your project relate to existing literature. Don't look for evidence that simply supports your findings; also look for evidence that might contradict what you have found. Such a discussion is helpful for readers to consider the relevance of your findings. Using tables or figures to summarize and compare previous work to that of yours can be helpful as presentation tools.

- Reflect on whether the study went as planned and achieved the outcomes you expected. If it did not, explain to the reader why you think this might have happened. For example, often things don't go to plan because something happens that you were not able to predict at the outset (for example, a change in leadership); describe the unexpected event and how it could influence what you (or others) might do differently in the future.

- Discuss how you think the findings from your work add to the existing body of evidence. It could be you added to the evidence for a particular issue, such as frequency of dressing changes for a peripheral intravenous line, or you might have learned more about how a particular intervention, such as audit or feedback, was used to improve management of a clinical issue.

- Consider the limitations of the project such as issues about the way that data were collected, tools used for data collection, sample selection, funder constraints, and the design of the project. Clearly describe them so others can make an informed judgment about the transferability, generalizability, credibility, and trustworthiness of your findings.

Now that you have discussed your findings, you are ready to complete the article by summarizing conclusions and implications.

Conclusions and Implications

Finish the article with clear and data-driven conclusions and implications that have broad, rather than local, applicability. First, highlight what you believe to be the lessons learned, including what the next steps for investigation might be. Point out specific questions, challenges, and potential methods/approaches. Second, describe the implications that arise from your work, including implications for policy, practice or service delivery, research, and management. Consider implications on a wide, rather than local, scale as readers will want to consider their relevance for their own settings.

Strengthening Your Article

The SQUIRE guidelines provide a good starting point to help you structure the writing about a QI project, but they aren't the only considerations.

How you or your team have approached the design of the project, and how you have chosen to evaluate the project will reflect some fundamental beliefs about what QI is, and how it should be studied. If you're writing up the project for a more "academic" audience, you may want to pay particular attention to the theory of change and fidelity.

Theory of change. Using theory provides an opportunity to design an approach or intervention with an evidence base to believe "this might work," and theory-guided evaluations of improvement processes will be helpful in better understanding mediating factors (see Rycroft-Malone & Bucknall [2010] for an in-depth consideration). Therefore, when writing articles about your QI or EBP project, it's important to fully describe how theory might have been used, and, if appropriate, how theory was advanced or tested through use. If you didn't explicitly use theory in the project, you could refer to theory in the discussion section of your article. This will help contextualize your work for readers in a wider evidence base and enhance the potential for theoretical transferability of the findings.

Fidelity. The practical world of improvement is often messy: Evidence can be contested, problems may emerge over time, and planned activities need tailoring to challenges that emerge in the field. A key question to help you consider fidelity is to what degree did what you planned actually happen? What components of your intervention changed, and why? This builds on the SQUIRE guidance, which requires you to include information about how any formative evaluation would be used to modify the interventions that you studied.

Disseminating Your Work

Every day nurses are conducting QI and EBP projects designed to improve processes and interventions that will help achieve better patient outcomes. By taking time to share the results of quality projects you're involved in, you can ensure your knowledge spreads beyond your organization to benefit patients in other settings.

Write Now!

1. Think about a QI or EBP project that you have either led or been involved in: Write an outline for an article, including subheadings and sample text for each section. Think about how you might involve other relevant stakeholders in this planning process.

2. Go to different journals and find different types of articles that report QI or EBP projects. Use the framework described in this chapter to assess the articles: What are some of the common missing elements from the articles you find? How would you improve them?

3. Write up the article that you planned as a result of undertaking the first task!

References

Batalden, P. B., & Davidoff, F. (2007). What is "quality improvement" and how can it transform healthcare? *Quality and Safety in Health Care, 16*(1), 2–3.

Chen, H. (2005). *Practical program evaluation.* Thousand Oaks, CA: Sage Publications.

Ching Lee, M., Johnson, K. L., Newhouse, R. P., & Warren, J. I. (2013). Evidence-based practice process quality assessment: EPQA guidelines. *Worldviews on Evidence-Based Nursing, 10*(3), 140–149.

Cochrane Effective Practice and Organisation of Care Review Group. (2011). Data Collection Checklist. Institute of Population Health. University of Ottawa, Ontario.

Consolidated Standards of Reporting Trials (CONSORT). (2010). The CONSORT Statement. Retrieved from http://www.consort-statement.org/consort-statement

Harry, M., & Schroeder, R. (2006). *Six Sigma: The breakthrough management strategy revolutionizing the world's top corporations.* New York, NY: Crown Business.

Langley, G. L., Nolan, K. M., Nolan T. W., Norman C. L., & Provost, L. P. (2009). *The improvement guide: A practical approach to enhancing organizational performance* (2nd ed.). San Francisco, CA: Jossey Bass.

McCormack, B., Manley, K., & Garbett, R. (2004). *Practice development in nursing.* Oxford, UK: Wiley Blackwell.

Ohno, T. (1988). *Toyota production system*. New York, NY: Productivity Press.

Rycroft-Malone, J., & Bucknall, T. (2010). *Models and frameworks for implementing evidence-based practice: Linking evidence to action.* Indianapolis, IN: Wiley-Blackwell & Sigma Theta Tau International.

Rycroft-Malone, J., & Burton, C. (2011). Is it time for standards for reporting on research about implementation? *Worldviews on Evidence-Based Nursing, 8*(4), 189–190.

Rycroft-Malone, J., Kitson, A., Harvey, G., McCormack, B., Seers, K., Titchen, A., & Estabrooks, C. A. (2002). Ingredients for change: Revisiting a conceptual framework. *Quality and Safety in Health Care, 11*(2), 174–180.

Rycroft-Malone, J., Seers, K., Titchen, A., Harvey, G., Kitson, A., & McCormack, B. (2004). What counts as evidence in evidence-based practice. *Journal of Advanced Nursing, 47*(1), 81–90.

Sackett, D. (1996). Evidence-based medicine: What it is and what it isn't. *BMJ, 312,* 71.

SQUIRE Standards for Quality Improvement Reporting Excellence. (n.d.). Retrieved from http://squire-statement.org

Tong, A., Sainsbury, P., & Craig, J. (2007). Consolidated criteria for reporting qualitative research (COREQ): A 32-item checklist for interviews and focus groups. *International Journal of Quality in Health Care, 19*(6), 349–357.

Van de Ven, H. (2007). *Engaged scholarship: A guide for organizational and social research.* Oxford, UK: Oxford University Press.

> *"If you want to be a writer, you must do two things above all others: read a lot and write a lot. There is no way around these two things that I am aware of, no shortcut."*
>
> –Stephen King

Writing Abstracts for Podium and Poster Presentations

16

Rose O. Sherman

Throughout our careers, most of us attend professional conferences in our specialty areas of interest. Whether that interest is critical care nursing, nurse management, or being a nurse editor, conferences can be useful ways to communicate with colleagues, meet collaborators, and share your research. The organizers of these conferences depend on nurses like you, who are either creating innovative new programs or doing research, to submit their work for presentation. Through researchers like you, new nursing knowledge is disseminated across the discipline at conferences and in publications.

This chapter explains how you can put together an effective abstract for a podium or poster presentation so you can share your work with others and offers tips on creating a poster. The chapter also outlines how you can take the next step and turn a presentation into a journal article.

All About Abstracts

An *abstract* is a brief, informative summary of the major content that you plan to present in your podium or poster presentation to give the reviewer a snapshot of your work. Completed work is

WHAT YOU'LL LEARN IN THIS CHAPTER

- Carefully reviewing and following the call for abstracts gives you a better chance at getting your presentation accepted.

- When developing your presentation or poster, use the abstract as a guide.

- To keep the focus on key points, avoid using too much content in presentations and posters.

- Don't let your enthusiasm fade. Begin writing your journal article when you return from the conference.

generally preferred, but some conferences allow you to submit work in progress. Conference abstracts are often limited to as few as 250 words, so brevity and clarity are vital. Happell (2007) suggests that well-constructed abstracts should answer the following questions:

- **Why** was this work important, and what were the issues and problems?

- **Where** was your setting, and what population did you use?

- **How** did you design your research, initiative, or educational program?

- **What** were the outcomes, findings, and lessons learned?

- **What now** and how should others use this information?

How Should I Review a Call for Abstracts?

If you are a member of a professional association or group, you will probably receive in the mail, or see published in the association's journal, what is often described as a *call for abstracts* well in advance of the conference itself. This call is an invitation to submit an abstract for conference presentation. Most conference organizers receive more abstracts—particularly for podium presentations—than they have speaker slots. The selection process is often quite competitive. Carefully review the call for abstracts guidelines to put yourself in the best possible position.

Here is a sample call for abstracts for a national conference.

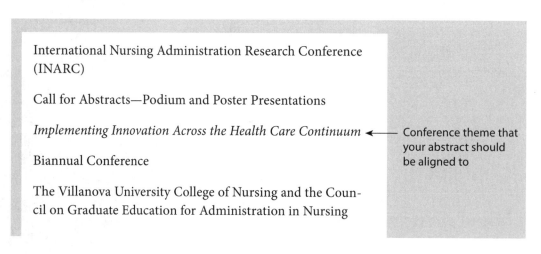

International Nursing Administration Research Conference (INARC)

Call for Abstracts—Podium and Poster Presentations

Implementing Innovation Across the Health Care Continuum ← Conference theme that your abstract should be aligned to

Biannual Conference

The Villanova University College of Nursing and the Council on Graduate Education for Administration in Nursing

(CGEAN) will be co-providing this year's International Nursing Administration Research Conference (INARC).This conference serves as a prominent vehicle for nursing educators, executives, administrators and researchers from all over the United States and Canada to strengthen their roles through learning, sharing and networking with professional colleagues. This is a call for abstracts for both podium and poster presentations.

← Along with the name of the sponsoring organization, indicates whom the conference is targeting

We encourage the submission of abstracts of work that has not been published in a peer-reviewed journal or presented at another national meeting. Topics can include any area of health services scholarly practice changes and research, nursing administration or health care delivery systems. Of particular interest are presentations that describe the implementation of research findings to improve quality, safety and cost outcomes in nursing care settings. ←

← List of possible topics

There are two presentation options. Podium presentations are 45 minutes in length and ten minutes of this time should be left for questions. Poster presentations are scheduled from 5:00 PM to 8:00PM during the Wednesday evening reception. Authors will have the opportunity to discuss materials and distribute handouts related to their work. The size of posters can be no larger than 4 feet high by 6 feet wide and must be capable of being hung. ←

← Length of presentation and poster specifications

All fees, expenses, and arrangements associated with attending the conference are the responsibility of presenter(s). Presenters are prohibited from marketing commercial products and/or services through either poster of podium presentations. ← The speaker guidelines are included in this announcement. The deadline for abstract submission is month/day/year. ←

← Financial/ethics responsibilities

← Deadline

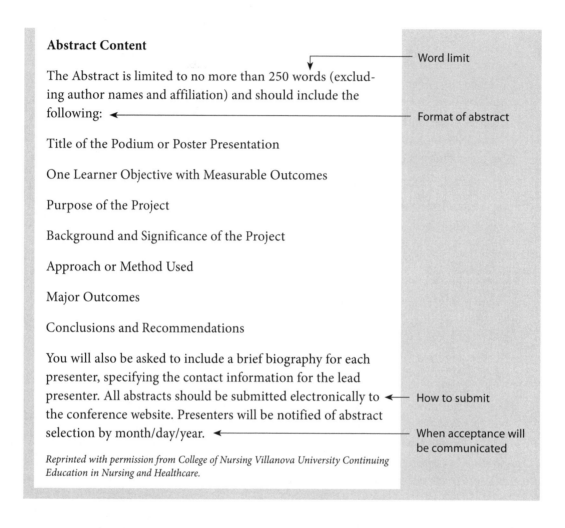

Abstract Content

Word limit

The Abstract is limited to no more than 250 words (excluding author names and affiliation) and should include the following:

Format of abstract

Title of the Podium or Poster Presentation

One Learner Objective with Measurable Outcomes

Purpose of the Project

Background and Significance of the Project

Approach or Method Used

Major Outcomes

Conclusions and Recommendations

You will also be asked to include a brief biography for each presenter, specifying the contact information for the lead presenter. All abstracts should be submitted electronically to the conference website. Presenters will be notified of abstract selection by month/day/year.

How to submit

When acceptance will be communicated

Reprinted with permission from College of Nursing Villanova University Continuing Education in Nursing and Healthcare.

Bindon and Davenport (2013) recommend that you target your work to the right conference. This is a key step because many professional conferences have themes or focus areas. Conference organizers are looking for presentations that are a good fit with the theme of the conference and with the educational needs and interests of those attending the conference. As you review a call for abstracts, consider the following questions:

- Is this a conference I would enjoy attending?

- Can I align my work to the conference theme and tracks?

- Who are the attendees, and will they be interested in this work?

- Will I be able to attend this conference with or without funding?

- How long is the presentation, and is that enough time for me to present my work?

- If I have done this work as part of a team, can we all present, or are there restrictions on the number of presenters?

- Do I have the resources to have a poster designed to the conference specifications?

- When and how will I learn whether the abstract has been accepted?

- Can I meet all the required deadlines for abstract submission?

Q: *May I submit my abstract to different conferences at the same time so that I have a better chance of being accepted?*

A: Unlike journal article submissions where you must clearly be rejected by one before submitting to the next, presenters often submit similar abstracts to more than one professional conference in similar timeframes. Submissions to some conferences may require verification that the work is original and has not been presented at other conferences. When your abstract is selected for presentation, you will be given a short time frame to accept or decline. After you accept, you have made a professional commitment and should plan to attend despite other opportunities that may be offered. It's discouraging to conference planners when speakers who are on the program cancel just before the event. This behavior is considered unprofessional, and your future abstracts may not be selected for conference presentation.

Podium or Poster?

Most call for abstracts offer you an option of submitting for a *podium*—a presentation in a meeting room or session that you present—or a *poster presentation*, where you present a storyboard of information on your poster.

Sometimes, you can submit for both. If you are turned down for the podium presentation, you will be offered a poster presentation slot. Although podium presentations are often considered more prestigious, poster presentations have several major advantages.

If you are a novice at presenting your work, posters are a great way to get started and receive feedback. If you're new to the conference or organization, you can meet the audience at poster sessions and sit in on podium presentations to gain insight into how other presenters showcase their work. If your work is still in progress, a poster session provides a forum for getting feedback and suggestions from other professionals.

For most professional conferences, a limited number of abstracts are usually selected for oral presentation. Podium presentations are often part of a menu of concurrent sessions offered during a specific timeframe. Although not all conference participants will hear about your presentation, your abstract will often be published in a conference proceedings book, professional association journal, or placed on a conference CD-ROM available to a broader audience than conference participants. In contrast, most conferences have scheduled times when all participants can attend the poster session. Contact hours are frequently awarded, and attendance is often excellent. Many professional groups also archive posters on their websites so even those not able to attend the conference can view them. Potentially, with the poster, your work can reach more attendees, and you have more opportunity to discuss your work and network with interested participants (DiSilets & Dickerson, 2010).

Writing Effective Abstracts

Remember that a number of different audiences will see your abstract (Sherman, 2010). The first audience will be the expert reviewers who select the abstracts that best meet the objectives of the conference. The second audience includes the conference attendees who use abstracts to guide their decisions about which presentations to attend or posters to view. A third but less-obvious audience consists of journal editors who troll conference pages in search of an interesting work that could be expanded into a journal article.

Here are some tips for making sure that your abstract stands out in a crowd.

Consider the Conference Audience

Will the audience be members of a specialty association, a cross-section of the nursing profession, or interdisciplinary professionals? Is the conference targeted to local, state, national, or international participants? Knowing the answers to these questions will help you to write a more effective abstract that will appeal to the conference audience (Bindon & Davenport, 2013).

Create an Immediate Impression With the Title

The title is the first thing that a busy reviewer will see on your abstract, and it can create an immediate impression. Try to make your title descriptive and compelling, and be sure that it connects to the theme of the conference.

For example, say that you are a neonatal nurse and want to submit a presentation for a National Association of Neonatal Nurses' annual conference, which is focused on parenting. Your project is a Kangaroo Parenting intervention that you implemented in your NICU. Consider the following two titles:

Kangaroo Parenting Intervention in a Neonatal ICU

or

Healthy Neonate Parenting: What We Can Learn from Kangaroos

The first title tells what your work is about, but the second title is more likely to capture the attention of your reviewers because it is both interesting and makes an immediate connection to conference theme of "parenting."

Follow the Guidelines

Similar to author guidelines for journal articles, the call for abstracts usually clearly specifies the sections to be included in the abstract. The sample call for abstracts from earlier in this chapter is a common outline for presentations involving evidence-based innovations. The sections in a call for research abstracts would be different and commonly include:

- Background and significance
- Aims of the study
- Methods
- Results
- Discussion and implications

Succinctly presenting all the information required in the abstract within the required word count can be a challenge but is very important. Often, fonts and font sizes are specified, and you must follow these guidelines. Many organizations have an online submission process, which typically includes the presenter information, objectives, and an abstract. I recommend typing all the components in a Microsoft Word document, carefully reviewing it (including running a spell-check), and then cutting and pasting pieces as appropriate into the online submission form. With online submission systems, you might not receive a final copy of what you have submitted, so remember to keep a copy for your records.

No matter how you submit your abstract, having someone else review your work for clarity, grammar, and spelling is also a good idea. Try to avoid common abstract mistakes (see the following sidebar).

Avoiding Common Mistakes for Abstract Submission

Submitting for a conference podium or poster presentation and then receiving a letter notifying you that your abstract was not accepted can be frustrating. Even experienced presenters sometimes receive denials, but you can increase the odds of acceptance of your abstract by avoiding these common mistakes.

- The abstract doesn't make a clear link to the conference theme.

- The abstract has grammatical and spelling errors.

- A generic abstract is developed for submission to multiple conferences without tailoring the presentation to the audience.

- The conference abstract guidelines aren't followed: for example, too short, too long, or lacks objectives or outcomes.

- The content of the abstract contains too much material to reasonably deliver in the time allotted for the presentation.

- The aims, objectives, and content of the presentation are not clear to the reviewers.

- The innovation or research is not presented in a manner that would be interesting, nor does it provide new information for the target audience.

- The learning objectives are poorly written, with no action verbs. (See Chapter 18 for tips on writing objectives.)

- The abstract fails to convey what the implications are for the profession.

Abstract Review

Abstracts are sometimes *blind reviewed:* that is, the reviewer doesn't know the presenter or the institution where the work was done. Here is a typical scoring sheet given to reviewers of abstracts.

Nursing Conference

Abstract Review Scoring Criteria
Abstract # _____
Abstract Title: _____
Reviewer: _____
Rating: NA= not applicable 1= poor 2= fair 3= good 4= very good 5= excellent

Criteria	Comments	Rating
The submitted abstract:		
The topic of the presentation is relevant to the conference theme.		
The content is evidence based.		
Outcomes for the study/project are clearly addressed in the abstract.		
The implications for other settings are described.		
The topic will be of interest to the target audience.		
The abstract is clear and follows the guidelines outlined in the call for abstracts.		
The presenters have experience with presentations to similar audiences.		
Total score		

Abstract reviewers are given specific guidelines that reference the call for abstracts, so careful adherence to the guidelines is important. As reviewers look at your abstract, they will ask themselves the following questions:

- Is this topic timely, and does it address an important problem?

- Does the author appear to have knowledge and expertise on this topic?

- Will the content in this abstract be well presented?

- Would I want to hear this presentation?

- Will this be of interest to our target audience?

Now that you understand how to submit an abstract, it's time to apply that information to a practical example.

Case Example

Let's take a look at an example, or case study. You are a nurse educator in a large community hospital in the Midwest. Last year, your hospital received grant funding from a local foundation to conduct a charge nurse leadership development course. You coordinated the program that involved the education of 50 charge nurses. The project had extremely positive outcomes for a number of different measurable dimensions. In doing a review of the literature on the topic of charge nurse development, you noted that little had been written on the topic. You recently received a call for abstracts from the Center for American Nurses for their annual LEAD Summit. You review the following information about the conference and decide that it would be a good opportunity to showcase the project:

> The LEAD conference will feature presentations on evidence-based practice, innovative strategies, and technologies to improve both the work environment of nurses and patient care delivery. We are planning a program that promises to be beneficial to nurses in all practice settings and roles.

LEAD Summit Conference Objectives:

1. Explore current innovations and approaches to building healthy work environments for nurses to enhance and promote quality patient care.

2. Examine conflict management strategies to decrease the occurrence of disruptive behavior and bullying in the workplace.

3. Evaluate evidence-based nursing practices that improve the delivery of patient care.

4. Analyze crucial leadership skills and practices for success in today's healthcare environments.

The call for abstracts asks for the following:

- Title of the abstract.

- Desired type of session (concurrent, poster, or in-brief) with a first and second choice listed. In-brief sessions are short sessions where presenters are paired with others presenting on similar subject areas.

- Objectives of the presentation (behaviorally stated, reflective of the content, no more than three).

- Description of the content of the presentation (not to exceed 150 words).

With these guidelines in mind, prepare the following first draft for your colleagues and chief nursing officer to review. Ask them to think of themselves as part of an expert panel appointed to review abstracts for this conference.

Draft 1

Title: Charge Nurse Leadership Development

Session Preference: Concurrent Session

Objectives:

1. Present an overview of a charge nurse development program.

2. Discuss program outcomes.

3. Identify the implications for other organizations.

Description of Content:

This presentation will describe a charge nurse development program that was conducted at *All Star Hospital* during 2013. This program received grant funding from a local foundation. Fifty charge nurses attended the 2-day development program, which was highly evaluated and had excellent unit-based outcomes. In this program, we will discuss our experiences developing the program as well as our lessons learned. We will show a short video, which illustrates teaching techniques that were used in the program as well as charge nurse reaction to the program. We will review the outcome evaluations and make recommendations for other organizations.

Your colleagues offer a number of excellent suggestions. They point out that although the abstract follows most of the guidelines (you failed to indicate your first and second choices), it does not appear innovative, nor does it capture the excitement or impact that this project generated at *All Star Hospital.*

Draft 2 – After Review and Input from Colleagues

Title: Leading the Charge: A Charge Nurse Development Program

Session Preference: First Choice – Concurrent Session; Second Choice – Poster Session

Objectives:

1. Identify the critical need for charge nurse leadership.

2. Describe an innovative charge nurse development program.

3. Present program outcomes and implications for other settings.

Description of Content:

Charge nurses play a pivotal role in clinical leadership. Yet, the development of charge nurses is rarely discussed in the nursing literature, and most agencies focus training on nurse managers. This presentation will highlight an innovative 2-day Charge Nurse Leadership Development Program designed to foster skills in the areas of supervision and delegation, communication, conflict resolution, and team building. Selection of these content areas for focus was based on feedback from charge nurses, nursing leadership, a review of the literature, and the ANCC standards for a healthy work environment. The program, which was attended by 50 charge nurses, included the use of pre- and posttests, assessment tools, case scenarios, group activities, and program evaluation by participants. The outcomes of the workshop included improved charge nurse leadership skills, a decrease in charge nurse turnover, and an increase in staff satisfaction. Lessons learned and implications for other organizations will be discussed.

The second draft does a much more effective job capturing the significance of your innovative program, beginning with the program title. The description of content meets the 150-word limit, but offers the reader a comprehensive overview of what you will cover.

Presenting Your Work

It is always exciting to receive the email or letter informing you that your work has been accepted for presentation. When you receive notice of acceptance, you will also usually receive speaker or poster presenter guidelines. Use these guidelines when developing your presentation. Your abstract should serve as your guide for your poster or podium session content.

Hedges (2010) observed that many presenters attempt to present too much content in their presentations. You have probably noted this in your own attendance at conference concurrent and poster sessions. The great American architect Ludwig Mies van der Rohe is well known for his quote, "Less is more." This is good advice for presenters. When tempted to share every detail of your research or project, remember that you generally will not have the poster space nor podium time to do this.

Designing an Effective Podium Presentation

Whether you have extensive experience speaking in public or you are brand new to presentations, effective planning is a key for success. You might have only 20–30 minutes to present. As you design your presentation, consider two to three major areas that you would like to cover. These should be the most important points for the audience.

Q: *What if my computer breaks down at the conference before my podium presentation?*

A: Always carry a copy of your presentation on a disc or a flash/thumb drive. That way, you will always have a backup. For larger conferences, the conference hosts will often ask you to send your presentation ahead of time so that it can be preloaded onto one computer. This avoids changing the computer for every speaker. Even when the host takes responsibility for preloading your presentation, bring a copy of your presentation on a disc or thumb drive as an added precaution and keep a copy in your computer "cloud" in case you need to access it. Most experienced presenters also suggest that you bring a printout of your presentation in the event that the technology fails and you need to present without your slides.

If you are presenting on an innovation—such as the charge nurse workshop addressed earlier in this chapter—you might decide to divide your presentation into three sections:

1. The need for the innovation

2. The innovation

3. The outcomes and implications

If you plan to use Microsoft PowerPoint slides, consider that most presenters spend between 2 and 3 minutes on each slide; be sure to leave about 5 to 10 minutes for questions and discussion. Avoid using embedded video or other bells and whistles unless you are an expert on solving audiovisual problems. The focus should be on your content.

After you design your presentation, practice it several times, ideally in front of an audience of your peers, who can give you feedback. Effective podium presentations end on time, so be sure that your content does not exceed the time frame given for your session. Otherwise, you might appear disorganized to the audience.

Q: *Do I need handouts?*

A: Some attendees will be interested in taking back information about your work to their settings. However, many conferences today have "gone green" and don't provide handouts during the conference. Make sure to submit your materials by conference deadlines so they can be included on the conference website or distributed on a flash drive or disc. Also, if you have business cards, take them with you and offer to email your presentation to anyone who requests it.

Creating a Professional Poster Presentation

Hedges (2010) reinforces the importance of starting early and developing a time line after your poster abstract has been accepted. Review the poster guidelines for your conference before you start your poster. The guidelines will specify the poster size and how it will be displayed: for example, posted with pushpins on a large corkboard or placed on a table. Tabletop posters should be created so they are freestanding; don't rely on the meeting organizers to supply an easel. The allowable poster size for conferences varies widely and will affect how much information you can place on the poster.

Many healthcare agencies and universities have graphic design resources to help you with the poster design, but some don't. Fortunately there are many resources on the Internet to help you design and print your poster, such as PosterGenius (www.postergenius.com). Some organizations have templates all presenters are asked to use. Weaver-Moore, Augspurger, King, & Proffitt (2001) surveyed nurses with poster presentation experience. Their findings indicate that the following were important poster components:

- Simplicity

- Readability

- Interesting graphics

Participants in the study reported that limiting the amount of information shared was the most common challenge in poster preparation.

Posters should be visually attractive, use bulleted text where possible, and be viewable from 6 feet away (Elghblawi, 2009). Figure 16.1 illustrates a standard layout for a research poster.

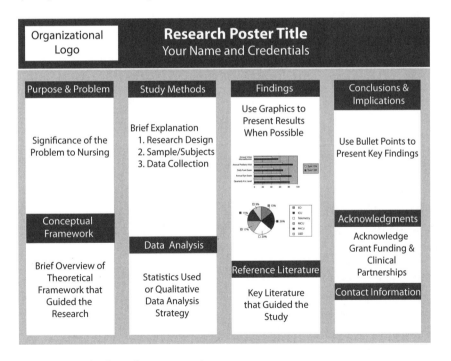

Figure 16.1   This example shows how to organize your poster.

First, create a rough layout of the poster on graph paper or with a computer software program to get an idea where to place the title, text, and any graphics, such as tables or illustrations. Write the text, being sure to carefully proofread each section. Try to use bullet points instead of lots of solid text. Consider making handouts to distribute to those who would like to take information back with them to their work area.

You can use Microsoft Word, Excel, or PowerPoint software programs to create your poster. Excel is particularly useful for creating data charts. Remember to consider that what might seem readable on the computer screen may be too small when enlarged.

Ideally, the poster should be on one sheet of paper. You will need to work with a copy center to enlarge and print the poster, or your organization may print it for you. If you need to assemble your poster in pieces, be sure to use glue or Velcro to attach materials securely.

You need to consider how you will transport your poster to the conference (Bindon & Davenport, 2013). Most presenters prefer to hand-carry their posters in a poster canister or portfolio because hotel delivery can be unreliable. Do not put the poster in your checked baggage.

Creating an ePoster

Electronic posters, or ePosters, are similar to traditional posters, but the presenter speaks with his or her poster on a large computer LCD screen. The American Academy of Nursing and the Council for the Advancement of Nursing Science are two nursing organizations that have moved to an electronic poster presentation format. An ePoster has many benefits. For example, the presenter doesn't have to worry about printing and carrying the poster to the event. These posters are also available in real time to conference participants on their tablets or smart phones and are archived after the conference.

Most ePoster guidelines require you to use PowerPoint templates, which can be easily downloaded from sites like PosterSession.com. The same design rules for traditional posters apply to ePosters.

A disadvantage of ePoster sessions is that because of the rental costs of LCD screens, poster presenters rotate during the poster session. You may only have 30 minutes during a 2-hour poster session where your poster is on display. You (or your employer) may also have to pay a fee to cover the LCD equipment that is rented by the conference organizers.

From Conference Presentation to Article

After presenting your work at a professional conference, consider taking the next step and converting the conference presentation into an article (Gross & Fonteyn, 2008). Your podium or poster presentation can serve as a beginning outline of what you will cover in a journal article (Elghblawi, 2009).

Q: *Is it acceptable to write an article related to the poster before I present it at the conference?*

A: As a courtesy to the conference sponsors, it is usually best to wait until after the conference to write an article. Some sponsors specify that the information must not have been published elsewhere. If you have written an article on the topic of your podium or poster presentation, be sure to reference it in materials that you present at the conference. In some situations, you might have signed over copyright on the material and will want to seek permission from a publisher before providing handouts at a conference.

Confidence Booster

Sally Elliot is a critical care educator in a community hospital. To help her new critical care nurses remember key concepts, she developed an innovative game. She had used this game in her own hospital with great success and presented a poster at the American Association of Critical Care Nursing National Teaching Institute (NTI). Other critical care educators were intrigued with her results and encouraged her to write about it. Sally had never envisioned herself as an author. She is enrolled in a master's program in education and decided to ask one of her faculty for help in taking the next step. The faculty member is delighted to assist her. She gives Sally suggestions for an article outline based on her poster presentation and offers to critique the article after it is written. As she begins to develop her article, Sally is surprised at her own passion as she explains her work in the article. Her article is accepted for publication in the "Teaching Tips" section of an education journal. Sally feels a great sense of pride. Although she felt like a novice beginning this process, she took a risk and wrote the article.

You might want to initially consider the journals of interest to the target audience who attended the conference. Often, journal editors attend specialty conferences and are in the exhibition hall booths of their publishers. This is a good time to personally query an editor about any interest in your topic. A strong advantage to having presented your work at a professional conference is that you learn from attendees the aspects of your work that particularly resonate with your audience. This can provide you with a better lens of how to present your work in a journal article so it will be informative and interesting as well as provide clear implications for the profession.

Often, your presentation abstract itself will provide you with a great working outline for your article beginning with your title, which could serve as an article title or header. The objectives you used for your presentation can serve as an overview of what you plan to present in the article. Your methods, findings, and recommendations will serve as the body of the journal article. Figures or tables that you used in your presentation can make great visuals to illustrate your work in an article. Professional implications were probably a key part of your poster or podium presentation and will also provide important summary content in your article.

Above all, don't let your enthusiasm from the conference fade before you begin work on your article.

Write Now!

1. Visit the website of a professional organization in your specialty area and look for the date and location of the next conference.

2. Find out when the call for abstracts will be posted.

3. Plan to submit an abstract for a poster or podium presentation using the information presented in this chapter.

References

Bindon, S. L., & Davenport, J. M. (2013). Developing a professional poster. *AACN Advanced Critical Care, 24*(2), 169–176.

DeSilets, L. D., & Dickerson, P. S. (2010). Poster presentations. *The Journal of Continuing Education in Nursing, 41*(10), 437–438.

Elghblawi, E. (2009). Double duty: Convert your poster presentations into papers. *Nurse Author & Editor,* March 19(1). Retrieved from http://www.nurseauthoreditor.com/article.asp?id=120

Gross, A. G., & Fonteyn, M. E. (2008). Turn you presentation into a published manuscript. *American Journal of Nursing, 108*(10), 85–87.

Happell, B. (2007). Hitting the target: A no tears approach to writing an abstract for a conference presentation. *International Journal of Mental Health Nursing, 16*(6), 447–452.

Hedges, C. (2010). Poster presentations: A primer for critical care nurses. *AACN Advanced Critical Care, 21*(2), 318–321.

Sherman, R. O. (2010). How to create an effective poster presentation. *American Nurse Today, 5*(9), 15–17.

Weaver-Moore, L., Augspurger, P., King, M., & Proffitt, C. (2001). Insights on the poster presentation and presentation process. *Applied Nursing Research, 14*(2), 100–104.

> *"The reason one writes isn't the fact he wants to say something. He writes because he has something to say."*
>
> *–F. Scott Fitzgerald*

From Presentation or School Assignment to Published Article

17

Lorraine Steefel

WHAT YOU'LL LEARN IN THIS CHAPTER

- Students can turn school projects into published articles, but the work must be transformed to fit the targeted publication.

- Basic questions—such as who, what, where, when, why, and how—can serve as a framework for a published article.

- To transform a school assignment into a published article, students must structure their article around key points, include the "need-to-know" information, and omit what is "nice-to-know."

You have just earned an "A" on your presentation, paper, capstone project, or thesis. Or perhaps you are basking in the glow of a well-received presentation at a regional or national meeting. You may be wondering, "How can I get this work published?"

Ideally, would-be authors should focus on publishing from the start, fashioning their words to a target journal while fulfilling their assignment objectives for a good grade or creating a presentation. But because this method doesn't follow the usual chain of events, starting with a completed assignment or presentation means you have some reworking to do to make it publishable. You're like the gardener who, rather than planting a small, new rosebush where it's supposed to grow, takes a full-grown bush and prunes away the unnecessary, calls out its best qualities, and then reshapes it to fit a particular garden spot. This reshaping is a different kind of writing work that can be more painful because you have to cut away what you've "given birth to" in your project. Deciding what should go and what should stay isn't easy, but you can do it.

This chapter focuses on how to reshape school projects into articles that can be published in print or online. It also discusses how you can repurpose a presentation, whether it was created for school or for a professional meeting, into a publication.

Rethinking Your Assignment

Although your reason for the school assignment was your grade, remaking it into a published article calls for broader goals. Now you want to share the findings of your project or perhaps some aspect of your findings that are new, unique, or similar to what is in the literature. Putting your work in print means you'll be contributing to nursing's body of knowledge, and your byline is your ticket into the world of experts on your topic.

As you consider your finished project for possible publication, begin by asking the following questions about your assignment:

- Why?
- What?
- Who?
- Where?
- When?
- How?

Then, compare your answers with the remake you will undertake (see Table 17.1).

Table 17.1   Questions to Guide the Transition from Assignment to Published Article

Question	Assignment	Remake to Published Article
Why did/will you do or redo the assignment?	Good grade	Share findings, add to the nursing body of knowledge, become a published author
What was/is the aim of your assignment/remake?	Specific to the assignment criteria	Select an aim based on your previous work and refashion it to fit your new work
Who did/would benefit?	Other students, yourself	Nurses who would be interested in the information you provide, yourself
Where did you/will you find nurse readers?	Students in your class	Publication that targets your specific group of nurses

Question	Assignment	Remake to Published Article
When did/should your work appear?	Class deadline	Depends on need and relevancy of topic as well as the publication's editorial calendar
How? What format did/ will you use to create your project?	Course guidelines used to create paper, presentation, capstone project, or thesis	Author guidelines of a specific journal use to create an article. The type of article, such as, case study, "how-to," editorial, question and answer, narrative review of literature

You can find detailed answers related to the Why? What? Who? Where? When? and How? questions in Chapters 1, 2, and 3, which discuss the publication process. However, here is a review of that process and how it relates specifically to remaking your assignment to get you started (Steefel & Saver, 2013).

Why?

Whereas the aim of your school project depended on a topic chosen by you and agreed on by your advisor, for the refashioned article you are free to select your aim and how you will present key point(s) to meet the needs of readers of a specific journal. You can begin by deriving several aims from your project's purpose, choosing which to use for your new article, based on the needs and interests of your target audience. You'll typically need to choose one aim that becomes the purpose of your article.

For example, if the purpose of your capstone project was to examine the rate of hospital re-admissions of patients with heart failure (HF) within 30 days postdischarge by examining the documented use of core measure HF-1 discharge instructions, you have several potential new purposes you can select for a new article:

- To discuss the findings of your capstone project, that is, whether use of core measure HF-1 discharge instructions resulted in fewer readmissions, and, if so, why

- To discuss core measures for HF-1 discharge instructions, what they are and their benefits

- To discuss how to put core measure HF-1 discharge instructions into use

By using a search engine such as Bing, Google, or Google Scholar, you can find articles that might help you decide on the purpose for your new article. Note that you should not copy these articles; rather, they are meant to serve as a stimulus for new thought regarding the article you will create.

In Table 17.2, you'll find examples of articles relating to core measure HF-1 discharge instructions and their references, which can be food for thought as you decide which purpose you will choose as the main focus of your article. That's not to say you can't include elements of your other purposes, but if you try to cover too much material, your article will be unfocused.

Table 17.2   Consider Purposes of Published Articles to Determine Your Article's Purpose

Purpose	Reference
To determine whether documentation of compliance with any or all of the six required discharge instructions is correlated with readmissions to hospital or mortality	VanSuch, M., Naessens, J. M., Stroebel, R. J., Huddleston, J. M., & Williams, A.R. (2006). Effect of discharge instructions on readmission of hospitalised patients with heart failure: Do all of the Joint Commission on Accreditation of Healthcare Organizations' heart failure core measures reflect better care? *Quality & Safety in Health Care, 15*(6), 414–417.
To discuss the barriers to self-care and how nurses help patients with HF overcome them through discharge education	Paul, S. (2008). Hospital discharge education for patients with heart failure: What really works and what is the evidence? *Critical Care Nurse, 28*(2), 66–82.
To discuss the current state of clinical practice aimed at promoting patient adherence to self-care and how healthcare systems and healthcare providers contribute to reaching self-care goals	Albert, N. (2008). Promoting self-care in heart failure: State of clinical practice based on the perspectives of healthcare systems and providers. *Journal of Cardiovascular Nursing, 23*(3), 277–284.

Who? and Where?

The answers to these two questions are related. You need to identify the publications the group you want to target reads (Pierson, 2009). For example, if you want to write about minimizing infection during insertion of peripherally inserted central catheter (PICC) lines for nurses who specialize in IV therapy, you might want to target the *Journal of Infusion Nursing*.

However, if you want to target nurses who care for patients with PICC lines as part of their other duties, you might consider a general nursing journal, such as *American Nurse Today*, the official publication of the American Nurses Association. You can also refer to your capstone project reference list for journals that have published your topic.

After you identify publications that publish the type of content you want to write and reach the nurses you want to reach, visit the publication's website to learn more about its mission, targeted readership, and Author Guidelines (Northam, Trubenbach, & Bentov, 2000). Notice the types of articles that the journal publishes, for example, position statements, reviews of literature, research, or case studies. Read some of the articles and choose the type that might best fit with your topic. (You can learn more about how to select a publication in Chapter 3.)

When?

Although you would hope to have your article in print as soon as possible, *when* to publish is the decision of the publications. Most publications, including journals or magazines, have annual editorial calendars to consider; some have themes for each issue, which means your article would be placed in the appropriate thematic issue.

The answer to the when question is especially critical to news items or opinion pieces relating to current nursing trends. You might want to consider publishing news and opinion pieces on the latest topics (garnered from your school assignment) in non-peer-reviewed print or online journals or magazines such as *Advance for Nurses* or *Nurse.com* for timely, compelling reads.

How?

How you wrote your assignment depended on guidelines from your professor. To rework your paper into a published article, consider tone and type of article. To get a sense of the tone, read several of the articles published in the targeted publication and refer to the Author Guidelines found on the publication's website. Author Guidelines prescribe whether the tone must be academic or less formal, that is, conversational. The tone of the *Journal of Advanced Nursing* is academic; whereas, *American Nurse Today's* tone is conversational.

Q: *OK, I've picked my publication and the type of article I think I want to write. Now what do I do?*

A: Send an email query to the editor of the publication to see if there is interest in publishing an article on your topic. The query should include an introductory statement about your topic that draws the editor's attention, a brief explanation of the article you would like to write, the reason why the journal's readers would benefit from reading the article, and what qualifies you to write about the topic.

A positive response from an editor may include an editor's advice as to what should be included (or not) in the article, and will spur you to write. Even with a positive query, however, publication is not guaranteed. The article still has to go through peer review. A negative response to your query saves you time, as you can go on to query a different journal.

Some publications do not accept queries; in this case, you have to write and submit the article. (You can learn more about queries in Chapter 3.)

To decide which type of article you should write, consider the best way to convey your message to your targeted group of nurses. For example, if your purpose is to describe the method of inserting a PICC line, write a "how-to" article, which guides readers through a step-by-step process to PICC line insertion. If your purpose is to discuss decreasing the delay for the use of PICC lines after insertion, you could search databases and write a review of literature that discusses methods nurses use to expedite use of PICC lines. (You can learn more about types of articles in Chapter 5.)

For more ideas on the type of article you can write, go to the targeted publication's website. In the search bar, type in the key words you used for your assignment and read the articles that relate to your topic. Notice how the authors have written them (the format they use, for example, a "review of literature" or a "how-to" article). Choose one as a model to which you can refer. You can then repeat the search process to find the format that interests you. For a review of literature on PICC line insertion, you would type "PICC line insertion review"; for a how-to article, type "PICC line insertion how-to."

Transforming Presentations, Papers, and Capstone Projects Into Published Articles

Whether your school project was a presentation, an academic paper, or a capstone project, putting aside time each day to write will enable you to transform it into a publishable article. The following describes the process for presentations, papers, and capstone projects.

Presentations

Turning your presentation for school or for a professional audience into a published article gives you the opportunity to reach a larger audience. If you have not already created the presentation, keep the idea of possible publication in mind when you create your presentation. Make detailed notes and include references in the notes section of each slide that will come in handy when you write an article. After you have given the presentation, revise as needed based on audience feedback (Schrager, 2010).

Q: *How do I know if my presentation has any likelihood of being published?*

A: A large part of the answer to that question depends on what's already been published and your particular slant on the topic. Suppose you gave a presentation to fellow students about the value of belonging to professional nursing organizations. First, determine whether your topic is print-worthy. Search the Internet (Google or Google Scholar) to see what has been published about your topic. Next, repeat a similar search in databases such as PubMed for peer-reviewed journal articles. This helps you identify whether there is room for another article on this topic in the nursing literature. If your topic has been covered in great detail, unless you have a unique slant, your chances of getting a related article accepted are slim.

Now suppose you gave a presentation on how your school partnered with the local chapter of a specialty nursing association to increase the number of students who joined the association. You have before-and-after statistics documenting the increase and you created some innovative tools such as a blog targeted to students and a special Twitter handle. You will probably find little in the nursing literature that provides this type of detail with specific outcomes data. You have significantly enhanced your opportunity for successful publication, depending, of course, on finding the appropriate journal.

You probably used Microsoft PowerPoint slides for your original presentation. In each slide, you presented key ideas for your listeners, which you should include in your article. Just as you began your presentation with statements to capture your listeners' attention, begin your article with statements that make them want to read more. At the beginning of the presentation, you told your audience what would be in the presentation, presented your purpose statement and key points, and concluded with a summary. Use this structure to write an outline for your article. Printing your slides in the outline form available in PowerPoint can also help you identify gaps in content and help you in developing an outline (Schrager, 2010).

Here is an example of an outline for an article on how to become a transformational leader that was developed from a presentation on the topic. As you review, consider how slide content contributed to the outline. For instance, can you see that there was probably a slide with a table comparing the two types of leadership in the presentation.

- **I   Introduction**
  - Why transformational leadership matters: morale and economic effects
- **II   Purpose Statement**
  - The purpose of this article is to discuss how you can become a transformational leader.
- **III   Key Points**
  - Differences between transactional and transformational leadership
  - Characteristics of transformational leaders
  - Strategies such as finding a mentor
- **IV   Conclusion**
  - Restating the value of transformational leadership
  - Motivational statement to encourage readers to apply the ideas in the article

Remember that oral language is different from written language. When you presented your talk, you relied on gestures, tone of voice, and eye contact to help carry your message to the audience. When transforming your presentation into an article, you can no longer rely on these communication tools. Your words must aptly relay your meaning, be free of slang or jargon, carry a tone and style appropriate to the journal, and keep within the word count specified by the Author Guidelines or the editor.

Which should come first: the presentation or the article? Ketefian (2011) suggests reversing the process of writing the presentation, and then the article. She recommends you write a good draft of your article before you develop your slides because working from a draft makes preparing the presentation easier. Of course, you still need to consider audience comments and revise the article as needed. You might want to try this approach to see how it works for you.

Academic Papers

Students who successfully write academic papers may think that their "A" grade is a ticket to publication. However, what is appropriate, even stellar, for class work may be inappropriate for an article. For example, you write an outstanding article on why nurses should be involved in politics. Unless you have experience with politics, you are not qualified to write on the topic for a publication.

Q: *My professor said that I should consider getting my academic paper published. Does mentioning that when querying the editor of a publication I would like to write for give me better credibility?*

A: No. Most editors react negatively to the terms "school paper" or "school project" because too many times they have subsequently received articles written like a school paper instead of articles targeted to their readers written in the style of the journal. Unless there is a compelling reason why you should mention the fact that the idea originated as the result of an assignment, then don't.

When you have targeted a publication and received a positive response to your query to the editor, you are ready to "re"-write. Pull out the key points from your academic paper, and keep the purpose of your article in mind as you retool the paper to fit the journal's mission and guidelines. It's best to state your purpose in the form of a sentence. Here is an example of how one topic might be transformed:

Topic of original school paper	This article discusses the benefits of a website to teach nurses about transitional care and discharge planning, as shown by the results of a pilot study.
Transformed topic for a **clinical journal**	This article discusses how to create and implement a website to teach nurses about transitional care and discharge planning.

Transformed topic for a journal that focuses on quality improvement projects	This article discusses the results of a pilot study of how a website increased nurses' knowledge of transitional care and discharge planning.

In most cases, you need to pare down your original paper, eliminating the nonessential information and keeping what's essential, to fit the purpose of this new article and stay within the journal's required word or page count. Construct a new outline for your article to serve as a framework for the new work. Then follow the publication's Author Guidelines to transform your paper into a manuscript to submit for publication.

Confidence Booster

Consider reading the book *Outliers: The Story of Success* by Malcom Gladwell (2011). Look at his exemplars and then think about your writing and life's work: What are your goals for both? Often they are intertwined. As Gladwell points out, success does not happen overnight, even if it seemingly appears to, but it is based on the hours spent improving your craft of writing, being immersed in a body of knowledge (a specific part of nursing for an example), and building on that foundation across time and over the years. So… start today toward your long-term vision!

–Tina M. Marrelli, MSN, MA, RN, FAAN, nurse author and editor

---

Capstone Project

A capstone is a lengthy project on which you've spent a great deal of time. This makes even the thought of changing or cutting it down difficult. But publishing means fashioning your work to meet the mission and style of the publication and the needs of the readers, as well as the word or page count requirements. Try to be objective as you rework your project; keep in mind that you want to present the information in the most useful way possible for readers, while staying within limitations such as word count.

Your publication choices are to search for a publication that will publish a shorter version of research or find an outlet that will publish an article based on the topic of your capstone project.

If, for example, your capstone project was culture-based research, such as, "Health Care Perceptions of African-American Parents of Children with Asthma", and you want to publish your findings, seek out journals that publish research studies focusing on topics such as cultural beliefs and healthcare, public health, or disparities in care. You might want to consider the *Journal of Transcultural Nursing* (JTCN), whose mission is to disseminate research findings concerning the relationship among culture, nursing, and other disciplines, and the delivery of healthcare (Mission Statement, 2013).

Follow the criteria described in the journal's guidelines regarding page or word count. According to the *JTCN's* online Author Guidelines, manuscripts should not exceed 20 pages. This means that you need to pare down your capstone to include essential elements that fit within this structure. If possible, ask your advisor which parts of your project are the standouts for an article, and for help paring down your project and eliminating the nonessential elements (Timmons & Park, 2008).

Or, you could write an article based on your study. You might discuss your findings regarding the perceptions of healthcare by African-American parents of children with asthma who reside in inner cities. Or, because *JTCN* publishes articles related to applications, you could write an article that describes how the findings are being used as the basis for an educational program for your study population.

Q: *Should I say my topic was a capstone project in my query to the editor?*

A: Editors vary on their preference, but all agree that it shouldn't be the main focus of the query. A good place to mention it is in the section as to why you are qualified to write the article. If you are targeting a "capstone-friendly" journal, that is, a journal committed to provide the information needs of nurse practitioners such as the *Journal of the American Academy of Nurse Practitioners* (JAANP; Guidelines for Authors, 2013), you can mention it earlier in the letter. Above all, avoid starting with, "I would like to publish my capstone project."

If you are fortunate enough to have a positive response to your query and write the article, be sure to wrap your narrative around your key points. Keep nurse readers in mind. Ask yourself what they need to know (essential points) as opposed to what is nice to know (nonessential points). Use the type of article, writing style, and voice, according to the Author Guidelines, that will capture readers' attention. An outline helps to organize your material.

Writing Tips for Articles Derived From Capstone Projects

These tips will help you transform your capstone project into a published article (Johnson, 1993; Steefel & Saver, 2013).

- Shorten the background and literature review.

- Condense the justification of the methods you used.

- Tighten your description of statistical methods so clinicians can understand them easily.

- Cut down the number of references. An over-referenced article is a sign of a school paper. Keep in mind that you don't have to reference every sentence in the article. And if you have several references for a point you are making, select the one or two that are most valuable to the reader.

- Don't use long passages from articles you've referenced, even if you include the citation. These interrupt the flow of the article. What's more, they could lead to charges of plagiarism.

- Review every figure and ask yourself if it's needed. Does it work for a wider audience? Could you substitute other figures to make the material clearer for the target reader, such as a clinician?

- For clinical publications, avoid using an author's name to start a sentence, such as "Smith (2013) found that nurses who are empowered...."

Master's Thesis and Doctoral Dissertation

Master's theses and doctoral dissertations are not widely circulated, but you can convert them into articles so your work can reach a wider audience.

You can't include your entire master's thesis in an article, so you have to recast the document. Ketefian (2011) recommends limiting the background and literature sections to important highlights. Significantly shorten the methods and results sections, and keep in mind that you have limited space for tables and figures. If your thesis is clinically oriented, draw clinical implications from the research to address nurses in clinical settings.

Q: *Should faculty advisors be listed as authors on articles derived from a master's thesis or a dissertation?*

A: The answer depends on whether the advisor significantly contributed to the writing of the article or made another substantial contribution. It's best to discuss authorship issues early in your relationship with your advisor. Also, check if your school has any policy related to this issue.

You might be able to harvest more than one article from your dissertation, but you need to avoid creating redundant publications (Ketefian, 2011). For example:

- You can prepare an article reporting the substance of your dissertation research.

- If you developed and tested an instrument, you might create a methodology article, describing the instrument development process.

- If your literature review is thorough, well-integrated, and novel, you might be able to write an article on how it elucidates a particular phenomenon.

Writing a dissertation demonstrates you have learned the process of research and can independently conduct a project (Ketefian, 2011). However, for a journal article you want to convey information that contributes to patient care or helps advance the profession. Understanding these different goals helps you determine what you can leave out and what you can present more succinctly. Some parts of a dissertation, however, might need expansion. For example, you might need to make the implications for practice and the recommendations for future research more specific and realistic (Ketefian, 2011).

Share Your Knowledge

Transforming your presentation, paper, and capstone project is a challenge, but is worth doing. You have already done so much work on a topic about which you care passionately. Now it's time to share your knowledge. If you do not tell others about what you have learned, your only reward will be the "A" on your report card. By publishing, you join the ranks of experts on your topic, and your byline provides the personal reward of recognition for your work.

Write Now!

1. If you are a student, choose one assignment that you are passionate about or did well on and research journals and magazines that would be appropriate for an article related to your work.

2. Consider a presentation that you have developed. Using that presentation, create an outline for an article for a specific journal.

References

Gladwell, M. (2011). *Outliers: The story of success.* New York: Little, Brown and Company.

Guidelines for Authors. (2013). In *Journal of the American Academy of Nurse Practitioners* (JAANP). Retrieved from http://www.aanp.org/images/documents/JAANPGuidelinesForAuthors111020_Fl.pdf

Johnson, S. H. (1993). Avoiding the "school paper style" rejection. *Nurse Anesthesia, 4*(3), 130–135.

Ketefian, S. (2011). Writing for scholarly and research journals. In C. Saver, *Anatomy of writing for publication for nurses* (pp. 193–209). Indianapolis, IN: Sigma Theta Tau International.

Mission Statement (2013). In *Journal of Transcultural Nursing.* Retrieved from http://www.tcns.org/JTCN.html

Northam, S., Trubenbach, M., & Bentov, L. (2000). Nursing journal survey: Information to help you publish. *Nurse Educator, 25*(5), 227–236.

Pierson, C. (2009). Avoid rejection: Write for the audience and the journal. *Nurse Author & Editor.* Retrieved from http://www.nurseauthoreditor.com/article.asp?id=123

Schrager, S. (2010). Transforming your presentation into a publication. *Family Medicine, 42*(4), 268–262.

Steefel, L., & Saver, C. (2013). From capstone project manuscript to published article, *American Nurse Today, 8*(5), 54–56.

Timmons, S., & Park, J. (2008). A qualitative study of the factors influencing the submission for publication of research undertaken by students. *Nurse Education Today, 28*(6), 744–750.

"Education is the most powerful weapon which you can use to change the world."

–Nelson Mandela

On the Road to Writing Continuing Education

18

Nan Callender-Price

WHAT YOU'LL LEARN IN THIS CHAPTER

- Continuing Education (CE) helps nurses around the world in their practice.

- A CE program typically includes a goal statement, instructional objectives, an introduction, the narrative, a concluding paragraph, and an exam.

- Teaching-learning strategies such as case studies, exercises, study questions, or self-assessment are used to enhance learning whenever possible.

In a rural village in a far-away land, a nurse who provides care for her community discovers your continuing education (CE) program on the Internet. Your program discusses a condition relevant to the health needs of her patient population, including the latest evidence-based treatments and interventions. She applies the new recommendations to her practice, and over time, sees an improvement in her patients. If well researched and well written, a CE activity can potentially affect and improve nursing practice and patient outcomes around the world. Of the many good reasons to write CE programs, that might be the best one.

Writing a CE program can be a fun and interesting experience, but it takes commitment and requires patience and persistence to plan, write, and revise your program to perfection. You might be asked to write a CE program or decide to approach a journal or website about developing one.

CE activities can have multiple venues, such as printed in a journal or magazine, online (which may involve an interactive presentation or a webinar), a DVD or CD, a video, or a podcast. But no matter what the format, the basic steps remain the same.

> **Q:** *I'm already so busy. Why should I take the time to write a CE article?*
>
> **A:** Writing a CE activity can enhance your career. After it's published, you can add it to your resume or curriculum vitae. The process of writing also reinforces your knowledge and keeps you current in this subject.

How to Get Started

Think of writing a CE program as an adventure, like taking a road trip. You have an idea about where you would like to go, but for a trip to be successful, you have to spend time preparing for it. Preparation is also the first step on your "CE journey."

Read the Author Guidelines

Say that an old friend agrees to go with you on the trip, and you volunteer to plan it. You need guidance from your friend about his or her interests as well as any limitations. On your CE journey, just like the journey to writing any kind of article, a publication's Author Guidelines guide you, setting the ground rules from which you can begin to plan the program. The guidelines inform you about a publication's word requirements (length), method for writing objectives, reference style, and any required special features, such as a clinical vignette.

CE Accreditation

Organizations that offer continuing nursing education are either accredited as providers of CE by an accrediting body, such as the American Nurses Credentialing Center's (ANCC) Accreditation Program (a subsidiary of the ANA and the largest nurse credentialing organization) or approved as providers by state nursing organizations. Individual activity approval is also available. ANCC and some state nursing and specialty organizations approve individual CE activities.

Providers of CE must meet specific criteria to maintain their provider status, such as ensuring that programs are of an appropriate length for the contact hours awarded, and these are included in the Author Guidelines.

Review the guidelines carefully and ask questions before you get started to save time for both you and the editor. You will typically need to submit the audience, topic, goal, objectives, and an outline. Take a closer look at these.

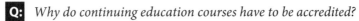

Q: *Why do continuing education courses have to be accredited?*

A: Requirements vary state to state, but many nurses have to have a set number of continuing education credits every year. An accreditation process helps ensure consistent quality of CE programs or courses, holding accredited organizations to the highest standards in nursing education.

Write for Your Audience

Just like you ask your traveling companion what he prefers to see and do before you go on your trip, you should know your target audience before you start writing. Do they represent a large or small group, a wide range of specialties or only one? What are their ages, educational backgrounds, and clinical experiences?

If you write a program for a publication with a million-plus audience, the focus probably will be different from a program for your facility or unit. For a large, clinically diverse audience, topics that pertain to multiple specialties might be a better option than topics specific to just one specialty.

Likewise, a program geared to new graduates generally reads differently than one for experienced staff nurses or advanced practice nurses. You should write a program that matches the level of the learner.

To learn more about the demographics of nurses in general, look to the National Council of State Boards of Nursing and the Forum of State Nursing Workforce Centers 2013 National Workforce Survey for RNs (Budden, Zhong, Moulton, & Cimiotti, 2013). This survey provides a summary of the number and characteristics of registered nurses in the United States, including age and educational background.

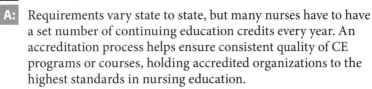

Q: *I recently heard someone at a conference talking about "interprofessional education;" what does that mean?*

A: In recent years, there has been increased support for collaboration and interprofessional education (IPE). IPE occurs when learners from two or more professions learn from and with each other to enable effective collaboration and improved health outcomes. (World Health Organization, 2010). IPE may occur in pre- and post-baccalaureate education. Similar considerations regarding your interprofessional target audience apply. However, when developing IPE or interprofessional continuing education (IPCE), the target audience is more diverse, and extra diligence is required to ensure the topic and discussion are relevant to all groups.

The editors of the publication you are writing for know their target audience well and can provide you with guidance, too.

Select a Topic

Knowing the demographics of your target audience will help you select an appropriate topic. First, take a look at the CE activities on the organization's website to be sure that your topic has not been featured. Look for the holes in the literature—topics that haven't been covered by other publications. Focus on what's newsworthy about your CE subject: Is there a cutting-edge medication or treatment on the horizon or discoveries about a particular disease or condition? CE editors, like news editors, seek out the "wow effect," those topics that make readers clamor for more. But even a novel approach to a common topic might be of interest.

 How do I know at what level I should write my CE?

A: CE content should go beyond the basic level of knowledge taught in undergraduate nursing school. For instance, a program on elementary assessment skills would not qualify as CE for practicing nurses because they should already be knowledgeable about basic assessment skills.

Set Goals and Objectives

Do you know your ultimate destination? What do you hope to accomplish by the end of your trip? Beginning with the end in mind helps to keep your CE program on the right track. The goal and objectives establish the direction of your CE activity.

The *goal* (or purpose) is broad, is not measurable, and helps you and the learner to focus on the big picture. An example of a goal or purpose is

The goal of this program is to inform nurses about transformational leadership in the healthcare setting.

Objectives, on the other hand, state what behavior is expected of the learner by the end of the program. The use of instructional objectives as a measure of learning started with Benjamin Bloom, an American educational psychologist from the University of Chicago (Bloom, Engelhart, Furst, Hill, & Krathwohl, 1956).

Bloom's Taxonomy of Learning

Bloom's taxonomy divides the *cognitive domain* (development of intellectual skills and knowledge) objectives into several categories of increasing complexity, which is a stair-step approach to thinking about levels of learning. The simple schematic in the sidebar will help you understand the level of learning conveyed in the objectives and the verbs typically associated with each level.

Keep in mind that you can use the taxonomy when writing test questions, too.

The categories illustrate the increasing complexity of the types of learning, starting with knowledge (the most basic level) and progressing to the most complex (evaluation).

Level of Learning	Type of Learning	Verbs
Knowledge	Memorization and regurgitation	Define, identify, list, repeat, name, relate
Comprehension	Understanding and interpretation	Discuss, describe, report, explain, review, summarize
Application	Use of information in new situation	Translate, apply, interpret, demonstrate
Analysis	Break up of the whole into parts	Distinguish, compare showing relationships, contrast, differentiate
Synthesis	Combination of elements, forming new structure	Formulate, prepare, design, assemble, plan
Evaluation	Situation assessment, based on criteria	Assess, compute, revise, measure, evaluate

Subsequent to Bloom's taxonomy, Robert F. Mager, PhD, a renowned instructional designer and developer, first published his groundbreaking work, *Preparing Instructional Objectives*, in 1962. Mager's strategy for developing instructional objectives is widely used today. Mager (1997) identifies three characteristics of an instructional objective. Objectives should be:

- Related to intended outcomes, not the process for achieving those outcomes

- Specific and measurable, rather than broad or intangible

- Focused on the learner, not the instructor

Mager further breaks instructional objectives into three main components:

- **Performance:** What learners are expected to be able to do

- **Conditions**: Conditions under which the performance is expected to occur

- **Criteria**: The level of competence that must be achieved

The condition and criterion are often not included, but are implied. Lynore DeSilets (2007) contends that the criteria are often not used in nursing unless a competency standard is required.

Here are some tips for writing objectives that will keep you on track:

- Keep objectives congruent with the goal, content, and teaching-learning strategies of the activity.

- Limit yourself to one behavior per objective.

- Keep the language simple.

- Use the performance, condition, and criteria model whenever possible.

- Use verbs that describe actions that can be quantified for example, "identify the signs and symptoms of stroke" can easily be converted into a posttest question, but "enhance knowledge of stroke" cannot.

- Describe learner outcomes.

- Write at the level of the learner, keeping in mind professional status and experience and educational level.

- Focus on the learner, not the instructor (that is, author).

- Make sure objectives are clearly stated.

- Make objectives realistic.

Take a closer look at some sample instructional objectives.

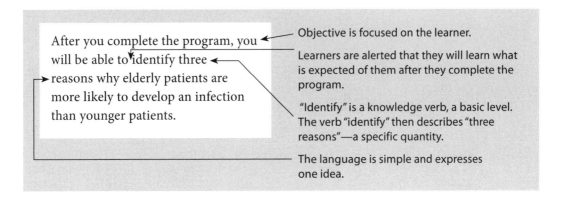

After you complete the program, you will be able to identify three reasons why elderly patients are more likely to develop an infection than younger patients.

Objective is focused on the learner.

Learners are alerted that they will learn what is expected of them after they complete the program.

"Identify" is a knowledge verb, a basic level. The verb "identify" then describes "three reasons"—a specific quantity.

The language is simple and expresses one idea.

Here are two more examples. Try to identify the characteristics that make them good objectives.

State the four components of transformational leadership.

Compare and contrast transactional and transformational leadership styles.

After you understand the basic characteristics of well-written objectives, you will be able to write instructional objectives for your own program.

Write Outcome Statements

Continuing education trends point to an increased use of outcomes rather than objectives as a measure of learning or competency. What's the difference? *Objectives* focus on the goal and process, with more emphasis on the instructor and learner whereas an *outcome*, a desired end result, speaks to the goal with the focus on the learner, who must achieve a specific result or outcome. Outcome-based education has its historical roots in competency-based education and has been discussed in the literature for many years (Wittman-Price, & Fasolka, 2010).

In part, the current healthcare environment has been the impetus for the shift in focus. With an increased emphasis on financial incentives tied to specific patient outcomes, evidence-based practice, accountability, and patient safety are the foundation for CE development.

There are multiple models of outcome-based education, so it's wise to review the literature about them. Writing outcome statements is similar to writing objectives. The stem, for example, precedes the outcome statement as it does with the objective:

> After completing this program, the learner will be able to…

Changing from the use of objectives to outcomes encourages the educator to stay focused on the end results, the practice change expected from the learner upon completion of the program, and ultimately, changes in patient outcomes.

Begin each statement with the highest-level verb—the more complex verb in the Bloom taxonomy—that relates to the content and is measurable. Use language that is familiar to nurses and represents their actual practice; as in objectives, the language should be clear, concise, and pertinent, and the statement should speak to the core competencies. Finally, state the most essential action first, with conditions or methods at the end (Lenburg, Abdur-Rahman, Spencer, Boyer, & Klein, 2011).

When writing outcome statements, consider what the learners are expected to do after completing the course: Is the expectation for a change in cognitive, affective, or psycho-motor performance? Will learners need to demonstrate their knowledge or write about it? (Lenburg, 1999)

Compare the following three traditional objectives with the outcome statements they have been converted to. Note that the verbs used in the objectives represent knowledge and comprehension, compared to the use of higher-level verbs, representing application and analysis, in the outcome statements. The outcome statements are more specific and performance-oriented, generally requiring the learner to apply the information to his or her practice.

Comparing Objectives and Outcome Statements

The goal of this disaster management program is to prepare emergency department nurses to respond to different types of disasters in the clinical setting by providing the appropriate nursing interventions. After completing this program, the learner will be able to:

Objective	Outcome Statement
State the four stages of disaster management.	Apply the four stages of disaster management to your clinical setting.
Describe the disaster triage criteria.	Triage patients using the appropriate disaster triage criteria.
Discuss the considerations that should be taken into account when the disaster involves a chemical, radiological, or biological agent.	Differentiate the considerations that should be taken into account when the disaster involves a chemical, radiological, or biological agent.

Write the Outline

With the goal and objectives or outcome statements completed, you can now write your outline, which many CE editors require before you start writing. An outline is like your trip's itinerary, showing the starting and ending points as well as where you go between. A one-page outline is usually adequate for a single-contact-hour CE program, but requirements vary with the publication. The editor needs to know how you plan to write the narrative to ensure that it flows in logical progression. You're not going to backtrack 100 miles on your road trip, and the same is true about a learning activity—the progression of the narrative should move the learner forward in a clear, coherent manner.

So what should you include in an outline? Generally, an outline shows that your topic moves from broad to more specific information. It includes your goal statement; objectives; and, if you already know them, a sentence or case study you plan to use as an opening. Show the main topics within the narrative with some detail for each. Figure 18.1 is an example of an outline for a single-contact-hour CE program about disseminated intravascular coagulation (DIC).

After the editor accepts your goal statement, objectives, outline, and teaching-learning strategies, you're ready to start the trip.

When the Coagulation Cascade Goes Horribly Wrong

I. **Goal:** The goal of this program is to inform nurses of the pathophysiology, assessment, and treatment of disseminated intravascular coagulation (DIC).

II. **Objectives:** After studying the information provided here, you will be able to

    A. Identify three factors that precipitate DIC.

    B. Describe the assessment parameters and laboratory values associated with DIC.

    C. Discuss four nursing interventions appropriate for care of patients who exhibit indications of DIC.

III. **Introductory Case Study**

IV. **Main Body**

    A. DIC defined

    B. Factors and diseases that contribute to DIC

        1. Obstetric disorders

        2. GI disorders

        3. Tissue-damage factors

        4. Infections

        5. Hemolytic processes

        6. Vascular disorders

    C. Pathophysiology of DIC

        1. Healthy clotting mechanisms outside of DIC

        2. Endovascular changes that contribute to DIC

Figure 18.1   Sample outline for single-contact-hour CE program.

Write the Narrative

Like any article, the CE activity has a beginning, a middle, and an end.

Off to a Good Start

What's going to make the learner want to jump onboard with you? A topic of interest helps, but something else increases the chances even more: An enticing lead sentence or paragraph (also known as a *lede*) or case study inspires the learner to begin the journey.

Check the journal's past CE articles to see what type of lede is preferred—an attention-grabbing lede or one that is more traditional, yet still engaging for the reader.

To make your lede attention grabbing, try using a compelling question, vivid metaphor, dramatic statistic, current event, or the mention of a well-known movie or book. Whatever the lede, you must relate it to your topic immediately with a transition sentence.

Here are two examples of well-constructed, attention-grabbing ledes.

> *Persistent Pertussis*
>
> In 2012, the U.S. had the highest number of whooping cough cases since the 1950s. Why and what is causing this increase in a vaccine-preventable childhood disease? Despite widespread vaccination, pertussis, more commonly known as "whooping cough," is one of the most poorly controlled vaccine-preventable diseases in the developed world, and is the only vaccine-preventable disease on the rise in the U.S.

In the preceding example, the author uses a compelling statistic to grab the reader's attention. Try to identify what makes the following introductory paragraphs good ledes.

> *Facebook: Know the Policy Before Posting*
>
> Why are some nurses and other healthcare professionals losing their jobs because of Facebook postings? Celebrities use the popular social networking site, TV reporters use it, and chances are you and your friends use it, too. However, users can overlook the negative effects that social networking sites can have on their careers. In healthcare, Facebook postings can influence the hiring process, violate patient privacy, and result in termination of employment.

Food Gone Bad

What do peanut butter, chocolate, granola bars, cookie dough, ground beef, ground turkey, chicken, bacon, hot dogs, salami, sushi, cheese, eggs, spinach, green onions, lettuce, tomatoes, olives, alfalfa sprouts, clover sprouts, orange juice, apple juice, cantaloupes, raspberries, sesame, tahini, ice cream, hazelnuts, pine nuts, and strawberries have in common? The answer: contamination with foodborne pathogens.

Note how provocative questions are posed for readers. In the first example, we're reminded of the consequences of misusing social media. In the second example, we're drawn in because everyone has consumed one or more of the listed foods and has been potentially exposed to foodborne pathogens. In either case, readers identify with the scenario, increasing their interest in the topic.

Teaching-Learning Strategies

You can use a variety of teaching-learning strategies in your CE article:

- **Case studies:** As nurses, our primary interest is people. Case studies play off that and allow readers to think about applying what they have learned in their own practice.

- **Illustrations:** For example, include an illustration of the surgical technique of repairing a mitral valve for an article on nursing care of the patient undergoing mitral valve replacement.

- **Tables and charts:** Pull out key concepts into tables. Use charts to illustrate study results.

- **Study questions:** You can give the reader questions to consider before taking the posttest.

- **Exercises:** Allow the reader a chance to practice skills. For example, in a CE on interpretation of arterial blood gas (ABG) results, give participants practice sets of ABG results for them to interpret.

- **Self-assessments:** If you are writing a lengthy CE, periodically insert self-assessments so readers can test themselves on what they have learned so far.

- **Glossary and references:** Even simple tools, such as a glossary of terms, and your list of references are teaching-learning strategies.

If the journal you are targeting prefers more matter-of-fact ledes, you might opt for a common technique of using an introductory case study. Cases studies can be used in multiple ways, including testing the learner midway or at the end of the program. Sandra DeYoung (2009, p.148) defines a case study as "an analysis of an incident or situation in which characters and relationships are described, factual or hypothetical events transpire, problems need to be resolved or solved."

Well-written, succinct case studies can also arouse the reader's curiosity. You want to choose a topic and scenario that fits your objectives and content.

You can choose a case study based on a clinical experience. Posing a question at the end of the case study—such as "What nursing care would be appropriate in this situation?"—and then answering it at the end of the program can be an effective way to draw in readers. Or providing readers with more details about the situation throughout the narrative can help move them along.

Here's an example of introductory case study:

> *Knife and Gun Club: The Biomechanics of Penetrating Trauma*
>
> An ear-splitting crack penetrates the silence of the night air. The smallest flash of orange pierces the darkness. Unseen to the human eye is a small metal object, cutting through the atmosphere at well over 1,500 feet per second.
>
> The recipient feels nothing more than a sudden rush of air from his throat as the blast wave preceding the bullet strikes his chest. Less than a millisecond later, the bullet tears first through his shirt and then through his skin and intercostal muscles. As the leading edge of the bullet meets the resistance of the man's body, it deforms outward, creating a flat surface that crushes the lung tissue in its way. When the object strikes the anterior edge of the scapula, it shatters into numerous pieces, each carving a different path through the surrounding tissue. One piece tears through the nerve roots of the neighboring spinal column, severing it and causing the man's legs to crumple beneath him. Another piece projects upward into the man's neck, cutting through an artery. Within seconds, blood gushes into the tissue spaces around the structures of the airway, and the man's respirations become labored and noisy.

> A race against time has begun. If the race is won, the gunshot victim
> will receive medical and surgical care quickly enough to save his life. If
> the race is lost, he will join the thousands who die every year around
> the world of penetrating trauma.

Note how the author sets the stage for the reader by describing the path of the bullet into the victim and its anatomical damage in detail.

Here is another example of an introductory case study. This one is slightly more formal in tone.

> *When the Coagulation Cascade Goes Horribly Wrong*
>
> The ambulance report seems routine: a patient transferring to the hospital from a nursing home for a possible urinary tract infection (UTI) caused by an indwelling catheter. But on arrival, it is apparent this 82-year-old patient does not have a routine UTI. Although the urine in the catheter bag does appear cloudy and tests positive for red and white blood cells, the patient is unusually confused and has a decreased level of consciousness. Clinicians observe petechiae all over the body.
>
> Lab tests are drawn and sent as an IV line is initiated. The prescribing provider orders antibiotics for apparent sepsis before transfer to the med/surg unit. Within hours, the patient's condition declines. Lab tests demonstrate low platelet and fibrinogen levels and elevated prothrombin times. Bright red blood begins to ooze from the patient's rectum, and the venipuncture and IV sites begin to bleed. The patient is unresponsive. The physician diagnoses disseminated intravascular coagulation (DIC), and summons the family to determine whether aggressive treatment is warranted.
>
> DIC refers to a complex disorder of the blood characterized by abnormal clotting leading to consumption of clotting factors that ultimately results in abnormal bleeding.

This example relates to the content outline earlier in the chapter. It also illustrates the importance of defining the topic after you introduce it. This ensures that everyone is starting from the same reference point.

Confidence Booster

Capturing readers' attention in the first paragraph is essential and can make the difference in their decision to read more or not. Writing ledes or introductory case studies can be fun and creative, but it takes time and practice. Try writing several different ledes, and then have your spouse, friends, and colleagues read them and tell you whether they're drawn into the narrative. Don't get discouraged if you don't achieve the wow effect at first; just keep trying and eventually you'll dazzle them.

In the Middle

You have already created an outline to follow. The narrative typically begins with more general information, introducing the main topics, and then subsequent paragraphs discuss them in detail. For example, say that you are writing about shingles. One logical way to discuss the topic is by etiology, risk factors, signs and symptoms, diagnosis, treatment options, and nursing interventions.

Some publications may prefer a traditional approach to subheads, such as "Signs and Symptoms," "Diagnosis," "Treatment," and "Nursing Interventions." Others may welcome a more creative use of words to give them pizzazz.

Visual aids, such as tables, graphs, and diagrams, can illustrate information and enhance the narrative. They can also break up text-laden layouts, making the program more reader friendly. (You can learn more about how to use these techniques in Chapter 7.)

Evidence-Based Practice

The trend to make evidence-based practice (EBP) an integral part of nursing is here to stay. By now, we've all heard about it. We know that EBP combines clinical expertise with the best available evidence and patient values and preferences for improved outcomes. It's your job to find the strongest evidence to support your learning activity. You can do it the old-fashioned way and go to a medical library, or you can locate it online through free sites, such as Medscape, subscription sites, or a combination of both.

If you're just getting started, you may need help in recognizing the levels of evidence. EBP taxonomies provide insight into the strength of the evidence; you can find them online. Well-respected nursing and medical journals and scientific and government websites are excellent starting points.

Writing for Different Specialties

Nursing specialties have a unique vocabulary, and you need to simplify the language in your program for nurses outside the specialty to increase readability and comprehension. For example, an infectious disease nurse writing about *C. difficile* for a general nursing population should define more terms than if she were writing for peers.

Often, just a one- or two-word explanation helps to jolt the memory of your audience or explain technical jargon. Provide a brief, but enlightening definition of a condition:

- Onychomycosis: Nail fungus

- Smoldering leukemia: A disease in which the bone marrow does not make enough healthy blood cells

Developing interprofessional continuing education (IPCE) presents additional challenges to ensure the appropriate wording is understandable to the healthcare disciplines targeted in the course. For example, consider this narrative from an interprofessional CE activity:

> Functional electrical stimulation (FES) may reduce foot drop and improve obstacle avoidance when used on the peroneal nerve. (Also called "neuromuscular stimulation," FES uses electrical current to stimulate nerves innervating affected extremities.)

In the preceding example, for a course developed for physical therapists (PT) and nurses, a definition about FES is required because nurses may not be familiar with the technical terms because they are more germane to PT.

Conclude Your Program

At the end of your program, be sure to include one or two summary paragraphs that highlight your main points. Learners need to be reminded about the gist of the program. You began with a broad approach, and now you finish with it.

Note how the author reiterates the key point in the following conclusion paragraph.

> *Traumatic Brain Injury (TBI)*
>
> TBI is a leading cause of trauma-related death. Nurses are critical in preventing or minimizing irreversible brain damage. The priorities

center on proper oxygenation, ventilation, and adequate circulation. Preserving neurologic function and preventing secondary injury due to shock and hypoxia are also important. By becoming familiar with brain injuries and their care, nurses can better plan and provide the special care that a patient with TBI needs.

You're on your way home, and it's time to look back and think about what you've experienced along the way. The next step is writing the posttest.

Test Knowledge

What level of knowledge do you want to test the learner on? Most often the editor or organization you're working with determines this, and it's stated in the writers guidelines.

The size of the target audience also influences the type of exam. Fixed-choice questions that require learners to select the correct response from several choices or supply a word or short phrase to answer a question (such as multiple-choice and true/false questions, and questions involving matching and completing phrases) are geared to larger groups. Open-ended questions (such as short-answer essays, extended-response essays, or problem solving) are suited to smaller groups. Evaluations for interactive online programs might include short video clips of scenarios for learners to respond to.

Q: *As author, will I always write the posttest?*

A: The publication editors may write the posttest or ask you to. Check the journal's Author Guidelines to see what is required.

Remember Bloom's taxonomy, which is used to write objectives? You should also apply it to writing test questions by considering the cognitive levels described earlier in the chapter. The taxonomy reminds you about the types of thinking required to answer test questions.

The following sidebar contains a summary of the taxonomy and an example of a question for each level.

Questions for Taxonomy Levels

Knowledge: Memorize and recall facts.

> Example: What is the major cause of toxoplasmosis?

Comprehension: Understand and interpret important information.

> Example: Pregnant women are at higher risk of DIC because _____ .

Application: Apply new concepts to another situation.

> Example: Which blood products would be used to improve tissue oxygenation if the CBC indicates a low hemoglobin and hematocrit?

Analysis: Break down new information into parts and differentiate between them.

> Example: What are the main characteristics of Jean Watson's theory of human caring?

Synthesis: Take various pieces of information and form a whole, creating a pattern where it didn't exist.

> Example: What nursing diagnosis can be formulated based on the patient's signs and symptoms, physical exam, and lab tests?

Evaluation: Assess and conclude the value of materials.

> Example: Of the two treatment options, which would be more efficacious for the patient's condition?

Multiple-Choice Questions

Multiple-choice questions are the most widely used method to test learners' knowledge and comprehension (Writing multiple-choice questions, 2007).

Typically, multiple-choice questions have three parts:

- The stem (the question)
- The correct answer
- Multiple incorrect options (distractors)

Most literature recommends writing the correct answer before writing the distracters (Writing multiple-choice questions that demand critical thinking, 2013). This order helps you focus on the one clearly correct answer.

Multiple-choice questions are a highly structured, effective method to measure a learner's achievement and an easy, reliable format for scoring and performance comparison. Although multiple-choice questions offer several advantages, they have limitations, as well:

- Constructing the questions is time consuming.
- Writing plausible distractors and testing higher levels of learning is difficult.

Here are a few tips for writing multiple-choice questions.

Strive to:

- Base questions on the instructional objectives whenever possible.
- Test for important information.
- Focus on a single problem or idea for each question.
- Gear to the level of the learner.
- Test for higher-level thinking whenever possible.

Avoid:

- Providing cues from one question to another.
- Being overly specific or including technical information.
- Using verbatim phrasing.
- Writing questions based on opinions.

Tips for writing the stem include:

- Phrase it as clearly and succinctly as possible.
- Include the central idea in the stem.
- Include language in the stem that would have been repeated in each answer option.
- Use a question or completion form.
- Put a blank space at the end of completion questions.
- Avoid negative phrasing, such as "not" or "except"; if negative words are used, highlight or capitalize them: for example, NOT.

Writing answers can be just as challenging as writing the questions, particularly when it comes to developing wrong answers, called "distractors." Here are some tips you can use:

- Make sure to offer only one correct answer.

- Keep the options about the same length and parallel in grammatical structure.

- Limit number of answers to three to five options.

- Use distractors that seem plausible but are incorrect.

- Avoid using phrases directly taken from the text.

- Use the following sparingly: all, always, never, usually, typically, all of the above, none of the above.

- Make options as similar as possible to increase the difficulty.

- Avoid offering trick answers.

- Avoid giving unintended cues, such as making the correct answer longer in length than the distractors.

Look at some examples of well-written multiple-choice questions. Try to identify what level of thinking the questions test the learner on, as well as what makes the following multiple-choice questions well written.

1. Which aneurysm is most common?

    a) Sacular

    b) Fusiform

    c) Mycotic

    d) Infectious

Note the clear central idea with only one correct answer and the distractors parallel in length.

1. In DIC, with low fibrinogen levels, the RN can expect to administer _____ .

    a) Vitamin K

    b) Cryoprecipitate

    c) Fresh frozen plasma

    d) Aminocaproic acid (Amicar)

Again, note the one central idea, a blank at the end of the question, and answers that are parallel in length and grammar.

1. a, 2. b

Multiple-Choice Questions and Case Studies

Multiple-choice questions are not used only in posttests. Using multiple-choice questions with case studies provides an opportunity to encourage critical thinking and test a higher level of thinking, such as the application level on Bloom's taxonomy scale. Case studies represent real-life clinical situations from which learners are challenged to apply the didactic information presented in the learning activity. They can range from short and simple to lengthy and complex.

Unlike the introductory case study for a lead into the program, though, the case study with multiple-choice questions specifically tests the learners' knowledge and comprehension of a topic. Sometimes used before reading the program, this method pretests the learners' knowledge base.

Multiple-choice questions should require learners to apply the information gleaned from the program. The rationale for correct and incorrect answers can be included for additional learning. This format especially works well online, so when users answer a question, the rationale or explanation reinforces learning.

Here is an example of a case study that can be used to test learners' knowledge before or after the program. What level of thinking does it test learners on?

Traumatic Brain Injury

Mr. Matthews, age 76, presents to the ED triage with a 2-inch laceration to the forehead. His wife states that he slipped and fell in the bathroom an hour ago.

Mr. Matthews is awake but says he has a headache. He feels nauseous and sleepy. Mr. Matthews is oriented to person and place but does not remember what happened. His wife says that he was unconscious for about 5 minutes after the fall. His vital signs are blood pressure 160/88 mmHg; pulse 64 beats per minute; respirations 16 breaths per minute; temperature 98.2 F. Oxygen saturation is 96% on room air.

Mr. Matthews reports a pain level of 7/10. The right pupil is 3 mm, and the left is 5 mm in size, and both are reactive to light. The patient moves all extremities on command. Bleeding has been controlled by direct pressure.

1. Which of the following is an immediate nursing priority for Mr. Matthews, based on his current presentation?

    a) Intubation

    b) IV insertion

    c) Cervical spine precautions

    d) Prep for the OR

2. Mr. Matthew's history includes a fall with brief loss of consciousness. A possible alteration in his neurological function would best be defined by which of these conditions?

    a) Concussion

    b) Diffuse axonal injury

    c) Herniation syndrome

    d) Skull fracture

3. Mr. Matthews begins to exhibit a late sign of increased intracranial pressure. Which symptom is he most likely exhibiting?

    a) Headache

    b) Increase in systolic blood pressure

    c) Tachycardia

    d) Restlessness

4. Which of these is a special consideration in maintaining a patent airway in Mr. Matthews?

    a) The neck must be hyperextended.

    b) The patient's mouth and nose should never be suctioned.

    c) The head of the bed should always be elevated.

    d) Stimulation of the gag reflex should be minimized or avoided.

1. c — Cervical spine precautions are one of the initial priorities in any patient with traumatic brain injury. Mr. Matthew's clinical presentation does not warrant immediate intubation, resuscitation, or surgery.

2. a — A classic concussion is defined as a condition caused by a jarring injury to the head resulting in a temporary loss of consciousness.

3. b — Early signs of increased intracranial pressure include headache, nausea, vomiting, restlessness, and drowsiness. Late signs, such as increased systolic BP and widening pulse pressure, can occur when compensatory mechanisms have been exhausted.

4. d — Stimulation of the gag reflex may cause a transient increase in intracranial pressure and may cause vomiting and subsequent aspiration.

Journey's End

Your journey has come to an end. You imparted new, important information that will affect the nursing practice of those who came along for the ride. You planned and organized your CE activity successfully by providing:

- A broad, one-sentence goal statement

- Clear, succinct instructional objectives or outcome statements that specify what the learner should know upon completion

- An outline that shows the logical progression of the content

- An attention-grabbing introduction

- A well-written, researched narrative that reflects the outline with key transitional sentences, subheads, and a concluding paragraph

- A well-constructed exam and/or case study that tests for high-level learning whenever possible

Whether nearby or in a distant land, nurses who read your program may change and improve their practice.

Write Now!

1. Write an objective, and then compare it with the sample objectives in this chapter.

2. Pick a CE program from a journal and write one posttest question for it. Compare what you have written with the criteria in this chapter to evaluate the question.

References

Bloom, B. S. (Ed.), Engelhart, M. D., Furst, E. J., Hill, W. H., & Krathwohl, D. R. (1956). *Taxonomy of educational objectives.* New York: David McKay Company, Inc.

Budden, J. S., Zhong, E. H., Moulton, P., & Cimiotti, J. P. (2013). Supplement: The National Council of State Boards of Nursing and the Forum of State Nursing Workforce Centers 2013 National Workforce Survey of Registered Nurses. *Journal of Nursing Regulation, 4*(2), S1–S72.

DeSilets, L. (2007). Using objectives as a road map. *Journal of Continuing Education in Nursing, 38*(5), 196–197.

DeYoung, S. (2009). *Teaching strategies for nurse educators* (2nd ed.). Upper Saddle River, NJ: Prentice Hall.

Lenburg, C. B. (1999). The framework, concepts and methods of the competency outcomes and performance assessment (COPA) model. *The Online Journal of Issues in Nursing.* Retrieved from http://gm6.nursingworld.org/MainMenuCategories/ANAMarketplace/ANAPeriodicals/OJIN/TableofContents/Volume41999/No2Sep1999/COPAModel.html

Lenburg, C. B., Abdur-Rahman, V. Z., Spencer, T. S., Boyer, S. A., & Klein, C. J. (2011). Implementing the COPA model in nursing education and practice settings: Promoting competence, quality care, and patient safety. *Nursing Education Perspectives, 32*(5), 290–296.

Mager, R. F. (1997). *Preparing instructional objectives: A critical tool in development of effective instruction* (3rd ed.). Atlanta: Center for Effective Performance.

Wittman-Price, R., & Fasolka, B. J. (2010). Objectives and outcomes: The fundamental difference. *Nursing Education Perspectives, 31*(4), 233–236

World Health Organization. (2010). Framework for action on interprofessional education and collaborative practice. (WHO/HRH/HPN/10.3). Retrieved from http://www.who.int/hrh/resources/framework_action/en

Writing multiple choice questions. (2007). Instructional Assessment Resources, The University of Texas at Austin. Retrieved from http://www.utexas.edu/academic/ctl/assessment/iar/students/plan/method/exams-mchoice-write.php

Writing multiple-choice questions that demand critical thinking. (2013). Teaching Effectiveness Program, University of Oregon. Retrieved from http://tep.uoregon.edu/resources/assessment/multiplechoicequestions/mc4critthink.html

"After nourishment, shelter and companionship, stories are the thing we need most in the world."

–Phillip Pullman

Writing the Nursing Narrative

19

Judith S. Mitiguy

As nurses, we could apply the quote at the start of this chapter to our work. Stories are essential to our practice and reveal the essence of our profession. We tell them to one another as well as to our patients and their families. Ask veteran nurses what they remember from student days, and they won't explain the flow of blood through the chambers of a normal heart or recite the stages of labor They'll tell you a story about a patient they cared for and possibly the instructor or preceptor who guided them. Or watch how people in an audience raise their eyes from the surreptitious texts and emails they've been keying on the screens of their cell phones and tablets when they hear the speaker say, "Let me tell you a story." People shift in their seats and lean forward in anticipation.

We use stories to drive home a point when we're teaching a student, a preceptee, or a patient. We also convey our feelings through stories, and we certainly juggle all kinds of feelings in our daily practice, such as awe, gratitude, weariness, sadness, joy, helplessness, anger, frustration, and satisfaction.

As readers or authors, some of us have already discovered the power of the written narrative to deepen our understanding of nursing and inspire our appreciation. This chapter will help you discover that power—and learn how to share it.

WHAT YOU'LL LEARN IN THIS CHAPTER

- Nurses write exemplars for professional advancement and narratives for publication in the first person; and as stories, with a definite beginning, middle, and end.

- For ideas, consider writing narratives about failures, errors, or missed opportunities.

- When writing, describe what you perceived with your senses; share your thoughts, reasoning processes, and feelings in a narrative.

- To illustrate important points, incorporate vignettes.

The Nature of Narratives

The narrative differs from the types of writing described in other sections of this book. It's personal and subjective, and it's written in the first person. It flows from emotional experiences, sensory perceptions, and intuitive as well as intellectual knowing. Narratives unearth golden nuggets of knowledge, sometimes hidden in clinical practice, and they enrich our understanding of our work. Just as important to the profession as clinical, research, and professional development articles, narrative writing educates, edifies, inspires, and clarifies; it may even serve as the springboard for a quality improvement (QI) project or formal research. Nursing and medical history tells us that specific observations in everyday practice have led to scientific discoveries and new theories.

In her 1984 book, *From Novice to Expert: Excellence and Power in Clinical Nursing Practice*, Patricia Benner opened the eyes of nurses and other healthcare providers around the world to the importance of the narrative. In the foreword to the 2000 commemorative edition of this book, Benner writes:

> "In developing a narrative account of experiential learning, the story-teller learns from telling the story. Teaching reflection allows clinicians to identify concerns that organize the story; identify notions of good embedded in the story; identify relational, communicative, and collaborative skills; and articulate newly developing clinical knowledge" (Benner, 2000, pp. vii-viii).

Another well-known nurse researcher—Donna Diers, former professor emerita of Yale University—takes this point even further, advising us that we have an obligation to tell others what we know about the human condition in narrative writing. She notes that nurses serve others at the intersection of policy and the real world (Diers, 2004). We are skilled in interpreting the actual human experience that results from policies and regulations.

Benefits of Narratives

Through telling stories, we learn a great deal from one another: for example, how to prevent complications; recognize subtle changes in a patient's condition; approach angry, anxious, or withdrawn patients; communicate with physicians; and teach and console family members. Anecdotes and stories can even serve as the basis of inquiry for evidence-based practice (EBP) projects and research studies.

Benner tells us that memory has a narrative structure. We remember context and scenes through sensory perception: not by rote learning of facts. She encourages nursing educators to use narratives when they teach students and to teach students how to write narratives or exemplars of practice as a way to learn about nursing and understand complexity, nuance, the unique characteristics of each patient and family, and individual responses to illness, recovery, and loss (Benner, Hooper-Kyriakidis, & Stannard, 1999).

Narratives also teach nurses about themselves and help them gain insight into their own beliefs, values, and biases. In a 2009 interview about writing narratives, nurse practitioner Cortney Davis (a nonfiction writer and prize-winning poet) says that sharing what we witness as caregivers is essential. Like Diers, Davis says that few people draw as close to others as nurses, and few share the rich experiences of birth, death, suffering, and healing on a daily basis.

Davis says that narratives help nurses make sense of what happens and help them get in touch with their inner selves. Writing helps nurses examine and express what could otherwise become a heavy burden to the heart and soul. "At the same time that you let go of the experience, you can also hold onto it," says Davis. "The experience doesn't dissipate. You can go back and read it, revisit the knowledge and insight you have gained. You can share it with others. Writing about a significant experience accomplishes this holding on and a letting go at the same time" (personal communication, October 16, 2009). In the book *Good Prose* (2013), about non-fiction writing, Pulitzer Prize winning author Tracy Kidder also describes what might be called the self-discovery aspect of the personal narrative. He writes, "What you know isn't something you can pull from a shelf and deliver. What you know in prose is often what you discover in the course of writing it, as in the best of conversations with a friend" (Kidder & Todd, 2013, p.4).

Confidence Booster

You may think the world isn't interested in nurses' everyday practice, but consider oncology staff nurse Theresa Brown. She submitted her personal essays about nursing to *The New York Times* and they soon began to appear in that prestigious newspaper on a regular basis. Brown also published a book of nursing narratives in 2010. In an essay titled "First Death" she writes, "Almost every job has its initiations and rites of passage. In nursing, especially in oncology nursing, the first death is a professional rite of passage."

Brown skillfully interweaves her own experiences at her patient's bedside with a factual account of specific events, the hallmark of an excellent narrative. She writes: "The family members listened so carefully to what I said that every word felt painful and far away as if I were speaking through water as if, and this was true, the end of someone's life hung in the balance" (Brown, 2010, p.35).

And even though nursing can exact an emotional toll on the most mature and well-adjusted person, narrative writing can serve as an antidote. In fact, researchers have found that story-telling is associated with beneficial effects in the form of decreased physical symptoms of disease and healing of emotional and mental trauma (DeSalvo, 2000; Smyth, Stone, Hurewitz, & Kaell, 1999; Spiegel, 1999).

Narratives can be exemplars of practice for a portfolio or published as stories in magazines or journals. Blogs are another form.

Exemplars

Most nurses are familiar with nursing narratives written as exemplars of excellent clinical ability, management savvy, or innovative program development skills. Benner and her co-authors define an exemplar as:

> "A narrative or story from one's practice that conveys concerns, mean-
> ings, knowledge, and skill common to the practice. [It] is a single
> clinical situation that illustrates clinical issues or patterns. Exemplars
> illustrate the context for qualitative distinctions and narrative under-
> standing" (1999, p. 568).

Many nursing departments require nurses to include at least one exemplar as part of a portfolio submitted for advancement: for instance, from staff nurse II to staff nurse III, or as part of an annual self-evaluation. For promotion, your exemplar should clearly portray a situation in which your competence and knowledge are congruent with the desired position and the department's professional practice model. It usually depicts an assessment and intervention resulting in a positive outcome—as dramatic as saving a life, but more often involving early recognition of signs and symptoms and prevention of complications. Applications for designation as a Magnet facility by The American Nurses Credentialing Center (ANCC) include exemplars of practice and certainly help illustrate that nursing practice meets the ANCC's high standards.

Exemplars of any aspect of practice can meet requirements for promotion depending on the setting and position. For example, Jessica Sexton, an emergency department (ED) staff nurse in a children's hospital wrote about major changes she championed in the ED to expedite treatment and admission for children with cancer who presented with fever and neutropenia. These patients and their parents deeply appreciate the "fast track" approach when they arrive at the ED; the team effort is aimed at preventing prolonged waiting periods and facilitating immediate care for a vulnerable population.

As part of her portfolio required for clinical promotion, Sexton, wrote of her experience in caring for a father whose son had been injured in the Boston Marathon bombing in 2013. Her first sentences engage the reader and set the stage for what follows:

> Amidst the excitement and helicopters overhead, I heard two loud booms. My friend turned to me and asked if they were setting off can-ons at the finish line for Patriot's day. I dismissed it and turned back to the race. A few moments later the crowd was becoming overwhelm-ing and the sound of sirens filled the air. We didn't know what was happening but we decided to walk down the street to my apartment. When we got inside we turned on the TV, and the images of smoke, confusion and terror filled the screen.

> My initial thoughts were children are hurt; this is a mass casualty event and what I needed to do was help. I called the emergency department coordinator (EDC) to let her know I was close and could come in if needed. Before I finished the sentence the EDC replied, "Yes." I threw on scrubs, put on my bike helmet, told my shell-shocked friends to lock up when they left, and jumped on my bike to ride to work. At that moment, I needed to be helpful. I needed to be with my coworkers, my friends, my work family.

> When I arrived to the ED I headed straight to the charge nurse. As a member of the leadership group, I knew that no matter what I walked into, it was important I stay calm, not only to ensure that I stayed focused and provided exceptional care, but also knowing that less

experienced nurses would be looking to me as an example of how to respond and react. I knew that in order to maintain control, we needed to remain calm and collected, to focus on each patient and work together as a team. None of us would get through this without each other. I feel comfortable in a clinical leadership role and confident in my abilities to not only perform but to educate and mentor other staff on tasks, procedures and equipment needed.

The initial wave of patients had already arrived in the ED when I arrived, and I was assigned to the position of bedside nurse in a team preparing for the next patients. Our team was assigned to a room we did not typically use for resuscitations/traumas, and I was the only primary ED staff member in the group. I immediately helped to facilitate introductions, and succinctly reviewed the trauma assessment steps with the team and made sure everyone in the room was aware of our critical care equipment. As we stood as a group in our yellow gowns, nametags, masks, and gloves awaiting the unknown, I took a few moments to check in with my nursing colleagues. One of the newer nurses to the ED whom I had recently precepted, turned to me with fear and uncertainty in her eyes and said, "Thank god you are here." I looked at her and simply said, "You can do this; we will do it together." After those few word, I saw her stand a little taller with a look of resolve on her face, and she shook her head yes.

At that time I noticed a man, probably a father, walking up and down the hall, frantically talking on his phone and looking lost and afraid. He had on a hospital gown; his hair was singed; he was barefoot and his legs were covered in wounds and blood. Instead of just calling the charge nurse or social worker to help this person, I did what was more difficult for me. I left the comfort of the task-oriented trauma team in the capable hands of my colleagues and went to see how I could help this man…. I will refer to this patient as the father. At that point all I knew was that this father had a son in another room.

I walked into the room not sure what I would face….

Tips on Writing Exemplars for Advancement

Here are a few tips to consider when you are writing an exemplar for advancement.

- Review the writing tips presented elsewhere in this book.
- Read the section that follows on writing narratives for publication.
- Select the situation for your exemplar based on the requirements of the new position.
- Use wording from the job description to depict your assessment and interventions. Exemplars usually illustrate expertise in more than one competency.
- Follow your facility's guidelines regarding specifics, such as length, formatting, and number of copies.
- Ask your manager for samples of excellent exemplars.
- Read published exemplars (Benner, Tanner, & Chesla, 2009).
- Consider the readers as you provide background information about the patient or situation. The Promotions Review panel might be unfamiliar with a diagnosis, the significance of certain signs and symptoms, or the intervention.
- Explain what you did and the rationale behind your actions. Describe how you demonstrated critical thinking and sound clinical judgment.
- Present patient outcomes and explain how they exemplify your clinical expertise.
- When appropriate, write about innovative program development or retooling, leadership skills, or effective teaching or communication for your exemplar.
- Explain how the narrative exemplifies the level of expertise required in the new position.

Publishing Your Narrative

Every day, in all types of settings, nurses are writing exemplars as part of the advancement process, but many of these stories are read or heard by only a few people. If you tucked away an exemplar for promotion in a file drawer, dust it off and consider submitting it for publication. Narratives written for nursing journals and magazines can offer you more latitude to explore your experiences than exemplars written specifically for advancement, although the two forms can be interchangeable.

For both types, you are free from the convention of the objective third-person voice, and you can simply tell a story from your own point of view. Whether you are writing about a meaningful relationship with a patient in the last days of her life, a highly technical assessment, or teaching an anxious mother how to nurse her newborn, you offer yourself to the reader in a way dramatically different from the presentation of information found in a research or clinical article.

 What other outlets are available for publishing narratives?

 Hospital and nursing newsletters are a perfect starting point. In fact, for years, Massachusetts General Hospital in Boston has been publishing exemplars describing outstanding practice in its patient care services newsletter, "Caring Headlines." You can read well-written and inspiring exemplars on the publication's website (http://www.mghpcs.org/News/CaringHeadlines/index.asp).

Flip to the final pages in a nursing magazine or journal, and you often find a personal narrative as a regular column. For years, you may have turned to the last page of the *American Journal of Nursing* to read the Reflections column or, every Sunday, to the last page of *The New York Times Magazine* to take in a well-crafted personal essay.

Keeping a journal or diary might help you get started if you'd like to publish a personal narrative. Of course, although a narrative written for publication may spring from journal jottings, a narrative is much more structured and polished and must be written as a complete story with a definite beginning, middle, and end. The conclusion or ending incorporates lessons learned, insights gained, truths discovered, or understandings about the essence of nursing realized—often an "Aha!" moment in your career.

Types of Narratives

Benner's work has certainly helped nurses understand the power of the personal narrative to teach, enlighten, reveal, and inspire. She provides guidelines for writing nursing narratives and describes many types of nursing situations that lend themselves to the narrative. Some potential narrative or exemplar topics include the following (Benner, 2000):

- Preventing a complication
- Providing comfort
- Teaching
- Assessing
- Intervening
- Advocating
- Coordinating a team
- Collaborating with a physician

- Saving a life
- Anticipating a change in condition
- Coaching
- Building trust
- Establishing a relationship
- Dealing with an ethical dilemma
- Providing end-of-life care
- Responding to a disaster

Here is a closer look at a variety of narratives.

The Descriptive Narrative

As you tell the story, draw readers in with an ongoing account of your thoughts and feelings as well as what you and the patient were saying and doing. Capture and hold the reader's attention with details and dialogue. Be specific. "Show, don't tell" is the advice repeated over and over by writing teachers.

The following excerpts from narratives illustrate the power of description.

> In "The Radio," Teresa Campbell paints a picture with a few words about a difficult patient she eventually built a relationship with, despite his surliness and resistance. She writes:
>
> > His white hospital gown had the remnants of various hospital meals splattered on the front of it. A wooden radio was playing on his bedside stand, and he yelled at me, "Get out." I started to leave then decided to stay and try talking with him (Davis & Schaefer, 2003, p. 47).
>
> Campbell's last sentences in this narrative exemplify a well-written conclusion:
>
> > He taught me that everybody has a story to tell, and everyone wants someone to listen. He taught me that listening to patients' stories is part of nursing. And I taught him that being able to tell that story is part of the healing process (Davis & Schaefer, 2003, p. 48).

In another narrative, "A Moment in the History of Nursing," nurse writer Frances Murphy Araujo uses a powerful simile, along with tactile and visual details, to transport us to the bedside. She describes her patient, a 15-month-old infant with a previous head injury, probably as the result of physical abuse. Araujo writes:

> Colleen's head was irregular in shape and soft as a melon gone to rot—like if you pressed the skin too hard, your fingers would break through the skin to the orange mushy flesh.

Araujo goes on to tell us in a few words how she felt:

> I was frightened by the feel of her head. It was the first time I had seen a child with that kind of damage. I sensed danger. I felt breathless (Davis & Schaefer, 2003, p. 3).

Each of these descriptions pulls us into the story with a few words, the hallmark of a good narrative.

Nurses play pivotal roles in local and national disasters, and the lessons learned from Hurricane Katrina in 2005, the earthquake in Haiti in 2010, and the Boston Marathon bombing in 2013 have been explored in nursing journals. The narratives of individual nurses also rank a place in the history of nursing and have lessons to teach.

Describing Experiences

Using narrative format, you can describe how you dealt with a difficult situation and influenced the course of a patient's recovery, a change in his or her behavior, a breakthrough in communication, or a peaceful death. The narrative allows you to discuss those moments of knowing, intuition, and perception that nurses often experience when trouble is brewing beneath the surface. The narrative is the perfect vehicle for conveying how you intervened to prevent a patient's collapse into septic or hemorrhagic shock, suicide, or cardiac arrest—or how you failed to assess a situation or disregarded a gut feeling. Narratives describing an error or oversight are really gifts to fellow nurses: cautionary tales of lessons learned and the aftermath of a mistake. In a 2009 edition of *Nursing Spectrum*, a seasoned nurse describes a major medication error:

> It's every nurse's nightmare. By missing a decimal point, by not carefully checking my math, I overdosed a pediatric patient by 10 times

his prescription. Thankfully, the child suffered no permanent damage as a result of the overdose. But in the fallout, I considered leaving my unit and taking another position in the hospital as I found the entire process humiliating. But in the end, I stuck it out and learned a valuable lesson…

The error happened the night before Thanksgiving. I had recently changed my hours from eight to 12-hour shifts and from evenings to day/night rotation. I worked Saturday night, then a 12-hour day Monday. My husband had been recently diagnosed with cancer and we met with the oncologist Tuesday to discuss treatment options. I napped poorly Wednesday before I came to work that evening…

Unfortunately, I was in no condition to care for such a critically ill child… I remember doing a quick physical assessment and checking his lines and drip rates. I thought that the Lasix was a 1:1 drip and it was running at 4 mL per hour. The Lasix was a 10:1 drip, and I ran it at 10 times the normal dose over 12 hours.

To make matters worse, I hung a new bag of Lasix at 5 a.m., and though I checked the bag with another nurse, I still did not pick up my error. The 7 a.m. nurse called me when I got home after she noticed the error.

Toward the end of the narrative, she writes:

I cannot say I will never again commit such an error as I am human. I am more aware of how outside factors affect my nursing practice and am more willing to give up the sickest patient if I am tired or distracted. No matter how busy it is, I now am less reticent to ask colleagues for help, especially in checking any IV medications that I am to give or to check calculations (Drawing the line, 2009, p. 35).

 Q: *How can I protect my patient's privacy when writing a narrative?*

 A: Davis provides some basic advice. She recommends changing details about the patient's age, sex, and condition as long as they don't affect the essence of the story. For example, you might write that the patient suffered a traumatic brain injury (TBI) from a fall rather than a motor vehicle accident. In some cases, decades have elapsed between the situation and the written narrative: for example, recollections from student days. Even though details remain vivid in the nurse's mind, they have been long forgotten by others (Davis, personal communication, October 16, 2009).

Usually, the writer or editor includes a note at the end of a narrative indicating that names and other details have been changed to protect patient privacy. (You can lean more about protecting the patient's privacy in Chapter 11.)

Describing Profound Moments

The following narrative by Cortney Davis depicts a profound moment in the life of a nurse.

In a narrative titled "Talking to No One," Davis tells the story of caring for Joe, a construction worker with a TBI resulting from a fall. He was comatose and ventilated, and totally unresponsive, but Davis talked to him and explained his care as she checked his lines, suctioned him, and changed his position. She turned the radio on and "danced" Joe's arms and legs through passive range of motion. She talked about the weather and the latest news. One morning as the night shift drew to a close, a nurse's aide said to Davis, "You're a hot ticket…. Talking all these nights to no one" (Davis, 2009, p. 23).

Joe was discharged to a nursing home, still ventilated and unresponsive on one of Davis' days off. Weeks or months passed; Davis didn't remember how many. Then one night around midnight, a stranger approached her in the ICU. "It's you," he said. "I recognize your voice." She was perplexed.

"Maybe I should lie down in bed and not move," he said. "Then we could dance."

Joe had come by to thank her. "You held me to this life, you know," he said (Davis, 2009, pp. 23-24).

This narrative, five short pages, speaks volumes about hope and respect for the dignity and personhood of every patient no matter what his or her condition. We can also read a lesson between the lines on caring for a patient with a TBI; on the importance of comforting words, explanations, reassurance, and news of the outside world; on the necessity to preserve joint and muscle function, safeguard corneas, protect bony prominences, and prevent pneumonia. The story of Joe enhances and brings to life information you might read in a textbook or neuroscience nursing journal and imprints it on your mind and heart.

Battlefield Narratives

By their very nature, narratives from the battlefield grip the reader with strong sensory language:

> The choppers continued arriving, bringing us more and more
> wounded… Gaping bloody holes were torn through every part of
> the body. Limbs dangled from bodies held by a single thread of flesh.
> Faces smeared with a mixture of blood, sweat, and dirt were recogniz-
> able as human solely by the piercing eyes looking up in fear and pain
> (Ruff & Roper, 2005, p. 129).

Note how words and phrases such as "bloody hole" and "piercing" grab the reader's attention.

Getting Started

Just the thought of putting pen to paper or fingers to keyboard intimidates some nurses. Consider following Natalie Goldberg's "writing practice rules" (Goldberg, 1986, p. 8) to grease your wheels as a prologue to your first draft:

- Keep your hand moving.

- Don't cross out.

- Don't worry about spelling, punctuation, or grammar.

- Don't think. Don't get logical.

- Lose control.

- Go for the jugular.

Short narratives in the form of vignettes can also add a great deal to books and articles on professional development topics and help you become more comfortable with the format. Nurses Kimberly McNally and Liz Cunningham illustrate this well in their prize-winning 2010 book, *The Nurse Executive's Coaching Manual*. In each chapter, the authors present short stories of an actual coaching situation including dialogue and reactions of leaders, staff members, and colleagues. The "stories" bring the theories and principles they discuss to life in a way expository writing cannot.

Similarly in the 2013 book, *Fostering Nurse-Led Care: Professional Practice for the Bedside Leader from Massachusetts General Hospital*, authors Ives Erickson, Jones, and Ditomassi use exemplars in each of the chapters—for example, on topics such as environmental care, healing spaces, intentional presencing, and mentoring the clinical nurse specialist.

Jumpstart Your Writing

It can be hard to start writing your narrative. Here are a few ideas for overcoming your inertia.

- Pay attention to the experiences that stay with you and the stories you tell repeatedly.

- Follow the train of thought when a chance encounter, TV show, sound, or smell triggers a memory. Sit quietly before writing, close your eyes, and imagine yourself back in the patient's room, at the nurses' station, and so on.

- Pretend your mind is a movie camera. What do you see, hear, smell? How do you feel? What time of day is it? What's the weather? What are you saying? What is the patient, family member, coworker saying? (Davis, personal interview, October 16, 2009).

- Tell the story to a friend, and record the conversation.

- Tell the story out loud to yourself, using a tape recorder or tell it out loud to a trusted colleague. Ask her to take notes on the parts that grabbed her attention and those the left her confused or disengaged.

- Spend time looking at the photos of patients and families on the unit's bulletin board; they'll trigger memories.

- Draw a picture or diagram to help you visualize the situation.

- Read other narratives.

- Find a mentor who would like to share his or her expertise.

- Find a writing partner, meet a few times, and write together in silence for at least 30 minutes with no interruptions. Read aloud what you've written to one another.

Tips for Writing Narratives

Here are tips you can use to create a powerful narrative.

- Grab the reader's attention with your lede.

    I have six patients this morning. One with a self-inflicted gunshot wound to the head who's expected to die on my shift. Two with recent strokes, one with a lumbar drain after back surgery, and one with a possible prion disease (Lasater, 2008, p. 88).

- Use sensory language.

- Include familiar similes and metaphors.

- Incorporate dialog. Exact word-for-word recall might be impossible, but do your best to re-create the conversation.

- Share your thought processes, judgments, and feelings.

    While my hands are busy with the familiar routine, my mind is also busy. I think about the medicine and the patient and the reason for the shots… My mind is busy, too, thinking about the side effects. Those are what trouble me. There is a squelching of the person that makes me sad. The face can become mask-like, so that laughing or crying are rare, and the person appears stiff and blunted. I wonder if the side effects are too high a price for the benefit, a disproportionate tipping of the risk-benefit ratio. While my hands and mind are busy, my spirit is burdened (Reed, 2005, p. 35).

- Tell a story with a beginning, middle, and end.

- In the conclusion, tell the reader how you grew or changed, what you learned or realized.

- Choose details that set the tone and capture the reader's attention. Less is more.

- Share situations in which you felt you succeeded and those in which you fell short of the mark.

- Use strong, active verbs to tell the story. An overabundance of adverbs and adjectives weaken the writing.

- Ask a trusted friend to read the narrative, and listen closely to the comments and questions. Clarify and revise as needed.

The Power of Storytelling

Sue Hagedorn's experience as a storyteller exemplifies the power of the narratives to influence practice. She used film rather than the written word as her medium and told other nurses' stories (not her own), but her reflections are similar to those from Davis. Hagedorn suspended her work as a nurse educator and pediatric nurse practitioner to study documentary filmmaking. For one of her projects, she recorded nurses telling their stories on camera. However, after 2 years, she found that she missed her work teaching and working with adolescents at a residential treatment center and returned to it part-time. "The most amazing thing happened," says Hagedorn. "I came back after telling stories for 2 years, and my practice was so much more sensitive. My intuition was heightened as a result of the storytelling project. I can walk into a room, and my connection with the child, my sense of how they experience what they're telling me is so enhanced. I think [storytelling] improves practice" (personal communication, October 16, 2009).

As nurses, we spend so much time in relationships, listening to our patients' stories and caring for people in crisis. Often, we are the only ones who experience life's momentous events with another human being. Hagedorn says, "We're the ones in a position to tell the story or help the patient tell the story and make some sense out of that story" (personal communication, October 16, 2009).

Like anything worth doing, writing narrative accounts takes time and practice, but you have stories to tell and experiences to share—and now you have the tools to begin writing.

Write Now!

1. Visualize a patient you cared for or a situation that has stayed with you. Recall what you saw, heard, smelled, and felt. Write the experience as you remember it. Include dialogue and your thoughts and feelings at the time.

2. Use a tape recorder or your mobile device to tell a story to yourself or a trusted colleague about a patient you cared for. Tell it quickly, without editing yourself. Then listen to the story for key points you might include in a narrative.

3. Read an article on the "Reflections" page in *American Journal of Nursing* and analyze how the author applied the tips for writing a narrative.

References

Benner, P. (2000). *From novice to expert: Excellence and power in clinical practice* (com. ed.). Upper Saddle River, NJ: Prentice-Hall.

Benner, P., Hooper-Kyriakidis, P., & Stannard, D. (1999). *Clinical wisdom and interventions in critical care: A thinking-in-action approach.* Philadelphia: W. B. Saunders.

Benner, P., Tanner, C., & Chesla, C. (2009). Expertise in nursing practice: Caring, clinical judgment, and ethics (2nd ed.). New York: Springer.

Brown, T. (2010). *Critical care: A new nurse faces death, life and everything in between.* NY: Harper Collins.

Davis, C. (2009). *The heart's truth: Essays on the art of nursing.* Kent, OH: Kent State University Press.

Davis, C., & Schaefer, J. (Eds.). (2003). *Intensive care: More poetry and prose by nurses.* Iowa City: University of Iowa Press.

DeSalvo, L. (2000). *Writing as a way of healing: How telling our stories transforms our lives.* San Francisco: Harper.

Diers, D. (2004). *Speaking of nursing: Narratives of practice, research, policy and the profession.* Sudbury, MA: Jones and Bartlett.

Drawing the line. (2009). *Nursing Spectrum* (New York, New Jersey Metro ed.), 21, 35.

Goldberg, N. (1986). *Writing down the bones: Freeing the writer within.* Boston, MA: Shambala Publications.

Ives Erickson, J. I., Jones, D., & Ditomassi, M. (2013). *Fostering nurse-led care.* Indianapolis, IN: Sigma Theta Tau International.

Kidder, T., & Todd, R. (2013). *Good Prose: The art of nonfiction.* NY: Random House.

Lasater, M. E. (2008). Heads and beds. *American Journal of Nursing, 108*(11), 88.

McNally, K., & Cunningham, L. (2010). *The nurse executive's coaching manual.* Indianapolis, IN: Sigma Theta Tau International.

Reed, M. (2005). Medicine vials. *Nursing Spectrum* (Tri-State ed.), 14, 47.

Ruff, L., & Roper, S. (2005*). Ruff's war: A Navy nurse on the frontline in Iraq*. Annapolis: Naval Institute Press.

Smyth, J. M., Stone, A. A., Hurewitz, A., & Kaell, A. (April 14, 1999). Effects of writing about stressful experiences on symptom reduction in patients with asthma or rheumatoid arthritis: A randomized trial. *Journal of the American Medical Association, 281*(14), 1304–1309.

Spiegel, D. (April 14, 1999). Healing words: Emotional expression and disease outcome. *Journal of the American Medical Association, 281*(14), 1328.

Alternative Publication Options: Letters to the Editor, Editorials, Columns, Book Reviews, and Newsletters

20

Demetrius J. Porche

Although nurses engage in communication everyday using the spoken and written word, writing for publication can be an intimidating process. Fortunately, if you're a novice nurse author, you have a variety of writing options beyond the traditional journal article open to you. Publishing through these alternative options helps you develop your writing skills and build confidence. These projects may also seem more achievable because many of the options are shorter pieces, such as book reviews.

If you're an experienced nurse author, you might be comfortable with publishing the traditional journal article, but now you're looking for a way to disseminate your opinion (editorial), share your expertise on a regular basis (column), or simply tackle a different type of writing.

WHAT YOU'LL LEARN IN THIS CHAPTER

- To build your confidence, consider options beyond traditional articles for expressing opinions, communicating substantive information, and engaging in professional dialogue.

- Writing letters to the editor allows you to share your opinions or thoughts with a large audience.

- The purpose of a book review is to assist nurses with deciding whether a book is worth their precious time to read.

- You can help keep people engaged with a professional organization by contributing to a newsletter.

Alternative publication options can document your knowledge and experience in a defined area, state an opinion regarding an issue, or just serve as an outlet to communicate with a professional group of like-minded nurses. These other publication options include letters to the editor, editorials, columns, book reviews, and newsletters.

Letters to the Editor

A letter to the editor is generally written in response to something the editor has written in previous editorials or a response to an article printed in the publication. Or for society or professional organization publications, the letter to the editor may be a statement about a position, issue, or current situation within the respective nursing organization. Like an editorial, letters to the editor are one of the most frequently read components of a publication. Letters to the editor are a great strategy for focusing attention on an issue and influencing others with your opinion.

When to Write a Letter to the Editor

Consider a letter to the editor when you:

- Want to suggest an idea, solution, or different perspective on an issue.

- Are trying to influence a public or political leader's opinion.

- Desire to educate the general public or readership on an issue.

- Have corrective or supplemental data and information to present on an issue.

- Are trying to publicize your scholarly work in an area related to an issue.

- Want to praise an article, editorial, or opinion.

- Want to use the letter to illustrate your authority or experience.

- Want to attract attention to your professional group.

Q: *I've decided to write a letter to the editor. How do I get started?*

A: First review the mission and purpose of the publication to which you plan to write a letter to the editor. Find the editor's name, title, credentials, and email address. Most editors prefer an email rather than a letter. Keep in mind that you must respond to an article quickly or your letter will have less

chance of being published. No editor wants to publish a letter
related to an article published 3 months ago if the publication is
published monthly.

Writing the Letter to the Editor

Letters to the editor can be influential if grounded in a conversation about an issue from a
larger community, organizational, or disciplinary perspective. A general rule of thumb is
to open the letter with a simple sentence that is important, dramatic, and grabs the reader's
attention (LaRocque, 2013). Consider the following examples:

> "In the next 5 years, our health care leaders will experience
> unprecedented challenges and opportunities" (Porche, 2010, p. 97)

> "Scientific journals serve as an essential avenue to disseminate
> knowledge and build a body of science" (Porche, 2011b, p.5).

After your opening statement, include the name of the article (whether in print or online)
and when it was published. Next, explain why you are writing the letter; state the problem or
issue to which your concerns are directed. Clearly articulate how the issue or concern affects
you, others, and especially the publication's readership. Finally, decide the best course of
action that you may take on the issue while presenting the positive and negative outcomes of
these courses of action.

It's good practice to link the issue of concern to an influential person. For example, if the
course of action you are proposing is the current position or a strategy supported by a professional association or leader, state that your position supports or is consistent with the
respective organization or person's stance.

As you write, remember the five B's of writing a letter to the editor:

- Be easy to read
- Be brief
- Be concise
- Be factual
- Be stimulating

Before concluding the letter to the editor, ensure that you have clearly communicated your recommendation, call to action, and/or expected action. Date and sign the letter with your name, title, credentials, email, address (if desired you can include your street address, but it's not essential because only the city and state are published), and recommended method of contact (phone or email). If you are mailing a letter, address the envelope to the attention of the editor.

Here is an example of an effective letter to the editor:

Ann Fleming Beach's tribute to her mother's nursing career extends well beyond her words ("A Smart Doctor Listens to the Nurses," *Reflections*, April). By modeling collaborative behaviors and teaching future health care providers the importance of interprofessional communication, Dr. Beach is positively impacting the quality of patient care today and tomorrow.

Multidisciplinary rounding results in better communication and collaboration. I hope Dr. Beach will consider a more formal approach to multidisciplinary rounding, including nurses and other health care professionals in daily rounds, so they all hear her "spiel." The resulting potential for improvements in patient quality of care would certainly be a lasting tribute to her mother.

Janice Hawkins, MSN, RN
Chesapeake, VA
American Journal of Nursing. 2013: 113(7): 12

Common errors with writing a letter to the editor are wordiness, addressing too many issues in one letter; taking several positions or presenting multiple opinions on the issue, which leads to an unfocused letter; using unprofessional slang and an aggressive, nonfactual informal tone; and not being original in your information or presentation of your opinion.

Tips for Getting Your Letter to the Editor Accepted

The following are several tips for getting your letter to the editor accepted:

- Write a provocative, catchy, and stimulating opening statement.
- Keep the letter shorter than 300 words.
- Make the letter relevant to the editor and readership by connecting the letter to recent publications, current events, or new information.
- Connect the letter to your readership through personal experiences.
- Use statistics that are relevant to the readership.
- Use easily validated information to make your points.
- Illustrate your points with personal stories.
- Conclude the letter with your name, title, and credentials.
- Proofread, proofread, and proofread again.

Q: *I want to write a letter to the editor, but I don't want to use my name. Can letters to the editor be published anonymously?*

A: If you do not want your name used, for example, if you want to share your personal experience with domestic violence but don't want to be identified, you may say so when you write the editor. An effective way to ask is to end your letter with a simple line like, "I would prefer to have my name withheld if the letter is published." Make sure, though, to include your contact information because many editors won't publish letters that they can't verify. An anonymous letter will most often be published as "Name withheld by request."

Letters to the editor are frequently missed opportunities to communicate evidence-based information. Seize the opportunity by ensuring that your letter to the editor contains data and other evidence to support your opinion. In addition, this simple letter begins to document in writing your knowledge of the topic under discussion.

Confidence Booster

"I read an article about buying pedigree dogs in an in-flight magazine. As a volunteer at an animal shelter, I was appalled that adoption wasn't even mentioned as an option. I felt so passionate about this issue that I wrote my first letter to the editor—and it was published!" This story from a nurse illustrates a key point about writing letters to the editor. Try to relate your topic to a passion you have; of course, remember to harness that passion so that your letter is objective.

Editorials

An editorial is an opinion, factual point of information or clarification, an argumentative stance, or a thought-provoking substantive narrative. Editorials are composed by editors, associate or assistant editors, or guest editors (LaRocque, 2013). The editorial, one of the most widely read features of a newspaper, newsletter, or journal, is a communication channel through which a nurse can disseminate information to a large audience in a short narrative. Publically elected officials are known to secure daily briefings on editorials written about current events and political affairs, especially through newspapers.

An opinion editorial can be positive, negative, or informative in tone. Regardless of tone, the editorial should always be factual and professional in word selection and presentation. The tone of an editorial can be emotional, but should always be objective in nature.

Consider the start of an editorial on nurse staffing (Cipriano, 2013):

> It's time to stop searching for nursing's cost-benefit ratio and believe the data. For more than two decades, health services researchers across the United States and around the globe have found that more RN hours and a higher skill mix are positively associated with reduced mortality, shorter hospital stays, and reduced rates of pressure ulcers, falls, hospital-acquired infections, pneumonia, medication errors, and failure to rescue.

Note that Cipriano doesn't pull any punches by starting with a simple declarative statement, but she then backs up the statement with evidence.

The best editorials are simple, easy to read, and short. Editorials are generally about 250 to 500 words, whereas a letter to the editor is rarely longer than 300 words (LaRocque, 2013; Porche, 2011a).

Some simple guidelines for constructing an editorial are:

- The opening paragraph should include an outline of the issue or problem; a statement challenging an opinion, agreeing with an opinion, or presenting a new perspective on an issue; and factual and dramatic information.

- The second paragraph should present your position and clearly communicate your rationale for your position.

- The third paragraph acknowledges opposing thoughts or opinions and presents a counter-argument, thought, or opinion from your perspective on each of the thoughts and opinions presented.

- The last paragraph concludes with a call to action. A call to action is typically behaviorally focused and states the action you expect someone to take or the action-oriented challenge you are putting forth for the readers. The call to action should be specific and not a laundry list of potential options.

- Conclude editorials with your name, title, credentials, affiliation, city, and state (Porche, 2011a).

Here is an example of a call to action from the same editorial on staffing (Cipriano, 2013):

> For our [nurses'] part, we need to be responsible for making evidence-based staffing decisions, adjusting staffing not only when our workload increases but also when it decreases. We must show we can change based on the evidence and can innovate to create more cost-effective care-delivery models. We must adhere steadfastly to safety measures and demand the same of each nursing and interprofessional colleague. We need to collect, report, and analyze the data that will help us keep up with evaluation of appropriate staffing and outcomes. We need to hold each other accountable for care outcomes.

The call to action is quite clear, and the repetition of "We" to start several sentences drives home her point. Good writers avoid starting multiple sentences with the same word or phrase, reserving the tactic for particular situations such as this one.

Tips for Getting Your Editorial Accepted

Here are several tips for getting your editorial accepted:

- Be sure the topic or issue is relevant and timely.
- Make the editorial informative by including new information.
- Make the editorial specific to a recently published article or national issue.
- Build on a previous editorial or present a contradictory or different paradigm of a previous editorial.
- Write in the active voice.

Columns

Columns are brief articles or features written for newspapers, newsletters, magazines, or professional journals. In professional journals, columns are sometimes referred to as departments. A column can be in every issue of a publication or scheduled periodically. Columns are generally short, about 700 to 1500 words, and may focus on a specific content area or theme such as research methods, research briefs, or new pharmacology information. An associate editor, rather than the editor, may be responsible for columns.

Tips for writing a column include

- Identify an informational need. Is there an information gap in the literature? Is there a new technique? Do you have a new model or strategy to share? Do you have new data or research findings?

- Determine your target audience. What component of the journal's readership are you targeting—for example, clinicians, administrators, or everyone?

- Determine the column's purpose. Is the column to inform the readers? Present information in a new manner? Influence best practices?

- Review the author guidelines for the expected column format, and comply with that format. Read and review the general structure of previously published columns in the publication.

- Obtain factual information by conducting a review of the literature. Ensure that you have the most current and relevant information and statistics.

- Synthesize the information. Because a column is short, the information needs to be presented in a concise manner with a logical flow. For example, if you are writing a column on a new intervention for an existing health problem, the flow of the column may be: incidence, etiology, pathophysiology, signs/symptoms, diagnostic criteria, clinical management (this would represent the bulk of the column since this column would be focusing on a new intervention), expected clinical outcomes, conclusion, and references.

- Outline the column.

- Write the column by inserting narrative content into the column outline.

- Proofread, edit, proofread, edit, have a colleague proofread, and edit. Do not read or think about the column for a few days, then read it again and edit and proofread a final time.

- Submit the column following the Author Guidelines.

Generally some level of peer review is conducted for column articles regarding the scientific merit (if appropriate) and accuracy of the information presented. For most professional journals, a column is peer reviewed by at least the editor, associate editor, or an editorial board member, so the peer-review process usually doesn't require as much time. This makes journal columns a great feature through which to rapidly disseminate your scholarly work or research. Keep in mind, however, that more clinically oriented articles will undergo a full peer review.

Book Reviews

Nurses face a time barrier when trying to keep up to date with the latest evidence-based practice while continuing to practice nursing full time. A strategy to help nurses decide what to read and what not to read is the book review. Book reviews help nurses focus their reading time on the most beneficial information source (Calvani & Edwards, 2008).

Book reviews are published by journals and other publications and generally appear in the beginning or ending of the journal amongst the non-peer-reviewed material. It is always a good idea to send a query to the editor before submitting a book review. Editors frequently receive complimentary copies of books that align with the journal's mission to promote the book being reviewed in the journal.

A book review is more than a description of the published book; it's a critical appraisal and evaluation of the quality and significance of the book to nursing practice. The review generally concludes with the author's overall impression of the book and a recommendation on the utility of the book for nursing practice. The length of a book review varies from about 50 to 1,500 words (Calvani & Edwards, 2008).

Before writing a book review, read the entire book, highlight any key sections (use the highlighting feature if you are reading it in an e-book format), and take notes that summarize the major points or theses. Generally, the first two-thirds of the book review should cover background information and summarize the book; the reviewer's critical appraisal and evaluation of the book should represent at least one-third of the book review's content.

Here is an example from the beginning of a review of the book *Nursing Leadership From the Outside In*:

> *Nursing Leadership* takes a unique view of leadership—from the outside in. The editors, who are exquisite models of leadership, gathered leaders primarily from outside nursing to describe from their perspectives how nursing is strategically positioned to transform health care. The obstacles that nurses will encounter are addressed, giving the book a realistic view of nursing's role in the transformation of care. The book's goal is to provide a foundation to prepare nurses to lead change. (Kenner, 2013)

The components of a book review, in order, are:

- A *bibliographic notation* on the book that includes the title, author, copyright date, place of publication, publisher, number of pages, type of book or genre, general content or focus of the book, special book features, price, and the ISBN number.

- The *background information*, which consists of the author's purpose of writing the book, intended audience, book theme or subject matter, author's primary thesis about the book's subject matter, and prior publications by the author.

- A *summary of the book's content*. The book content summary reviews the overall structure of the book, organization and flow of the book's content, a short review of the book's table of contents, and information on the substantive content covered throughout the book's chapters.

- The author's *critical appraisal and evaluation of the book*, which should consist of the extent to which the book achieved its stated purpose, comparison of the book to other books on the same or similar topic, content omitted or unique content presented in the book, persuasiveness of the content, placement or position of this book within the existing books on the same or similar topic, extent to which the book meets the intended audience's needs, and the content's accuracy, objectivity, and thoroughness.

- A *concluding recommendation* about the book's usefulness and extent to which the author recommends the book to other nurses. The concluding recommendation is an honest explanation regarding the author's opinion about the book's utility, significance, and contribution to the nursing literature.

In part, Kenner (2013) summarizes the content of *Nursing Leadership From the Outside In* as, "The chapters do not follow the traditional path of leadership books; instead, they offer lessons learned in leadership and present unique aspects of leadership, including 'Hiring as a Pathway to Understanding Leadership.'" Notice that she quickly establishes that the book has a unique point of view.

Kenner concludes her review with

> Nursing has a bright future, and it is poised for change. This book provides the foundation for skill development and presents an innovative view of leadership development. It also challenges nurses to rise to the occasion to take full advantage of the opportunities to lead the health care revolution of change. *Nursing Leadership* sends a powerful message to nurses in all settings and to nursing students to broaden their views of leadership.

 I have never written a book review. Do you have any more tips?

 It seems obvious, but still worth stating again, that you should read the book. Start with the book's preface, which outlines the book's intended purpose and structure. Reading the preface will help you understand the organization of the book's content. Check if the preface identifies the intended audience. After reading the book, ask yourself, "Do I agree that the book was focused on the intended audience?" Reflect on the book to generate a critical appraisal and evaluation. Finally, write your opinion about the books' value, keeping your tone neutral. You never want to disparage the author, but rather focus on the usefulness of the content.

Newsletters

Newsletters are a communication tool for professional associations, organizations, and institutions. Some boards of directors consider newsletters as the communication glue that holds the organization together and keeps members engaged with the professional association. Generally the newsletter is a document to inform, announce, remind, advise, educate, advertise, or communicate with a large audience in a short publication. Professional association and institutional newsletters frequently have an open call for submissions.

An organization's newsletter (whether disseminated as print or electronically, known as e-newsletters) is a critical element to the strategic success of an organization. As a critical communication tool, the newsletter is used to disseminate information to the membership or constituents of an organization or institution in a timely manner. The key to a successful newsletter is in its name—NEWsletter. The information must be "new."

Regular newsletter readers tend to focus on three things in the newsletter:

- Who they know and what they are doing

- New events or announcements

- Recent activities of the association or organization that directly affect them.

All of these areas make good ideas for potential newsletter articles.

Newsletters have an editor who compiles all the features, solicits information, edits information, and ensures that the newsletter is disseminated on schedule. Some newsletters are indexed in various literature databases.

The ease in getting published in a newsletter varies according to the source. For example, getting published in your hospital's newsletter is easier than getting published in a more scholarly newsletter that is indexed in a database. As with other types of articles, first contact the editor with your idea and access any Author Guidelines that are available.

Some general suggestions for writing a newsletter article are (Eyman, 2006):

- When developing a title, remember that readers scan for key words and that newsletter titles are typically short in length.

- Start with a catchy opening statement that states the purpose of the article: the who, what, where, when, why, and how.

- Include new content. Remember the "new" in "NEWsletter."

- Keep messages short and concise and focus on one topic at a time.

- Keep sentence structure simple; sentences should be no more than 15 to 20 words long.

- Keep paragraphs simple with a structural length of five sentences.

- Write in a conversational tone.

- Use bulleted and numbered lists to facilitate reading.

Remember, newsletters are an excellent way to get started in writing for publication.

Expand Your Writing Potential

Expand your writing potential by using other avenues for publishing, such as letters to the editor, editorials, columns, book reviews, and newsletters. These other avenues help you with developing your writing skills and building your confidence while engaging in a less laborious and lengthy publication process. These publications also build your documented level of knowledge and expertise in a nursing area.

Write Now!

1. Write a letter to the editor and submit it. You might first try your local newspaper.

2. Select a journal you read routinely. Does the journal publish columns? If so, read the author guidelines for writing a column. Review the last 3 years of the journal for relevant and "hot" topics not covered. Use the tips for writing a column from the chapter to begin writing your first column. Contact the editor to see if there is interest in your topic.

3. Review your professional association's newsletter. Identify the three main areas that are the focus of your professional organization's newsletter. What can you contribute as an article in one of these areas?

References

Calvani, M., & Edwards, A. K.(2008). *The slippery art of book reviewing*. Kingsport, TN: Paladin Timeless Books.

Cipriano, P. (2013). Hospital nurse staffing for dummies. [Editorial.] *American Nurse Today, 8*(3), 6.

Eyman, C. L. (2006). *How to publish your newsletter: A complete guide to print and electronic newsletter publishing*. Garden City Park, NY: Square One.

Hawkins, J. (2013). Listening to nurses. *American Journal of Nursing, 113*(7), 12.

Kenner, C. (2013). Book review: Nursing leadership from the outside in. *Journal of Nursing Regulation, 4*(3), 60.

LaRocque, P. (2013). *The book on writing: The ultimate guide to writing well*. Arlington, TX: Grey and Guvnor.

Porche, D. (2010). Health care leaders' challenges in the time of health care reform. *American Journal of Men's Health, 4*(2), 97.

Porche, D. (2011a). *Health policy: Application for nurses and other health care professionals*. Sudbury, MA: Jones & Bartlett Learning.

Porche, D. (2011b). Linking scholarly publications to popular press: An avenue for dissemination. *American Journal of Men's Health, 5*(1), 5.

"If there's a book you really want to read, but it hasn't been written, then you must write it."

–Toni Morrison

Writing a Book or Book Chapter

21

Sandra M. Nettina

Have you ever read a book and thought, "I could have written that"? Or maybe you simply have a secret desire to write a book of your own but are afraid to try. Writing a book (or even a chapter in a book) can seem overwhelming. Some nurses have taken on the task and have found themselves in a nightmare of disorganization, miscommunication, and missed deadlines. Others have encountered challenges but ultimately achieved a highly satisfying outcome. Although writing a book or book chapter is not for the faint of heart, a systematic approach will help you achieve positive outcomes.

This chapter takes you through the steps of that approach. Much like other writing projects, the process starts with a rough idea that is further elucidated by developing a table of contents. A major difference, however, is the organization, timeframe, and flow of a multistep or multilayered project: You need to be a good project manager to produce a book with multiple chapters. And, you might need to recruit, supervise, and coordinate the efforts of multiple contributors and reviewers.

Whether you are a single author or working with contributors, all books start with an idea.

WHAT YOU'LL LEARN IN THIS CHAPTER

- To prepare a proposal for your book, articulate your idea and consult publisher websites.

- To maintain organization and cover assigned content areas while avoiding overlap, develop a table of contents, templates, and a sample chapter.

- When choosing contributors, pick them carefully and outline their responsibilities in a letter of intent.

- While you're writing, frequently remind yourself and the contributors to follow the schedule and follow submission guidelines.

Idea to Proposal

Good books start with ideas of all sizes. A small, undeveloped idea often grows into an out-pouring passion. If an idea is not well articulated, however, it may languish in the recesses of your mind or be forgotten. You must nurture an idea until it blossoms into content with a specific purpose for a specific audience.

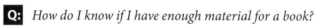

Q: *How do I know if I have enough material for a book?*

A: You might debate whether you have enough material for a book—or whether your idea is best portrayed in an article. Writing an article is certainly easier, but it's limiting. A two- or three-part series of articles might be appropriate for a topic that can clearly be broken down into parts that could stand alone. Comparatively, you might have enough content for a book if your idea is multifaceted, covers many different aspects of the general theme, is a collection of topics, or contains so much detail that it encompasses multiple chapters.

When you create a book, you must have an overall theme and construct it in a way that provides a broader service to the reader than a single article or series of articles could do. If your book focuses on research, tease out the important strands from other studies and pull them together into a theme. The longer length of a book allows a thorough systematic review of the theme with both historical review and application to practice included.

Targeting the Right Publisher

Your proposal will more likely be accepted if you target a publisher who has released books in line with your idea. Your idea should not be in direct competition with the publisher's books but should be relevant to a similar audience. For instance, you wouldn't pitch an idea for a memoir of hospice nurses to a publisher who prepares only study guides for nursing certification exams. Nor would you pitch your idea for a scholarly review of research stud-ies on cardiovascular risk reduction to a publisher of exclusively consumer health books. Some publishers' websites, including Sigma Theta Tau International (STTI) and Lippincott, Williams & Wilkins (LWW), list focus areas for books.

Check for books with similar topics to yours. You would not want to pitch an idea for a book similar to something the publisher already has produced. However if your book can be com-plementary to what the publisher already has in print, say so. For example, a publisher might have a strong emphasis on end-of-life care, but doesn't have a book on end-of-life care for pediatric patients, giving you an opening for your idea in this area.

After you have a publisher in mind, you're ready to tackle the proposal.

Crafting a Successful Proposal

Submit a proposal in the requested format, which is usually found on the publisher's website for prospective authors. Although publishers' formats vary, they generally want to see the same thing: your plan and vision for the book. For example, here are the STTI book proposal guidelines.

> STTI asks for a prospectus, a table of contents, and a sample chapter (Sigma Theta Tau International, n.d.). The prospectus should include the following:
>
> **Working title:** The publisher often changes the title that the author submits, but you should still create a title. Be sure that it reflects the content and purpose of the book.
>
> **Name of the authors, editors, and any contributors already identified:** Include brief biographies for contributors, and a more detailed biography for the authors.
>
> **Description of topic and how this book uniquely addresses a need in the market:** Why is this book needed? How will this book meet a current need?
>
> **Primary audience:** Who are the main readers you are targeting? Will it be a clinical text or a reference for professionals? Be as specific as possible and include what organizations or groups could be effectively marketed.
>
> **Number of chapters and projected word count:** What is the general length and number of chapters that will form the book?
>
> **Special features**: Will there be stories from nurses in the field? Will it include tips, checklists, and resources?
>
> **Images:** How many photos, illustrations, tables, or figures will be in the book?

Projected word count: How long do you expect the book to be?

Time frame: How long will it take to prepare the manuscript?

Goals for writing this book: Will it inform, expand, or influence current thinking?

Competitive works: List books that will compete with your planned book. Include publishers, authors, titles, and prices. Then explain how your book differs from these.

Don't submit your proposal to more than one publisher at a time unless you're working with a literary agent. (Agents aren't necessary for most nursing books.) Most proposals are submitted electronically via email directly to an acquisitions editor who will review them.

Keep in mind that reviewing proposals is a significant time and workforce investment, so you might not get an answer for a few weeks. Be patient and follow up with your editor after 3 weeks if you haven't received a response.

Q: *I thought I had a one-of-a-kind idea. However, the publisher I submitted it to said that it already had a book just like it in the works. What keeps them from stealing my idea?*

A: Ethical issues prevent publishers from stealing ideas. However, know that publishers might receive the same idea from multiple writers; it is the writer who first develops the most effective proposal and is the best fit for the book who will likely be approached as an author.

Here is another example of a proposal format (Wolters Kluwer, 2013):

Statement of scope and intent: Includes the purpose of the book and field(s) of content. Is it primarily to teach students on a particular topic, inform readers of new developments, or serve as a reference? If the project is going to include electronic media, what warrants its creation in an electronic format? What software features do you expect the program to contain? In terms of subject matter, what field and subfields are you going to cover? Will coverage be comprehensive or selective? What approach will be used to put forth the content? Will it be straightforward or conceptual, for the beginner or advanced reader? Will there be tables and other presentation features? Who is the primary audience and what books compete with yours? How is this project timely? Indicate the type and number of illustrations that you intend.

Detailed table of contents: Should clearly display what material will be covered and how it will be organized. Include a brief description of parts of the book and each chapter. Show headings and subheadings and sections with consistent formatting. For CD-ROM projects, include a breakdown of units or lessons that will enable a reviewer to conceptualize the project.

Physical specifications: Includes the proposed size of the book: pocket book, handbook, or large manual size; the length of the book in number of pages; and the number of illustrations, in black and white or color.

Sample material: Includes at least one sample chapter, including objectives, content outline and tabular or graphic material.

Curriculum vitae (CV): Include CVs for the main authors or editors.

Some book publishers request a marketing plan as part of the proposal. (You can learn more about how to create such a plan in Chapter 12.)

Waiting for a Reply

Usually, a review of your proposal takes 4 to 8 weeks but might take longer, particularly if the publisher uses external proposal reviewers. Faculty, practicing nurses, and students may be used as reviewers. Follow up by telephone or email after submitting the proposal to make sure that it was received by the appropriate contact person and is complete. If you hear no news after 8 weeks, follow up again. Your contact might ask for more information or for revisions based on internal or external review of your proposal.

After a proposal has been favorably reviewed, cost and sales forecasts are made, a development and marketing plan may be designed, and the project is presented to the in-house editorial board for final approval (F.A. Davis Company, n.d.).

Is writing or editing a book worth the effort?

 This question can't be easily answered. Each authorship experience is unique. In many cases, writing or editing a book becomes an all-encompassing personal quest, beyond the margins of professional duties or responsibility. Authorship is seldom financially lucrative, but there are other benefits, such as sense of accomplishment, prestige, and secondary benefits to one's career. Going into the project well prepared and with some experience in the publishing process will help. You can gain experience by submitting articles for publication or reviewing articles or chapters for your targeted publisher before you launch into a book project of your own. Writing or revising a chapter for someone else's book project can also provide a taste for what writing an entire book will be like.

Developing a Table of Contents

Many publishers will ask for a table of contents as part of your proposal. A *table of contents—* an outline or blueprint of your chapter or book project—is the most complete way to show publishers exactly what you intend to cover. Not only will this outline help guide you while you complete the project, but it will also be used in the publication to lead readers to specific information. Detailed tables of contents are especially helpful for large projects that include multiple writers or contributors so that each can see what the other is doing.

A table of contents is organizational and topical. It should flow in a logical and evident pattern. For example, a head-to-toe format is logical, as is an organ system from critical (heart, lungs) to less critical (skin).

To decide how to break down content into chapters or sections, start with major topic areas of your subject. Decide whether any major area is so broad that it needs to be divided: for example, *cardiovascular* into *cardiac* and *peripheral vascular*, or *reproductive* into *male reproductive* and *female reproductive*. Likewise, determine whether any major area is shorter than the rest and could naturally be combined, such as *eye, ear, nose, and throat disorders*.

After you document in a logical format all the major areas you want to cover, determine what subheadings of information need to be addressed. List these in bullet points or write a paragraph under each major topic area. Include estimated page or word counts for each section of your table of contents (see the following sidebar).

Estimating Page Counts

Assigning page or word counts to the table of contents is important for your own writing schedule as well as for a publisher to assess the proposal as a business proposition. Estimating page count depends on the trim size of the book, font size, spacing, number and size of illustrations and tables, and additional elements such as table of contents and index. There is software available that calculates page count by creating a dummy book with adjustable layout parameters (Jackson, 2009). You can also query the publisher for standard book trim sizes and page conversions. For a standard size 8.5" × 11" use three double-spaced manuscript pages in a 12-point font to one printed book page. Use roughly two manuscript pages to one print page for smaller trim-size books (Wolters Kluwer, 2013). Setting page limits will also help keep multiple contributors to similar levels of detail. Here are some tips to keep in mind:

- Determine page counts by evaluating other available literature on the topic areas, dividing the sum by the number of parts, and weighing the importance of various chapter or section areas.

- In most cases, per-chapter page counts are flexible as long as you stay within the total for the entire book.

- Have some optional content in mind to add in the event that your project falls short. Also put some thought to what you could cut if the project runs long.

- You can refer the reader to Internet resources for additional information, and cross-reference to previous sections of the book to save space. Books that will be offered in electronic formats can link to endless resources, and even print books can be enhanced by their own web pages for additional content.

While you are preparing the table of contents, keep in mind your target audience and purpose of the book or chapter. Is it a nursing textbook that might include ancillary materials, or a general nursing book that might be used for reference or inspiration? If you have not gathered enough information about the topic(s) you are going to write about, do an extensive but general review before you finalize your table of contents. Have your table of contents reviewed by several people in the field and then reorganize, rework, or supplement as indicated.

Using a Template

Most clinical books as well as some nonclinical books are composed of chapters and entries within chapters that follow a consistent format. If you find that "Clinical Manifestations" is the third subheading in the first chapter or entry, it could well end up being the third subheading in subsequent chapters or entries.

Just like an outline helps you write an article without leaving out any critical content areas, you can use a template to help organize your writing and ensure that everything has a place in the book or chapter. For example, for nursing books about the care of patients with certain diseases and disorders, the reader consistently wants to know about the pathophysiology, clinical manifestations, diagnostic test findings, and what treatments and nursing interventions to provide. Use these guideposts as you write each chapter.

One template does not fit all topic areas, however. Variations on the template might be necessary.

Within the template, identify the level of headings and subheadings that best portray the information. For example, the highest level of heading after the title of the chapter could be the name of a disease or disorder. The second level of heading could be "Pathophysiology" or "Diagnostic Test Findings." To organize information further, a third level of heading such as "Laboratory," "Imaging," or "Physiologic Tests" might be used.

You can set up templates in most word processing systems, including formatting for headings and other key sections. Consider using a template or the level headings feature in your word processing program. However, be aware that some publishers may request specific formatting or require that formatting be removed before final submission of the manuscript. It's best to ask the editor you work with if the publisher has any word processing templates that should be used. You can then share them with your contributors.

If you are working with other authors, you can insert instructions into the various sections, which can then be deleted by the contributor. Here is an example of a template.

> Chapter 15 Dermatologic Disorders
>
> *(Introduction explaining how common these types of disorders are, how they can affect the rest of the body systems and affect the patient, and what are the main assessments and interventions by the nurse; 2 paragraphs)*
>
> **Overview** *(include an overview of anatomy and physiology and common pathophysiology of the system)*
>
> **Anatomy and Physiology**
> > Structure *(2-3 paragraphs)*

Normal Physiologic Functions *(3-4 paragraphs)*

Common Pathophysiology *(3-4 paragraphs, this should be the same level as anatomy and physiology)*

Diagnostic Evaluation *(describe the major laboratory tests, imaging studies, and function tests in this system; indications and results for specific disorders will be given under conditions)*

Laboratory Tests

Test *(include for each the common uses, basic procedure, and precautions; 1 paragraph)*

Test

Test

Imaging Studies

Test *(include for each the common uses, basic procedure, and precautions; 1 paragraph)*

Test

Test

Other Tests

Test *(include for each the common uses, basic procedure, and precautions; 1 paragraph)*

Test

Test

Disorders

Name of Disorder *(for each disorder, give name and pseudonyms, type of disorder, and brief description; 2-3 sentences)*

Disease Process *(give specific pathophysiology down to a cellular level, use short paragraphs to describe the progression; 3-6 paragraphs)*

Clinical Presentation *(give signs and symptoms from early to late stages, including complications; 2-4 paragraphs)*

Diagnosis and Management *(outline the diagnostic work-up and give specific results of specific tests that are used at various stages;*

outline the treatment modalities of pharmacologic, surgical, and other at various stages; 6-8 paragraphs)

Supportive Care *(describe nursing interventions, including therapeutic, supportive, and educational at various stages; 6-8 paragraphs)*

Creating a Sample Chapter or Entry

At the start of a project, writing a sample chapter or entry within a chapter is often helpful, especially if you are heading a team of contributors. A sample might also be required in a proposal. Pick an area that you are most familiar with or that will fit the template best. By putting the information into the template format, you will see what doesn't work and make revisions accordingly. You can identify areas that fall outside the template and identify how to handle them differently. Contributors will be able to work more efficiently and uniformly when a sample is available to guide them. Yvonne D'Arcy, author of several books on pain management (including *Compact Clinical Guide to Women's Pain Management: An Evidence-Based Approach for Nurses* and *Pain Management: Evidence-Based Tools and Techniques for Nursing Professionals*) states, "If the chapter is written so that it is easily reproducible then the remaining chapters will complement and expand the original concept that the author created" (Y. D'Arcy, personal communication, October 8, 2009).

Within the sample, try to include recurring or suggested features, including tables, boxes, tips, case studies, key points, online resources, or questions and answers. Show their placement within the sample. Highlight the type of information to include in these features as well as the format to use. Identifying features early helps ensure that a good number of these will be included in the finished project and also that they will be consistent and appropriate.

Writing style should also be highlighted in a sample. You will likely have writing guidelines, but use your sample to show thoughtful and deliberate implementation of the guidelines. The sample will also set the tone of the writing style, depth of information, and frequency and format of references.

Contributors and Coauthors

Just like the actors in a movie can make or break its success, having the right contributors, who understand and are committed to the project, can ease your workload and improve the outcome. A book might have one main author, who writes some parts of the book but also acts as an editor who coordinates a team of contributors, or several coauthors who divide sections or topics within the book. The more contributors you have, the shorter each section that contributors need to write, which can speed the process. However, the more contributors, the more coordination and time you will spend orienting them to the project and editing for uniform style, repetition, and flow between sections or chapters.

Finding Contributors

Matching content area with expertise to assign sections of the project can take several weeks to even months. Start by using your network of dependable experts. Perhaps you can find colleagues who are willing to do more than one section or chapter.

If you assign too much to one person, however, you run the risk of a delay. Yvonne D'Arcy warns, "Contributors can be a double-edged sword. You try to approach potential writers with a creative and professional approach. If some are honest enough they will decline due to previous commitments. Others may think the idea is interesting and commit to the work but fail to produce the contracted material" (Y. D'Arcy personal communication, October 8, 2009).

If you have been asked to write or revise a chapter for a book, you can feel honored, but should not feel obligated to accept. You'll make the right decision and be of greater assistance to the main author or editor if you learn as much as you can about the project, understand what is expected of you and what the deadlines are, and keep communication channels open (Nicoll, 2013).

After you exhaust your own network, look further. Ideas for finding good writers in fields out of your area of expertise include the following:

- Check recent journals for authors of articles on the general topic or check specialty journals for their editorial board.

- Contact specialty organizations to see whether they can put out a call for authors to their members.

- Online, check conference programs or proceedings to see who has spoken on the topic.

- Partner with a school of nursing or hospital department of continuing education to find contributors who are being encouraged by their institution to write for publication.

- Consult with your initial contact—usually the acquisitions editor—at the publisher. There may be a file of contacts at the publisher.

Some (but not all) book projects and some chapter projects have an author allowance budgeted; depending on the contract, this might be an advance on royalties or a flat amount for the creation of the book. You might need to use some of this money to pay for those hard-to-find contributors. Give potential authors complete information—a synopsis of the project, the breadth and depth of the topic you want covered, page count, deadlines, and any honorarium or incentive—to help them determine whether the work is a good fit. The last thing you need is a contributor who says yes but fails to deliver.

Collecting Contributor Forms

Even if you are using a network of friends and trusted colleagues to help you with your project, don't neglect to have a contributor agreement and other official forms in place, including the letter of intent, biography form, and contributor agreement. Your contract with your publisher will require it, and your editor might even ask to see them before your book publishes.

Q: *I asked a friend to contribute to my book. I didn't think I'd need a contributor agreement because we're so close, but now she's late on her deadline, and my publisher is unhappy with us. What can I do to avoid losing a contributor—and a friend?*

A: You might need to consider replacing her with a back-up plan because ultimately, your professional career is your priority. For the future, remember that it's hard to do business with friends. A contributor agreement is a business agreement; it's a simple transaction to protect you both.

Letter of intent. One of the first forms you should provide for the contributor is a letter of intent or project letter. This should describe the project and identify the contributor's role, including topic area, length, due dates, publishing date, and honorarium. The letter, which summarizes what you described to the contributor verbally or in written correspondence, serves as a document that the contributor can refer to during the project for basic information. Some authors have their contributors sign this letter as an agreement between the author and the contributor. This is different from signing a contributor agreement with the publisher, which assigns copyright. The following is an example of a contributor agreement.

Components of a Contributor Letter of Intent

Sam Peters, RN, MSN
Associate Professor
"University School of Nursing"
"Address"

Dear Mr. Peters:

Thank you for your interest in contributing to *The Community Nurse's Guide to Chronic Diseases*. Sigma Theta Tau ◄——— Title of book, publisher, and planned publication date
Publishers will publish this handbook in fall of 2011. This
book will be used as a field guide and quick reference book
for community health nurses to care for individual patients
as members of high-risk populations in the community. I ◄——— Purpose of the book
would like it to reflect best practices and research in the areas
of chronic disease management, access to care, and cost-
effective implementation systems.

Your chapter is Chapter 12, "Renal Problems," which has ◄——— Chapter topic and page allotment
been allocated 13 pages. I will be sending you an electronic
template that will explicitly outline the headings and flow of
information. I need your completed manuscript by February
15, 2011 to allow for editing and production time. Approxi- ◄——— Deadline and editing process
mately 6 weeks after submission of your manuscript, you will
receive an edited copy with questions for your review. Later in
the process, you will be asked to read page proofs of the chapter to ensure its accuracy and possibly add any last-minute
changes. Please keep a copy of your manuscript, revisions
along the way, and the reference materials you used in case I
have any questions during the process. When the entire book
is complete, you will be sent an honorarium of $100 and a ◄——— Honorarium
copy of the book. Your name will be listed in the front of the
book as a contributor.

Because this is a field guide and reference book, the material should be written in a practical manner, but please supply ◄——— Writing style authoritative references within the chapter, such as those that come from published clinical trials, meta-analyses, approved guidelines, and position papers, using American Psychological Association (APA) format as appropriate. The majority of references should be no more than 3 years old at the time of ◄——— Reference style publication.

Special features in this book are three to six learning objectives for each chapter, tables that outline assessment of each body system, a list of community resources for each topic ◄——— Special features of the book area, and caregiver education alerts. You will see examples of these on the electronic template that I will send to you.

Please contact me when you have reviewed all the material and would like to discuss the details further. You can reach me by email or cell phone at any time during the process. ◄——— How to contact you with any questions Thank you again for your participation.

Sincerely,

Biography form. A biography form is another important form to have completed early in the process. You need each contributor's correct spelling of name and credentials, professional title and affiliations, preferred address, email address, and contact numbers (phone and fax). Collecting this information early will ensure that you can reach your contributors with questions and comments as deadlines approach. You can also use this information when compiling a list of contributors in the book, or for finding expertise if you need additional help in certain areas. Here is a sample biography form.

Sample Contributor Biography Form

Date: _____

Name of book: _____   Name of chapter(s): _____

Please complete the following information. This is how your name and other information will appear in print:

Name, degrees, and certifications: _____

Current job title: _____

Employer and employer's city/state: _____

Please provide the following contact information.

Address _____

Preferred phone number: _____   Secondary number: _____

Preferred email address: _____

Secondary email address (if available): _____

Fax number: _____

Please provide a short bio (no more than 125 words) that describes your expertise in relation to the book:

_____

_____

_____

_____

Contributor agreement. An essential form is the contributor agreement for the publisher. The publisher might offer a standard form that identifies the responsibilities of the contributor to the main author(s) and publisher, verifies that the work has not been published previously, and assigns copyright to the publisher. Both the contributor and the publisher sign the form. This legal agreement attests that the contributor has not published the work elsewhere and is relinquishing the rights to the publisher. In some cases, the contributor agreement is between you and the author; in this situation, the publisher has required the author to ensure agreements are signed and kept on file.

Contract

After the publisher accepts your proposal, a contract is drawn up and signed between the author and the publisher. Publishers usually have a template contract that includes items such as payment of author royalties, copyright ownership, number of copies to be published, publication date, and general responsibilities of the author and publisher. As with any contract, read carefully before signing and consult an attorney as needed.

 Q: *How can I best manage the schedule?*

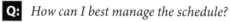 **A:** Through no fault of your own, you might find yourself slipping behind because of over-commitments, natural disasters, and the constant flow of new information. At the start of the project, have a back-up plan to handle this situation. For example, think about lining up a potential second editor in case you run short of time. If you are using contributors, regularly check their progress to identify problems early on. And, of course, you should be ready to "burn the midnight oil" as deadlines approach!

Setting a Schedule

The publisher has accepted your proposal with projected manuscript transmittal and publication dates. Whether you are writing your project alone or working with a team of 50 people, you need a schedule. You now need to work backward to establish a timeline. Front-end planning time is needed to ensure that content can be reviewed, edited, and revised as needed before submission to the publisher.

Q: *Why does it take so long to produce a book?*

A: The larger and more complex the project is (for example, if it has many contributors), the longer the preparation time. Time is needed for the initial preparation of the manuscript by the main author(s). Then it is sent to the publisher, where more editing and copyediting will be done. After that, you need to answer editor's questions and make revisions as needed. A production staff takes over, you review page proofs, the work goes out to a printer, and (finally) it arrives in a distribution center for sale! That whole process can take from 8 months to 2 years. Fortunately, you—as author—are concerned only about the preparation of the manuscript and reviewing the edited pages and page proofs.

Naturally, your schedule becomes a bit more complex if you're using contributors or co-authors. Because you will be providing outlines, templates, and a sample chapter to the contributors, you might not need to see rough drafts or expanded outlines from them. You should give enough time, however, for you to send their contributions for peer review and to edit them, then return to the author for revisions. Add in extra time for revisions in case the chapter or section does not come in as you intended. Some authors give a monetary bonus to contributors who get in their material ahead of the deadline. Despite incentives, frequent communication, and even pleading, expect that some contributors will be late. As an author, you must balance the schedule with enough time for contributors to produce their manuscript, adding your time spent editing all sections and melding them into one cohesive work.

Confidence Booster

Even though you may have had a negative experience with writing or publishing in the past, don't give up on your dream project! With enough organization, support, commitment, and guts, you can succeed.

One tip for managing a schedule and encouraging on-time submissions by contributors is to have virtual office hours at least once a week at a time that will be convenient to many. You can let your team know you are available for questions and communication by phone or electronic means. You may pass information back and forth through various programs such as

Google Documents, blog, or even your Facebook page. You can also use this time to send out reminders, words of encouragement, tips, and examples of best practices. Be aware that you will need to be available 24/7, however, for those who work best during off hours.

Although you'll want to keep the documents private, you might want to use social media such as Facebook and Twitter to give people a taste of what is coming in your book to build anticipation—and sales.

Following Submission Guidelines

Each publisher has *submission guidelines*, also called *Author Guidelines* or *publisher's guidelines*, that give you information on each step of the process, from how to submit your manuscript and figures to the primary contacts for each step of your book. Guidelines also cover any *house style* issues, such as how to handle titles or credentials or how to spell certain words (for example, *health care* versus *healthcare*.) Base your instructions to any contributors on these guidelines, and check them again during the editing and final preparation of your manuscript.

The electronic format in which you transmit the manuscript depends heavily on these guidelines. Typically, each chapter and other parts of the manuscript, such as the appendices, should be in separate files. The Johns Hopkins University Press stresses that a hard copy of the manuscript and an electronic copy should be submitted and be identical. Some publishers only want hard copy of your figures or charts and graphs. Most publishers, like STTI, no longer require a hard copy submission. However you submit, no changes should be made to the content or format of the electronic file after it is printed (The Johns Hopkins University Press, 2013).

The publisher's submission guidelines detail how to set up paragraphs, pages, tables, illustrations, footnotes or endnotes, references, and other aspects of the manuscript. As author, this is your responsibility, but you will save time and effort by highlighting these guidelines for your contributors. An important aspect of submission guidelines is how to submit illustrations. Many contributors do not know how to obtain illustrations or obtain permission for published illustrations. In most cases, you can submit hard copy photos or illustrations in the form of glossy prints, electronic files of illustrations, or digital media. You must obtain permission from the copyright holder of anything that has been published. Submission guidelines explain this process. (You can learn more about permissions in Chapter 11.)

Q: *Who picks the title and creates the book cover?*

A: Although your ideas on title and cover design are usually welcome, the publisher makes the final decision on these items. Both title and design depend on several marketing considerations, such as other book titles in your content area; whether the book is positioned as a textbook, gift book, or another type; and what will work well on the planned cover size.

Yes, You Can

Potential book authors usually ask themselves, "Can I do this?" If you believe you can't, you won't. If you think you can, then enlist some help from colleagues and start writing. Through upfront planning and careful project management, you *can* produce a finished book.

Write Now!

1. Think of an idea for a book or book chapter. Using the STTI proposal format in this chapter, make notes on how you would accomplish each step.

2. Compare the table of contents from three different books to identify different formats. Analyze how well the table of contents reflects the book's stated purpose and title.

References

F. A. Davis Company. (n.d.). Guidelines for preparing a publishing proposal. Retrieved from http://www.fadavis.com/page/preppubproposal

Jackson, G. (2009). How to calculate book length. Getting Published. Retrieved from http://gettingpublished.wordpress.com/2009/09/20/how-to-calculate-book-length/

The Johns Hopkins University Press. (updated 8/13). Manuscript Preparation. Retrieved September 6, 2013, from http://www.press.jhu.edu/books/manuscript_prep.html.

Nicoll, L. (2013). Writing a book chapter. *Nurse Author & Editor, 23*(3). Retrieved from http://www.nurseauthoreditor.com/article.asp?id=223 (free registration required)

Sigma Theta Tau International Honor Society of Nursing. (n.d.). Book proposal guidelines. Retrieved from http://www.nursingsociety.org/Publications/Books/Pages/BookProposal.aspx

Wolters Kluwer. (2013). Lippincott, Williams & Wilkins proposal guidelines. Nursing: general interest. Retrieved from http://www.lww.com/webapp/wcs/stores/servlet/content_resources_authors-proposalguidelines_11851_-1_12551

"When you know better, you do better."

–Maya Angelou

Writing for a General Audience

–Pamela J. Haylock

Nurses are often introduced to writing for general audiences as they write self-care instructions, discharge plans, and other patient education materials. As expertise evolves, nurses can—and should—contribute to procedural, research, and informed consent documents, institutional review board (IRB) research proposals and review processes, sophisticated patient and community education projects and programs, and marketing materials using print, audio-visual, computer, and Internet-based media.

This chapter covers the unique contributions that nurses can make in writing for the general audience and how you can take specific steps to make these contributions effective.

Current Trends Create an Imperative for Nurses to Write

Patient and community education are central to nursing's philosophy of practice (Redman, 2011), so it's not surprising that the Code of Ethics for Nurses (ANA, 2001) specifies a nurse's duty to advocate for and strive to protect the health, safety, and rights of patients. Most nurses would agree that communication of health-related information is essential to patient safety and well-being (Redman, 2011). Nurses can reach more patients—and the general public—by writing than through one-to-one conversations or small

WHAT YOU'LL LEARN IN THIS CHAPTER

- You can promote community, national, and international efforts to meet health needs by writing for general audiences.

- When writing patient education materials, pay attention to reading level, health literacy, and cultural sensitivity.

- Identify publishing outlets for a general audience.

- Following the four basic principles of writing for a general audience will make your efforts more effective.

group meetings. In addition, several trends call for nurses to get involved in creating useable, compelling written materials, for example, patient education brochures, that capture and maintain readers' interest.

Q: *What resources are available if I want to become more skilled in writing health information materials for the public?*

A: Take every opportunity that comes your way to hone your writing skills and improve your abilities to share health-related information. Peruse the local library and bookstores for "how-to" books that seem to match your interest areas. Look for writing interest groups in your community and local or university-sponsored writing workshops. Online continuing education courses in writing are increasingly available as healthcare facilities seek ways to meet national Culturally and Linguistically Appropriate Services (CLAS) Standards. The American Medical Writers Association (www.amwa.org) and the Association of Health Care Journalists (www.healthjournalism.org) are two of many member associations established to support writers who focus on medical communication. These organizations' websites provide resources for writers of any level, and many resources are available to nonmembers at no cost.

Nurses, HITECH, and Meaningful Use

Nurses' contributions in communicating with patients, caregivers, and the general public date back to Florence Nightingale. Writing for lay-women readers, Nightingale's *Notes on Nursing* (1859) encouraged "every woman" to "think how to nurse" (Nightingale, 1859, Preface). In the late 19th century and well into the 20th, Lillian Wald, credited with the invention of public health nursing in 1893, used her writing skills to inform the community, which was served by the Nurses' Settlement in New York, to advance public health nursing as a new role (Buhler-Wilkerson, 1993; Wald, 1902).

Technology advances in this century create new opportunities for nurses to share their expertise. For instance, the need to maximize the potential of electronic health records (EHRs) to deliver educational materials is a regulatory component detailed in "meaningful use" rules in the Health Information Technology for Economic and Clinical Health (HITECH) Act of 2009 (HealthIT.gov). Multidisciplinary collaboration, including nurses, is essential so that EHRs can achieve health and efficiency goals in any delivery system. Potential EHR patient education capabilities include (Donelan, Michael, DesRoches, & Shoemaker, 2013):

- A library of information, suggested to clinicians by the EHR system, that may be viewed, printed, and provided during clinical visits

- A library of information accessible to patients through a patient portal or gateway

- Tools or information that can be proscribed through EHR functions and disseminated to patients outside the clinical setting via mail, Internet, or telephone

- Population or system-prescribed information generated by a practice for all patients who meet conditions or criteria

These are all areas where nurses could write material for patients.

Confidence Booster

A friend's life is threatened as she fights an infection that started with breakdown of a surgical wound and pressure ulcers. He didn't know the "sore spots" he couldn't see were so dangerous. Or a young woman starts chemotherapy months after her obstetrician told her not to worry about the lump in her breast. The doctor told her, "Don't worry; you're too young to have breast cancer." Much later, the woman learned the doctor was wrong; she is not too young.

Nurses hear stories like this far too often. How many times have you heard words such as, "If only I'd known better, I would have done things differently." Nurses do know better. As advocates for the people, communities, and populations we serve, it's our duty and responsibility to learn and to teach. Sharing what we know, and seeing people benefit from our knowing, is one of the great joys of being a nurse.

Communication the Public Understands

President Obama signed the Plain Writing Act of 2010 on October 13, 2010, requiring federal agencies to use "clear Government communication that the public can understand and use" (PlainLanguage.gov, 2011). Acknowledging the critical link between effective communication and successful delivery of healthcare services, The Joint Commission supports several efforts to improve patient-professional communications, including Patient-Centered Communication Standards for hospitals released in 2010 (The Joint Commission, n.d.). No profession is better prepared than nurses to integrate and translate complex scientific and medical terminology to the plain language demanded in today's healthcare environment. And the public is hungry for that information. According to a Pew Internet survey (2013), one in three U.S. adults say they have gone online to determine what medical condition they or someone else might have.

Patient Activation and Engagement

Engaging patients in their care and expectations of consumer empowerment and responsibility are basic elements of health system reform outlined in the Patient Protection and Affordable Care Act of 2010 (Hibbard & Green, 2013; Lober & Flowers, 2011). Patient activation can enhance health outcomes and the patient experience (Hibbard & Greene, 2013), and possibly reduce healthcare costs (Hibbard, Greene, & Overton, 2013).

Hibbard and Greene (2013) differentiate the terms patient activation and patient engagement:

- Patient *activation* equates with understanding one's role in the care process and having the knowledge, skill, and confidence to manage one's health and healthcare.

- Patient *engagement* denotes a concept that includes activation—interventions designed to increase activation and patients' resulting behavior.

Effective patient-provider communications and effective educational efforts are vital if such engagement is to occur (Hibbard & Mahoney, 2010; Holman & Lorig, 2000; Ricciardi, Mostashari, Murphy, Daniel, & Siminerio, 2013).

Nurses work every day to activate and engage patients. Why not use all available tools—including writing—to achieve those goals?

Population-Based Diversity

The ever-growing diversity in local, national, and international populations leads to variations in health information–seeking among populations and reinforces the importance of the cultural context of health and healing (Kirmayer, 2012). Substantial evidence supports that ethnic and socioeconomic diversity are significant factors in disparate health outcomes. Patient comprehension of basic and every-day occurrences within the healthcare systems—procedural patient consent forms, medication administration, and other self-care instructions—must be tailored to end users, and have a profound effect on healthcare outcomes

(MacDougall, Connor, & Johnstone, 2012; Marks, Schectman, Groninger, Plews-Ogan, 2010; Polishchuk, Hashem, & Sabharwal, 2012). That's where nurses come in.

What to Write

Pick a topic you find interesting, and about which you are knowledgeable and passionate. Consider, "What is it that you want people to know?" Brenda Ueland, author of *If You Want to Write,* which three-time Pulitzer Prize recipient Carl Sandburg described as the "best book ever written about how to write," advises (Ueland, 1987, xii)

> …to have things alive and interesting it must be personal, it must come from the "I": what *I* know and feel. For that is the only great and interesting thing. That is the only truth *you* know, that nobody else does (Ueland, p. 71).

William Zinsser, author of another classic guide to writing, suggests:

> Writers of every age will write better and more confidently if they are allowed to write about what they care about. Affection for the subject is a tonic (Zinsser, 1990, p. 240).

In conversations with friends, neighbors, patients, and healthcare consumers, you've probably noticed topics that generate confusion, such as terms and phrases that can be unclear or are frequently misunderstood by the lay public. Think about topics that induce fear, stress, and anxiety for some people or populations. Any of these subjects could make valuable additions to available resources.

In addition to writing on health topics, consider writing about nursing issues, such as the need to have adequate staffing to promote optimal outcomes, for the public. Few laypersons are aware of the true scope of your education or your potential contributions to healthcare (Buresh & Gordon, 2006; Nelson & Gordon, 2006; Summers & Summers, 2009). Your input can prompt debates at institutional, local, state, and federal levels about healthcare services. Sharing your perspective about healthcare delivery helps members of the public understand health, healing, and nurses' roles.

Magazines, newsletters, websites, blogs, social networking forums, and other outlets in the general media often feature letters to the editors, columns, commentaries, opinion papers, and editorials written by nurses. You can use these outlets to offer realistic images of contemporary nursing, showing nursing's unique and valuable perspective to a broad audience—including policy-makers.

Principles of Writing for a General Audience

Using the following four essential principles will help you meet your goal of providing high-quality information that's useful for the general public and healthcare consumers. The good news is that following these principles will also make you a better writer.

Know Your Audience

Despite the title of this chapter, the term "general audience" is misleading. In response to the question "Who am I writing for?" Zinsser (1990) advises, "Don't try to visualize the great mass audience. There is no such audience—every reader is a different person" (Zinsser, p. 27). He suggests that as an author, you let yourself be who you are, allowing your humor, your vision for life, your passion, in short, your style, to show. At the same time, Zinsser insists that mastering the craft of writing is essential, that "there's no excuse for losing the reader through sloppy workmanship" (Zinsser p. 28).

Knowing your intended audience is really about carefully simplifying, pruning, and ordering your topic in ways that encourage someone to read and take note of what you write. Federal Plain Language Guidelines (PlainLanguage.gov, 2011) recommend that you "write for your audience" as a first rule of plain language: Use language your audience knows and feels comfortable with. Address separate audiences separately. By addressing different audiences in the same place, you make it harder for people to find the information that applies to them. For example, you could be asked to write text for a pamphlet on vaccination for human papillomavirus (HPV). Before you begin this project, you'll want to define who is expected to use this resource. Are you writing for parents? What do you think parents already know, want, or need to know on the subject? Or, are you writing for children? What do you want to happen as a result of the information you've provided? What do you need to say to get this outcome?

The U.S. Centers for Disease Control (CDC), charged with explaining HPV vaccination to the American public, addressed the "Who is the audience?" question by creating two versions of HPV vaccine information that cover pertinent questions for children and parents. (Centers for Disease Control and Prevention, 2012a, 2012b).

Deliver a Clear and Compelling Message

Before you start to write, give yourself time to make a conscious decision about your message. Then, translate that message into a statement that is clear and compelling. Every sentence in the final material concisely and simply supports the message. Are you trying to explain what you're doing and why you are doing it? Einstein is quoted as saying:

> "If you can't explain something simply, you don't understand it well. Most of the fundamental ideas of science are essentially simple, and may, as a rule, be expressed in a language comprehensible to everyone. Everything should be as simple as it can be, yet no simpler" (PlainLanguage.gov, 2011).

Bring Commitment, Energy, and Passion

When, as Zinsser suggests (1990), you write to please yourself, you're more likely to be writing with confidence, and less likely to fret over whether the reader is with you. The work of preparing to write, searching for supporting evidence in the literature, for example, becomes an interesting and thought-provoking process when you have a topic that matches your own interests and passions. Without the commitment to provoking readers' interest and offering important information, the writing process is a dull, painful slog, and readers are likely to detect your pain and stop reading.

An author should tell readers why they should care about the topic. A short narrative revealing your personal connection to the issue can help start your material with an appealing story, providing something readers can relate to and drawing them into what you are writing. For example, the story of a friend's (or parent's, or child's) experience in a healthcare setting could set the stage for a magazine article or a newspaper opinion piece that praises the services or highlights problems and advocates for change. People like to read about people and others' experiences; the vicarious nature of stories makes it easier for readers to relate to information that is provided. Of course, you need to protect the identity of your subjects.

Plainly State the Desired Change or Action

Organize your written material by opening with a statement of its purpose and bottom line. Put the most important information at the beginning and include background information as it's needed toward the end. People read informational materials to find answers—how to do something or to learn what happens if they don't. They want to get this knowledge quickly. Organize your document to respond to these concerns. Identify questions your audience may ask and organize your material in the order they would likely ask them (PlainLanguage.gov, 2011). For example, if someone is searching for information on Rocky Mountain Spotted Fever, one of the first items they would probably want to know is what it looks like and its most common signs and symptoms.

Be specific about what you want the reader to do. Details help readers more easily implement your suggestions. Which of the following two examples do you think readers are more likely to follow?

> It is important for cancer survivors to eat a healthy diet. *(Common advice given to survivors and caregivers.)*

> Or

> "In this book, you'll find vegetables, fruits, sweets, poultry, and fish. They're all here, presented in sensible ways that take advantage of the nutrition, taste, and immunity-building properties in every morsel of yum." (Katz, 2004, p 13)

In the first sentence, "*healthy diet*" is up to the reader's interpretation. The second sentence leaves no doubt in the reader's mind what's going to be presented, doesn't use the word "diet"—which is a turnoff for many people—and captures a reader's interest in just two sentences.

Suitability of Written Materials

Suitability, as used here, refers to the integration of reading level, cultural sensitivity, and health literacy in the creation and assessment of written materials.

Reading Level

Reading level and readers' ability to comprehend information are basic elements of writing about health topics for the general public. Only 12% of American adults have proficient literacy with any written material, not just health-related material (Kutner, Greenberg, Jin, & Paulsen, 2006). An average adult reads at about the same level as seventh- or eighth-grade students; people reading materials written above this reading level may not be able to follow what they read. One in five Americans reads at or below the fifth-grade level (Doak, Doak, & Root, 1996). This doesn't mean your material needs to be written for fifth graders. Thinking in terms of reading level is just a way of making information more accessible to more people.

Current criteria for readability of health information, derived from the Centers for Disease Control and Prevention (CDC, 2009), National Institutes of Health/National Cancer Institute (NIH/NCI) (MedlinePlus, n.d.), and Doak and colleagues (1996) state that material should be written below the fifth-grade level. Yet, in such critically important areas as neurosurgery (Agarwal, Chaudhari, Hansberry, Tomei, & Prestigiacomo, 2013), interventional radiology (Shukla, Sanghvi, Lelkes, Kumar, & Contractor, 2013), and radiation therapy (MacDougall, Connor, & Johnstone, 2012), readability of consent forms, patient educational materials and websites currently range from tenth grade to college level.

Assessing Readability

Several tools can be used to assess readability. Most are based on how well the material fulfills two central features that translate to easier readability:

- Minimize the number of words with three or more syllables

- Minimize average sentence length

SMOG (Simplified Measure of Gobbledygook) Readability Formula. The SMOG formula is based on the number of polysyllabic words in a given text. It's a quick and simple way to grade readability and is especially useful for materials that are short in length, such as an information pamphlet or consent form. The SMOG reading level is calculated by using these steps (Columbia University School of Nursing, "Assessing Suitablity," n.d.):

1. Count off 10 consecutive sentences near the beginning, middle, and end of the text. For materials with fewer than 30 sentences, use the entire text.

2. Count the number of words with 3 or more syllables, including repetitions of the same word.

3. Use the SMOG conversion table (see Table 22.1) to determine the approximate grade level.

Table 22.1   SMOG Conversion Table

Total Polysyllabic Word Count	Approximate Grade Level
1–6	5
7–12	6
13–20	7
21–30	8
31–42	9
43–56	10
57–72	11
73–90	12

Note: The SMOG conversion table, developed by Harold C. McGraw, Office of Educational Research, Baltimore Co. Public Schools, Towson, MD. The actual table extends through Grade Level 18.

Flesch-Kincaid Grade Level Index. The Flesch-Kincaid formula computes readability based on the average number of syllables per word and the average number of words per sentence. The score indicates a grade-school level (Columbia University School of Nursing, Assessing Suitablity, n.d.). The Flesch-Kincaid test is automatically calculated on Microsoft Word documents as an element in the Spelling and Grammar Check feature.

SAM (Suitability Assessment of Materials). You can use SAM to guide development of your material and assess suitability in six areas: content, literacy demand, graphics, layout and typography, learning stimulation and motivation, and cultural appropriateness. The SAM assessment process provides a score that falls in one of three categories: superior, adequate, or not suitable (Doak, Doak, & Root, 1996).

REALM (The Rapid Estimate of Adult Literacy in Medicine) Tool. The REALM assessment tool uses a medical word-recognition and pronunciation test to screen a patient's reading ability in medical settings (Zulick, Zulick, & Rothrock, 2009). Trained staff can administer and score the test in fewer than 3 minutes. Like other readability assessment tools, REALM uses the number of syllables, along with pronunciation difficulty. Each correctly read and pronounced word increases the score by one point. Scores are translated into four reading levels based on grades: grade 0-3, 4-6, 7-8, and grade 9 and above. The REALM scale is only available in English.

Making the Conversion

Converting professional or scholarly information to information for consumers is common. Hill-Briggs and colleagues (2012) devised a five-step method for evaluation and adaptation of print materials to meet the "less than 5th Grade Readability" criterion. Three low-literacy criteria are targeted for evaluation and text modification:

- Sentence length less than 15 words.

- Writing in active voice. (You can learn more about active voice in Chapter 6.)

- Use of common words (use of multisyllabic words, words more than two to three syllables long, is minimized or avoided).

Here, an example shows commonly used medical information translated to material useful to consumers. At the end is an estimate of the reading level based on the Flesch-Kincaid tool.

Healthcare professionals: Early assessment of current and potential vascular access needs (preferably at admission) in all patient settings promotes timely and appropriate vascular access insertion, reduces vascular access-associated complications, promotes vessel health and preservation. A consultation between the vascular access specialist and the patient and/or family is critical in achieving the optimal outcome of selecting the right device, placing it in the right location, at the right time.

(Readability Statistics: Passive sentences – 0; Words per sentence – 34.5; Flesch-Kincaid Grade Level – 21.4.)

General public: You will meet with the vascular access nurse soon after you arrive. She helps us to know and plan for the treatment you are to have. This allows us to plan ahead to meet your needs. This helps to reduce your chances of problems while you are here and when you are at home. You will get the best result from your treatment when we

- use the right kind of device

- put the device in the right place

- use the device at the right time.

(Readability Statistics: Passive sentences – 0; Words per sentence – 12.6; Flesch-Kincaid Grade Level – 3.7)

This example shows how you can convert the language that nurses commonly use to communicate with each other to language that conveys the same information to patients. Notice how the second example strips away medical jargon, replacing it with simple words. Shorter sentences and, with a few exceptions, sticking to words with fewer than three syllables, decreases the reading grade level.

The PlainLanguage.gov website (www.plainlanguage.gov) provides an online link to a list of common medical terms with suggested alternative words or phrases aimed at creating patient education and consent materials at a fifth-grade reading level. For example, the Simple Words and Phrases section of the site suggests replacing "a number of" with "some," and "convene" with "meet."

Health Literacy

Health literacy is the "degree to which individuals have the capacity to obtain, process, and understand the basic health information and services needed to make appropriate health decisions" (Committee on Health Literacy, 2004). Health literacy involves reading, listening, analytical, and decision-making skills, plus the ability to apply these skills to health-related situations so that the person can take appropriate action such as following treatment instructions.

Low health literacy is an obstacle to appropriate communication between patients, families, and healthcare providers (Diaz & Allchin, 2013). Substantial evidence indicates links between limited health literacy and fewer health promotion and early detection activities, lower abilities to manage chronic illnesses, increased hospitalization and re-hospitalization, and increased morbidity and mortality (Rudd, Groene, & Navarro-Rubio, 2013). Only 12% of adults have proficient health literacy, and low levels of health literacy are linked to poor health outcomes (Coleman, 2011; DeWalt, Berkman, Sheridan, Lohr, & Pignone, 2004). Health-literacy levels are even lower among older Americans, inner-city minorities, and immigrants (Potter & Martin, 2005). People with low health literacy are unable to absorb complicated concepts related to health, so explanations must be clear and concise.

A classic study of parent comprehension of two polio vaccine information pamphlets showed the payoff of considering readability and health literacy (Davis et al., 1996). Researchers used two versions of a pamphlet on polio vaccine. One version was developed by the CDC; the second was a simplified version that maintained the essential information. Parents' comprehension and reading time improved with the shorter, revised version. Parents were more likely to read the revised pamphlet, suggesting that plain language motivates readers to read.

Enhancing Value of Education Material

If you're creating educational materials for the general public, keep in mind these general suggestions to enhance the education value of the materials (adapted from Fact Sheets [Potter & Martin, 2005], prepared for the Center for Health Care Strategies):

- Supplement the text with simple illustrations and pictures to help readers visualize important material. Be sure your graphics are clear and appropriate for age, culture, and content.

- Emphasize the desired behavior rather than medical facts.

- Use clear headings and bullets instead of paragraphs.

- Use short sentences, active voice, and conversational language.

- Deliver a clear and compelling message.

People choose to read, and they can choose *not* to read. Capture your readers' interests in the topic as early as possible—in the first few sentences. Consider these questions as you form those all-important first sentences:

- Why is this information important to the reader?

- What difference will this information make?

- How will the information be helpful?

Cultural Sensitivity

Emerging and under-studied aspects of health education are cultural sensitivity and cultural appropriateness (Kirmayer, 2012; Knoerl, Esper, & Hasenau, 2011; Williamson & Harrison, 2010). Kirmayer (2012) provocatively writes that the evidence-based practices (EBP) demanded in today's healthcare settings are culturally determined, possibly biased, and inappropriate. He suggests, too, that culturally diverse communities have "ways of knowing" that don't rely on the methods that characterize EBP.

In 2000, the Department of Health and Human Services' Office of Minority Health published Competency and Linguistically Appropriate Service (CLAS) Standards; these were updated in 2013 (U.S. Department of Health and Human Services, Office of Minority Health, n.d.). Unfortunately, compliance and enforcement throughout U.S. hospitals remain inconsistent but are expected to come as guidelines gain wider use (Diamond, Wilson-Stronks, & Jacobs, 2010). There is undoubtedly a place here for nurses' contributions.

Linguistic issues affect many minority and ethnic populations' communication with health-care providers. Pain control is especially vexing: minority patients with cancer are more likely to be undermedicated for cancer pain (Haozous & Knobf, 2013). Many traditional American Indians (AI) and Alaska Natives (AN) were taught to endure pain as a survival skill. Verbal and nonverbal expressions of pain are unacceptable in many American Indian cultures: People who violate the social norm by admitting to pain experience a high degree of social isolation and guilt (Haozous, Knobf, & Brant, 2010). Older AI/AN have difficulties describing pain and as a result, may be less likely to ask for pain medication and more likely to use internal resources to manage pain (Hendrix, 2001). A request for assistance may not be repeated, or may be told to a family member who will relay the request (Kramer, 1996).

In many AI languages, no single word translates to the English word "pain"; instead, pain is illustrated through lengthy storytelling. Descriptions used in pain-assessment tools using the word "pain" may have limited or no uses in AI/NA settings. Pelusi and Krebs (2005) note that AI/ANs have difficulty reducing their pain to a number or simple descriptors: instead, pain is conceptualized as a physical, social, and spiritual experience. Among older and/or more traditional AI/NA people, numeric or linear pain scales are not particularly useful (Burhansstipanov & Hollow, 2001; Haozous & Knobf, 2013). People of different cultures also interpret pain differently, for example, pain might be perceived as punishment for past behaviors or as a sign of weakness. In either case, the presence of pain might not be readily acknowledged. In other cultures, pain is a spiritual experience that is meant to test one's beliefs and is to be endured. Similarly, many disease states carry culturally imposed stigmas that are barriers to candid discussions of signs, symptoms, and treatment options (Burhansstipanov & Hollow, 2001).

Creation and use of culturally appropriate materials about pain offers authors a host of complex and interrelated challenges, though the basic principles mentioned earlier are especially useful in writing for an AI/NA audience. Knowing *which* audience is essential: tribal culture and socioeconomic variations make important cultural sensitivity, health literacy, and readability considerations imperative in preparing written materials. In nursing clinical practice, an obvious example is use of the ever-present pain scale, in which a patient is asked to rate his or her pain on a scale from 0 to 10. For many AI/NAs, a numeric scale is not useful, but modifications of pain assessment scales have yet to be devised to meet the needs of Native populations (Burhansstipanov & Hollow, 2001; Jimenez, Garroutte, Kundu, Morales, & Buchwald, 2011). Attention to the multidimensional nature of AI's perceptions of pain, metaphors, words used, and storytelling traditions, use of other quality-of-life measures and terms, and inclusion of culturally based traditional treatments for pain management are suggested as concepts to be incorporated in written materials and holistic strategies for healthcare settings serving AI/ANs and Aboriginal Canadians (Haozous & Knobf, 2013; Jimenez et al., 2011).

Publishing Opportunities

Magazines featuring health articles are an important but underused avenue for nurses to reach the public. Parenting, fitness, and beauty magazines all feature health-related articles contributed by freelance writers who often get their information from nurses. Why shouldn't nurses do the writing and get the credit (and maybe even be paid) for what they know?

If you're ready to pitch a writing idea to an editor at a consumer magazine, you can explore many sources for publishing opportunities. You can sign up for the *Writer's Market* (writersmarket.com, fee required), which lists hundreds of publications, with contacts, or you can probably find the book, published annually, in your local library. Public libraries and bookstore magazine racks also offer opportunities to peruse, compare, and contrast consumer-directed publications to determine a potential niche for the publication you have in mind. Lastly, don't forget online venues. Many publications have websites and blogs, or are entirely online, offering venues for essays, stories, and practical advice from nurses for the consumer public.

Q: *I'm a faculty member. How can I help nurses become better writers?*

A: Model the culture of writing. Become the best writer you can be and establish your publishing track record. Faculty role models can nurture habits of writing among students by being proactive writers, focusing efforts where they can influence; beginning with the end in mind, believing in the topic's worth and importance; and putting first things first, deciding that writing is a professional priority and then following through by making the choice to write (McGuiness, 2008). Faculty can provide realistic guidance to the variety of publishing possibilities and submission expectations.

Students today are likely to be proficient in texting shorthand grammar and syntax—obviously inappropriate for communications with patients, families, and colleagues.

(Metcalf & Putnam, 2013) It's left to nurse educators to help students become more proficient in written English. Incorporate writing skills into basic, advanced, and continuing nursing education programs, and socialize nurses to value writing skills (Newton, 2008). Assign formal papers, and require correct grammar and punctuation even though this may tarnish your popularity among the student body. Curriculum and elective courses could incorporate writing and journalism content. Expose students to nurse-authors, publishers, and agents. Facilitate mentor partnerships for first-time authors. Create and support a collaborative writing group, a writing support group, a writing workshop or retreat for students and other faculty members. These group settings diminish the loneliness of writing, encourage skills development, and generate publication outcomes. (Jackson, 2009; Ness, Duffy, McCallum, & Price, 2013; Saver, 2011; Stone, Levett-Jones, Harris, & Sinclair, 2010)

Make the Leap

Nurse-authors enjoy limitless opportunities to provide accurate information to patients, families, and the public through writing. We often begin our writing careers by creating patient-education tools to meet specific informational needs in clinical practice settings. From there, it's a short leap to submitting your work to newsletters, magazines, social media, and journals with potential for broad dissemination. Details of practice innovations, using the time-honored journalism tenets of *who, what, where, when,* and *how,* result in much-sought-after manuscripts for professional clinical journals, but can be adapted to meet the needs of lay readers.

By following a few basics of writing for consumers, especially using readability levels and health literacy concepts that are consistent with your audience, you can open doors to writing for the public. You might also find that you widen your sphere of influence.

Q: *Are there workshops I can attend to improve my writing for the public (and my professional writing too)?*

A: Several workshops and programs are available. The Association of Writers and Writing Programs (AWP) (www.awpwriter.org) provides advice and an overview of the many options available to you. ShawGuides' "The Guide to Writers Conferences & Workshops" is an online directory describing nearly 1,000 writing programs worldwide (http://writing.shawguides.com). Writing workshops planned especially for nurses are popping up; if there isn't something local or convenient, plan and offer a program in your setting (Walker & Tschanz, 2013).

Degree and nondegree writing courses are increasingly available onsite at many universities and online. For example, at Education-Portal.com (http://education-portal.com), you can find universities that offer free writing courses online.

The combination of fascinating and inspiring environs, accomplished mentors, and willing fellow students can motivate participants to adopt the habit of writing—and with each effort, write better.

Write Now!

1. Write a paragraph designed for the public, and then test its readability level, using one of the tools discussed in this chapter.

2. Compare the two versions of the CDC's patient education on the HPV vaccine mentioned in this chapter. You can retrieve the one for parents at http://www.cdc.gov/vaccines/vpd-vac/hpv/downloads/PL-dis-preteens-hpv.pdf and the one for young women at http://www.cdc.gov/std/hpv/STDFact-HPV-vaccine-young-women.htm. Compare the two as far as language, information contained, and style.

References

Agarwal, N., Chaudhari, A., Hansberry, D. R., Tomei, K. L., & Prestigiacomo, C. J. (2013). A comparative analysis of neurosurgical online education materials to assess patient comprehension. *Journal of Clinical Neuroscience, 20*(10), 1357–1361.

American Nurses Association. (2001). Code of ethics for nurses with interpretive statements. Silver Spring, MD: Author.

Buhler-Wilkerson, K. (1993). Bringing care to the people: Lillian Wald's legacy to public health nursing. *American Journal of Public Health, 83*(12), 1778–1786.

Buresh, B., & Gordon, S. (2006). *From silence to voice: What nurses know and must communicate to the public* (2nd ed.). Ithaca, NY: Cornell University Press.

Burhansstipanov, L., & Hollow, W. (2001). Native American cultural aspects of oncology nursing care. *Seminars in Oncology Nursing, 17*(3), 206–219.

Centers for Disease Control and Prevention. (2009). Simply put: A guide for creating easy-to-understand materials. (3rd ed.) Retrieved from http://www.cdc.gov/healthliteracy/pdf/simply_put.pdf

Centers for Disease Control and Prevention. (2012a). HPV Vaccine for Preteens and Teens: Information for Parents. Retrieved from http://www.cdc.gov/vaccines/vpd-vac/hpv/downloads/PL-dis-preteens-hpv.pdf

Centers for Disease Control and Prevention. (2012b). HPV Vaccine Information for Young Women – Fact Sheet. Retrieved from http://www.cdc.gov/std/hpv/STDFact-HPV-vaccine-young-women.htm

Coleman, C. (2011). Teaching health care professionals about health literacy: A review of the literature. *Nursing Outlook, 59*(2), 70–78.

Columbia University School of Nursing. (n.d.). Assessing suitability of written materials. Retrieved from http://cumc.columbia.edu/dept/nursing/ebp/HealthLitRes/assessWrittenMat.html

Committee on Health Literacy. (2004). *Health literacy: A prescription to end confusion.* Washington, DC: National Academies Press.

Davis, T. C., Bocchini, J. A., Jr., Fredrickson, D., Arnold, C., Mayeaux, E. J., Murphy, P. W., … Paterson, M. (1996). Parent comprehension of polio vaccine information pamphlets. *Pediatrics, 97*(6 Pt 1), 804–810.

DeWalt, D. A., Berkman, N. D., Sheridan, S., Lohr, K. N., & Pignone, M. P. (2004). Literacy and health outcomes: A systematic review of the literature. *Journal of General Internal Medicine, 19*(12), 1228–1239.

Diamond, L. C., Wilson-Stronks, A., & Jacobs, E. A. (2010). Do hospitals measure up to the national culturally and linguistically appropriate services standards? *Medical Care, 48*(12), 1080–1087.

Diaz, D. A., & Allchin, L. (2013). Importance and promotion of linguistic safety in the healthcare setting. *Clinical Journal of Oncology Nursing, 17*(4), 374–375.

Doak, C., Doak, L., & Root, J. (1996). *Teaching patients with low literacy skills* (2nd ed.). Philadelphia: Lippincott, Williams & Wilkins.

Donelan, K., Michael, C. U., DesRoches, C., & Shoemaker, S. (2013). Improving patient education with EHRs. In C. M. DesRoches, M. W. Painter, & A. K. Jha, (eds.), *Health information technology in the United States: Better information systems for better care* (pp. 57–80). Robert Wood Johnson Foundation. Retrieved from www.rwjf.org

Haozous, E. A., & Knobf, M. T. (2013). "All my tears were gone": Suffering and cancer pain in Southwest American Indians. *Journal of Pain and Symptom Management, 45*(6), 1050–1060.

Haozous, E. A., Knobf, M. T., & Brant, J. M. (2010). Understanding the cancer pain experience in American Indians of the Northern Plains. *Psycho-Oncology, 20*(4), 404–410.

HealthIT.gov. The Health Information Technology for Economic and Clinical Health (HITECH) Act of 2009. Retrieved from http://www.healthit.gov/policy-researchers-implementers/hitech-act-0

Hendrix, L. R. (2001). Ethnogeriatric Curriculum Module: Health and Health Care of American Indian and Alaska Native Elders. Retrieved from http:www.stanford.edu/group/ethnoger/americanindian.html

Hibbard, J. H., & Greene, J. (2013). What the evidence shows about patient activation: Better health outcomes and care experiences; fewer data on costs. *Health Affairs, 32*(2), 207–213.

Hibbard, J. H., Greene, J., & Overton, V. (2013). Patients with lower activation associated with higher costs; delivery systems should know their patients' 'scores'. *Health Affairs, 32*(2), 216–221.

Hibbard, J. H., Mahoney, E. (2010). Toward a theory of patient and consumer activation. *Patient Education and Counseling, 78*(3), 377–381.

Hill-Briggs, F., Schumann, K. P., & Dike, O. (2012). 5-step methodology for evaluation and adaptation of print patient health information to meet the 5th grade readability criterion. *Medical Care, 50*(4), 294–301.

Holman, H., & Lorig, K. (2000). Patients as partners in managing chronic disease. Partnership is a prerequisite for effective and efficient health care. *BMJ, 320*(7234), 526–527.

Jackson, D. (2009). Mentored residential writing retreats: A leadership strategy to develop skills and generate outcomes in writing for publication. *Nursing Education Today, 29*(1), 9–15.

Jimenez, N., Garroutte, E., Kundu, A., Morales, L, & Buchwald, D. (2011). A review of the experience, epidemiology, and management of pain among American Indian, Alaska Native, and Aboriginal Canadian peoples. *The Journal of Pain, 12*(5), 511–522.

The Joint Commission. Facts about patient-centered communications. Retrieved from http://www.jointcommission.org/assets/1/18/Patient_Centered_Communications7_3_12.pdf

Katz, R. (2004). *One bite at a time*. Berkeley, CA: Celestial Arts.

Kirmayer, L. J. (2012). Cultural competence and evidence-based practice in mental health: Epistemic communities and the politics of pluralism. *Social Science & Medicine, 75*(2), 249–256.

Knoerl, A. M., Esper, K. W., & Hasenau, S. M. (2011). Cultural sensitivity in patient health education. *Nursing Clinics of North America, 46*(3), 335–340.

Kramer, B. J. (1996). American Indians. In J.B. Lipson, S.L. Dibble, & P.A. Minarik (Eds.), *Culture and nursing care: a pocket guide*. (pp. 11–22). San Francisco: University of California – San Francisco Nursing Press.

Kutner, M., Greenberg, E., Jin, Y., & Paulsen, C. (2006). The health literacy of America's adults: Results from the 2003 National Survey of Adult Literacy NCES 2006-483. Washington, DC: National Center for Education Statistics, U.S. Dept. of Education.

Lober, W. B., & Flowers, J. L. (2011). Consumer empowerment in health care amid the Internet and social media. *Seminars in Oncology Nursing, 27*(3), 169–182.

MacDougall, D. S., Connor, U. M., & Johnstone, P. A. S. (2012). Comprehensibility of patient consent forms for radiation therapy for cervical cancer. *Gynecologic Oncology, 125*(3), 600–603.

Marks, J. R., Schectman, J. M., Groninger, H., Plews-Ogan, M. L. (2010). The association of health literacy and socio-demographic factors with medication knowledge. *Patient Education and Counseling, 78*, 372–376.

McGuiness, T. M. (2008). The habit of writing. [Commentary.]. *Journal of Professional Nursing, 24*(4), 324–325.

MedlinePlus. (n.d.). How to write easy-to-read (ETR) materials. Retrieved from http://www.nlm.nih.gov/medlineplus/etr.html

Metcalf, S., & Putnam, A. (2013). The Net Generation of nursing: Keeping empathetic communication alive. *Creative Nursing, 19*(1), 21–25.

Nelson, S., & Gordon, S. (2006). *The complexities of care: Nursing reconsidered.* Ithaca, NY: Cornell University Press.

Ness, V., Duffy, K., McCallum, J., & Price, L. (2013) Getting published: Reflections of a collaborative writing group. *Nurse Education Today.* Retrieved from http://www.sciencedirect.com/science/article/pii/S0260691713001184

Newton, S.E. (2008). Faculty role modeling of professional writing: One baccalaureate nursing program's experience. *Journal of Professional Nursing, 24*(2), 80–84.

Nightingale, F. (1859, 1946). *Notes on nursing: What it is, and what it is not.* Philadelphia: J.B. Lippincott Co.

Pelusi, J., & Krebs, L. U. (2005). Understanding cancer–understanding the stories of life and living. *Journal of Cancer Education, 20*(Suppl 1), 12–16.

Pew Internet. Health Online 2013. (Jan. 13, 2013). Retrieved from http://www.pewinternet.org/Press-Releases/2013/Health-Online-2013.aspx

Plain Writing Act of 2010. Public Law 111-274, 111th Congress. Retrieved from http://www.plainlanguage.gov/plLaw/index.cfm

PlainLanguage.gov. (2011). Federal plain language guidelines. Retrieved from www.plainlanguage.gov/howto/guidelines/FederalPLGuidelines.pdf

Polishchuk, D. L., Hashem, J., & Sabharwal, S. (2012). Readability of online patient education materials on adult reconstruction web sites. *Journal of Arthroplasty, 27*(5), 716–719.

Potter, L., & Martin, C. (2005). Health literacy fact sheets. Center for Health Care Strategies, Inc. Retrieved from http://www.chcs.org/usr_doc/Health_Literacy_Fact_Sheets.pdf

Redman, B. K. (2011). Ethics of patient education and how do we make it everyone's ethics. *Nursing Clinics of North America, 46*(3), 283–289.

Ricciardi, L., Mostashari, F., Murphy, J., Daniel, J. G., & Siminerio, E. P. (2013). A national action plan to support consumer engagement via e-health. *Health Affairs, 32*(2), 376–384.

Rudd, R. E., Groene, O. R., Navarro-Rubio, M. D. (2013). On health literacy and health outcomes: Background, impact, and future directions. *Revista de Calidad Asistencial: Organo de la Sociedad Española de Calidad Asistencial, 28*(3), 188–192.

Saver, C. (2011). From practice to print: Creating a thriving culture of writing. *Nurse Leader, 9*(3), 23–25.

Shukla, P., Sanghvi, S. P., Lelkes, V. M., Kumar, A., & Contractor, S. (2013). Readability assessment of Internet-based patient education materials related to uterine artery embolization. *Journal of Vascular and Interventional Radiology, 24*(4), 469–474.

Stone, T., Levett-Jones, T., Harris, M., & Sinclair, P. J. (2010). The genesis of 'the Neophytes': A writing support group for clinical nurses. *Nursing Education Today, 30*(7), 657–661.

Summers, S., & Summers, H. J. (2009). *Saving lives: Why the media portrayal of nurses puts us all at risk.* New York: Kaplan.

Ueland, B. (1938, 1987). *If you want to write* (2nd ed.). St. Paul, MN: Graywolf Press.

U.S. Department of Health and Human Services, Office of Minority Health. (n.d.). National CLAS standards. Retrieved from http://minorityhealth.hhs.gov/templates/browse.aspx?lvl=2&lvlID=15

Wald, L. D. (1902). The Nurses' Settlement in New York. *American Journal of Nursing, 2*(8), 567–575.

Walker, M., & Tschanz, C. (2013). Stories are like water: An academic writing workshop for nurses. SpringBoard. Retrieved from http://blog.springerpub.com/nursing/stories-are-like-water-an-academic-writing-workshop-for-nurses

Williamson, M., & Harrison, L. (2010). Providing culturally appropriate care: A literature review. *International Journal of Nursing Studies, 47*(6), 761–769.

Zinsser, W. (1990). *On writing well* (4th ed.). New York: Harper Perennial.

Zulick, K. M., Zulick, P. A., & Rothrock, J. C. (2009). Patient education and health literacy. *Perioperative Nursing Clinics, 4*(2), 131–139.

Ten Tips for Editing Checklist

Here are some questions to ask yourself when editing your article.

Yes	No	
❑	❑	Does the article meet the intended purpose? After reading the article, refer to the beginning to see whether you followed through with what you said you were going to do.
❑	❑	Is there a take-home message for the reader?
❑	❑	Is the organization of the article logical?
❑	❑	Does the opening make the reader want to read more and, as needed, set up the research report?
❑	❑	Is the tone appropriate for the readership?
❑	❑	Are citations and references used where appropriate but not overused?
❑	❑	Is the voice consistent? For example, check for switching back and forth from first person (I, me, my) to third person (we, us, ours).
❑	❑	Are transitions used to move from one point to another and from one paragraph to another?
❑	❑	Are grammar, punctuation, and spelling correct? Remember to run a final spelling and grammar check.
❑	❑	Have you used active voice when possible and appropriate?
❑	❑	Will the article hold the reader's interest?

Proofing Checklist

Immediately before submission, do a final proof, checking for the following:

Yes	No	
❏	❏	Are titles and subheads spelled correctly?
❏	❏	Are all organization names spelled correctly?
❏	❏	Are all names of people spelled correctly? Is your biography correct?
❏	❏	Is the sequence of tables, figures, and other graphics correct?
❏	❏	Is each graphic referenced in the text (per Author Guidelines)?
❏	❏	Are captions accurate and any people identified correctly?
❏	❏	Do you have permission, as needed, from copyright owners to publish graphics from other sources? Is the credit information for the source included?
❏	❏	Are tables aligned properly?
❏	❏	Is the math correct in all calculations?
❏	❏	If a source is cited within the text, is the complete reference to the work also provided (per style guidelines)?

Yes	No	

If you receive an electronic copy of your article before print publication, check for the above points as well as the following:

Yes	No	
❏	❏	Are pages numbered sequentially?
❏	❏	Are the fonts consistent?
❏	❏	Are figure and other captions complete? (Sometimes they can get cut off when imported into the layout program.)

If you are proofing a computer-based program, also check the following:

Yes	No	
❏	❏	Can you navigate in the file (for example, go back a page, return to home, return to the table of contents?)
❏	❏	Are the links active, and do they take you to the correct page?
❏	❏	Do pages contain too much text?
❏	❏	Are all levels of headings consistent in size, color, and font?
❏	❏	Do graphics load onto the page at an acceptable speed?
❏	❏	Can you access help files?

Copyright 2013. Cynthia Saver.

Parts of Speech

Julie A. Goldsmith

This appendix contains grammatical classifications of the parts of speech in the English language.

Adjective

An *adjective* modifies a noun or pronoun by offering a comparative quality.

Examples:

antimicrobial soap

competent article

health communications

Adverb

An *adverb* modifies a verb, adjective, or another adverb and most often ends with the suffix *-ly*. Adverbs may be used with the words *more* and *most* if they indicate a superlative quality.

Examples:

He brought her *excellent* antimicrobial soap.
(*excellent* modifies adjective *antimicrobial*)

The ED nurse cleansed the wound *thoroughly*. (*thoroughly* modifies verb *cleansed*)

He questioned the victim *most* sensitively. (*most* modifies adverb *sensitively*)

The incision was *not large enough*. (*not large enough* modifies verb *was*)

Article

An *article* modifies and precedes a noun to determine whether the noun is specific or non-specific. The two indefinite articles are *a* and *an*; the one definite article is *the*. In general, use *a* before a singular noun that begins with a consonant or consonant sound, and use *an* before a singular noun that begins with a vowel or a vowel sound. Indefinite articles are not specific: They do not identify the noun they modify, such as *a patient* or *an injury*. In these examples, the references are to any patient and any injury. Use *the* before a singular noun that is a specific group, idea, person, or thing, such as *the patient* or *the injury*. In these examples, the references are to a specific patient and a specific injury. A plural noun does not require the article, *the*, to precede it.

Conjunctions: Coordinating and Correlative

A *conjunction* links words, phrases, independent clauses, or sentences. A *phrase* lacks a subject and verb and consists of several words connected through an idea, such as *measles, varicella, tuberculosis*.

Examples:

Patient education remains central in the science *and* art of healing.

She gave the patient his medications *when* he returned to his room.

Use a *coordinating conjunction* to link independent and dependent clauses. These conjunctions, including the words *and*, *but*, *or*, *so*, and *yet*, require commas to precede them, if connecting main clauses, or linking main clauses to subordinating clauses.

If you do not use a comma, you will have a classic example of a run-on sentence, which is unacceptable. However, if a sentence is uncommonly short, you may not require one.

Examples:

> Scientific definitions in publications serve a critical purpose for a specialized group, *but* can put off a general audience. (Subordinating a clause)

> My shift begins at midnight tomorrow, *so* I can't go with you to the play tonight. (Coordinating a clause)

Use *correlative conjunctions* to compare and contrast. These conjunctions are used in pairs and include *either/or, neither/nor,* and *not only/but also.*

Examples:

> Tell *either* Sammy's father *or* mother that he would like to have his stuffed bear while he is in the hospital.

> *Neither* Sammy *nor* his mother knew where his father purchased his favorite stuffed bear.

> *Not only* did Sammy tell the nurse he wanted his stuffed bear, *but also* the physician's assistant.

Clauses: Dependent and Independent

A *clause* consists of a subject and a verb.

Examples:

> The patient's *adherence declined.*

> As *he treated* the first-degree burns on the epidermis....

An *independent clause* can stand on its own to convey the meaning.

Examples:

> The intervention consisted of a 6-month telephone support group for 25 women in rural Idaho.

> The patient controlled the meperidine with the button on her analgesia pump.

A *dependent clause* is without meaning unless connected to an independent clause with subordinating conjunctions, such as *although, because,* or *while;* or relative pronouns, such as *what, which,* or *whom.*

Examples:

> *Although* the patient controlled the meperidine with the button on her analgesia pump, her anxiety did not decrease.
>
> The nurse, *who* explained the procedure during the postoperative phase of the patient's cardiac care plan, administered crushed aspirin through his nasogastric tube.

Nouns and Pronouns

A *noun* and its plural forms may represent an idea or a group, person, place, or thing. Proper nouns are capitalized. However, occupational titles are not capitalized when placed after a name, but they are capitalized when they precede the name, such as Chief Executive Officer Patricia Thompson, RN, PhD, or Dr. Patricia Thompson, RN, chief executive officer.

A pronoun functions as a noun and refers to a noun. A pronoun must be in agreement with the noun it references and stands for in gender, number, person, and case (first person, second person, third person). Common mistakes occur with the use of *me* or *my,* in particular.

Examples:

> Between you and *me,* we can screen 235 airline passengers for tuberculosis. (*me* is the object even though it begins the sentence.)
>
> The hospital provided my coworkers and *me* with new defibrillators for the satellite clinic. (*me* is the object and receiver of action.)

Objects: Direct and Indirect

A *direct object* is the receiver of the action.

Examples:

> He brought the *bandages.*
>
> He ordered the *soap.*

An *indirect object* precedes the direct object and identifies for whom, to whom, or what action was done.

> He brought *her* the bandages.

> He brought *her* the soap.

Prepositions

A *preposition* provides information about the direction of a noun or another element in the sentence (beneath the wound, over the bed, under the skin). If placed at the end of a sentence, a preposition may reduce the clarity. If an essential preposition at the end prevents an awkward phrase or sentence, go ahead and break the norm.

Verbs and Verbals

A *verb* represents an action or a state of being. Verbs have an active or passive voice. Active voice occurs when the subject drives the action with a verb; passive voice occurs when the subject receives the action through the verb.

A *verbal* uses verbs to construct other parts of speech (gerunds, infinitives, and participles). An *infinitive*, consisting of the word *to* before a verb, often poses the most grammatical difficulties. Avoid inserting a word(s) between *to* and the verb (*split infinitive*) unless you cannot find a natural and unforced alternative word choice.

Examples:

> The patient tried *to sincerely express* her feelings. (split infinitive)

> The patient tried *to express* her feelings sincerely. (correct use of an infinitive)

> The nurse needed *to quickly transfer* the patient to a different floor. (split infinitive)

> The nurse needed *to transfer* the patient quickly to a different floor. (correct use of an infinitive)

Publishing Terminology

Editors and publishers use jargon that can be just as confusing as medical jargon is to a layperson. This appendix explains some of the terms you might hear.

In addition to the terms list here, you can access an annotated illustration of publishing terms at http://www.jandos.com/Resources/Anatomy Pages4.pdf.

Acknowledgment A statement in the front of a book or at the end of a journal article that expresses the author's gratitude for help with the content.

Appendix Supplemental information to text in a book, placed in the back of the book.

Art (Artwork) A general term for tables, figures, graphs, photographs, and illustrations.

Back matter The material that follows the main body of a book, such as the index or appendices.

Bad break Occurs when a word or line breaks at the right margin of a page in a way that results in too much space; also occurs when a word is hyphenated incorrectly.

Bibliography A list of articles, books, and other references that are not cited in the text.

Bleed   A printed image that runs off the page.

Byline   The author of an article, which appears at the start or the end of an article.

Callout   See *pull quote*.

CMYK   Refers to the four colors used in printing color materials—cyan, magenta, yellow, and black.

Caption   The text that explains a photo or illustration; also called a legend.

Citation   The complete information for a reference, including criteria such as author, journal, volume, number, and page numbers.

Copy edit   Editing the manuscript for details such as proper use of grammar and punctuation.

Credit (credit line)   The text that credits the source of an image or text that has been reproduced with permission; it usually appears under the reproduced material.

Crop marks   Define the edge of a photo or printed page. In photography, used to indicate where the image should be trimmed.

Dedication   An inscription in the front of a book dedicating it to a person; dedications are personal in nature as opposed to acknowledgments.

Dash   Two types of dashes are commonly used. An *en* dash is slightly longer than a hyphen and is about the width of a letter "n". An *em* dash is the widest dash, and is the width of a letter "m".

Deck   Refers to some additional information about the article that falls after the headline but before the byline and main text.

Drop cap   Refers to when the initial letter of the first word in a paragraph is larger and drops down into the paragraph (and sometimes is a different color) than the rest of the text starting an article.

DOI   Stands for Digital Object Identifier; a unique code assigned in an article on publication (whether in print or online) that enables someone to retrieve the article using the DOI as a search term.

Endnote   Note or reference at the end of a portion of a text.

en dash   A dash character that is slightly longer than a hyphen and is about the width of a letter "n". Often used to connect numbers, as in 50–60.

em dash   The widest dash, and is the width of a letter "m". Often used to indicate a change in thought.

Errata   Note of correction for previously published information.

Figure   A general term for charts, graphs, photographs, and illustrations.

Footnote   Information placed at the bottom of the page in a book or document. Footnotes should be avoided in most cases.

Four color   Refers to a full-color publication that is printed using cyan, magenta, yellow, and black.

Flush   Used in combination with left or right, such as "flush left," which means the text is aligned with the left margin or "flush right," which means the text is aligned with the right margin.

Folio   The text that appears at the bottom of each page of a magazine or journal. It includes the page number, and may also include the name of the publication, website, and year, volume, and issue number.

Font   A typeface.

Foreword   A short introduction to a book by someone other than the author.

Front matter   The pages before the main text of the book; typically includes the title page, table of contents, foreword, and preface.

Galley   A term for a prepublication version of an article or book; in the case of books it's used to obtain prepublication endorsements from experts.

GIF   Stands for graphics interchange format, a type of graphics file.

Illustration   A figure that is drawn or needs to be drawn; can include graphs and flowcharts, as well as pictures.

Infographic   Refers to presenting information visually rather than within text.

JPG (JPEG)   Stands for joint photographic experts group, a type of graphics file.

Kerning   The space between the letters of a word. Kerning is sometimes adjusted for a better "look" to the text.

Layout   Refers to the composition or graphic design of a page or article. In essence, it is how the final publication will look. Usually authors review the layout in a portable document file (PDF).

Leading   The space between lines of type, typically measured in *points*. Leading is sometimes adjusted for a better "look" to the text.

Lead or lede   The start of an article, designed to draw the reader in.

Legend   The caption for a figure, photograph, or illustration.

Marginalia   Another term for sidebars, mainly used with books.

mov   Represents a QuickTime video file.

mpg (mpeg)   Stands for motion picture experts group; these files are used for computer video.

Orphan   A word that appears by itself at the end of a paragraph. Adjustments are usually made to avoid this. Definitions of widow and orphan vary; the point is that a word or line of text is separated from the rest of the text by too much distance.

Page proof   Shows how the final publication will look. Usually authors review the layout in a portable document file (PDF).

PDF   Stands for portable document file; it shows how an article will look when it is published.

Photograph   A photograph can be a black-and-white or color figure, but keep in mind that color photographs that need to be converted to black and white do not convert well and may appear washed out in the final product.

PNG   Stands for portable network graphic, a type of graphics file.

Preface   The introduction to a book written by the author; it states the purpose of the book and its scope.

Pull quote (or call out)   Copying a part of the text of an article and highlighting it as a graphic, usually in a larger text size and in a different color.

Reference list   A list of references (citations) cited in the article.

RGB   Refers to the three colors used to achieve online color—red, green, and blue.

Running header or footer   Copy that appears at the top (header) or bottom (footer) of each page of a book or journal.

Sidebar   A box of text with or without visuals that is set off from the main text.

Spread   Refers to two pages of a magazine or journal set side by side.

Stet   Proofreading or editorial mark that means to ignore a previously indicated change.

Style guide   A set of standards for editors or designers to follow so that information is presented consistently. In addition to general guides such as those from the American Psychological Association and the American Medical Association, publications usually also have a "house" style guide that addresses issues such as whether healthcare will be one word or two words (both are considered correct) and may pull from elements of general style guides.

Two color   Printing in which the final product is black and one other color.

Substantive edit   During this edit, the focus is on the big picture of the work, such as organization and flow. Sometimes referred to as the developmental edit.

Supplement   A special section to a journal or magazine that is separate from the publication, but distributed with a particular issue.

Table   Presentation of numeric information or short bullet points set aside from the text in a column format. Note that having more than four columns can create a design problem, so should be avoided if possible.

TIFF   Stands for tagged image file format, a type of graphics file. This is the preferred format for images such as photographs.

TOC   Stands for Table of Contents; the section in the front of the publication that lists what is contained within.

Typeface   A type font that has a name such as Times New Roman.

Subhead   These are smaller in size than (and subordinate to) the main headings and are used to break up text.

Upload   Refers to the transfer of files from a person's computer to a website.

White space   The area of a page that does not have any text or graphics. Sufficient white space makes pages easier to read.

Widow   A line of text at the end of a paragraph that is separated from the rest of the text. Definitions of widow and orphan vary; the point is that a word or line of text is separated from the rest of the text by too much distance.

Wrap text   Refers to moving sentences or words so that they wrap around a shape or graphic.

XML   Stands for extensible markup language, used in formatting text and graphics that will appear online.

zip file   A type of file that is compressed so that it can contain more files while not using too much computer space.

Copyright 2013. Cynthia Saver, with input from David Beverage, Kathy Goldberg, and Patricia Dwyer Schull.

SQUIRE (Standards for Quality Improvement Reporting Excellence) Guidelines

These guidelines provide a framework for reporting formal, planned studies designed to assess the nature and effectiveness of interventions to improve the quality and safety of care.

It may not be possible to include information about every numbered guideline item in reports of original formal studies, but authors should at least consider every item in writing their reports.

Although each major section (i.e., Introduction, Methods, Results, and Discussion) of a published original study generally contains some information about the numbered items within that section, information about items from one section (for example, the Introduction) is often also needed in other sections (for example, the Discussion).

Text section; Item number and name	Section or Item description
Title and abstract	*Did you provide clear and accurate information for finding, indexing, and scanning your paper?*
1. Title	a. Indicates the article concerns the improvement of quality (broadly defined to include the safety, effectiveness, patient-centeredness, timeliness, efficiency, and equity of care)
	b. States the specific aim of the intervention
	c. Specifies the study method used (for example, "A qualitative study," or "A randomized cluster trial")
2. Abstract	Summarizes precisely all key information from various sections of the text using the abstract format of the intended publication
Introduction	*Why did you start?*
3. Background knowledge	Provides a brief, nonselective summary of current knowledge of the care problem being addressed, and characteristics of organizations in which it occurs
4. Local problem	Describes the nature and severity of the specific local problem or system dysfunction that was addressed
5. Intended improvement	a. Describes the specific aim (changes/improvements in care processes and patient outcomes) of the proposed intervention
	b. Specifies who (champions, supporters) and what (events, observations) triggered the decision to make changes, and why now (timing)
6. Study question	States precisely the primary improvement-related question and any secondary questions that the study of the intervention was designed to answer

Text section; Item number and name	Section or Item description
Methods	*What did you do?*
7. Ethical issues	Describes ethical aspects of implementing and studying the improvement, such as privacy concerns, protection of participants' physical well-being, and potential author conflicts of interest, and how ethical concerns were addressed
8. Setting	Specifies how elements of the local care environment considered most likely to influence change/improvement in the involved site or sites were identified and characterized
9. Planning the intervention	a. Describes the intervention and its component parts in sufficient detail that others could reproduce it
	b. Indicates main factors that contributed to choice of the specific intervention (for example, analysis of causes of dysfunction; matching relevant improvement experience of others with the local situation)
	c. Outlines initial plans for how the intervention was to be implemented: e.g., *what* was to be done (initial steps; functions to be accomplished by those steps; how tests of change would be used to modify intervention), and *by whom* (intended roles, qualifications, and training of staff)
10. Planning the study of the intervention	a. Outlines plans for assessing how well the intervention was implemented (dose or intensity of exposure)
	b. Describes mechanisms by which intervention components were expected to cause changes, and plans for testing whether those mechanisms were effective
	c. Identifies the study design (for example, observational, quasi-experimental, experimental) chosen for measuring impact of the intervention on primary and secondary outcomes, if applicable
	d. Explains plans for implementing essential aspects of the chosen study design, as described in publication guidelines for specific designs, if applicable (see, for example, www.equator-network.org)
	e. Describes aspects of the study design that specifically concerned internal validity (integrity of the data) and external validity (generalizability)

Text section; Item number and name	Section or Item description
11. Methods of evaluation	a. Describes instruments and procedures (qualitative, quantitative, or mixed) used to assess (a) the effectiveness of implementation, (b) the contributions of intervention components and context factors to effectiveness of the intervention, and (c) primary and secondary outcomes
	b. Reports efforts to validate and test reliability of assessment instruments
	c. Explains methods used to assure data quality and adequacy (for example, blinding; repeating measurements and data extraction; training in data collection; collection of sufficient baseline measurements)
12. Analysis	a. Provides details of qualitative and quantitative (statistical) methods used to draw inferences from the data
	b. Aligns unit of analysis with level at which the intervention was implemented, if applicable
	c. Specifies degree of variability expected in implementation, change expected in primary outcome (effect size), and ability of study design (including size) to detect such effects
	d. Describes analytic methods used to demonstrate effects of time as a variable (for example, statistical process control)

Text section; Item number and name	Section or Item description
Results	*What did you find?*
13. Outcomes	a. Nature of setting and improvement intervention
	i. Characterizes relevant elements of setting or settings (for example, geography, physical resources, organizational culture, history of change efforts), and structures and patterns of care (for example, staffing, leadership) that provided context for the intervention
	ii. Explains the actual course of the intervention (for example, sequence of steps, events or phases; type and number of participants at key points), preferably using a time-line diagram or flow chart
	iii. Documents degree of success in implementing intervention components
	iv. Describes how and why the initial plan evolved, and the most important lessons learned from that evolution, particularly the effects of internal feedback from tests of change (reflexiveness)
	b. Changes in processes of care and patient outcomes associated with the intervention
	i. Presents data on changes observed in the care delivery process
	ii. Presents data on changes observed in measures of patient outcome (for example, morbidity, mortality, function, patient/staff satisfaction, service utilization, cost, care disparities)
	iii. Considers benefits, harms, unexpected results, problems, failures
	iv. Presents evidence regarding the strength of association between observed changes/improvements and intervention components/context factors
	v. Includes summary of missing data for intervention and outcomes

Text section; Item number and name	Section or Item description
Discussion	*What do the findings mean?*
14. Summary	a. Summarizes the most important successes and difficulties in implementing intervention components, and main changes observed in care delivery and clinical outcomes
	b. Highlights the study's particular strengths
15. Relation to other evidence	Compares and contrasts study results with relevant findings of others, drawing on broad review of the literature; use of a summary table may be helpful in building on existing evidence
16. Limitations	a. Considers possible sources of confounding, bias, or imprecision in design, measurement, and analysis that might have affected study outcomes (internal validity)
	b. Explores factors that could affect generalizability (external validity), for example: representativeness of participants; effectiveness of implementation; dose-response effects; features of local care setting
	c. Addresses likelihood that observed gains may weaken over time, and describes plans, if any, for monitoring and maintaining improvement; explicitly states if such planning was not done
	d. Reviews efforts made to minimize and adjust for study limitations
	e. Assesses the effect of study limitations on interpretation and application of results
17. Interpretation	a. Explores possible reasons for differences between observed and expected outcomes
	b. Draws inferences consistent with the strength of the data about causal mechanisms and size of observed changes, paying particular attention to components of the intervention and context factors that helped determine the intervention's effectiveness (or lack thereof), and types of settings in which this intervention is most likely to be effective
	c. Suggests steps that might be modified to improve future performance
	d. Reviews issues of opportunity cost and actual financial cost of the intervention

Text section; Item number and name	Section or Item description
18. Conclusions	a. Considers overall practical usefulness of the intervention
	b. Suggests implications of this report for further studies of improvement interventions
Other information	*Were other factors relevant to conduct and interpretation of the study?*
19. Funding	Describes funding sources, if any, and role of funding organization in design, implementation, interpretation, and publication of study

Available for download at http://squire-statement.org/assets/pdfs/SQUIRE_guidelines_table.pdf. Reprinted here with permission.

What Editors and Writers Want

What Editors Want

Editors appreciate it when writers:

- Follow our journal's author guidelines carefully.

- Use your last name, title of article, and name of journal when corresponding by email.

- In a query letter, give us two or three sentences on why our readers would be interested in your topic and why you should be the one to write the article.

- Carefully read your manuscript before submitting it to catch errors.

- Meet your deadline. If you can't, let us know ASAP, and be honest about whether you can meet a later deadline.

- Stay calm if your manuscript is rejected because of peer-review comments; ask to see the reviewers' comments if they aren't included, but know that not all journals will share them.

- Respond to peer-review comments when you revise. If you choose not to make a suggested revision, briefly tell us why so we know you didn't overlook it.

- Understand that it can take more than a year for your article to be published if it is accepted for publication. If you haven't heard anything for 4 or 5 months, it's fine to email us for an update.

- Understand that each journal has a unique style. Our editors know how to edit for our readership. We ask that you respect their expertise in this area just as we respect your expertise in the subject matter.

- Know that English is a living language. Rules you learned in high school may no longer apply.

- Realize that we know it's frustrating when we have your article for a year and then ask you to turn around your review of the edited manuscript in 5 days. Unfortunately, that sometimes occurs with the publishing cycle.

- Write for us more than once, and tell others that you enjoyed the experience of working with us.

- Follow our author guidelines carefully. (Yes, this is a repeat!).

Cynthia Saver, MS, RN, with input from multiple journal editors. Copyright 2013.

What Writers Want

Writers appreciate it when editors:

- Make the author guidelines readable and as short as possible.

- Explain publishing terms we might not understand.

- Provide a realistic idea as to time frames. If we know it takes 8 weeks for peer review, we won't bother you about the status of the manuscript after 4 weeks.

- Choose peer reviewers who are experts and provide feedback that is specific and considerate.

- Respect our input. We know you have a journal style, but please don't change our words just for the sake of changing them.

- Double- and triple-check the spelling of our names, credentials, and affiliations.

- Keep us informed of the status of the submitted manuscript. It's hard to wait to hear whether an article has been accepted, and, if it's been accepted, when it's going to be published.

- Understand that writing is just one component of our busy world.

- Send us at least one copy (hopefully more) of the published article or the link to where it is online.

- Let us know if you have received feedback (positive and negative) about our articles after publication.

- Give us encouragement along the way.

- Thank us for taking the time to write the article.

Cynthia Saver, MS, RN, with input from Susan Tocco, MSN, CNS, CNRN, CCNS. Copyright 2013.

Additional Resources

Chapter 1

American Psychological Association. (2009). *Publication manual of the American Psychological Association* (6th ed.). Washington, DC: American Psychological Association. Another stylebook that contains some helpful information.

Associated Press. (2013). *The Associated Press stylebook 2013*. Philadelphia: Basic Books. AP is the gold standard for newspapers and general media.

Iverson, C., Christiansen, S., Flanagin, A., Fontanarosa, P. B., Glass, R. M., Gregoline, B., et al. (2007). *American Medical Association manual of style: A guide for authors and editors* (10th ed.). New York: Oxford University Press. In addition to a style guide, this book is packed full of wisdom for writers who want to break into scholarly journals.

King, S. (2002). *On writing: A memoir of the craft*. New York: Pocket. The writer of horror tales gives readers a concise, insightful lesson on writing that is relevant to any type of writing you take on.

Zinsser, W. (2006). *On writing well, 30th anniversary edition: The classic guide to writing nonfiction*. New York: Harper Paperbacks. The title says it all—a classic.

Chapter 2

Barnett, D. E. (2007). Writing with a co-author: Tips to having a successful, creative relationship. *Associated Content*. Retrieved from http://voices. yahoo.com/writing-co-author-tips-having-successful-610998.html?cat=38

Webb, C. (2009). *Writing for publication: An easy-to-follow guide for any nurse thinking of publishing their work*. Hoboken, NJ: Wiley-Blackwell Publishing.

Chapter 3

Nurse Author & Editor (http://www.nurseauthoreditor.com). You have to create a free account, but it's worth it to access this useful newsletter.

Nursing Writing blog by Thomas Lawrence Long (http://nursingwriting.wordpress.com). In addition to being a good general resource, if you put "query" or "call for" into the search box, you will receive a list of journals with upcoming special issues.

Chapter 4

About Google Books. Retrieved from http://books.google.com/intl/en/googlebooks/about/index.html. In addition to Google Scholar, which searches content in professional journals, Google Books searches for content in books.

Boolean Searching Basics. (2011). Retrieved from http://www.youtube.com/watch?v=jMV7X3W_beg. This video gives a concise overview of how to use the Boolean operators AND, OR, and NOT in a search.

Hacker, D. Research and Documentation Online. Retrieved from http://www.dianahacker.com/resdoc/home.html. APA and AMA are not the only style manuals that are used, although they are popular. This website has a nice overview of a variety of style manuals used in different disciplines, with examples.

Chapter 5

Alley, M. (1996). *The craft of scientific writing* (3rd ed.). New York: Springer-Verlag. Still a classic.

Garrard, J. (2010). *Health sciences literature review made easy: The matrix method* (3rd ed.). Sudbury, MA: Jones and Bartlett.

Rogers, S. M. (2007). *Mastering scientific and medical* writing: *A self-help guide*. Berlin, NY: Springer.

Chapter 6

Brooks, B. S., Pinson, J. L., & Wilson, J. G. (2009). *Working with words: A handbook for media writers and editors* (7th ed.). Boston, MA: Bedford/St. Martin's Press.

Butcher, J., Drake, C., & Leach, M. (2006). *Butcher's copy-editing: The Cambridge handbook for editors, copy-editors and proofreaders* (4th ed.). New York: Cambridge University Press.

National Disability Rights Network. (n.d.). Reporting and writing about disabilities. Retrieved from http://www.ndrn.org/en/media/press-kit/265-reporting-and-writing-about-disabilities.html

O'Connor, P. T. (2010). *Woe is I: The grammarphobe's guide to better English in plain English* (3rd ed.). New York, NY: Riverhead Trade.

Purdue Online Writing Lab (OWL) (http://owl.english.purdue.edu). Has many writing resources.

Chapter 7

File reading and conversion programs

Adobe Acrobat (http://get.adobe.com/reader). This free version enables you only to read PDF files.

Adobe Acrobat (http://www.adobe.com). Several versions for purchase enable you to save files in PDF format.

Online virtual storage services

Some storage service vendors offer a small amount of free storage; most offer storage for a fee based upon the amount of desired storage space.

Box.net (http://www.box.net)

Mozy Online Storage (http://www.mozy.com)

Online image resources

Centers for Disease Control and Prevention—Public Health Image Library (http://phil.cdc.gov/phil/home.asp)

U.S. National Library of Medicine (http://www.nlm.nih.gov/services/stockshot.html)

Wikimedia Commons (http://commons.wikimedia.org/wiki/Category:Images). Read the licensing information for the image to verify it can be reused; be sure to credit the source. Unfortunately, many of the images are too low in resolution to be used in print, but can be used online.

Chapter 8

Ingham-Broomfield, R. (2008). A nurses' guide to the critical reading of research. *Australian Journal of Advanced Nursing, 26*(1), 102–109. Has a great checklist!

Modern Language Association (http://www.mla.org)

Chapter 9

Christenbery, T. L. (2011). Manuscript peer review: A guide for advanced practice nurses. *Journal of the American Academy of Nurse Practitioners, 23*(1), 15–22. doi:10.1111/j.1745-7599.2010.00572.x.

Hirst, A., & Altman, D. G. (2012). Are peer reviewers encouraged to use reporting guidelines? A survey of 116 health research journals. *PLOS One, 7*(4): e35621. Retrieved from http://www.plosone.org/article/info%3Adoi%2F10.1371%2Fjournal.pone.0035621

Chapter 10

Gedney Baggs, J. (2010). Through the looking glass: Publishing in a journal in another language or another country. *Research in Nursing & Health*, *33*(2), 85–86.

Chapter 11

Carlson, K., & Ross, J. (2010). Publication ethics: Copyright, permission and authorship. *American Society of PeriAnesthesia Nurses*, *25*(4), 263–271.

Committee on Publication Ethics (COPE), at http://publicationethics.org. The Committee is an international one composed of editors of academic journals and others interested in publication ethics. Its website contains a wealth of information for members and nonmembers on such issues as codes of conduct, sample letters, and databases of all cases concerning publication ethics discussed at COPE forums.

Conn, V. S., Algase, S., Rawl, M., Zerwic, J. J., & Wyman, J. F. (2010), Publishing pilot intervention work. *Western Journal of Nursing Research*, *32*(8), 994–1010.

Copyright Clearance Center. Retrieved from http://www.copyright.com/content/cc3/en.html

Improve your writing: Plagiarism check, grammar check & tutoring. Retrieved from http://en.writecheck.com/ (fee based)

iThenticate: Professional Plagiarism Prevention. Retrieved from http://www.ithenticate.com (for publishers and researchers)

LeFrance, M. (2011). *Copyright law in a nutshell* (2nd ed.). St. Paul, MN: West.

McJohn, S. (2012). *Examples and explanations: Copyright* (3rd ed.). New York, NY: Wolters Kluwer Law & Business.

Plagerism.org. Retrieved from https://www.plagerism.org (educational resources on plagiarism and also checking plagiarism)

Turnitin for Educators. Retrieved from http://www.turnitin.com (fee based)

Chapter 12

Bykofsky, S., & Sander, J. B. (2011). *The complete idiot's guide to getting published* (5th ed.). New York, NY: Penguin.

Comm, J. (2010). *Twitter power 2.0: How to dominate your market one tweet at a time* (revised ed.). Hoboken, NJ: John Wiley & Sons, Inc.

Katz, C. (2008). *Get known before the book deal: Use your personal strengths to grow an author platform*. Cincinnati, OH: Writer's Digest Books.

Shih, C. (2011). *The Facebook era: Tapping online social networks to build better products, reach new audiences and sell more stuff* (2nd ed.). Boston, MA: Prentice Hall.

Singh, S., & Diamond, S. (2012). *Social media marketing for dummies* (2nd ed.). Hoboken, NJ: John Wiley & Sons, Inc.

Chapter 13

Elsevier Authors Home Page: resources and information for any health science author at http://elsevier.com; click Authors. If interested in becoming a reviewer, click the Reviewer tab.

The OWL at Purdue for both MLA and APA styles for entire papers, not just citations: http://owl.english. purdue.edu. Also http://www.apastyle.org, http://www.mla.org, and www.citationmachine.net

Chapter 14

Cooper, H. (2010). *Research synthesis and meta-analysis: A step-by-step approach* (4th ed.). Thousand Oaks, CA: Sage.

Garrard, J. (2007). *Health sciences literature review made easy: The matrix method* (2nd ed). Boston, MA: Jones and Bartlett.

Chapter 15

Ching Lee, M., Johnson, K. L., Newhouse, R. P., & Warren, J. I. (2013). Evidence-based practice process quality assessment: EPQA guidelines. *Worldviews on Evidence-Based Nursing, 10*(3), 140–149.

Chapter 16

Albarran, J. (2007). Planning, developing and writing an effective conference abstract. *British Journal of Cardiac Nursing, 2*(11), 570–572.

Blakesley, D., & Brizee, A. (2008). Designing research posters. Purdue University Writing Lab. Retrieved from http://owl.english.purdue.edu/media/pdf/20080626013023_727.pdf

Dusaj, T. K. (2013). Pump up your PowerPoint® presentations. *American Nurse Today, 8*(7), 43–46.

University of Buffalo Libraries. (2013). Poster presentations: Designing effective posters. Retrieved from http://libweb.lib.buffalo.edu/guide/guide.asp?ID=155

Vanderbilt University Medical Center. (n.d.). Poster presentations. Retrieved https://www.mc.vanderbilt. edu/root/vumc.php?site=evidencebasedpractice&doc=37886

Chapter 17

Driscoll, J. & Aquilina, R. (2011). Writing for publication: A practical six step approach. *International Journal of Orthopaedic and Trauma Nursing, 15*(1), 41–48.

Chapter 18

Acito, A. (2002). Learning objectives—A practical overview. Chicago: Praxis Learning Networks.

Bell D. F., Pestka, E., & Forsyth, D. (2007). Outcome evaluation: Does continuing education make a difference? *Journal of Continuing Education in Nursing, 38*(4), 185–90.

Morrison, S., & Free, K. W. (2001). Writing multiple-choice test items that promote and measure critical thinking. *Journal of Nursing Education, 40*(1), 17–24.

Writing objectives using Bloom's Taxonomy. (n.d.). Retrieved from http://teaching.uncc.edu/articles-books/best-practice-articles/goals-objectives/writing-objectives-using-blooms-taxonomy

Chapter 19

Baird, K. (2004). Reclaiming the passion: Stories that celebrate the essence of nursing. Fort Atkinson, WI: Golden Lamp Press.

Cameron, J. (2002). *The artist's way: A spiritual path to higher creativity.*[10th anniversary ed.] New York, NY: Jeremy P. Tarcher/Putnam. A classic book on creativity.

Davis, C., & Schaefer, J. (Eds.). (1995). *Between the heartbeats: Poetry and prose by nurses.* Iowa City, IO: University of Iowa Press. More wonderful examples.

Lamott, A. (1995). *Bird by bird: Some instructions on writing and life.* New York: Doubleday.

Pennebaker, J. W. (2004) *Writing to heal: A guided journal for recovering from trauma & emotional upheaval.* Oakland, CA: New Harbinger Publications.

Seltzer, R. (1976). *Mortal lessons: Notes on the art of surgery.* New York, NY: Simon & Schuster.

Sergi, P., & Gorman, G. (2009). *A call to nursing: Nurses' stories about challenge and commitment.* New York, NY: Kaplan.

Sherman, D. W. (2009). *Final moments: Nurses' stories about death and dying.* New York, NY: Kaplan.

Chapter 20

Akinwole, B. (August 13, 2012). Communications corner: How to write a letter to the editor. Retrieved from http://campaignforaction.org/letter-editor-CFA-communications. Particularly helpful for writing letters to the general media.

Mikoluk, K. (2013). How to write an editorial: Follow these 5 tips. Retrieved from https://www.udemy.com/blog/how-to-write-an-editorial

Sullivan, E. J. (2001). Writing an op-ed commentary on nursing. *Journal of Professional Nursing, 17*(1), 1–2. Sullivan's advice still resonates today.

Chapter 21

World Association of Medical Editors (www.wame.org). The resources section has several articles and statements that deal with ethical decision-making, plagiarism, authorship, and peer review issues.

Chapter 22

Anker, A. E., Reinhart, A. M., & Feeley, T. H. (2011). Health information seeking: A review of measures and methods. *Patient Education and Counseling, 82,* 346–354.

Blumenthal, D. (2010). Launching HITECH. *New England Journal of Medicine, 362(5),* 382–385.

Carman, K. L., Dardess, P., Maurer, M., Sofaer, S., Adams, K., Bechtel, C., & Sweeney, J. (2013). Patient and family engagement: A framework for understanding the elements and developing interventions and policies. *Health Affairs, 32(2),* 223–229.

Manafo, E., & Wong, S. (2012). Exploring older adults' health information seeking behaviors. *Journal of Nutrition Education and Behavior, 44*(1), 85–89.

Somers, S. A., & Mahadevan, R. (2010). Health literacy implications of the Affordable Care Act. Center for Health Care Strategies, Inc. Retrieved from http://www.chcs.org/publications3960/publications_show.htm?doc_id=1261193

Speros, C. I. (2011). Promoting health literacy: A nursing imperative. *Nursing Clinics of North America, 46*(3), 321–333. A call to action for nurses.

Trimble, J. R. (2000). *Writing with style: Conversations on the art of writing* (2nd ed.). [Silver Anniversary Edition]. Englewood Cliffs, NJ: Prentice-Hall, Inc.

Truss, L. (2003). *Eats, shoots & leaves: The zero tolerance approach to punctuation.* New York, NY: Gotham Books. A fun approach.

U.S. Department of Health and Human Services, Office of Disease Prevention and Health Promotion. (2010). National Action Plan to Improve Health Literacy. Washington, DC: Author. Retrieved from http://www.health.gov/communication/hlactionplan/pdf/Health_Literacy_Action_Plan.pdf

U.S. Department of Health and Human Services, Office of Minority Health. (n.d.). Culturally Competent Nursing Care. Retrieved from https://ccnm.thinkculturalhealth.hhs.gov

A

Index

B

T